An Introduction to Sociology

Fourth edition

An Introduction to Sociology

Fourth Edition

Ken Browne

polity

First edition published in 1992 by Polity Press
This edition published in 2011 by Polity Press

Polity Press
65 Bridge Street
Cambridge CB2 1UR, UK

Polity Press
350 Main Street
Malden, MA 02148, USA

ISBN-13: 978-0-7456-5007-4
ISBN-13: 978-0-7456-5008-1(pb)

A catalogue record for this book is available from the British Library.

Typeset in 9.5pt on 13pt Utopia
by Servis Filmsetting Ltd, Stockport, Cheshire
Printed and bound by 1010 Printing International Ltd., China

For further information on Polity, visit our website: www.politybooks.com

Twenty years on, and it's still
For Eirene

Contents

4 Education

5 Crime and Deviance

6 *The Mass Media*

7 *Power*

8 *Social Inequality*

9 Health and illness

Appendix: Reading Statistical Data

Preface

Every week for the last twelve years I've presented *Thinking Allowed* on BBC Radio 4. It's a programme devoted to the latest research in social science. I mention it here, however, not as a self-advertisement but because it gives me a way to acknowledge the excellence of Ken Browne's *Introduction to Sociology*.

On the face of it my programme has a simple task. All I need to do is invite a social researcher into the studio and then ask them to explain their findings. What exactly have they discovered about social class, race relations, crime and deviance, social inequality or the impact of the new forms of media?

But it's rarely that simple. Academic sociologists are often so immersed in their subject matter that they can easily overlook the need to make their findings understandable to the general public. They can often fail to connect their work to the everyday world and to current political and social debates.

They need a lesson from Ken Browne. My admiration for his ability to make sociology both understandable and relevant was evident from the preface I wrote for the first edition of this book back in 1992. But as I've laboured over the years to bring the same qualities to my radio programme, that initial admiration has grown and grown.

You only need to look at a single page of this text to appreciate the author's skill in relating sociological findings to 'commonsense' truths, his ability to conjure up appealing examples and analogies, his readiness to use cartoons and photographs and contemporary news items to stimulate the reader's curiosity and arouse their enthusiasm. Browne is also bang up to date. This latest edition not only includes valuable new material on crime and deviance, the mass media and social problems, but also benefits from additional illustrations and from a greatly improved overall appearance.

In a world increasingly characterized by information overload, we are in ever more need of a guide who can separate the wheat from the chaff, who can show the difference between opinions and evidence, and perhaps, most importantly, indicate the ways in which research, when properly used by politicians and practitioners, can help to improve the lives of our fellow citizens.

I am delighted once again to have the chance to recommend Ken Browne as just such a guide for anyone embarking upon the path to sociology.

Laurie Taylor

Introduction to the Fourth Edition

This book is intended as an introduction to sociology for both the general reader and those studying at GCSE and other courses at a similar level. No previous knowledge of sociology is assumed. All the key issues and areas included in GCSE and other introductory sociology courses are covered, and this fourth edition has been completely restructured and rewritten to reflect the latest GCSE specifications. Thoroughly revised and updated, this fourth edition includes a wide range of new material and statistics reflecting more contemporary social changes and social trends, and new cartoons, photographs and graphics have been added.

The book is particularly suited to students studying for GCSE on one- or two-year courses, who require a clear and concise account of each topic area. The book provides full coverage of the AQA GCSE specification, and it is structured around this. There is also full coverage of the core material and of the most popular options offered by the WJEC and OCR, and it also covers much of the material required by the Cambridge IGCSE Sociology. The book will enable students to obtain the highest grades in all the sociology GCSE exams available in the UK at the time of writing.

It is also suitable for use by students on other introductory courses which have a sociological component, such as nursing, social work and health and social care courses. This book will enable the content of such courses to be covered easily and thoroughly, and allow time for students and teachers or lecturers to discuss, and acquire the skills of application, interpretation and evaluation. Students studying at home or on other distance-learning courses will find the book a valuable companion to their studies. Those who are considering taking an AS- or A-level or Access Sociology course or an applied AS- or A-level in Health and Social Care will find the book very useful both as preparatory reading and as an easy-to-read foundation text to get them started in sociology.

Acknowledgements

I'd like to thank Eirene Mitsos once again for her help and ideas, for constructive criticism and for her alertness in reading various drafts of a book she has been re-reading now in various versions for nearly twenty years. I'd also like to thank Polity's anonymous readers who provided valuable feedback in preparing this fourth edition. Ken Pyne has applied his creative energies, flair and imagination to the production of some new cartoons, and I am indebted to him once again. I'd like to thank all the staff at Polity, particularly Jonathan Skerrett for being such a conscientious and supportive editor, Leigh Mueller for her informed and professional copy-editing, Clare Ansell and her team for making it the most attractive edition yet, and Breffni O'Connor for his marketing skills.

I am grateful to all those who gave permission to reproduce copyright material. The source of copyright material is acknowledged in the text. Should any copyright holder have been inadvertently overlooked, the author and publishers will be glad to make suitable arrangements at the first possible opportunity.

How to Use this Book

Most chapters in this book are fairly self-contained, and it is not necessary to read them in any particular order or to read all of them. Select chapters according to the course you are studying. Those not familiar with the interpretation of statistical data will find it useful to study the appendix fairly early on. Those doing research projects of various kinds should read chapter 2, and refer to the website list for useful reference sites. When issues are discussed in more than one chapter, cross-references are made in the text.

Throughout the book, a range of activities and discussion topics is included. These provide valuable exercises to develop your skills and understanding, and should be attempted whenever possible, though they are not essential for understanding each chapter. Important terms are highlighted in colour when they first appear in the text, and in most cases appear in **bold type** in the page margins. These are normally explained in the text, and listed at the end of the chapter. They are also included in a comprehensive glossary at the end of the book. Unfamiliar terms should be checked in the glossary or index for further clarification or explanation. The contents pages or the index should be used to find particular themes or references.

Chapter summaries outline the key points that should have been learnt after reading each chapter. These should be used as checklists for revision – if you cannot do what is asked, then refer back to the chapter to refresh your memory. The glossary at the end of the book also provides both a valuable reference source and a revision aid, as you can check the meaning of terms.

A last word: do not look on this book as your final and absolute source of authority – see it as your friend rather than your boss. Much of sociology is controversial and the subject of intense and heated debate, and even apparently factual statistics are open to a variety of interpretations. Be prepared to draw on your own experiences of the social world to help to reach a sociological understanding of contemporary society. Discuss with others what you read in this book, and adopt a questioning and critical approach to your studies. The truth may be out there somewhere, but, like the executioner's face, it is always well hidden, so take nothing for granted and do not accept things at face value. Above all, enjoy sociology.

Useful Websites

The Internet is an invaluable source of information for sociologists, and for exploring the topics in this book. This might particularly be the case if you are doing small-scale research of your own. You should be prepared to click on links and surf the Web to explore the topics you're interested in, though always be cautious as there is a lot of rubbish on some sites, and you can't always believe what they say.

Internet site addresses often change or disappear, but below are a few sites that are very well run, kept very up-to-date, and which carry an excellent range of contemporary information, articles and statistics of relevance to the topics covered in this book. The information found on them can generally be regarded as accurate and trustworthy, and used by sociologists as evidence or to develop arguments. Other useful websites are referred to throughout this book.

Don't forget also to refer to the useful resources at **www.politybooks.com/browne**.

Exam boards

www.aqa.org.uk – the site of the Assessment and Qualifications Alliance (AQA), which has the largest GCSE Sociology entry. Very useful for downloading latest specifications and teaching resources.

www.ocr.org.uk – the site of the Oxford Cambridge and RSA Examinations (OCR) Board. Similar usefulness to AQA site above.

www.wjec.co.uk – the site of the WJEC, the main Welsh examining body. This has similar uses to the AQA site for teachers, but the sociology aspect is particularly well developed. The link to www.ngfl-cymru.org.uk contains a range of very useful sociology resources for GCSE, whatever exam board you're following.

Current affairs and useful general information

www.google.com is one of the best search engines to search for topics generally.

www.guardian.co.uk – this is the site of the *Guardian* newspaper, which is packed with useful stuff.

www.bbc.co.uk – the BBC. Widely regarded as one of the best websites in the world, you're bound to find something useful.

www.en.wikipedia.org – Wikipedia. A useful on-line encyclopaedia, but as people can create and edit entries on this, you need to be careful with the material.

Sociology for schools and colleges

www.sociology.org.uk – an excellent sociology site created for GCSE, AS- and A-level students, and run by Chris Livesey.

www.atss.org.uk – the site of the ATSS (The Association for the Teaching of Social Science). You will find a range of material, including worksheets, notes and a valuable list of websites of use to sociologists.

Government and other official sites

At the time of writing, a new government had just been formed, so it is possible some government department names and website addresses may change.

www.statistics.gov.uk/default.asp – the site of the Office for National Statistics, which contains a huge range of contemporary data on all the topics covered in this book.

www.direct.gov.uk – the British government site is an excellent starting point for locating all government ministries and departments.

Some of the government ministries that may be of particular use are:

www.homeoffice.gov.uk – the Home Office, for a whole host of material on crime and deviance, and a range of other issues.

www.education.gov.uk – the Department for Education, for all information on education. Prior to 12 May 2010, this was known as the Department for Children, Schools and Families (DCSF) and contained a wide range of information on children and young people, including education. At the time of writing, this could still be found at www.dcsf.gov.uk.

www.standards.dfes.gov.uk – the standards site of the DCSF.

www.doh.gov.uk – the Department of Health.

www.dwp.gov.uk – the Department for Work and Pensions where the latest benefit and poverty statistics are available, as well as the 'Targeting Benefit Thieves' site.

www.parliament.uk – Parliament, for political research and contacting your MP.

www.equalityhumanrights.com – the Equality and Human Rights Commission.

http://europa.eu/index_en.htm – the European Union, in case you want to see what is happening in other European countries in comparison to Britain.

www.ofcom.org.uk – the Office of Communications – the media regulator.

www.pcc.org.uk – the Press Complaints Commission.

www.tuc.org.uk – the site of the Trades Union Congress, a useful site for exploring trade union and labour force issues.

www.who.int/en – the site of the World Health Organization.

Voluntary and campaigning groups

www.jrf.org.uk – the site of the Joseph Rowntree Foundation, for all the latest research about poverty and inequality.

www.poverty.org.uk – a site supported by the Joseph Rowntree Foundation dedicated to monitoring poverty and social exclusion in the UK, and packed with the very latest information on poverty and inequality.

www.cpag.org.uk – the site of the Child Poverty Action Group, the major campaigning group against poverty.

www.newint.org – the site of the *New Internationalist* magazine, where global poverty and international inequalities between nations are discussed.

www.fawcettsociety.org.uk – the site of the Fawcett Society, which is the UK's leading campaigner for equality between women and men, containing a wide range of useful material on inequalities between women and men on pay, pensions, poverty, justice and politics.

CHAPTER
1

Studying
Society (1)

Contents

1 Studying Society (1)

Introducing Sociology: Key Ideas and Concepts

KEY ISSUES

- What is sociology?
- Social structure
- Social processes
- Social issues, social problems and social policy
- Different views of society

Newcomers to sociology often have only a vague idea as to what the subject is about, though they frequently have an interest in people. This interest is a good start, because the focus of sociology is on the influences from society which mould the behaviour of people, their experiences, and their interpretations of the world around them. To learn sociology is to learn about how human societies are constructed, and where our beliefs and daily routines come from and how our social identities are formed; it is to re-examine in a new light many of the taken-for-granted assumptions which we all hold, and which influence the way we think about ourselves and others. Sociology is above all about developing a critical understanding of society. In developing this, sociology can itself contribute to changes in society, for example by highlighting and explaining social problems like divorce, crime and poverty. The study of sociology can provide the essential tools for a better understanding of the world we live in, and therefore the means for improving it.

WHAT IS SOCIOLOGY?

Sociology is the systematic (or planned and organized) study of human groups and social life in modern societies.

It is concerned with the study of **social institutions**. These are the various organized social arrangements which are found in all societies. For example, the family is an institution which is concerned with arrangements for marriage, such as at what age people can marry, whom they can marry and how many partners they can have, and the upbringing of children. The education system establishes ways of passing on attitudes, knowledge and skills from one generation to the next. Work and the economic system organize the way the production of goods will be carried out, and religious institutions are concerned with people's relations with the supernatural. These social institutions make up a society's **social structure** – the building blocks of society.

Sociology tries to understand how these various social institutions operate, and how they relate to one another, such as the influence the family might have on how well children perform in the education system. Sociology is also concerned with describing and explaining the patterns of inequality, deprivation and conflict which are a feature of nearly all societies.

> **Sociology** is the systematic study of human groups and social life in modern societies.
> **Social institutions** are the various organized social arrangements which are found in all societies.

> **Social structure** refers to the social institutions and social relationships that form the building blocks of society.

Sociology and common sense

Sociology is concerned with studying many things which most people already know something about. Everyone will have some knowledge and understanding of family life, the education system, work, the mass media and crime simply by living as a member of society. This leads many people to assume that the topics studied by sociologists and the explanations sociologists produce are really just common sense: what 'everyone knows'.

This is a very mistaken assumption. Sociological research has shown many widely held common-sense ideas and explanations to be false. Ideas such as that there is no real poverty left in modern Britain; that the poor and unemployed are inadequate and lazy; that everyone has equal chances in life; that the rich are rich because they work harder; that men are naturally superior to women; that it is obvious that men and women will fall in love and live together – these have all been questioned by sociological research. The re-examination of such common-sense views is very much the concern of sociology.

A further problem with common-sense explanations is that they are tightly bound up with the beliefs of a particular society at particular periods of time. Different societies have differing common-sense ideas. The Hopi Indians' common-sense view of why it rains is very different from our own – they do a rain dance to encourage the rain gods. Common-sense ideas also change

What is seen as common sense varies between societies and over time. What is seen as common sense in one society may appear as nonsense in another

over time in one society. In Britain, for example, we no longer burn witches when the crops fail, but seek scientific explanations for such events.

Not all the findings of sociologists undermine common sense, and the work of sociologists has made important contributions to the common-sense understandings of members of society. For example, the knowledge which most people have about the changing family in Britain, with rising rates of divorce and growing numbers of lone parents, is largely due to the work of sociologists. However, sociology differs from common sense in two important ways:

- Sociologists use a sociological imagination. This means that, while they study the familiar routines of daily life, sociologists look at them in unfamiliar ways or from a different angle. They ask if things really are as common sense says they are. Sociologists re-examine existing assumptions, by studying how things were in the past, how they've changed, how they differ between societies, and how they might change in the future
- Sociologists look at evidence on issues before making up their minds. The explanations and conclusions of sociologists are based on precise evidence which has been collected through painstaking research using established research procedures.

Sociology and biological explanations

Biological or *naturalistic* explanations are those which assume that various kinds of human behaviour are natural or based on innate (in-born) biological characteristics. If this were the case, then one would expect human behaviour to be the same everywhere, as people's biological make-up doesn't change between societies. In fact, by comparing different societies, sociologists have discovered that there are very wide differences between them in **customs**, **values** and **norms**, beliefs and social behaviour.

For example, there are wide differences between societies in the **roles** of men and women and what is considered appropriate masculine and feminine behaviour.

How masculine and feminine behaviour is created in Britain will be discussed later in this chapter.

Similarly, some people have tried to distinguish between humans on the grounds of race, dividing people into different racial groups according to physical and biological characteristics like skin colour. However, sociologists generally attach little importance to such categories, as people may be of the same race, but behave differently. White English people behave rather differently from white Polish or German people, and often they have many different cultural traditions; there are many differences in the culture and behaviour of Pakistani Asian Muslims and Indian Sikhs, even though they belong to the same race.

These differences between people can only be because people learn to behave in different ways in different societies, as their biological make-up is the same. Sociological explanations recognize that most human behaviour is learnt by individuals as members of society, rather than being something with which they are born. Individuals learn how to behave from a wide range of social institutions right throughout their lives. Sociologists call this process of learning **socialization**.

> **Customs** are norms that have existed for a long time.
> **Values** are general beliefs about what is right or wrong, and the important standards which are worth maintaining and achieving in any society.
> **Norms** are social rules which define correct or appropriate behaviour in a society or group.
> **Roles** are the patterns of behaviour which are expected from people in society.

> **Socialization** is the process of learning the culture of any society.

FERAL CHILDREN

Evidence of the importance of socialization in binding the individual into the culture of society is found in the study of feral ('feral' means wild or undomesticated) children. Feral children are children who, for one reason or another, miss out on some important stages of human learning as they have been removed from human contact and the normal processes of human socialization. They remain unaware of human social behaviour and language from a very early age and therefore fail to develop many aspects of behaviour we would regard as human. There are many possible examples of feral children at www.feralchildren.com. One example is Tissa, the 'Monkey Boy of Sri Lanka', who was found in Sri Lanka in 1973, and who showed more animal than human characteristics. For example, he walked on all fours with a group of monkeys, yelped and snarled at humans, ate his food off the ground and did not smile.

Sociology and journalism

Journalism is the gathering of news and information about the state of society, such as current events, trends and issues. Journalists report these

Activity

Go to www.feralchildren.com.
1 Identify *two* case studies in which children were raised differently from normal human children.
2 Identify in each case study the characteristics these children display that children raised in human societies usually don't.
3 Explain carefully the ways these examples might show that human behaviour is learnt rather than naturalistic or based on instinct.

news stories aiming to inform large numbers of people through media such as newspapers, magazines, radio, television and the Internet. In some ways, *good* journalism and sociology have a lot in common, as both seek to collect information about society, try to avoid deliberate bias, present the information in a balanced and fair way, and use the evidence they have collected to justify the conclusions they reach. However, most journalism is *not* good, and often is very sloppy in the use of evidence, reaching conclusions that the facts don't justify. Information is often presented in sensational ways which are designed more to interest media audiences and sell newspapers or attract viewers than to spread accurate information about the world. This often means journalists are selective in their use of evidence, producing sensationalized or one-sided reports in a way that sociologists generally try to avoid.

Sociology differs from journalism in the following main ways:

- Sociology is based on evidence collected through systematic, planned research methods and rigorous sampling techniques, and that evidence is generally presented in a balanced objective way. Journalists don't necessarily use such systematic methods of collecting evidence – though they may draw on sociological research – and the presentation of news may be biased (one-sided).
- Sociological research is subject to scrutiny for bias, errors and omissions by other sociologists.
- Sociology has a toolkit of theory, concepts and research methods which influence the way the investigation of society is carried out, and sociological work is primarily aimed at other sociologists and social policy makers. Journalism does not require theory, and is in most cases aimed at large mass audiences, rather than the specialized audiences of sociology.
- Sociological research is not driven by the same time pressures as journalism. Journalists work within very tight time constraints, as news is about very recent events, with news being updated on an almost instantaneous rolling basis, with new and revised bulletins going out many times each day. This means journalists are often forced to cut corners in collecting evidence.

Sociology and psychology

Like sociology, psychology also studies people, and has a range of research techniques (like experiments and sampling) and theories to support this. However, psychology tends to focus on the behaviour of individuals, why they come to think and behave as they do and how their minds work. This includes things like their learning, perception, intelligence, memory, aggression and the development of their personalities. Sociology focuses more on the social groups, communities, organizations and social institutions, like the family and the education system, forming the social structure of society. Sociologists also focus on the wider social processes like socialization and social control that influence individuals.

Sociology and science

Sociology is one of a group of subjects, including economics, psychology and politics, which are known as the social sciences. The idea that sociology might be considered a science poses a number of problems. This is because the term *science* is usually associated with the study of the natural world, in subjects like physics, chemistry and biology which make up the natural sciences.

However, the study of society by sociologists presents a range of problems which do not exist in the natural sciences, as the comparison opposite suggests.

Is sociology scientific?

The differences between the natural sciences and sociology mean that sociologists cannot follow exactly the same procedures or produce such precise findings as those in the natural sciences. Despite this, sociology might still be regarded as adopting a scientific approach to the study of society as long as it has the following features:

- **Value freedom** – the personal beliefs and prejudices of the sociologist should not be allowed to influence the way research is carried out and evidence interpreted. Obviously the personal interests and beliefs of the sociologist will influence the choice of topic he or she studies, but the research itself should not be distorted by these beliefs. In other words, sociologists should not 'cook the books' to make their point.
- **Objectivity** – the sociologist should approach topics with an open mind, and be prepared to consider all the evidence in a detached way.
- The use of systematic research methods – sociologists collect evidence about topics using planned and organized methods. These are discussed fully in the next chapter.

Value freedom is the idea that the beliefs and prejudices of the sociologist should not be allowed to influence the way research is carried out and evidence interpreted.
Objectivity means approaching topics with an open mind, avoiding bias, and being prepared to submit research evidence to scrutiny by other researchers.

NATURAL SCIENCE	SOCIOLOGY

- Experiments can be carried out to test and prove ideas and it is possible to isolate causes in laboratory conditions.

- As a result of experiments, natural scientists can accurately predict what will happen in the same circumstances in the future. For example, the chemist can predict with certainty, as a result of experiments in laboratory conditions, that some combinations of chemicals will cause explosions.

- In the natural sciences, the presence of the scientist doesn't affect the behaviour of chemicals or objects.

- The natural scientist does not have to persuade objects, chemicals or, usually, animals to cooperate in research.

- Human beings have rights, and might well object to being experimented upon. For example, the idea of removing children from their parents and raising them in isolation to test the influence of society on human behaviour would be regarded by most people as outrageous. Sociology also wants to study society in its normal state, not in the artificial conditions of an experiment.

- Human behaviour cannot be predicted with such certainty: in two similar situations, people may react differently, according to how they interpret what is going on around them, and people can change their minds.

- Sociologists studying people may change the behaviour of those being studied, who may become embarrassed, be more defensive and careful about what they say, or act differently because they have been selected for study. If this happens, then the results obtained will not give a true picture of how people behave normally.

- People may refuse to answer questions or otherwise cooperate, making sociological research difficult or impossible. They can lie or otherwise distort and conceal the truth when they are being researched, making the findings of research suspect.

- The use of evidence – sociological descriptions of social life, and the explanations and conclusions drawn, are based on carefully collected evidence.
- The capacity for being checked – the findings and conclusions of sociological research are open to inspection, criticism and testing by other researchers. Bad sociology, using inadequate evidence to reach unjustifiable conclusions, is likely to be torn to shreds by others interested in the topic.

SOCIAL STRUCTURE

Social structure refers to the social institutions and network of social relationships and the links between them which combine to build up the structure of society. These building blocks include institutions like the family, work and the economy, the education system, the legal system, the political system, and the pattern of inequality. Many of these social institutions are considered throughout this book.

> **Activity**
>
> To what extent is our behaviour moulded by the social structure? Suggest *three* ways that each of the following social structures has contributed to the way you are now, and which prevent you from behaving in any way you like:
> - the family
> - the education system
> - the legal system
> - the workplace (if you have a full- or part-time job)
> - the pattern of inequality, e.g. the amount of income you (and your family) have, or racial and sexual discrimination.

SOCIAL PROCESSES

Social processes are the various influences that control and regulate human behaviour, and help to keep societies running more or less smoothly and with some day-to-day stability. Two important social processes which are considered below, and throughout this book, are socialization and social control.

Socialization

Socialization, culture and identity

Socialization is the life-long process of learning the **culture** of any society. The term *culture* refers to the language, beliefs, values and norms, customs, roles, knowledge and skills which combine to make up the way of life of any society. This culture is socially transmitted (passed on through socialization) from one generation to the next.

Socialization plays a crucial part in forming our identities. **Identity** is about how we see and define ourselves – our personalities – and how other people see and define us.

For example, we might define ourselves as gay, black, a Muslim, Welsh, English, a woman, a student or a mother. Many aspects of our individual

> **Culture** refers to the language, beliefs, values and norms, customs, roles, knowledge and skills which combine to make up the way of life of any society.
>
> **Identity** is about how individuals see and define themselves and how other people see and define them.

identities will be formed through the socialization process, with the family, friends, school, the mass media, the workplace and other agencies of socialization helping to form our individual personalities. Figure 1.1 illustrates the various factors which influence our identities and how others see us, and many chapters in this book refer to aspects of this socialization process, and the forming of our identities.

Primary and secondary socialization

Primary socialization refers to socialization during the early years of childhood, and is carried out by the family or close community. It is during primary socialization that children first begin to learn about the basic values and norms and other features of the culture making up the way of life of their society. They also begin to acquire their sense of who they are as individuals – their individual identities – and significant elements of their social identities such as their gender, ethnicity and sexuality. In most cases, these identities formed during childhood will remain throughout people's lives and are much more difficult to change in adulthood than other identities.

Secondary socialization refers to socialization which takes place beyond the family and close community. It is carried out through agencies of secondary socialization such as the education system, the **peer group** (a group of people of similar age and **status**), the workplace, the mass media and religious institutions.

While life-long socialization plays a very important part in forming our identities, individuals also have the free will to enable them to carve out their own personal identities and influence how others see them, rather than simply being influenced by them. Individuals are not simply the passive victims of the socialization process. Figure 1.1 shows a range of factors which influence our identities. Note the arrows go both ways, suggesting that, while individual identities are formed by various forces of socialization, the choices individuals and groups make and how they react to these forces can also have an influence. For example, while the mass media might influence our lifestyles, attitudes and values, and how we see ourselves and how others see us, individuals may also react to what they read, see or hear in the media in different ways. A woman from a minority ethnic background may define herself as black or Asian, but she may also see herself mainly as a woman, a mother, a teacher or a Muslim. Similarly, we have some choices in the **consumer goods** we buy, the clothes we wear, and the leisure activities we choose to follow. Through these choices, we can influence how others see us, and the image of ourselves we project to them.

Socialization – roles and role conflict

Roles are the patterns of behaviour which are expected from people in different positions in society – they are very much like the roles actors play in a television series, and learning them is an important aspect of the socialization

---

Primary socialization is socialization during the early years of childhood.
Secondary socialization is socialization which takes place beyond the family and close community.
The **peer group** is a group of people of similar age and status, with whom a person often mixes socially.
Status refers to an individual's or group's social standing or importance in the eyes of others.

Consumer (or consumption) goods are products and services that people buy to satisfy their needs and desires, such as food, clothes, furniture, TVs and DVD players, computers for personal use, iPods and leisure activities, like paying to go to cinemas, clubs and concerts.

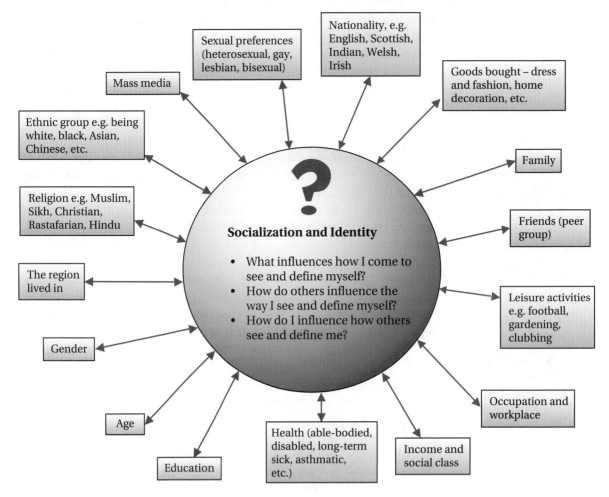

Figure 1.1 Socialization and Identity

Activity

Refer to figure 1.1

1 Suggest one example in each case of how the various factors may influence the individual's sense of identity.

2 Suggest three ways that individuals can influence how others see them.

3 Describe the three most important factors that you think have influenced how *you* define yourself and how others see you. Explain your answer with examples.

4 Suggest three ways *you* can influence how others see and define you, for example as a particular type of person – cool, odd, sporty, scary, Goth, etc.

In what ways do different forms of mass media (for example, public screenings of sporting events such as the Olympics, or free newspapers on commuter transport) influence the individual's socialization and sense of identity?

process. People in society play many different roles in their lifetimes, such as those of a boy or girl, a child and an adult, a student, a parent, a friend, and work roles like factory worker, police officer or teacher. People in these roles are expected by society to behave in particular ways. For example, police officers

Activity

Below are some important agencies of secondary socialization. In the right-hand column, give three examples in each case of how that agency carries out secondary socialization. The education system has been done for you, but try to do the same for the other agencies.

Agency	Role in socialization
Education system	• Teaches knowledge about society, like history, language and customs, making up key elements of society's culture • Teaches values and norms to which young people will be expected to conform as adults • Teaches skills and qualifications needed for adult life and further education and training, like literacy, numeracy and GCSEs and A-levels
The peer group	
The workplace	
The mass media	
Religious institutions	

Role conflict for working women

are expected to show patterns of behaviour – roles – that involve things like honesty, obeying the law and generally conforming to social rules. Teachers are expected to show similar patterns of behaviour, and the role of teacher involves providing examples to students of proper, socially acceptable, forms of behaviour. Often, the rules that define roles are not always clear until they are broken, but the police officer who steals, or the teacher who is drunk in the classroom, shows what these rules and expectations of behaviour are.

One person plays many roles at the same time. For example, a woman may play the roles of woman, mother, worker, sister and wife at the same time. This may lead to **role conflict**, where the successful performance of two or more roles at the same time may come into conflict with one another, such as the conflict between the roles of full-time worker and mother which some women experience.

> **Role conflict** is the conflict that arises between the successful performances of two or more roles at the same time.

Activity

1 List all the roles you play, and briefly outline what others expect of you in each of these roles. For example, how are you expected to behave as a student, and what activities are you expected to carry out which you wouldn't have to if you were not a student?
2 From your list of roles, try to pick out those which conflict with each other, as suggested in the cartoon above.

Socialization – learning values and norms

Values are ideas and beliefs about what is right and wrong, and the important standards which are worth maintaining and achieving in any society.

They provide general guidelines for behaviour. In Britain, values include beliefs about respect for human life, privacy, and private property, about the importance of marriage and the importance of money and success. There are often strong pressures on people to conform to a society's values, which are frequently written down as laws. These are official legal rules which are formally enforced by the police, courts, and prison, and involve legal punishment if they are broken. Laws against murder, for example, enforce the value attached to human life in our society.

Norms are social rules which define correct and acceptable behaviour in a society or social group to which people are expected to conform. Norms are much more specific than values: they put values (general guidelines) into practice in particular situations. The rule that someone should not generally enter rooms without knocking reflects the value of privacy, and rules about not drinking and driving reflect the value of respect for human life. Norms exist in all areas of social life. In Britain, those who are late for work, jump queues in supermarkets, laugh during funerals, walk through the streets naked, or never say 'hello' to friends are likely to be seen as annoying, rude or odd because they are not following the norms of accepted behaviour. Norms are mainly informally enforced – by the disapproval of other people, embarrassment, or a telling-off from parents.

Customs are norms which have existed for a long time and have become a part of society's traditions – kissing under the mistletoe at Christmas, buying Easter eggs, or lighting candles at Divali are typical customs found in Britain.

Values and norms are part of the culture of a society, and are learned and passed on through socialization. They differ between societies – the values and norms of an African tribe are very different from those of people in modern Britain. They may also change over time and vary between social groups in the same society. In Britain, cohabitation (living together without being married) is much more accepted today than it was in the past, and wearing turbans – which is seen as normal dress among Sikh men – would be seen as a bit weird among white teenagers.

Social control

In order for people to know how to behave in society, to be able to predict how others will behave, and therefore to live together in some orderly way, some shared values and norms are necessary. Without some measure of agreement on the basic ground rules, social life would soon fall into confusion and disorder. For example, imagine the chaos on the British roads if drivers stopped following the rules about driving on the left-hand side of the road, or stopping at red traffic lights.

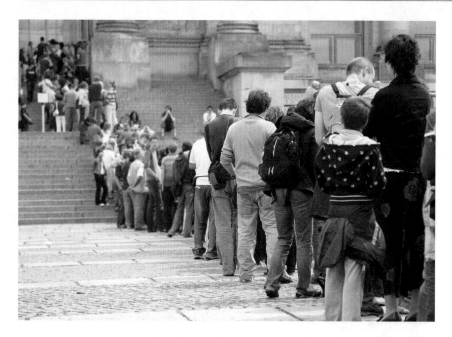

What might happen to you if you didn't know or follow the expected norms of queuing?

Norms and values are learnt through socialization, but knowing what the norms are does not necessarily mean people will follow them. **Social control** is the term given to the various methods used to persuade or force individuals to conform to those social values and norms which have been learnt through socialization, and to prevent **deviance** – a failure to conform to social norms. Deviance is any behaviour that is in some way socially unacceptable or not approved of – non-conformist behaviour.

Sanctions are the rewards and punishments by which social control is achieved and conformity to norms and values enforced.

These may be either *positive sanctions*, rewards of various kinds, or *negative sanctions*, various types of punishment. The type of sanction will depend on the seriousness of the norm: positive sanctions may range from gifts of sweets from parents to children, to merits and prizes at school, to knighthoods and medals; negative sanctions may range from a feeling of embarrassment, to being ridiculed or gossiped about or regarded as a bit eccentric or a bit odd, to being fined or imprisoned.

> **Social control** is the social process of persuading or forcing individuals to conform to values and norms. **Deviance** is the failure to conform to social norms. A **sanction** is a reward or punishment to encourage social conformity.

Activity

Discuss the various positive and negative sanctions which affect the way you behave in your daily life.

Together, socialization and social control help to maintain social conformity – conforming to social values and norms.

Social control: people make rules and then enforce them on the carrot-and-stick principle

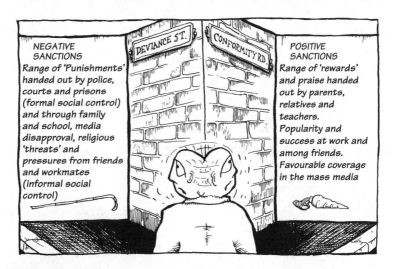

NEGATIVE SANCTIONS
Range of 'Punishments' handed out by police, courts and prisons (formal social control) and through family and school, media disapproval, religious 'threats' and pressures from friends and workmates (informal social control)

DEVIANCE ST.   CONFORMITY RD.

POSITIVE SANCTIONS
Range of 'rewards' and praise handed out by parents, relatives and teachers. Popularity and success at work and among friends. Favourable coverage in the mass media

Activity

Look at the cartoon above.

1 Explain in your own words the point the cartoon is illustrating.
2 List four possible consequences that might face a person who followed a deviant path as an adult.
3 Suggest two reasons why a person might fail to conform to social norms.
4 Identify and explain two ways in which not conforming to social norms might lead to success in society.
5 Much deviance is disapproved of to some extent, but can you think of forms of deviance in any society which might be welcomed by the majority of the public as opening the way for society to change and improve?

Agencies of social control: formal and informal social control

Social control is carried out through a series of agencies of social control, many of which are discussed in fuller detail in other parts of this book, but it is useful to summarize them here.

Formal social control is that which is carried out by an agency specifically set up to ensure that people conform to a particular set of norms, especially the law. The criminal justice system – police, courts, the probation service and prisons – force people to obey the law through formal sanctions such as arresting, fining or imprisoning those who break society's laws.

Informal social control is carried out by agencies whose primary purpose is not social control, but they play an important role in it none the less. For example, the family is an important agency of primary socialization, where children first begin to form their identities, and learn about the basic values and norms of society. Children begin to learn the difference between right and wrong, good and bad behaviour, norms governing gender roles, and acceptance of parental authority. Children may become embarrassed or develop a guilty conscience if they break these rules. The approval or disapproval of parents can itself be an important element in encouraging children to conform, along with other sanctions such as praise and rewards, threats, teasing and physical violence. Table 1.1 below shows some examples of how other agencies carry out social control, and seek to limit deviance.

Table 1.1 Informal social control

Agency	How it carries out social control
Education system	Sets standards of 'correct' behaviour, the forms of dress and so on which are expected by society. This is achieved by sanctions such as detentions, suspensions, exclusions, merit points and other aspects of the **hidden curriculum** (see glossary, later in this chapter and chapter 4 for more discussion of this). Through the actions of teachers and the way the school is organized, for example through streaming and examinations, pupils are encouraged to accept norms like the competitiveness, the gender roles, the ranking of people with unequal pay and status, and the inequalities in power and authority to which they are expected to conform in the wider society. In this way, the school helps to maintain the way society as a whole is presently organized, such as the inequalities between men and women and between managers and workers.
Peer group	The peer group is a very important group in providing an individual's view of herself or himself – their sense of identity. The desire for approval and acceptance by peers, and fear of rejection and ridicule, may promote conformity to the wider norms of society, such as acceptance of traditional gender roles. However, conformity to the peer group may also promote deviance. This is particularly likely among young people, where peer pressure may encourage them to adopt forms of deviant behaviour, such as playing truant from school, taking illegal drugs or under-age drinking.
The workplace	There are frequently strong pressures from fellow workers to conform to work-related norms, and an individual who is labelled as a trouble-maker or uncooperative may find herself or himself denied promotion opportunities, allocated unpleasant jobs or even dismissed. Fellow workers may use such negative sanctions as refusing to talk to or mix with workmates, ridiculing them, or playing practical jokes on those who fail to conform to their norms.
The mass media	These are major sources of information and ideas, and can have powerful influences on people's attitudes, opinions and behaviour. The media generally encourage conformist behaviour, by devices like news reports on the serious consequences which follow for those who break society's norms, selection of what to report – thereby telling people what they should be thinking about and behaviour they should disapprove of – or advertising promoting conformity to traditional gender roles.

The **hidden curriculum** refers to the attitudes and behaviour which are taught through the school's organization and teachers' attitudes but which are not part of the formal timetable.

Table 1.1 (continued)

Agency	How it carries out social control
Religion	Religion lays down often clear rules about right and wrong behaviour, which may persuade believers to conform. For example, the Christian religion promises rewards (heaven) to those who conform to its teachings, and punishments (an eternity in hell) to those who do not. Religious beliefs and teachings often support and reinforce the values and norms of society by giving them a sacred quality. The Ten Commandments in Christianity – 'thou shalt not kill . . . steal . . . commit adultery, etc. – reinforce values such as respect for human life, private property and monogamous marriage, and Muslims believe that practices like fasting during the month of Ramadan help them to avoid violence, anger, lust, envy and other anti-social behaviour. Feelings of guilt (a guilty conscience) may result if religious rules are broken by believers – a sort of inner police officer controlling behaviour.

Activity

1 Give examples of three norms in each case, to which you are generally expected to conform, in *two* of the following: (a) at your school or college; (b) in your peer group; (c) at work.
2 Explain in each case how these norms are enforced, and outline the sanctions applied to encourage you to conform to them.

An example of a social process: gender role socialization

Sex and gender

- The term **sex** (whether someone is male or female) refers to the natural or biological differences between men and women, such as differences in genitals, internal reproductive organs and body hair.
- **Gender** (whether someone is masculine or feminine) refers to the cultural, socially constructed differences between the two sexes. It refers to the way a society encourages and teaches the two sexes to behave in different ways through socialization.
- A **gender role** is the pattern of behaviour and activity which society expects from individuals of either sex – how a boy/man or girl/woman should behave in society. Gender roles may sometimes be referred to as sex roles.

The difference between the terms *sex* and *gender* is best illustrated by the case of transsexuals – people who biologically belong to one sex, but are convinced they belong to the opposite sex, for example a woman 'trapped' in a man's body. When these people try to change their biological sex, through surgery and hormone treatment, they also have to learn to act in a different way and adopt new masculine or feminine gender roles.

Gender and biology

It is sometimes suggested that the different gender roles played by women and men are obvious extensions of the biological differences between the sexes. Therefore women are thought to be natural mothers, with a maternal and caring instinct and a biological inclination towards child rearing and domestic tasks. Men, on the other hand, it is suggested, are naturally assertive and dominant members of society, inclined towards the breadwinner role of supporting the family.

If this argument were correct, then socialization would be of little importance, as men and women would naturally adopt their roles, and one would expect the typical roles played by men and women in Britain to be the same in every society: after all, the biological differences between men and women are the same everywhere. However, the comparative study of other societies suggests this is not the case.

Three Tribes in New Guinea   Margaret Mead described three tribes in New Guinea (*Sex and Temperament*, 1935) where the roles of men and women were quite different from those found in modern Britain.

- Among the *Mundugumor*, both sexes showed what we in Britain would regard as masculine characteristics – both sexes were aggressive, both hated childbirth and child rearing, and both treated children in an off-hand way.
- Among the *Arapesh*, there were few differences between the behaviour of the sexes. Both sexes were gentle and passive, women did the heavy carrying, and the men tried to share the pains of childbirth with their wives by lying with them during it. Both sexes shared equally the tasks of bringing up children (women's traditional role in Britain).
- In the *Tchambuli* tribe, the traditional gender roles found in modern Britain were reversed – it was the men who displayed what we would regard as feminine characteristics, such as doing the shopping and putting on make-up and jewellery to make themselves attractive. Women were the more aggressive, practical ones, who made the sexual advances to men and did all the trading.

These three examples suggest that gender roles are not natural, since they differ between societies even though biological differences remain the same. It is evidence like this which has led sociologists to conclude that masculine and feminine gender identities are primarily constructed through socialization, rather than simply a result of the biological differences between men and women.

Gender socialization and stereotyping in Britain

A gender stereotype is a generalized view of the typical or ideal character-istics of men and women. In modern Britain, for example, girls and women are often expected to show the feminine characteristics of being pretty, slim, gentle, caring, sensitive, submissive, non-competitive, dependent and focused on people (people-oriented), for example with concerns for their family, maintaining friendships, and keeping customers happy.

The masculine stereotype, on the other hand, emphasizes characteristics like physical strength, aggression and assertiveness, independence, com-petitiveness, ambition and focused on 'doing things' (task-oriented), like playing sport, achieving success at work, making things, doing DIY in the home or activities to escape from work. Girls and women who fail to conform to the feminine stereotype are liable to be seen as 'tomboys', while men and boys who fail to conform to the masculine stereotype are likely to be seen as 'wimps'. It is still the case that one of the worst taunts a male child can face is to be called 'a girl' by his peer group.

> A **stereotype** is a generalized, over-simplified view of the features of a social group, allowing for few individual differences among its members. The assumption is made that all members of the group share the same features. An example might be 'all those on welfare benefits are on the fiddle'.

Gender stereotyping of the worst kind. This was how Mr Justice Harman responded when someone explained to him the difference between Miss, Mrs and Ms

Some jobs and activities are also stereotyped as more suitable for men or women: housework and childcare, for example, are still seen as predominantly women's work, while men's work is predominantly seen as something that takes place outside the home in paid employment.

There is a wide range of social institutions which influence the socialization of males and females into their gender roles in modern Britain, but here the family, the education system, the peer group, and the mass media will be focused on.

Activity

1 What other groups of people tend to get stereotyped in the world today, apart from men and women?
2 What are the main features of these stereotypes?
3 Do you consider these stereotypes to be flattering or insulting to the groups concerned? Give reasons for your answer.
4 Look at the following list of words, and divide them into three groups: those you might use to describe women, those you might use to describe men, and those you might use to describe both men and women.

clever	passive	sulky	thoughtful	bastard
powerful	assertive	gentle	caring	attractive
bimbo	emotional	spinster	elegant	soft
aggressive	pretty	tart	kind	tender
cold	sweet	logical	quiet	competitive
sly	ruthless	delicate	brave	active
muscular	bitchy	weak	clinging	slag
domineering	slim	submissive	frigid	gracious
hideous	hunk	handsome	raving	plain
hysterical	blonde	beautiful	bachelor	stud
cute	babe	fit	mover	dickhead
loose	dog	trophy bird	easy	slut

5 Now compare the two lists of words used to describe men and women. Do they present gender stereotypes? You will probably have found there are some words in both lists that have a similar meaning. Why are some words generally restricted to one gender? Discuss why these words are not used to describe both sexes, and how they show stereotyped assumptions about women and men.

The Role of the Family

Children begin to learn their gender roles at a very early age, and often well before they start school they have already learnt much about feminine and masculine roles and identities. The family plays a very important part in this primary socialization.

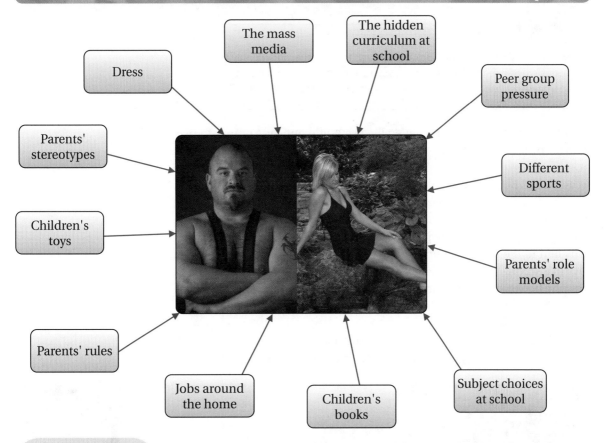

Figure 1.2 The Social construction of gender stereotypes through socialization

A **social construction** is something, like official statistics or the definitions of crime and deviance, that is created by people's interpretations and actions, and only exists because people have constructed it by giving it a particular meaning, interpretation and label.

Parents' stereotypes   Gender socialization begins with the simple question from new parents: 'Is it a boy or a girl?' Parents and relatives tend to hold stereotyped views of the typical or ideal characteristics of boys and girls, and they often try to bring up their children in accordance with this view of normal masculine or feminine behaviour. For example, research shows that baby boys are treated differently from baby girls, with boys more likely to be bounced in physical play, whereas girls are treated more gently and are more .likely to be cuddled. Parental praise like 'you're a good boy / good girl' is likely to reward behaviour which is seen as appropriate for the child's gender, and young children soon learn that approval from parents and relatives often depends on conforming to gender stereotypes. From birth, girls and boys are frequently dressed in different clothes and colours – 'blue for a boy, pink for a girl' – and parents generally buy girls clothes which are more colourful and pretty, and boys more practical clothing. Such different forms of dress generally continue, of course, right throughout life, and pink, for example, is almost exclusively seen as a female colour, even for adult women.

Activity

Go to www.pinkstinks.co.uk/. Browse through the website, and identify four reasons why those involved with the website think the association between pink and female socialization is harmful – in short, why they think pink stinks.

Children's toys   Children are generally given different sorts of toys to play with according to their sex. This increases the pressure on them to perform at an early age the different roles to which they will be expected to conform in adult life. Boys tend to be given (and choose to play with), for example, construction kits, cricket bats, footballs, chemistry sets, electronic toys, guns, cars and trucks, aeroplanes, computers and computer games: more active and technical toys, which take them outside the home, both physically and in their imagination. On the other hand, girls are generally given toys like sewing machines, dolls, prams, toy hoovers, cookers, tea sets and drawing books – toys which are often played with inside the home, and serve to restrict girls to the domestic situation.

Children's games   Children's games frequently involve practising adult gender roles, such as girls acting out the role of nurse to their brother's

More than 1 billion Barbies (and members of her family) have been sold worldwide since 1959. If all the Barbies sold were placed head to toe, they would circle the world more than eleven times. But do such toys make girls overconcerned with their own bodies and image?

Games and toys aimed at boys tend to be more active and take them outside the home both physically and in their imaginations. To what extent do you think children's toys and games contribute to socialization into gender stereotypes?

doctor, or girls playing at being mothers or housewives by playing with dolls, experimenting with make-up, cooking, or serving tea to brothers with toy tea sets. A short time in a nursery shows that, by the age of 3, most little girls are already acting out the stereotyped female gender role. Boys play more aggressive and dominant games, such as war games, or cowboys and Indians.

Table 1.2 Sex-stereotyping of toys

Masculine toys		Either sex		Feminine toys	
Toy	Rating	Toy	Rating	Toy	Rating
Football	1.5	Banjo	4.5	Skipping rope	7.0
Plane	1.7	Rocking horse	4.6	Sewing machine	8.2
Toolset	2.0	Alphabet ball	4.9	Dish cabinet	8.3
Racing car	2.2	Paddling pool	5.0	Cleaning set	8.4
Dumper truck	2.5	Blackboard	5.3	Dolls' pram	8.5
Construction set	2.7	Roller skates	5.3	Dolls' wardrobe	8.7
Tractor	3.0	Telephone	5.6	Cosmetics	8.8
Wheelbarrow	3.2	Teddy bear	5.8		
Sports car	3.6				

The ratings were made by 20-year-old psychology students, and were found to correspond strongly with the choices made by children of either sex. 1 = strongly masculine, 5 = appropriate for both sexes, 9 = strongly feminine.

Source: Data adapted from A. Oakley, *Sex, Gender and Society* (Gower)

Activity

Table 1.2 illustrates the way toys tend to be stereotyped according to their suitability for either boys or girls. This was based on research that was carried out about forty years ago in the 1970s.

1 Look at the three lists of 'strongly masculine', 'strongly feminine' and 'either sex' toys in table 1.2. How, if at all, do you think the gender stereotyping of toys has changed over the last forty years? Draw up three new lists, removing any toys in table 1.2 you think are no longer stereotyped, adding any modern toys you think are strongly sex-stereotyped, and adding modern toys or removing old toys that have become less gender stereotyped and more suitable for either sex. Give reasons for your choices, with examples.

2 Explain all the main differences between the strongly masculine and feminine toys in your modified lists, and suggest how these differences might encourage boys and girls to learn different skills and behave differently as adults. Make sure you refer to examples of particular toys and particular adult roles in your answer.

Parents' rules   Research has suggested that girls face different rules from boys of the same age, and are more strictly supervised by parents. Girls are more likely to be collected by parents from school than boys are, and are less likely to be allowed to play outside or in the street. Girls are also more likely to be told to be in at a certain time, and to have to tell their parents where they are going.

Jobs around the home   As table 1.3 shows, participation by children in household duties shows a marked difference between the sexes, with girls more likely to do indoor housework, generally helping their mothers with domestic jobs, while boys are more likely to do outdoor jobs with their fathers, like cleaning the car, sweeping the paths, and being shown how to do repairs and make things.

Watching and imitating parents   Small children mainly learn by watching and imitating the role models provided by others. A **role model** is a pattern of behaviour on which others model their behaviour.

   Children often observe their parents carrying out their respective gender roles every day. If children see their mothers spending more time in the home

> A **role model** is a pattern of behaviour which others copy and model their own behaviour on.

Table 1.3 11-year-olds' participation in household duties

Duty	Boys %	Girls %	Both %
Washing up	40	63	51
Indoor housework (tidying, vacuum cleaning, dusting, bedmaking, etc.)	19	44	32
Miscellaneous dirty/outside jobs (gardening, sweeping, cleaning car or windows, making or mending fires, peeling potatoes, shoe cleaning, emptying bin, etc.)	36	8	22
Going on errands	39	21	30

Source: adapted from J. Newson, E. Newson, D. Richardson and J. Scaife, 'Perspectives in Sex Role Stereotyping', in J. Chetwynd and O. Hartnett (eds.), *The Sex Role System: Psychological and Sociological Perspectives* (Routledge & Kegan Paul)

Activity

Study table 1.3 and answer the following questions:
1 What household duty is most likely to be performed by both sexes?
2 What household duty is least likely to be performed by (a) boys and (b) girls?
3 How do you think the divisions in household duties among 11-year-olds could be seen as preparation for adult gender roles? Give examples of particular adult roles.

while their fathers go out to work, their mothers spending more time doing cooking, cleaning and other housework than their fathers, and their mothers, rather than their fathers, taking time off work to look after them when they are sick, or taking them to the doctor, then children may well begin to view these roles as the normal ways for men and women to behave. In general, small children are brought up by women, surrounded by women, and it is women who nearly always care for them, whether as mothers, child-minders or teachers. It is perhaps not surprising, then, that many girls still grow up today seeing childcare as being a major part of their role in life.

The Role of the School

The process of gender socialization begun in the home often carries on through schooling. Much of this socialization goes on through the school's hidden curriculum.

Role models are important in socialization, particularly in the early formative years, but also throughout life. How might these role models encourage different behaviours in men and women? Who is important in your life today as role models for behaviour, and to what extent do you try to copy their examples?

This consists of the hidden teaching of attitudes and behaviour, which are taught at school through the school's organization and teachers' attitudes but which are not part of the formal timetable. This is discussed in more detail in chapter 4. Despite equal opportunities policies, the hidden curriculum still often emphasizes the differences between males and females, and encourages different forms of behaviour. Three examples help to illustrate this.

Teachers' attitudes   Teachers have also been socialized into gender roles, and there is evidence suggesting that teachers may give different career advice to boys and girls, such as steering girls towards nursing and office work, and boys towards a much wider range of occupations.

Boys demand more of the teacher's time, and disruptive, unruly behaviour from boys is more likely to be tolerated than the same behaviour from girls. Girl trouble-makers, who fight in the playground or are disruptive in class, for example, are likely to be punished more severely than boys displaying similar behaviour, since girls are not expected to act in such an 'unfeminine' way.

Schoolbooks   Reading-books in infant schools have often shown women and little girls in the housewife/mother role, for example girls helping mother in the home, or watching their brothers climbing trees, mending the car and getting into mischief. Boys are more likely to be portrayed as playing with cars or trains, playing football, exploring, building things, climbing trees, and so on. Schools and textbook publishers are now tackling such stereotypes, but the effects of these changes will take time, and of course schools alone cannot reverse the stereotyping that goes on in a wide range of areas.

In secondary school, gender differences are reinforced by the illustrations in textbooks for different subjects – science books less commonly show girls doing science, and boys rarely appear in home economics books, suggesting that some subjects are more suited to one sex than to the other.

Subject choice   Girls and boys have traditionally been counselled by parents and teachers into taking different subjects. Girls have been more likely to take arts subjects (like English literature, history and foreign languages) and study subjects like food technology, business studies, leisure and tourism, and hair and beauty, while boys have been more likely to take sciences, CAD, and design and technology – subjects which are more likely to lead to more skilled and technical occupations after school. This gender division is also found in sport, with rugby and cricket for the boys and hockey and netball for the girls. Under the National Curriculum, *all* 11- to 14-year-olds have to take technology, which includes home economics, business studies, food technology, and design and technology. This means that these gender divisions between subjects were broken down to some extent during the 1990s. However, even within the National Curriculum, there are gender differences within option choices. For example, girls are more likely to take home economics, textiles and food technology, while boys are more likely to opt for electronics, CAD, woodwork or graphics, and after age 16 other subject divisions still remain, as chapter 4 on education shows.

> ### Activity
> 1 On the basis of your own experiences at both primary and secondary school, make a list of any difficulties or pressures you might have experienced at school, because of your sex, in choosing subjects and options that you wanted to do. Take into account factors such as the views of your parents, friends and teachers, and the advice of careers and subject teachers.
> 2 Suggest explanations for why these difficulties and pressures exist, and discuss your findings and ideas with others in your group.

The Importance of the Peer Group

A peer group is a group of people of similar age and status with whom a person mixes socially. Generally, people try to gain acceptance among their peers by conforming to the norms of their peer group. These norms frequently involve stereotyped masculine and feminine roles. For example, among male peer groups, interests and norms often centre on activities like football, music, cars, motor-bikes, computers and computer games. Female interests often centre on things such as fashion, diet, celebrities, make-up and dancing. The peer group can exert strong pressure to conform to these interests: a boy, for example, who collected soft toys would be quite likely to

How do you think the interests and concerns of male and female teenage peer groups differ? How does your peer group influence your behaviour?

find himself ridiculed by his peer group; a girl who played rugby or was into boxing might be seen as a bit of a tomboy. Young people who fail to conform to gender stereotypes may find themselves ridiculed by their peer group, or excluded from group activities. Such pressures can help to discourage participation in activities which don't conform to gender stereotypes.

Double standards   Among teenage boys (and often adult men too) sexual promiscuity and sexual conquest are often encouraged and admired as approved masculine behaviour, and are seen as a means of achieving status in the male peer group. However, males will condemn this same promiscuity among women – promiscuous girls and women are likely to be seen as 'up for it', and called 'loose', 'slags' or 'slappers' or some other insulting term. This attitude is sometimes reinforced even by the female peer group, where sexual relations by girls are often only approved of in the context of a steady, close relationship. Girls and women who have sex outside some steady relationship are therefore likely to find themselves condemned by men and women alike. In short, promiscuous men are seen as stags or studs; promiscuous women are seen as slags or sluts. This double standard helps to encourage conformity to separate gender identities for men and women, with the stereotyped man as sexual athlete and woman as the passive and faithful lover, wife or girlfriend.

Activity

1 Explain the influences your peer group has had in forming your gender identity, and, drawing on your own experiences, suggest ways it does this.
2 Do you have any evidence that there is a double standard applied to the behaviour of males and females when it comes to sexual activity? Note down your evidence and discuss it with others, and try to establish whether this double standard is a common occurrence.

The Role of the Mass Media

The mass media include films, videos and DVDs, television, newspapers, CDs, radio, advertising, books, comics, magazines and the Internet. The mass media create and reinforce gender stereotypes in a number of ways. Comics, for example, present different images of men and women: girls are usually presented as pretty, romantic, helpless, easily upset and emotional, and dependent on boys – strong, independent, unemotional and assertive – for support and guidance, and boys and girls are often presented in traditional stereotyped gender roles such as soldiers (boys) or nurses (girls). A similar pattern is shown on children's television, and much TV advertising shows gender stereotypes. Around 80 per cent of TV advertising voice-overs are male voices – suggesting authority. The media, particularly advertising, often promote the 'beauty myth' – the idea that women should be assessed primarily in terms of their appearance.

> **Activity**
>
> Examine some children's reading-books, comics, or male or female adult magazines, or study TV adverts, and see if you can identify any pattern in the different roles and interests allocated to boys and girls or men and women. Provide evidence for your conclusions.

You may have found from the previous activity that there are often very different types of story and magazine aimed at males and females. Romantic fiction is almost exclusively aimed at a female readership. A glance at the magazine shelves of any large newsagents will reveal a 'Women's interests' section, consisting almost exclusively of magazines on 'true-life' stories, the lifestyles of celebrities, beauty, fashion and haircare, health and slimming, alongside traditional fare of cooking, homecare, housekeeping, and weddings, mothers and babies.

Women's magazines still often portray stereotypical views of women's interests

This shows very clearly the way the media both encourage and cater for a particular view of a woman's role. Similar 'Men's interests' sections are much less common. However, men (and not women) can often be seen queuing up to read magazines (often classified as of 'general interest') concerned with photography, electronic gadgets of all kinds, computers and computer games, DIY, and all manner of transport: cars, motor-bikes, aircraft, trains and boats. The top-shelf soft-porn magazines are aimed exclusively at men.

Activity

Take two similarly priced magazines – one aimed at men, and one aimed at women.
1 List the differences between them, in terms of things like the stories or issues covered and the pictures used.
2 From the list of differences you have made, suggest ways that these might contribute to differences in the socialization and adult behaviour of males and females.

Images of men and women   When women appear in the mass media, it has traditionally been in a limited number of stereotyped roles. These include:

- *As a sex object* – the image of the slim, sexually seductive, scantily clad figure typically found on page 3 of the *Sun* newspaper is used by the advertising industry to sell everything from peanuts to motor-bikes and newspapers. Supermodels are the beauty queens of today, at a time when Miss World beauty contests are seen by many as redundant and unacceptable
- *In their relationships with men*, such as bosses, husbands and lovers
- *As emotional and unpredictable*
- *In the housewife/mother role* – as the content, capable and caring house-wife and mother, whose constant concern is with the whiteness of clothes, the cleanliness of floors, and the evening meal; and as the per-son who keeps the family together and manages its emotions.

Men are presented in a wider range of roles which have no particular refer-ence to their gender. Women's roles often involve being women first – that is, women play limited roles restricted to their gender. The masculine stere-otype of the physically well-built, muscular, handsome, brave, unemotional, non-domestic male still often appears. These differing roles of men and women are most evident in advertising, even when young children are used. For example, television advertisements for washing-up liquid or washing powder nearly always show mothers and small daughters working together, and boys are usually the ones who come in covered in dirt. While men and small boys hardly ever appear in such advertisements, when they do appear

To what extent do you think this shelf of men's magazines seems to reflect gender stereotypes? Do you think men's and women's magazines today still present stereotypes of men and women? Try to think of some specific examples with which you are familiar

Activity

1 Go to www.youtube.com/watch?v=M9fFOelpE_8 and list and explain briefly the gender stereotypes shown in the video clip. Do you think the clip gives a fair, if exaggerated, picture of gender stereotypes in advertising? What effects do you think such images might have on the behaviour of men and women, particularly over a long period of time?

2 A psychological study of the 'lonely heart' personal columns found that gender stereotyping was still the norm. Putting together the main features of the advertising, the study drew up the typical male and female lonely hearts advertisements:

Male advert
Male, high wage earner, own home, with caring genuine nature, attractive, with sense of humour and interested in home building, seeks attractive, loving young woman for genuine partnership.

Female advert
Female, attractive, slim, tall shapely blonde, loving and sensitive, seeks financially secure caring man with good sense of humour and own home for genuine relationship.

(a) What are the differences between the two advertisements in the qualities expected of a male and female?

(b) Look at the personal columns of a local or national newspaper, and see if you can spot any common themes in the qualities that men look for in women, and that women look for in men. Link your findings, if you can, to gender stereotyping.

in a domestic role it is nearly always made clear it is an exception, or that they are not very good at domestic tasks.

In recent years, media images of gender have been changing. 'Girl power' was a phenomenon in the 1990s, challenging more traditional stereotypes of women as housewives or low-status workers, with more emphasis on women being themselves, and doing things by themselves. Movies, for example, now show more self-confident, tough, intelligent and independent female lead characters – though they can also maintain perfect make-up and hair.

The masculine ideals of toughness, self-reliance and emotional coldness now exist alongside an emphasis on men's emotions, and the problems of masculinity. Such changing gender identities are shown by the feminized David Beckham – one of the world's most famous role models for both sexes – who has fronted many advertising campaigns for various cosmetic products.

Men—a user's guide

Mark Haddon and Clara Vulliamy

Activity

1 What do the two cartoons opposite suggest are the main forces which contribute to the gender socialization process?
2 Study the result of the socialization of men shown in the cartoons, and describe the stereotype of a 'typical male'.
3 Do you think the cartoons give an accurate impression of present masculine behaviour? Back up your view with evidence of both child and adult male behaviour.
4 To what extent do you think media stereotyping of females and males is changing? Give examples to illustrate your answer.

Activity

Go through the following questions, and write down a couple of points in relation to each one. Then discuss your findings in a group, and try to reach some conclusions about how the socialization of males and females might be changing in contemporary Britain.

1 To what extent is the social process of gender role socialization discussed in the sections above still accurate in contemporary Britain?
2 Does socialization mean that women and men still have different experiences and expectations of life?
3 Does socialization still have the general effect of emphasizing girls' domestic responsibilities of housework and childcare, limiting their self-confidence, and pushing them, eventually, towards marriage and the roles of housewife and mother (often alongside paid employment) as their primary roles in life?
4 Are boys still more likely to grow up conforming to the stereotype of the non-domestic, practical, unemotional, independent and assertive male, whose role in life is that of 'the provider, the protector, and the impregnator'?
5 Are the stereotypes of men and women changing? If so, how?

SOCIAL ISSUES, SOCIAL PROBLEMS AND SOCIAL POLICY

Social issues tend to be matters that people worry about, and their causes, effects and solutions are frequently controversial, generating quite heated debate and discussion. They are also matters that may affect in some way many members of society and that are rooted in the wider community, rather than being purely personal issues under the control of any one individual. Such issues might include the causes and consequences of social class, gender and ethnic inequalities, the causes of and solutions to poverty, the welfare state, crime and the fear of crime, the quality of education and healthcare, and **racism**. Many of these and other issues are considered in other parts of this book.

> **Racism** is believing or acting as though an individual or group is superior or inferior on the grounds of racial or ethnic origins, usually based on skin colour or other physical characteristics, and suggesting that groups defined as inferior have lower intelligence and abilities. Racism often involves acting in a hostile way towards individuals or groups defined as inferior.

Examples of social issues

- **Social class, gender and ethnic inequalities** and unequal and unfair treatment can generate hostility and conflict between the haves and the have-nots, between women and men, and between different ethnic groups. These can contribute to social instability and social conflict. These issues are discussed later in this book.

- **Poverty** is an issue as the poor find themselves lacking the resources to obtain the types of diets, participate in the activities and have the consumer goods and living conditions that others in society take for granted. This can generate resentment and conflict, contributing to an unstable society. This can be made worse as the poor often lack the power to do much to change their position. Poverty is also an issue for government, as there are huge costs in social welfare benefits and tax credits to help the poor, plus potential social disorder if poverty and resentment among the poor about social inequality become too great.

- **Crime** is a source of fear for many people. Even though crime rates have been falling in recent years, fear of crime remains persistently higher than the real risk of being a victim of crime. Older people have particularly high levels of fear of crime, as they tend to be more home-centred and dependent on the media for information, and the media tend to focus on bad news and make exaggerated reports on crime to sell papers and attract viewers. Similarly, the media often give the impression that most young people are frightening and threatening anti-social, gun- and knife-carrying thugs. In fact, most young people are conformist and law-abiding.

- **Racism** is a serious issue for black and minority ethnic groups, as they often find themselves discriminated against in many areas of life. African Caribbeans and Asians are around fourteen times more likely to be the victim of a racially motivated incident than white people, and they often

A slum neighbourhood in Freetown, the capital city of Sierra Leone. In what ways might such poverty pose threats to the stability of society? In contemporary Britain, such poverty is very rarely found, but how might large numbers of people lacking everyday things others take for granted pose threats to social stability in the UK?

Life chances
are the chances of obtaining those things defined as desirable and of avoiding those things defined as undesirable in any society.

A **social problem** is something that is seen as harmful to society in some way, and that needs something doing to sort it out.

Social policy refers to the packages of plans and actions adopted by national and local government or various voluntary agencies to solve social problems or achieve other goals that are seen as important.

face discrimination in jobs, housing and the law. Racism can also generate wider conflicts, as it can breed resentment, periodically erupting in riots, and cause a fragmented society lacking cohesion.

- **The quality of education** is a social issue as education is a key to **life chances** – the chances of gaining the desirable, and avoiding the undesirable things in life, such as gaining a well-paid job, a nice home, consumer goods and good health, and avoiding unemployment, poverty, poor housing and ill-health. Poor schools, with a high turnover of teachers, low standards and multiple social problems, mean that young people are being denied opportunities in life.

Social problems

Many social issues are also often considered to be **social problems** – things that are in some way harmful to society, and that need something doing to sort them out. The issues referred to above are also social problems, as they cause difficulties, resentment and instability in society, and harm many people.

Social policy

Social problems are tackled by the application of **social policy**. Social policy refers to the plans and actions of national and local government and various voluntary agencies designed to solve social problems. Social policy seeks to achieve goals that have an impact on and improve the life chances and welfare of citizens, such as goals concerned with health, housing, employment, social care, education, crime and transport.

There are always different ways of tackling social problems, and the social policy option chosen – if indeed any is chosen – will depend on those with power to make policy, which is nearly always either national or local government. For example, poverty is a social problem, and possible social policies to tackle it include:

- doing nothing – the poor are inadequate, workshy and lazy, and have only themselves to blame for their own inadequacy, and therefore don't deserve any help. Not providing help will force them to help themselves
- forcing people into work, even if jobs are very low-paid
- redistributing wealth, through higher welfare benefits for the poor, paid for by higher taxes on the rich
- a national minimum wage, tax credits and other incentives to help the low-paid.

The option chosen will depend on the views about poverty and its causes held by those with the power to implement social policies.

Activity

Take *one* of the following social problems (or another social issue, of your own choosing, that is also a social problem): teenage pregnancy; obesity; sex discrimination; racism; crime; family breakdown.
1 Explain three reasons why the issue you have chosen is a social problem.
2 Outline three social policies that might be adopted to resolve the problem.

Sociology, social problems and social policy

Governments are more likely to produce social policies that are effective and work as intended in tackling social problems if they base them on proper evidence gained through research. The work of sociologists in areas such as education, health, poverty and crime has contributed to understanding and explaining social problems, and has sometimes had quite important effects on the social policies of governments. Government will often commission research from sociologists in universities to assist policy making.

Sociology can assist social policy making by:

- *changing assumptions* – detailed research can change existing (incorrect) assumptions about what the nature of a social problem is, and therefore the means of tackling it. For example, sociological research has contributed a great deal to understanding the extent of poverty in contemporary Britain, and has shown that the causes are primarily located in society rather than the individual inadequacies of poor people (these issues are discussed later in this book).

- *identifying social problems* – sociological research may uncover social problems, and help to identify their causes and solutions.
- *providing the evidence* – sociological research, through surveys, opinion polls, collecting the statistics and analysing the problems, can provide the evidence to assist in policy-making decisions, and either back up or show the inadequacies of particular social policies.
- *identifying the unintended consequences of policies* – for example, have policies designed to reduce crime in one area simply moved it to another?
- *assessing the results* – sociological research can help to establish whether policies have worked, whether they have achieved what they set out to do, and whether they need changing or scrapping.

It is by analysing social issues, identifying social problems and suggesting policy solutions to them that sociologists and their research can help to provide the means of improving society.

DIFFERENT VIEWS OF SOCIETY

Macro and micro approaches

A **macro approach** is one that focuses on the large-scale structure of society as a whole, rather than on individuals and small groups.

A **micro approach** is one that focuses on small groups or individuals, rather than on the structure of society as a whole.

Sociologists have different ways of seeing society. Some focus on the structure of society, taking a large-scale or **macro approach** to the study of the social world.

Such sociologists will look at the various social institutions making up society's structure, and the links between them. For example, they might study the role of the family or the education system in society as a whole, rather than looking at an individual family or family member, or individual school or student. Others tend to take a small-scale or **micro approach**, studying small-scale interaction, such as how an individual family operates and the interaction of individual family members, or an intensive case study of one school.

Consensus and conflict views of society

Is society based on harmony and agreement between individuals and groups? Or is society based on conflict and antagonism between them? These two questions reflect different views among sociologists about the way society works. These two approaches are often referred to as consensus and conflict theories.

Consensus theory

Consensus theory is the approach adopted by functionalist sociologists.

Functionalism sees society built up and working like the human body, made up of interrelated parts working together to maintain society. For example, just as the heart, lungs and brain in the human body work together to maintain human life, social institutions like the family, education and the law work together to maintain society.

Stability in society is based on socialization into norms and values on which most people agree. These shared norms and values are known as a value consensus.

Consensus theorists, when studying society, emphasize these shared norms and shared values that exist between people, and see society made up of individuals and social institutions working together in harmony, without much conflict between individuals and groups.

> **Consensus theory** is an approach that sees society made up of individuals and social institutions working together in harmony, without much conflict between people and groups.
> **Value consensus** means a general agreement around the main norms and values of society.

Conflict theory

Conflict theory has its origins in the work of Karl Marx (1818–83), and Max Weber (1864–1920).

Rather than viewing society as essentially peaceful and harmonious, conflict theorists emphasize social differences and conflicts, with inequalities in wealth, power and status all creating conflicts between individuals and social groups. For example, feminist writers argue that society is essentially a patriarchy – a male-dominated society – with a range of inequalities and conflicts between men and women.

Other conflicts exist between black and white people, between employers and employees, and between the rich and the poor. These groups have different interests and values, and there is no value consensus. The conflict approach sees differences and conflicts between individuals, groups and classes as important features of contemporary society, and tends to emphasize these conflicts when describing and explaining society.

> **Conflict theory** is an approach that sees society as having many social differences and conflicts, with inequalities in wealth, power and status all creating conflicts between individuals and groups.
> **A feminist** is someone who believes that women are disadvantaged in society, and should have rights, power and status equal to those of men.
> **Patriarchy** is where power, status and authority are held by men.

Activity

1 Imagine you were creating an ideal society from scratch. Drawing on the ideas of social structure and social processes discussed in this chapter, plan how you would organize your ideal society, with particular reference to the following issues:
- the care and socialization of children
- the passing on of society's knowledge and skills from one generation to the next
- the production of food and other goods necessary for survival
- how you would allocate food and other goods to members of society
- the establishment and enforcement of rules of behaviour, and how decisions will be made

- how you would deal with people who didn't conform to social rules
- how you would coordinate things and resolve disputes between members of society
- how you would prevent or deal with any social conflicts.

2   Consider what social issues might arise in your society, and how they might be brought to the attention of everyone.

3   Identify two social problems that might arise, and suggest ways you might resolve them.

4   Do you think your society would mainly be marked by consensus or conflict? Give reasons for your answer.

5   Suggest ways your ideal society is similar to, or different from, the organization of contemporary Britain. How would you explain these similarities or differences?

CHAPTER SUMMARY

After studying this chapter, you should be able to:

- explain why sociology is different from common-sense and biological (or naturalistic) explanations, and differs from journalism and psychology

- explain some of the problems sociologists face compared with those working in the natural sciences

- explain why sociology is scientific

- define the meaning of socialization, culture, identity, roles, role conflict, values, laws, norms, social control, deviance, and positive and negative sanctions, and explain their importance in understanding human behaviour in society

- explain what is meant by social structure and social processes, and discuss gender role socialization as a social process

- explain, with examples, what is meant by a social issue, a social problem and social policy, and how sociology can contribute to social policy

- explain briefly what is meant by micro and macro, and consensus and conflict approaches to the study of society.

KEY TERMS

conflict theory
consensus theory
consumer (or consumption) goods
culture
customs
deviance
feminist
gender

gender role
hidden curriculum
identity
life chances
macro approach
micro approach
norms
objectivity
patriarchy
peer group
primary socialization

racism
role conflict
role model
roles
sanctions
secondary socialization
sex
social construction
social control
social institutions
social policy

social problem
social structure
socialization
sociology
status
stereotype
value consensus
value freedom
values

Studying
Society (2)

Contents

Studying Society (2)

Doing Sociological Research

KEY ISSUES

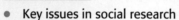

- Key issues in social research
- Quantitative and qualitative data
- Primary and secondary sources
- Social surveys
- Longitudinal studies
- Observation
- Planning your own research project

Sociology is concerned with a wide range of issues in social life, spanning the continuing existence of poverty, the influence of the mass media on our views about the world, the things that make work interesting or not, and how the very centre of our personalities is constructed through socialization into gender roles. The interests and concerns of sociologists are not that different from those of most people in society. However, what makes the views of sociologists different from those likely to be aired in a pub, in the canteen at work, or in other daily situations where people swap views and form opinions is that sociologists try to provide evidence to back up what they say. This evidence is collected from a variety of sources and through the use of a number of research methods. In this chapter, we will examine the types of data (or information) sociologists collect, the range of sources used and the methods sociologists use to collect their own information.

KEY ISSUES IN SOCIAL RESEARCH

There are three key issues that should always be considered when carrying out or assessing research. These are the issues of validity, reliability and the ethics of research.

- **Validity** is concerned with notions of truth: how far the findings of research actually provide a true, genuine or authentic picture of what is being studied. Data can be reliable without being valid. For example, official crime statistics may be reliable, in so far as researchers repeating the data collection would get the same results over and over again, but they are not valid if they don't give us the full picture on the extent of crime.
- **Reliability** is concerned with *replication*: whether another researcher using the same method for the same research on the same or a similar group would achieve the same results. For example, if different researchers used the same questionnaire on similar samples of the population, then the results should be more or less the same if the techniques are reliable.
- The **ethics** of research are concerned with morality and standards of behaviour when sociologists carry out research. These important ethical issues are considered in the box below.

THE ETHICS OF RESEARCH

When doing research, sociologists should always consider the following points:

- They should take into account the sensitivities of those helping with their research. For example, it would not be appropriate to ask about attitudes to abortion in a hospital maternity ward where women may be having babies or have suffered miscarriages.
- Findings should be reported accurately and honestly.
- The physical, social and mental well-being of people who help in research should not be harmed by research – for example, by the disclosure of information given in confidence which might get the person into trouble, or cause them embarrassment.
- The anonymity, privacy and interests of those who participate in your research should be respected. Their personal information should be kept confidential. Sociologists should not identify them by name, or enable them (or an institution) to be easily identified.
- As far as possible, research should be based on the freely given consent of those studied. Researchers should make clear to those participating what they're doing, why they're doing it, and what they will do with their findings. This is known as obtaining *informed consent*.

> ### Activity
>
> Suggest at least *two* ethical problems that may arise in each of the following research situations, and suggest ways of overcoming them:
>
> (a) You want to investigate what sort of men get involved with prostitutes. In order to do this, you photograph the car number-plates of kerb crawlers in a well-known local red light district. You then track down the names and addresses of the owners, with help from a friend in the police, and call on the men in their homes to interview them about their lives, pretending your survey is about healthy eating.
>
> (b) You want to study, using a questionnaire, to what extent students at a local college have been in trouble with the police. The questionnaire involves asking students about all their illegal activities as well as encounters with the police. In collaboration with the college authorities, completion of the questionnaire is made a compulsory requirement of enrolment at the college, although students are not told what the questionnaire is for.
>
> (c) You want to study how much time parents spend playing with and talking to their small children. You plan to ask children about this, selected from those at a local infant school, but you can't mention it to their parents in case they distort the results by telling the children what to say.
>
> (d) You want to observe teachers as they are teaching in an infant school to see how far they stereotype boys and girls and treat them differently in classes. You decide not to tell the teacher what you're doing, because otherwise you're afraid they'll behave differently. You therefore pretend you're interested in the behaviour of children in the classroom.

QUANTITATIVE AND QUALITATIVE DATA

> **Quantitative data** is information that can be expressed in statistical or number form.
> **Qualitative data** is information concerned with the feelings people have, and the meanings and interpretations they give to some issue or event.

Quantitative data is anything that can be expressed in statistical or number form or can be measured in some way, such as age, qualifications or income. Such data is usually presented in the form of statistical tables, graphs, pie charts and bar charts. There is more about interpreting statistical data in the appendix.

Qualitative data is concerned with people's feelings about some issue or event, and tries to get at the way they see things. Such data is normally in the form of the sociologist describing and interpreting people's feelings and lifestyles, often using direct quotations from the people studied. Personal diaries, letters, interview data, video, audio-recordings, photographs and documents like newspaper reports and emails are all forms of qualitative data.

This data may be gathered from either primary sources or secondary sources.

Content analysis

Content analysis is a way of trying to analyse the content of documents and other qualitative material, like books, newspapers, magazines, films and advertisements, by quantifying it. This is done, for example. by sorting out categories, and then going through documents, books, magazines, television programmes and so on systematically, recording the number of times items in each category appear. Examples might include researchers analysing reading books or comics for children when seeking evidence of gender role stereotyping, using categories such as 'male leader / female led', 'female works or plays indoors / male outdoors' and so on.

The advantages of content analysis

- It is a relatively cheap means of research.
- There is no involvement with people that can sometimes lead to distorted results if people's normal behaviour changes.
- It is a *reliable* research method, as it produces quantitative statistical data that other researchers can easily check.
- It enables the discovery of things that may not be obvious before the content analysis is carried out – for example, whether gender role stereotyping is really occurring in children's books.

The disadvantages of content analysis

- It depends on the categories chosen by the researcher and how he or she interprets what they see. For example, the researcher decides in analysing a children's comic to use the categories of 'male leader / female led', but these categories and what is happening depend on the researcher's personal judgements.
- It is mainly concerned with describing what is being studied, and is not very good at explaining it.

Activity

Refer to the section above on content analysis.

1 Look at a selection of red-top daily or Sunday newspapers (these are the *Sun*, *Daily Mirror*, *Sunday Mirror*, *Daily Star*, *Daily Star Sunday*, *News of the World* and the *People*, plus, in Scotland, the *Daily Record* and *Sunday Mail*), and carry out a content analysis of the photographs of men and women, and how they are portrayed. You will need to decide what you want to discover, work out suitable categories, and then work through the newspapers classifying photos into the categories you've chosen, and counting them up.

2 Draw conclusions from your findings, saying what you think you discovered and outlining any problems you had in categorizing the photographs.

● The interpretation of what is being described may differ from one research-er to the next, and items may not fit neatly into one particular category.

PRIMARY AND SECONDARY SOURCES

Secondary data is information that already exists and which the researcher hasn't collected herself or himself.
Primary data is information that sociologists have collected themselves.

Figure 2.1 Secondary sources of data

Secondary sources of data are those which already exist. **Secondary data** has already been collected by others. Figure 2.1 shows a range of secondary sources which might be used by sociologists in carrying out research.

Because the existing data required for research may be unreliable or may simply not have been collected, sociologists often have to collect their own data from primary sources. **Primary data** is that which is collected by soci-ologists themselves – it only exists because the sociologist has collected it. Such information is usually obtained by carrying out a social survey or by non-participant or participant observation (these will be discussed shortly).

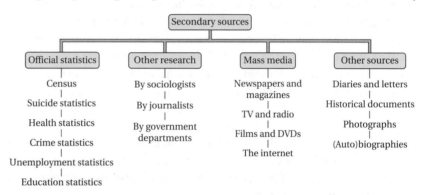

Activity

1 Go through the following examples, marking each as primary or secondary *and* quantitative or qualitative data:
   ● exam results of schools in your area published in a local newspaper
   ● newspaper stories from the 1930s
   ● information collected by you showing the proportions of students doing different GCSE subjects
   ● teenage magazine articles
   ● statistics produced by the local NHS showing inequalities in health
   ● video-recordings of a week's news reports
   ● letters in a newspaper complaining about the risks of accidents arising from cyclists riding on footpaths
   ● the published diaries of a former prime minister
2 Explain, with reasons, in what circumstances you might, or might not, consider each of the above pieces of data to be (a) reliable, and (b) valid, as sources of evidence.

The advantages of secondary sources

Secondary sources have the main advantage that the material is readily available and so is cheap and easy to use. There is no need to spend time and money collecting data, and some data, such as that provided by the census, would be impossible for an individual to collect. In some cases, secondary sources may be the only sources of information available in an area, such as in historical research, and sociologists may therefore have no alternative but to use them.

The problems of secondary sources

Secondary sources do present problems for use in sociological research. The information may be unrepresentative, and therefore may not apply to the whole population. For example, before the beginning of compulsory education in Britain in 1880, it was mainly only the well-off who could read and write, and so it was mainly they who left documents behind them.

The information may be inaccurate in some way and therefore *unreliable* or lacking in *validity*. It may be forged or biased, contain errors or be exaggerated. Newspaper reports, for example, are notoriously unreliable as sources of evidence, as discussed in chapter 6.

Official statistics

Sociologists very often use official statistics, which are those produced by the government, in their research – such as those on crime, health and unemployment. Such statistics must be treated very cautiously by sociologists, as the following examples suggest.

- *Official crime statistics* don't include a large number of crimes not discovered by or reported to the police. Between around 58 per cent and 70 per cent of crimes reported in the British Crime Survey are never reported to the police. The official crime statistics don't really provide evidence of the real extent of crime in society. (There is more on crime statistics in chapter 5.)
- *Official health statistics* may be inaccurate because:
  - Not all sick people go to the doctor, and not all people who persuade doctors they are ill are really sick.
  - They depend on people persuading doctors they are ill, and are therefore simply a record of doctors' judgements and decision-making.
  - Doctors may diagnose illnesses incorrectly, reflecting how patients describe their symptoms and the state of the doctor's knowledge, so records of illnesses may not be accurate. For example, there may

have been many AIDS deaths recorded as pneumonia or other diseases before AIDS was discovered in the 1980s.

- *Unemployment statistics* often underestimate the real numbers of unemployed, as they exclude a number of groups:
  - Those in part-time work who are really looking for full-time work – a form of disguised unemployment.
  - Those on government job training schemes, who can't find a proper job but don't count as unemployed.
  - Those reluctantly staying on at school or college because they can't find jobs.
  - Some married women who can't claim unemployment-related benefits as they don't have enough national insurance contributions to qualify.

When sociologists use such secondary data, including official statistics, they must be very aware of their limitations, question their *validity* and *reliability*, and therefore approach such data with care.

Activity

1 To get a flavour of some of the official statistics available, go to www. statistics.gov.uk/focuson. Take any of the *Focus on* topics (or, more likely, sub-topics) that interest you, and make a few brief notes on what you find out and the source from which the information is derived. How useful do you think such official statistics and websites are for sociologists trying to find out about society?

2 Read the following passage and then answer the questions:

Suicide is, by definition, the death of a person who intended to kill him or herself. The problem for coroners is they can't ask dead people if they meant to kill themselves, so they can only guess at the truth by looking for 'clues' in the circumstances surrounding the death. Atkinson has suggested there are four main factors or clues which coroners take into account when deciding whether a death is a suicide or not.

- Whether there was a suicide note.
- The way the person died, for example by hanging, drowning or a drug overdose. Death in a road accident rarely results in a suicide verdict.
- The place the death occurred and the circumstances surrounding it – for example, a drug overdose in a remote wood would be more likely to be seen as a suicide than if it occurred at home in bed. A coroner might also consider circumstances such as whether the person had been drinking before taking the drugs, and whether the drugs had been hoarded or not.
- The life history and mental state of the dead person, such as her or his state of health, and whether the victim was in debt, had just failed exams, lost her or his job, got divorced, or was depressed or not.

Coroners do not always agree on the way they interpret these clues. For example, Atkinson found one coroner believed a death by drowning was likely to be a suicide if the clothes were left neatly folded on the beach, but another coroner might attach little importance to this.

(a)   How is suicide defined in the passage?
(b)   Why do you think coroners attach such importance to suicide notes?
(c)   Suggest two reasons why the presence or absence of a suicide note might be an unreliable clue to a dead person's intention to die.
(d)   Suggest ways relatives and friends might try to persuade a coroner that a death was not a suicide but an accident.
(e)   On the basis of the evidence in the passage, suggest reasons why: (i) some deaths classified as suicides may have been accidental; and (ii) some deaths classified as accidents may in fact have been suicides.
(f)   With reference to the evidence in the passage, suggest reasons why a sociologist should be very careful about using official statistics on suicide as a record of the real number of suicides in society.

SOCIAL SURVEYS

A **social survey** involves the sociologist in systematically gathering information about some group of people. This is done by questioning them using questionnaires and interviews.

A **social survey** is a means of collecting primary data, often from large numbers of people, in a standardized statistical form, by questioning them using interviews and questionnaires.

Social surveys often use questionnaires to collect information from large numbers of people, with results usually presented in statistical form

The survey population

One of the first steps in any social survey is the selection of the target group of people to be studied. This target group is called the **survey population**. The choice of survey population will depend on the **hypothesis** which the sociologist is investigating. This is any idea or hunch which the sociologist guesses might be true, but which has not yet been tested against the evidence.

For example, a hypothesis like 'teachers treat males more favourably than females' might mean the survey population would include all pupils and teachers in a particular school.

If the survey population is small, such as a class of college students, it may be possible to question everyone in it. In some cases, because the organization doing the research has enough time and money, it may be possible to investigate everyone, even in a very large survey population. For example, the government has the resources to survey the entire population of the United Kingdom in the census every ten years – at a cost of £250 million in 2001 (you can view the latest census and general information about the census at www.ons.gov.uk/census). Such costs are way beyond the reach of most sociologists and market research organizations, and, because of cost and time, most surveys are limited to studying a sample of the survey population.

Sampling

A **sample** is simply a small group drawn from the survey population. Taking a sample is a way of making general statements about the whole survey population based on the responses of only a small percentage of the total survey population.

If the results obtained from the sample are to be used to make valid (true) generalizations about the whole survey population, it is important that the sample is *representative*. A **representative sample** is one that contains a good cross-section of the survey population, such as the right proportions of people of different ethnic origins, ages, social classes and sexes. The information obtained from a representative sample should provide roughly the same results as if the whole survey population had been questioned.

Sociologists obtain representative samples by using various sampling methods.

Methods of obtaining a representative sample

1 Drawing up a sampling frame

A **sampling frame** is simply a list of names of all those included in the survey population from which the sample will eventually be selected – for example, the names of all children in a school taken from registers, or doctors in a town. A commonly used sampling frame is the Electoral Register, which includes nearly all the names and addresses of adults over the age of 18 in Britain who are eligible to vote in elections. The Royal Mail's Postcode Address File is another widely used sampling frame, as it contains all addresses in the UK. Doctors' lists of patients are also used, as most people are registered with a doctor.

The choice and completeness of the sampling frame are very important if the results obtained are to be generalized to the whole survey population. For example, a telephone directory would be an unreliable sampling frame if we wanted to select a sample which was representative of the entire adult population, as it only contains those on the telephone and excludes those who may not want or be able to afford a telephone, who are ex-directory, and who are on cable or use only mobiles, and are therefore not included in the phone book.

2 Deciding on the sample size

The size of the sample will depend on the amount of time and money available. However, if the sample is too small the results obtained may not be representative of the whole survey population. The ideal size of a sample is that at which the results obtained won't be made much more accurate by increasing the size of the sample.

3 Deciding on a sampling method

A sampling method is the process by which the sociologist selects from the sampling frame representative individuals to question. There are a number of sampling methods used by sociologists to try to gain a representative sample.

Simple random sampling Simple random sampling means that every individual in the survey population has an equal chance of being picked out for questioning. For example, all names are put in a hat and enough names picked out to make up the required sample size. This is most commonly done by numbering all the names in the sampling frame and then getting a computer to select enough numbers at random to make up the size of sample required.

The problem with this method is that, purely by chance, the random sample may not be representative of the survey population. For example, there may be too many people of one sex, of one age group, or who live in the same area.

Systematic sampling Systematic sampling is a method where names are selected from the survey population at regular intervals until the size of

A random sample is a bit like a lottery draw – every person has an equal chance of being selected but, like the lottery, you've got to be in it to win it, or, in surveys, to be in the sampling frame to have a chance of being selected

sample is reached. For example, every tenth name in the sampling frame is selected.

Quota sampling   Quota sampling is a method in which interviewers are told to go and select people who fit into certain categories, according to their proportion in the survey population as a whole. For example, an interviewer may be asked to question thirty men and women over the age of 45. The choice of the actual individuals chosen is left to the honesty of the interviewer (unlike other sampling methods in which actual named individuals are identified).

Stratified random sampling   Stratified random sampling is a way of attempting to avoid the possible errors caused by simple random sampling. In this case, the sampling frame is divided into strata (layers) or sub-groups relevant to the hypothesis being investigated, such as groups of a similar age, sex, ethnic group, or social class, and a random sample is then taken from each sub-group. For example, in a survey of doctors, we may know from earlier research that 8 per cent of all doctors are Asian, and so the sociologist must make sure 8 per cent of the sample are Asian. To do this, the sociologist will separate out the Asian doctors from the sampling frame of all doctors, and then take a random sample from this list of Asian doctors to make up the 8 per cent of the sample of all doctors. In this way, the final sample is more likely to be representative of all doctors in the survey population. Stratified random sampling has the advantage of being much more representative than simple random sampling, because all the characteristics of the survey population are more certain to be represented in the sample.

   If one of the sampling methods discussed above and shown in the box (below) is used, the information provided by the sample can be generalized with great accuracy to the whole survey population. For example, opinion polls on the voting intentions of electors often produce extremely accurate predictions of the outcome of general elections from questioning only about 1,000 voters.

EXAMPLES OF SIMPLE RANDOM, SYSTEMATIC, AND STRATIFIED RANDOM SAMPLING

Survey population	400 students in a school
	50 per cent are male and 50 per cent are female
	This information would be known from earlier research, such as school records
	In each group, 75 per cent are white and 25 per cent are black
Sample size required	10 per cent (40 students)

A simple random sample

To obtain a simple random sample:

1   Draw up a sampling frame: a list of the names of 400 students in the survey population.
2   Pick out forty names at random.

A systematic sample

To obtain a systematic sample:

   Pick out every tenth name from the sampling frame until forty names are collected.

   The possible problem with these random and systematic samples is that, purely by chance, they might consist of too many males or females, or too many black or white students. If this happened, the sample would be unrepresentative of the survey population, and therefore the survey results would give biased, inaccurate and unrepresentative results. Stratifying the sample can avoid this problem.

A stratified random sample

To obtain a stratified random sample, complete the following stages:

1   Draw up a sampling frame (list of names) of the 400 students in the survey population.
2   Divide this sampling frame into the same proportions as the survey population. We know 50 per cent are male and 50 per cent are female, so in this case divide the sampling frame into two groups, one with 200 males, one with 200 females.
3   We know 25 per cent of males and of females are black, and 75 per cent are white, so divide *each* of these sampling frames into two further groups.
4   Now take a 10 per cent random sample from each sampling frame. This produces a sample made up like the one here.

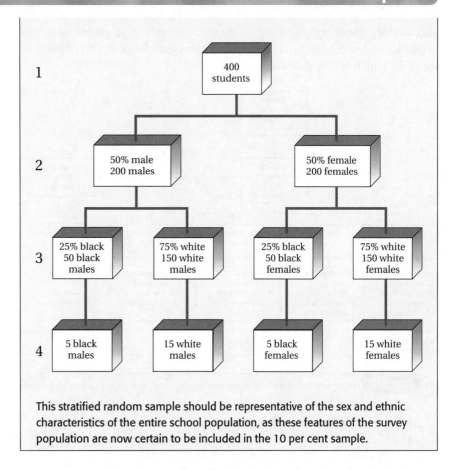

This stratified random sample should be representative of the sex and ethnic characteristics of the entire school population, as these features of the survey population are now certain to be included in the 10 per cent sample.

Snowball sampling

Snowball sampling is used when a sampling frame is difficult to obtain or doesn't exist, or when a sample is very difficult to obtain. The researcher may identify one or two people with the characteristics they're interested in, and ask them to introduce the researcher to other people willing to cooperate in the research, and then ask these people to identify others. In this way the sample gradually builds up, just like a snowball getting bigger as you roll it in the snow. For example, Laurie Taylor in *In the Underworld* (1995) used this technique to investigate the lifestyles of criminals. There was no readily available sampling frame of criminals. He happened to know a convicted criminal, who was willing to put him in touch with other criminals who were willing to cooperate in his research. These criminals in turn put him in touch with other criminals, and so he was able gradually to build up his sample.

Such samples may be useful, but they are not random or representative. They rely on volunteers recommending other volunteers to the researcher, and the sample is therefore self-selecting, and this may create bias. For example, such volunteers may have particular views for or against a particular issue, which is why they volunteered.

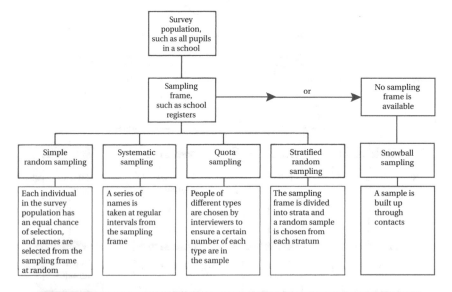

Figure 2.3 Sampling methods

Research methods used in surveys

There are two main methods which are used in social surveys to collect data: questionnaires and interviews.

Questionnaires

Most surveys involve the use of a questionnaire of some kind. A questionnaire is a printed list of questions to be filled in either personally by the *respondent* (the person answering the questions) or by an interviewer. All respondents answer exactly the same questions.

There are two main types of questionnaire: the pre-coded questionnaire and the open-ended questionnaire.

The pre-coded questionnaire The pre-coded questionnaire (sometimes called a *closed questionnaire)* involves the individual being asked a number of pre-set *closed* questions with a limited number of multiple choice answers. The person filling in the questionnaire will tick off the answer. A typical question might be 'Do you think wages should be paid for housework?' with available answers being 'Yes'/'No'/'Don't know'. The problem with this type of pre-coded closed questionnaire is that it does not allow respondents to explain their views fully or to develop their answers. An example of a pre-coded questionnaire (to be carried out by an interviewer) is shown in figure 2.4.

The open-ended questionnaire Like the pre-coded questionnaire, the open-ended questionnaire (sometimes called an *open questionnaire*) usually has a number of pre-set questions, but there is no pre-set choice of answers. They are *open* questions that allow respondents to write their own answer or dictate it to an interviewer.

An example of an open-ended question is: 'What is your opinion of the idea that wages should be paid for housework?' Such open questions give respondents scope to express their own views. Such a questionnaire may form the basis for an unstructured interview (see below).

In a survey, both pre-coded (closed) and open-ended (open) questions may be combined in the same questionnaire.

The postal/mail or self-completion questionnaire This kind of questionnaire is either left with the respondent and picked up later, or sent through the post with a pre-paid addressed envelope for the reply, or posted on an Internet site for people to reply to, or it may be sent and returned via email. The respondents fill in the form themselves (self-completion). Many surveys, including opinion polls and government surveys like the British Crime Survey (see chapter 5), are now using computerized and

(*cont.* on p. 62)

Newspaper survey

Conduct the interview politely. Ask questions clearly. Do not give extra emphasis to any words. Use only the words that are underlined. Mark the answer given by putting a circle round the appropriate code number.

Good morning/afternoon/evening. I am conducting a survey on newspapers and I would be grateful if you would help me by answering some questions.

		Code
A	Sex of respondent:	
	Male	1
	Female	2
B	Estimated age of respondent:	
	16 or under	1
	17–21	2
	22–40	3
	41–60	4
	61 or over	5
C	Would you please tell me which of the following categories best describes your occupation: (show list)	
	Professional/senior manager	1
	Manager in business	2
	Administrator/clerical	3
	Self-employed/business owner	4
	Manual	5
	Housewife	6
	Student	7
	Retired	8
	Unemployed	9
	Other	10

Question			Code			Route
Q.1	Do you read a daily morning newspaper					
	every day		1			Q.2
	4–5 times a week		2			Q.2
	2–3 times a week		3			Q.2
	once a week		4			Q.2
	less than once a week		5			Q.2
	never?		6			Classify
Q.2	Do you usually read:					
	all the newspaper		1			Q.3
	most of it		2			Q.3
	part of it		3			Q.3
	or just glance through it?		4			Q.3
Q.3	Which newspaper or newspapers do you read?					
	Sun / Star / Independent		1	5	9	Q.4
	Mirror / Telegraph / Financial Times		2	6	10	Q.4
	Mail / Guardian / Others (please		3	7	11	Q.4
	Express / Times / write in)		4	8		Q.4
Q.4	Where do you usually get most of your news about what's going on in Britain today? Is it from:					
	Newspapers		1			Q.5
	Television		2			Q.5
	Radio		3			Q.5
	Other (specify)		4			Q.5
	Don't know?		5			Q.5
Q.5	Which of the following do you think gives the most truthful account of the news:					
	Newspapers		1			Q.6
	Television		2			Q.6
	Radio		3			Q.6
	Don't know?		4			Q.6

Figure 2.4 Example of a pre-coded questionnaire conducted by an interviewer.
Note the instructions given to the interviewer at the top of the questionnaire. These seek to ensure objectivity and consistency between different interviewers

Designing a questionnaire

To design a successful questionnaire, you should follow these rules:

- It should be clearly laid out and well printed, and instructions for completing it should be easily understood by the respondent. The questionnaire should be easy to follow and complete.
- Questions should only be asked which the respondents are likely to be able to answer accurately. For example, people can only give opinions on things they know about and can remember accurately.
- The number of questions should be kept to the minimum required to produce the information. Respondents may be unwilling to spend a long time answering questions, or might stop answering the questions seriously.
- Questions should be simple and direct, and able to be answered briefly.
- Questions should be phrased in simple, everyday language so they are easily understood by the respondent. Technical words and jargon should be avoided as the respondents may not understand the question. For example, a question about 'marital status' should be avoided – it is better to ask if someone is married/partnered, single or divorced.
- Questions should be unambiguous, and their meaning quite clear. For example, a question like 'Do you watch television often?' is a bad question because people might interpret 'often' in different ways – it is better to specify actual time periods such as 1–2 hours a day, 3–4 hours a day, and so on.
- Leading questions which encourage people to give particular answers should be avoided – otherwise the respondent might feel he or she is expected to give a particular response. This might then produce invalid (or untruthful) answers.
- Pre-coded questionnaires should provide enough alternative answers to apply to all the respondents. There should be an opportunity for the respondents to give a 'Don't know' answer.

Questionnaires should be phrased in straightforward, everyday language

web-based self-completion questionnaires, sometimes recorded onto computer for those who are illiterate, and this can help in getting answers to embarrassing questions, like those on a person's criminal or sexual activity, that might otherwise remain unanswered if asked by a researcher in person.

Activity

A useful site for devising computer-based surveys, which can be used either on-line or offline, is www.surveymonkey.com. If you want to try your hand at a computer-based survey, have a go at devising a questionnaire using Survey Monkey, preferably relating to a topic of some sociological interest. Practise using your friends as a sample. Outline any conclusions you might reasonably reach and discuss with others any difficulties or problems you experience.

A key problem with postal and other self-completion questionnaires is that of non-response – often people don't bother to reply. The percentage returning them may sometimes be less than 20 per cent of the sample, and this may mean the results obtained are not valid, but inaccurate, biased and unrepresentative. For example, those not replying might have answered differently from those who did reply, and those replying may be more educated, be interested in the topic being investigated, or have some axe to grind.

To try to overcome the problem of non-response, postal questionnaires often have covering letters from well-known individuals or organizations, or offer free gifts, competition prizes and other rewards. A reply-paid envelope is essential if the questionnaire is not to be dropped into the nearest paper recycling bin.

Activity

1   The following questions, which are intended to be filled in by the respondent, all have *at least* one thing wrong with them. In each case, describe what is wrong with the question and re-write the question in a more correct or more appropriate way.

   a) Do you watch television: 1–2 hours a night?
                                  2–4 hours a night?
                                  4–6 hours a night?

   b) Don't you agree sex before   YES/NO
       marriage is wrong?

   c) Don't you think you should vote   YES/NO/DON'T KNOW
       Labour if there were a general
       election tomorrow?

d) Which recommendation of the Government Road Safety Committee regarding the change in the upper speed limit on class A roads and motorways do you support?

e) Are you happy with your washing machine?   YES/NO/DON'T KNOW

f) Do you have joint conjugal roles in your household?   YES/NO/DON'T KNOW

g) Which social class do you belong to?

h) Do you bonk with your partner a lot?   YES/NO

i) Are you a good driver?   YES/NO/DON'T KNOW

j) Do you read newspapers: A LOT?
QUITE A LOT?
OFTEN?
SOMETIMES?
A BIT?
NOT MUCH?
NEVER?

2   Do you think any of the questions above in their present form would be either unlikely to be answered or answered dishonestly? How would this affect the *validity* of the research? Give reasons for your answer.

THE STRENGTHS AND LIMITATIONS OF POSTAL/MAIL AND OTHER SELF-COMPLETION QUESTIONNAIRES

Strengths

- Fairly cheap compared to paying interviewers
- Large numbers of people over a wide geographical area can be questioned
- Results are obtained quickly
- People have more time to reply than when an interviewer is present, so more accurate answers may be obtained
- Questions on personal, controversial or embarrassing

Limitations

- Non-response, leading to unrepresentative, invalid, biased results
- Extra questions cannot be asked or added, to get the respondents to expand or explain themselves more fully. The depth of information is therefore limited
- With pre-coded questionnaires, the limited range of questions and answers may mean the

subjects are more likely to be answered than if they are asked by an interviewer
- The problem of interviewer bias is avoided
- Answers are easy to compare and put into statistical form (numbers and percentages) – for example, '87 per cent of women questioned said they had to do all the housework'

researcher isn't getting at what the respondent really thinks, so results may not be valid
- The wording may be confusing to the respondent, and the questions therefore misunderstood. There is no interviewer present to explain the question if necessary

Interviews

Questionnaires are often carried out by an interviewer. There are two main types of interview: the structured or formal interview and the unstructured or informal interview.

The structured or formal interview   The structured interview is based on a pre-coded questionnaire. The interviewer asks the questions and does not probe beyond the basic answers received. It is a formal question-and-answer session.

The unstructured, informal or in-depth interview   This type of interview is based on an open-ended questionnaire, or simply a list of topics the interviewer wishes to discuss. The interviewer will ask the respondent open-ended questions which may trigger off discussions or further questions. The interviewer will try to put the respondent at ease in a relaxed, informal situation and encourage him or her to express his or her feelings and opinions. This means the interviewer can obtain much greater depth of information than is possible in a structured interview or in a postal or other self-completion questionnaire. It is a bit like a TV chat show.

Group interviews and focus groups   Group interviews and focus groups are both forms of in-depth interview. A group interview is an interview in which the researcher interviews several people at the same time. The interviewer's role is to question, and to control the direction the interview takes as she or he is seeking to obtain particular information; usually, responses will be to the interviewer, though people may well develop their answers through discussion with others in the group.

A focus group is a form of group interview in which the group focuses on a particular topic to be explored in depth, and people are encouraged to talk to one another as well as the interviewer so people's views on the issue under

How do you think interviewing people in a group might affect the validity of the information obtained compared to interviewing someone on their own?

discussion are drawn out and well explored. The researcher's role is to feed in ideas or questions and get people discussing an issue and to draw out their feelings, experiences, ideas and opinions. The researcher also has to make sure the group remains focused on the topic under discussion.

Interviewer bias

A major problem with interviews, particularly unstructured ones, is that of **interviewer bias**.

Interviewer bias is the way in which the presence or behaviour of the interviewer may influence in some way the answers given by the respondent. Interviews involve face-to-face social interaction between people, and the success of interviews often relies on the personality and personal skills of the interviewer, and on how participants feel about one another. There

> **Interviewer bias** refers to the answers being given in an interview being influenced or distorted in some way by the presence or behaviour of the interviewer.

Interviewers may not always get the cooperation they hope for . . . especially if they choose the wrong moment

is always the possibility that the respondent might adapt his or her answer according to the status, class, ethnicity, age, sex, speech, accent, tone of voice, style of dress, or behaviour of the interviewer. The interviewer may give the impression of wanting to hear a certain answer, and the respondent may try to impress the interviewer by giving answers she or he thinks the interviewer wants to hear and would approve of, rather than giving her or his real opinions. This isn't really surprising, as nearly everyone likes to obtain the approval of the person they're talking to.

Interviewer bias is a serious problem, as it could mean that respondents do not give answers which they really believe, and therefore the results of the survey may not be valid or reliable – that is, not give a true, genuine or authentic picture of what is being studied, and other interviewers may not get the same results. To overcome interviewer bias, interviewers are trained to avoid giving any impression of approval or disapproval based on their own opinions and feelings about the answers they receive. They should give the impression of polite and friendly indifference to the answers received. Another way of overcoming interviewer bias is to avoid face-to-face interviews altogether, and use telephone interviews instead.

What possible sources of interviewer bias might there be in this interview? What steps might you take to overcome them?

Activity

Consider the following situations, and in each case:

1 Suggest possible ways in which interviewer bias might occur.
2 Suggest what might be done to help remove the bias.
   - A white person being questioned by a black interviewer about his or her racial attitudes
   - An adult interviewing pupils in a school
   - A British person interviewing a French person about her or his attitudes towards the English
   - An adult interviewer asking teenagers about their attitudes to drug abuse
   - A well-dressed, middle-class sociologist asking Travellers (including New Age Travellers, Irish Travellers and Romani (commonly called 'gypsies')) questions about their lifestyle
   - A middle-class interviewer asking lower-working-class people about their attitudes to social security benefits
   - A female interviewer asking a married or cohabiting couple about how household tasks are divided between them
   - An interviewer asking questions on birth control techniques
   - An older woman asking questions of a young mother about the way children should be brought up
   - An interviewer who is a committed Christian asking questions about religious belief

THE STRENGTHS AND LIMITATIONS OF INTERVIEWS

Strengths

- They are the best way of getting questionnaires completed – the problem of non-response found with postal questionnaires is much rarer. Skilled interviewers can persuade people to answer questions.
- There is more flexibility than with postal questionnaires – questions may be explained and, except with pre-coded questionnaires, extra questions can be asked and more detail obtained.
- Unstructured interviews allow the respondent to be more

Limitations

- Interviews are more time-consuming and costly than postal and other self-completion questionnaires – interviews are often slow and interviewers have to be paid. Many more people can be questioned with a postal or other self-completion questionnaire for the same cost.
- Because interviews tend to be slow and expensive, often only a small number can take place – this means the sample size is often small, and therefore risks being unrepresentative of the survey population.

open and honest, and therefore more valid information about the respondents' attitudes, values and opinions can be obtained.

- Unstructured interviews enable the ideas of the sociologist to develop during the interview, and the interviewer can adjust questions and change direction as the interview is taking place if new ideas and insights emerge. By contrast, structured interviews have already decided the important questions.

- Group interviews and focus groups can help to trigger off discussions, and draw out the feelings, experiences and opinions of group members and thereby gain more detailed and in-depth qualitative information.

- Interviews tend to be artificial situations, and there is no way of knowing whether what people say in an interview is what they really believe or how they behave in real life.

- The success of interviews depends heavily on the skill and personality of the interviewer, especially in unstructured interviews – for example, in getting people to provide answers to questions that give useful information and in keeping the conversation going.

- There is a risk of interviewer bias, leading to results that are neither reliable nor valid.

- Group interviews or focus groups may act as a form of peer pressure and individuals may conceal their true feelings in case others disapprove. They may be reluctant to reveal personal issues in such a group setting. They may also exaggerate or distort their views to impress others.

Activity

1 Make up a short five-question structured questionnaire (with a choice of answers) to find out about attitudes to some social topic you're interested in.
2 Test this out on three people, using a structured interview, and record your findings.
3 Now, using the same questions as prompts, do unstructured interviews with two people. Be prepared to probe further and ask extra questions and enter discussions. Record your findings.
4 Compare the data collected by each type of interview, and the time it took to complete the interviews. Is there any difference between the information collected by these two types of interview, and the time taken to carry them out? Explain why you think this might be the case.
5 Identify and explain *two* reasons why a sociologist might choose to use an unstructured interview rather than a structured interview in sociological research.
6 Identify *two* ways in which unstructured interviews might be unreliable as a method of research.

7 Suggest *two* ways in each case below in which group interviews or focus groups might:
  (a) provide a greater depth of qualitative information than interviews with a single individual;
  (b) provide less valid information than interviews with a single individual.

OPINION POLLS

Opinion polls are social surveys that aim to find out people's attitudes and opinions. They are often used in market research to discover people's opinions towards some product or service, and they are widely used to discover how people intend to vote in elections (opinion polls and elections are discussed in chapter 7). Opinion polls don't always give a valid, or true and genuine, picture of what the public really thinks, despite often employing sophisticated research methods. Why are opinion polls sometimes inaccurate?

- They may not contain a representative sample, which may lead to inaccurate results.
- Respondents might give any answer just to get rid of the pollster.
- Interviewer bias may mean people give inaccurate answers. People in face-to-face interviews may give the answer that they think is socially acceptable rather than what they really believe.
- The format and wording of questions may affect the results. For example, respondents prefer to agree rather than disagree with statements which are put to them.

The stages of a survey

Before carrying out a large-scale survey, it is important to carry out a **pilot survey**.

This is a trial run of the final survey, using fewer people than the final sample. Its purpose is to iron out any problems which the researcher might have overlooked. For example, some questions may be unclear, some of the sample may have died or moved away, or there may be unexpected problems with non-response or non-cooperation by respondents.

After the pilot survey is completed, the results are reviewed, any necessary changes are made, and the main survey can then proceed. The stages of a survey are shown in figure 2.5.

A **pilot survey** is a small-scale practice survey carried out before the final survey to check for any possible problems in the way it is designed.

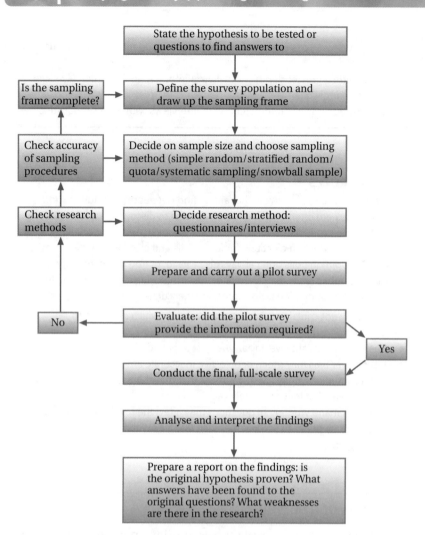

Figure 2.5 The stages of a survey

LONGITUDINAL STUDIES

Most sociological researchers study a group of people only for a short period of time, producing a snapshot of events. It is therefore difficult to study change over time. Longitudinal studies attempt to overcome this problem by selecting a sample – sometimes called a panel or cohort – from whom data are collected at regular intervals over a period of years (each one of these data collecting surveys is known as a 'sweep'). The census, carried out every ten years since 1801 (with the exception of 1941), is in effect a longitudinal study of the entire population. This enables researchers to trace broad patterns of social change, and to make comparisons between the social conditions of one period and those of another.

Longitudinal studies show change over a period of time. Why might this provide more useful information than the one-off snapshot provided by most research?

The British Household Panel Survey (BHPS) is a longitudinal study that began in 1991, and continues to follow the same representative sample of individuals. Each year, researchers interview every adult member of around 9,000 sampled households drawn from all areas of the UK. These interviews enable researchers to follow people's lives over time, providing insights into things like parenthood, household arrangements, income, employment, housing, health and political views, and how they change over time. (You can find out more about the BHPS at www.iser.essex.ac.uk/survey/bhps.)

THE STRENGTHS AND PROBLEMS OF LONGITUDINAL STUDIES

Advantages and strengths

- They make it possible to study change over time, and provide detail on the changes that occur, compared to the somewhat artificial one-off snapshot picture provided by most research, which is out of date often before it is even published.

- As long as the sample remains the same, it may be possible to discover the causes of changes. By comparing earlier studies with later ones, researchers can be sure that the changes measured do not result from changes in the composition of the sample.

Disadvantages and problems

- It is necessary to select a sample who are available and willing to assist in the research project over a long period. However, it is likely that the original sample size will drop as people die, can't be traced, or become unwilling to cooperate. This may reduce the representativeness of the sample.

- Those in the sample are conscious of the fact that they are being studied. This may change their behaviour because they think more carefully about what they do (especially if they know they may be questioned about it in the future). This may bring into question the validity of the findings.

- They may provide more valid data in some circumstances. Studies which ask people about past events rely on human memories, and people may also distort or exaggerate past events. Longitudinal studies help to avoid this, as there are previous studies to refer back to.

- There is the problem of cost. Most funding agencies are unwilling to take on a commitment over a long period of time.

Activity

1 If people drop out of the original sample during a longitudinal study, suggest reasons why sociologists should be cautious about using the results to make general statements about society.
2 Suggest *one* reason why longitudinal studies might provide a more valid picture of society, and *one* reason why they may not.
3 Go to the Centre for Longitudinal Studies at www.cls.ioe.ac.uk.
   (a) Identify two aims of the Millennium Cohort Study.
   (b) Find out how large the sample is, and what steps have been taken to make the sample representative.
   (c) Find out how many sweeps have taken place, and when they were carried out.

OBSERVATION

Apart from surveys, sociologists also collect data by observation. There are two main kinds of observation: non-participant observation (or direct observation) and participant observation.

Non-participant observation

The researcher observes a group or situation without taking part in any way. This has the advantage that the sociologist can study people in their natural or normal setting without their behaviour being influenced and changed by the presence of the researcher. For example, a researcher may observe people queuing in a supermarket to see how impatient they get. However, observation without involvement in the group means it is often not possible to understand what is really happening, or to find out more by questioning people about the behaviour the researcher is observing. The data produced may well reflect simply the assumptions and interpretations of the researcher, raising serious issues over the reliability and validity of the data. Therefore sociologists more often join in with a group to observe it. This is known as participant observation.

Is this a romantic encounter or are the couple fighting? Are they having a séance or has there been a power cut or haven't they paid their electricity bill? Observation alone is not always adequate for finding out what is really going on

Participant observation

Participant observation is a very commonly used observation technique. In this method, the researcher actually joins in the group or community she or he is studying. The researcher tries to become an accepted part of the group and to learn about the group as a member of it. For example, the sociologist may spend time as a mental patient in a hospital, join a gang, live as a Romani (gypsy) or as a 'down and out', spend time in prison, or teach in a school.

Overt and covert roles

Joining a group raises many questions about the researcher's role. The researcher may adopt an **overt role** where the researcher declares his or her true identity to the group and the fact he or she is doing research. Alternatively, the researcher may adopt a **covert role** (concealing his or her role as a researcher) or a cover story (partially declaring his or her role as a researcher, but concealing elements of it).

A covert role has the advantage of avoiding the risk of people's behaviour changing if they know they are being studied, but there are ethical concerns over observing and reporting on people's activities in secret, without obtaining their consent first.

Adopting an overt role has the advantage that things might be hidden from a member of a group in a way that they might not be from a trusted and known outsider – since she or he will have nothing to gain in the group. Other advantages are that the researcher may be able to ask questions or interview

An **overt role** is one in which the researcher reveals to the group being studied his or her true identity and purpose.
A **covert role** is one in which the researcher conceals from the group being studied his or her true identity as a researcher, to gain access to the group and avoid disrupting its normal behaviour.

people without arousing suspicion. Ethically, it is right that people should be aware they are being studied. However, adopting an overt role carries the risk that the behaviour of those being studied may be affected, raising questions over the validity of the research.

Activity

1 What does the cartoon above suggest might be some of the difficulties involved in a participant observation study of a gang?
2 Many participant observation studies have been concerned with the study of groups not fully accepted into society, such as street gangs, religious cults or drug users. Suggest ways you might get in touch with and be accepted by such a group to study it, and outline any difficulties you might have with staying in the group.
3 Suggest two advantages and two disadvantages of adopting a covert role in participant observation.
4 What ethical problems are there with adopting a covert role? Can adopting a covert role ever be justified?
5 Explain the ways, with examples, in which being a successful participant observer might depend on the personality and personal characteristics of the researcher, such as their age, sex or ethnic group.

In an actual piece of research, sociologists will probably use a variety of methods to collect the data they require. The methods chosen will be influenced by the questions or hypothesis being investigated, the information required (whether quantitative or qualitative), the scale of the research, and the time and money available to complete it. Figure 2.6 illustrates the relationship between some of these factors.

THE STRENGTHS AND LIMITATIONS OF PARTICIPANT OBSERVATION

Strengths

- The sociologist gains first-hand knowledge of the group being studied. She or he sees the world through the eyes of members of the group. This provides much more detail and depth than other methods like questionnaires and interviews.
- Questionnaires and interviews tend to provide information only at one point in time. Participant observation takes place over a long period and can therefore give a much fuller and more valid account of a group's behaviour.
- With other methods, the sociologist has already decided on a hypothesis, which affects what questions are asked and therefore what is found out. With participant observation, interesting new ideas to explore may emerge during the research itself and the sociologist may discover things she or he would not even have thought of asking about, producing more valid results.
- Participant observation may be the only possible method of research. For example, a criminal gang is hardly likely to answer questionnaires or do interviews for fear of the consequences, and a group like Travellers (including New Age Travellers, Irish Travellers and Romani (commonly called 'gypsies')), may well see an interviewer as official and prying, and may fear harassment by councils, police and other official bodies. By adopting a *covert* role – keeping her or his identity secret – the researcher may be able to investigate such groups. Even if the group knows who the researcher is (an *overt* role), the researcher may, after a time, win the trust of the group.
- People can be studied in their normal social situation, rather than in the somewhat artificial context of an interview or questionnaire.

Limitations

- It is very time-consuming and expensive compared to other methods, as it involves the sociologist participating in a group for long periods.
- Because only a small group is studied, it is difficult to make generalizations.
- It depends a great deal on the personality and personal characteristics of the investigator and his or her ability to fit in with the group.
- There is a danger of the researcher becoming so involved with the group and developing such loyalty to it that he or she may find it difficult to stand back and report his or her observations in a neutral way. The research would not then be valid.
- There is no real way of checking the findings of a participant observation study. There is no real evidence apart from the observations of the researcher, and what one researcher might regard as important may be missed or seen as unimportant by another.
- There may be a problem of gaining the group's confidence (getting into the group) and maintaining it (staying in), especially if criminal and other deviant activities are involved. What does the researcher do if a group involves itself in criminal activities like theft, drug-dealing or acts of violence? Failure to take part may result in loss of the group's confidence and trust, and the effective end of the research.
- The presence of the researcher, if she or he is known to the group as a researcher (an overt role), may change the group's behaviour simply because they know they are being studied. This may produce invalid information.
- With a covert role, the researcher has to be very careful when asking questions, in case her or his real identity is revealed or people become suspicious. This may limit the information obtained. There are also serious ethical difficulties involved in a researcher concealing his or her real identity and purpose.

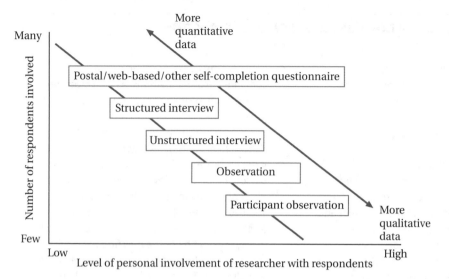

Figure 2.6 Methods of data collection

PLANNING YOUR OWN RESEARCH PROJECT

As a result of studying this chapter, you should have some ideas about how sociologists carry out their research and the methods they use. You should by now be able to plan your own small-scale research project.

Figure 2.7 shows the stages that a sociologist might go through in carrying out research. Study figure 2.7 carefully, and then complete the activity that follows.

Figure 2.7 The stages of research

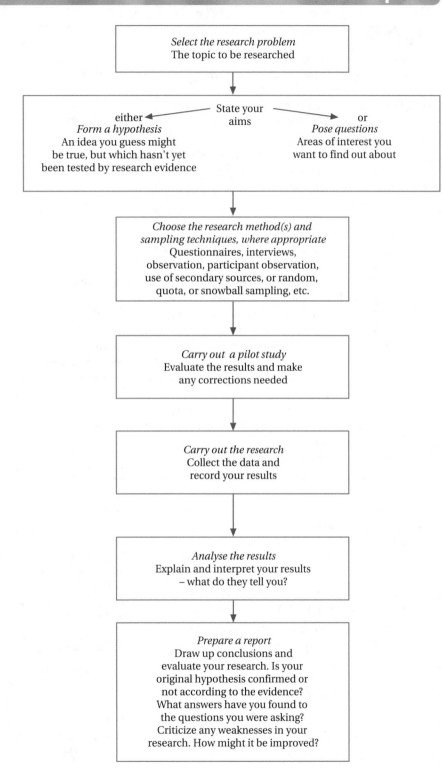

Activity

Imagine you have two months to carry out a small-scale research project on one of the following issues (or one of your own choosing), using both primary and secondary sources:
- the difficulties facing the elderly
- the opinions of adults in your neighbourhood about how they will vote in the next election
- how household tasks are divided between men and women in the home
- gender stereotyping in a school or college
- the attitudes of people towards religion
- the lifestyle of teenagers.

Select one of the issues above, and:

a) Suggest a hypothesis you might wish to test or questions you want to find answers to.
b) Identify at least one secondary source of information you might use, and explain what information you would expect to obtain from it.
c) Explain how you might select the group of people to be studied, and how you would try to make sure any sample was representative.
d) Explain carefully what research method you would use to collect your primary data, why it would be particularly suited to the hypothesis you would be investigating, and why it would be more suitable than other methods you could use.
e) Identify three problems or difficulties you might face in carrying out your research, and in each case suggest how you might overcome them.
f) Identify two ethical issues you might encounter, and how you would try to avoid or overcome them.

CHAPTER SUMMARY

After studying this chapter, you should be able to:
- explain the issues of reliability, validity and ethics in social research
- explain the difference between quantitative and qualitative data
- explain, with examples, the difference between primary and secondary sources of data, and their advantages and disadvantages
- describe the various methods sociologists use to obtain samples to study
- outline the stages of a survey

- describe the use of questionnaires, interviews, and non-participant and participant observation in sociological research, and explain their various strengths and limitations
- outline the advantages and difficulties of longitudinal studies
- outline the stages a sociologist would go through in carrying out a piece of research
- plan a small-scale piece of research of your own, using the various sources, sampling techniques and research methods covered in this chapter.

KEY TERMS

covert role
ethics
hypothesis
interviewer bias

overt role
pilot survey
primary data
qualitative data
quantitative data

reliability
representative sample
sample
sampling frame
secondary data

social survey
survey population
validity

Families

Contents

CHAPTER

3

Families

Most people are raised in families, and so we might think we know all about them. We may make assumptions that people will fall in love with someone of the opposite sex and get married, or starting cohabiting, start having children, and form their own family. We may have the impression that the 'best' kind of family consists of married parents and a couple of children, with Dad out working and Mum mainly concerned with the home and looking after the kids, but with both partners sharing a lot of jobs around the home. We may believe the family is the only place where children can be properly brought up, and that it is a source of unconditional affection – a place to retreat to whenever things get too much or go wrong in the outside world.

On the other hand, you may believe that the family is in decline, pointing to rising rates of divorce, extra-marital sex and abortion, with rising numbers of lone-parent families. You might point to rising levels of child abuse, violence against women, vandalism and crime, and drug abuse. You would not be alone in holding such a belief – the mass media, politicians, the police, social workers, teachers and religious leaders have all at some time or other tried to blame the family and lack of parental control for a wide range of problems in society.

There is, whatever way you look at it, a controversy over the family.

SOCIAL ISSUES, SOCIAL PROBLEMS AND FAMILIES

The previous paragraph referred to a range of social problems which have been linked at various times to the quality of family life and the way families work. Below is a list of some social issues and social problems that have been linked to families:

- the lack of male role models for young boys growing up in mother-headed lone-parent families
- the poor quality of parenting, as parents lack the skills to bring up their children properly
- the rise of cohabitation, with more couples choosing to live together without getting married, raising concerns over the long-term security of children
- the growing numbers of the elderly, and the strains this puts on families
- the way the poorest families pass on a culture of dependency, bringing up their children in a culture where living off welfare benefits provides an acceptable way of life

Growing concern over the quality of parenting in recent years has given rise to policies aimed at providing advice and support to parents to help them bring up their children. *Every Parent Matters* is a 2007 government publication outlining the vital role of parents in shaping their child's development and the role the government will play in supporting them. Further examples of government advice and support for parents can be found at www.direct.gov.uk/en/parents/index.htm

- the high level of teenage pregnancies in the UK – the highest in Europe
- child poverty, with 4 million children (around 30 per cent of all children) in the UK living in poverty in 2008–9.

Activity

1 Refer to the list of issues and problems linked to families in the list above. In each case:
   (a) explain why it may be a matter of concern to many people
   (b) explain what consequences there might be for the individuals and families concerned
   (c) suggest possible solutions to these problems.
2 Go to one or all of the following websites, and identify and explain three measures that are suggested as improving the quality of family life:
www.dcsf.gov.uk/everychildmatters/earlyyears/surestart/whatsurestartdoes/ – the site of Sure Start Children's Centres, aiming to give the best start in life for every child by bringing together early education, childcare, health and family support.
www.family.go.com/parenting/ – a site that contains a range of useful advice to parents on how to bring up their children.
www.direct.gov.uk/en/parents/index.htm – a site providing advice and information to parents on a wide range of matters, including how to deal with children of all ages.

WHAT IS THE FAMILY?

Kinship
refers to relations of blood, marriage / civil partnership or adoption.

A family is a group of people who are related by kinship ties: relations of blood, marriage / civil partnership or adoption. Cohabitation (living together without the legal bonds of a marriage or civil partnership) is becoming a very common alternative to marriage or a civil partnership, so for couple families, cohabitation ought also to be included as a family relationship.

The family unit is one of the most important social institutions, which is found in some form in nearly all known societies. It is a basic unit of social organization, and plays a key role in socializing children into the culture of their society, and forming their identities – how they see themselves and how others see them.

A household
is either one person living alone or a group of people who live at the same address and share living arrangements.

WHAT IS A HOUSEHOLD?

A household is either one person living alone or a group of people who live at the same address and share living arrangements. Most families will live in a household – but not all households are families. For example, students sharing a house together make up a household, though they are not a family. In 2009, around one in three households consisted of people living alone.

CONSENSUS AND CONFLICT APPROACHES TO THE FAMILY

The consensus approach

The consensus approach of functionalist writers tends to see the family as working like a part of the human body, with the family like a vital organ maintaining the health of the 'body' of society. The family does this through things like reproduction of the population, the primary socialization of children, and providing food and shelter and an emotional refuge for family members. In this way the family makes a major contribution to social stability, and the creation of a harmonious society. This approach to the family emphasizes the way the family socializes children into a **value consensus** (shared norms and values) which makes up the culture of the society to which they belong, and helps to keep human personalities stable.

> A **value consensus** means a general agreement around the main norms and values of society.

Conflict approaches

Conflict theorists, like Marxist and many feminist writers, tend to emphasize the way the family reproduces social inequality from one generation to the next, such as the inequalities between social classes and between men and women. Conflict theorists stress the way the **nuclear family** is concerned not with building value consensus, but with teaching its members to submit to the values and beliefs of the wealthy upper class, and not to be critical of the society around them.

> **Nuclear family** refers to a family with two generations, of parents and children, living together in one household.

The family is seen as working to dampen down the inevitable social conflict that is bound to appear in unequal societies. Conflict theorists also emphasize the negative aspects of family life – the 'darker side' of family life – such as violence against partners and children.

Feminist writers see the family as a unit based on patriarchy, reproducing and supporting a society in which men have most of the power, status and authority. Chapter 1 showed how socialization into gender stereotypes takes place through the family, and later in this chapter there will be some discussion of how family life seems not only to benefit men more than women, but often to do so at the expense of women. For example, women perform more housework and childcare in the family than men. This may limit women's ability to enter full-time employment and pursue careers, and sometimes has negative consequences for their physical and mental health.

DIFFERENT FORMS OF THE FAMILY, MARRIAGE AND HOUSEHOLDS

Even though the family is found in nearly every society, it can take many different forms. Marriage and family life in earlier times in Britain could – and today in many other societies can – be organized in quite different ways from family life in modern Britain. Sociologists use a number of different terms to describe the wide varieties of family types and relationships and households. Table 3.1 summarizes these varieties, which are discussed below and throughout the rest of this chapter.

Table 3.1 Forms of the family, marriage and household

Forms of:	Description
Marriage	
Monogamy	One husband and one wife
	Found in Europe, the USA and most Christian cultures
Serial monogamy	A series of monogamous marriages
	Found in Europe and the USA, where there are high rates of divorce and remarriage
Arranged marriage	Marriages arranged by parents to match their children with partners of a similar background and status
	Found in the Indian sub-continent and Muslim, Sikh and Hindu minority ethnic groups in Britain
Civil partnership	A legal form of marriage for gay and lesbian couples. Civil partnership gives legal recognition to the relationships of same-sex couples, giving civil partners equal treatment to married couples in a wide range of legal matters
Polygamy	Marriage to more than one partner at the same time
	Includes polygyny and polyandry
Polygyny	One husband and two or more wives
	Found in Islamic countries like Egypt and Saudi Arabia
Polyandry	One wife and two or more husbands
	Found in Tibet, among the Todas of southern India, and among the Marquesan Islanders
Family and household structure	
Nuclear family	Two generations: parents and children living in the same household
Extended family	All kin including and beyond the nuclear family
Classic extended family	An extended family sharing the same household or living near each other

Table 3.1 (continued)	
Forms of:	Description
Modified extended family	An extended family living far apart, but keeping in touch by phone, letters, email, networking websites like Facebook and frequent visits
Beanpole family	A multi-generation extended family, which is long and thin, with few aunts, uncles and cousins, reflecting fewer children being born in each generation, but people living longer
Patriarchal family	Authority held by males
Matriarchal family	Authority held by females
Symmetrical family	Authority and household tasks shared between male and female partners
Reconstituted family or stepfamily	One or both partners previously married, with children of previous relationships
Lone-parent family	Lone parent with dependent children, most commonly after divorce or separation (though may also arise from death of a partner or unwillingness to marry or cohabit)
Gay or lesbian family	Same-sex couple living together with children
Single person household	An individual living alone

Monogamy

In modern Britain and the rest of Europe, the USA and most Christian cultures, monogamy is the only legal form of marriage. Monogamy is a form of marriage in which a person can have only one husband or wife at any one time. Monogamy has not traditionally been the most common form of marriage in the world, though it is rapidly becoming so as Western ideas of marriage spread through the world, as societies modernize. In a society where monogamy is the only form of legal marriage, a person who marries while still legally married to someone else is guilty of the crime of bigamy – a serious offence punishable by imprisonment.

Serial monogamy

In modern Britain, most of Western Europe, and the USA there are high rates of divorce and remarriage. Some people keep marrying and divorcing a series of different partners, but each marriage is monogamous. The term serial monogamy is sometimes used to describe these marriage patterns. This form of marriage has been described as 'one at a time, one after the other and they don't last long'.

Arranged marriages

Arranged marriages are those in which the marriages of children are organized by their parents, who try to match their children with partners of a similar background and status. Such arranged marriages are more a union between two families than between two people, and romantic love is not necessarily present between the marriage partners. They are typically found among Muslims, Sikhs and Hindus. The arranged marriage is still common in the Asian community in Britain, where the custom is often more strictly enforced than in the Indian sub-continent. This is because the present generations of parents and grandparents here often still stick to the customs which existed when they left India for Britain many years ago.

It is important not to confuse arranged marriages with *forced* marriages. While arranged marriages involve the family in selecting marriage partners, the couple are normally free to accept or reject the arrangement. They are therefore consensual, involving the consent of both parties to the marriage. In contrast, a forced marriage is one that takes place without the consent of both parties, and involves forcing marriage on someone against their will. The Forced Marriage (Civil Protection) Act in 2007 was designed to protect both adults and children at risk of being forced into marriage and to offer protection for those who have already been forced into marriage.

> **Activity**
>
> What are the advantages and disadvantages of arranged marriages? How do you think arranged marriages might be changing in Britain, and what pressures do you think there might be on the survival of the custom in Britain?

Civil partnership – same-sex (gay and lesbian) marriages and families

The Civil Partnership Act in 2005 gave legal recognition to the relationships of same-sex couples who enter a civil partnership, involving similar arrangements to a legal marriage. Entering a civil partnership gives gay and lesbian couples equal treatment to married couples in a wide range of legal matters. Couples who form a civil partnership now have a new legal status of 'civil partner'.

Same-sex couples are becoming more common, though they are still relatively rare. Most same-sex couples with children tend to be lesbian couples. However, there are more cases emerging of gay male couples adopting children or having children through surrogate mothers.

Up to the end of 2009, over 40,000 civil partnerships were formed in the UK after the Civil Partnership Act came into force in December 2005.

Polygamy

While marrying a second partner without divorcing the first is a crime in Britain, in many societies it is perfectly acceptable to have more than one marriage partner at the same time. **Polygamy** is a general term referring to marriage between a member of one sex and two or more members of the opposite sex at the same time. There are two different types of polygamy: polygyny and polyandry.

Polygyny

Polygyny is the marriage of one man to two or more women at the same time. It is widely practised in Islamic countries such as Egypt and Saudi Arabia. It is also practised (illegally) among some Mormons in the state of

Monogamy

Polygyny

Polyandry

Utah in the USA. The possession of several wives is often seen as a sign of wealth and success, and generally only those men who can afford to support several wives practise polygyny. Because of this, even where polygyny is allowed, only a small number of men actually practise it. In any case, the numbers of men and women in most societies are usually fairly evenly balanced, and there are not enough women for all men to have more than one wife. Further information on polygyny, including its practice among people who are not members of minority ethnic groups, can be found at www.polygamy.com.

Polyandry

Polyandry is the marriage of one woman to two or more men at the same time. This is rare and is found in only about 1 per cent of all societies. Polyandry appears to arise where living standards are so low that a man can only afford to support a wife and child by sharing the responsibility with other men. It is found among the Todas of southern India and the Marquesan Islanders, and has been reported as occurring in parts of Tibet.

The nuclear family

The **nuclear family** means just parents and children, living together in one household. It is sometimes called the two-generation family, because it contains only the two generations of parents and children. In Britain in 2008, 37 per cent of people lived in this type of family.

37 per cent of people in Britain lived in nuclear families in 2008. In what other types of family and household do you think the remaining 63 per cent of people live in today?

The extended family

The extended family is a grouping consisting of all kin. There are two main types of extended family: the classic extended and the modified extended family.

The classic extended family

The classic extended family is made up of several nuclear families joined by kinship relations. The term is mainly used to describe a situation in which many related nuclear families or family members live in the same house, street or area and the members of these related nuclear families see one another regularly. It may be horizontally extended, where it contains just two generations, with aunts, uncles, cousins, etc., or vertically extended, where it contains more than two generations, such as grandparents and grandchildren as well as parents and their own children.

The modified extended family

The modified extended family is one in which related nuclear families, although they may be living far apart geographically, nevertheless maintain regular contact and mutual support through visiting, the phone, letters, email and social networking sites like Facebook: continuing close relations made possible by modern communications. This is probably the most common type of family arrangement in Britain today.

Activity

1. Do a brief survey among your friends or workmates and find out how many live in nuclear families, how many live in classic extended families, and how many have modified extended families. You will have to think of suitable ways of measuring the features of these families, such as how near relatives live, how often they see one another, what other relatives live in the household apart from parents and children, and so on.
2. Ask them what it is like living in these different types of family. On the basis of your findings and using also your own experience of family life, make a list of the advantages and disadvantages of living in each type of family.

Patriarchal and matriarchal families

Patriarchy is a term used to describe the dominance of men over women. A patriarchal family is one in which the father, husband or eldest male is usually the chief authority and decision-maker. An example of this was the family in Victorian Britain, but many writers would argue the modern British family remains patriarchal. Matriarchy describes the dominance of women

Matriarchy refers to the dominance of women over men, with power and authority held by women.

over men. A matriarchal family is one where power and authority is held by the most senior woman. These are very rare, but there is some evidence of them in rural Japan.

The symmetrical family

The **symmetrical family** is one in which the roles of husband and wife or of cohabiting partners have become more alike (symmetrical) and equal. There are more shared tasks within relationships, rather than a clear division between the jobs of male and female partners. Both partners are likely to be wage earners. It remains a popular impression that most families in modern Britain are symmetrical, but evidence which will be discussed later in this chapter suggests this is not the case.

The reconstituted or stepfamily

The **reconstituted** or **stepfamily** (sometimes also called a *blended family*) is a family in which one or both partners have been married previously, and they bring with them children of a previous marriage. This 'reconstitutes' the family with various combinations of stepmother, stepfather and stepchildren. Such families are increasingly common in Western societies, as a result of rising divorce rates and remarriages or other re-formed relationships. In Britain, nearly four in every ten marriages in 2008 involved remarriage for one or both partners, and around one in ten of all families with children today are stepfamilies, with parents having had one or more previous marriages.

The lone-parent family

The lone-parent or single-parent family is increasingly common in Western societies. In 2008, 10 per cent of people in Britain lived in this type of family. Although lone-parent families can also arise from the death of a partner or a lack of desire to cohabit with a partner, they are today largely a result of the rise in the divorce rate. In 2008 around 23 per cent of all families with dependent children were lone-parent families, and nearly nine out of ten of these lone parents were women. Increasingly, lone-parent families are arising from a simple lack of desire or opportunity to get married or cohabit – in 2008 around half of lone mothers fell into this category.

Single person households

About one in three households today contains only one person, compared to about one in twenty in 1901. Around half of these households are over pensionable age compared to two-thirds in 1971. This means there is a growth in the number of younger people living alone.

Activity

Refer to table 3.1 and the previous section. Fill in the blanks in the following passage, using *some* of the following terms: nuclear family; extended family; classic extended family; modified extended family; beanpole family; lone-parent family; reconstituted family; symmetrical family; civil partnership; bigamy; patriarchal; forced marriage; monogamy; serial monogamy; arranged marriages; polygamy; polyandry; gay families.

Each term should only be used once, and each dash below represents one word.

The ___ ___ means just the parents and children, living together in one household. This is sometimes called the two-generation family, because it contains only the two generations of parents and children. The ___ ___ is a grouping consisting of all kin. The ___ ___ ___ consists of several related nuclear families or family members who live in the same household, street or area and who see one another regularly.

The ___ ___ ___ is one in which related nuclear families, although they may be living far apart, maintain close relations made possible by modern communications, such as car travel, phone, letters or email. This is probably the most common type of family arrangement in Britain today.

The ___ ___ is a form of the extended family in a pattern which is long and thin, reflecting the fact that people are living longer but are having fewer children.

The ___ ___ ___ is today largely a result of the rise in the divorce rate, although it may also arise from the death of a partner, the breakdown of cohabiting relationships, or a simple lack of desire to get married. Nine out of ten of these families are headed by women.

The ___ ___ is one in which one or both partners have been married previously, and they bring with them children of a previous marriage.

It remains a popular impression that the most usual kind of family in contemporary Britain is the ___ ___ in which both husbands and wives or cohabiting partners are likely to be wage earners, and to share the housework and childcare. However, some argue that men still dominate in the family and make most of the decisions, and it therefore remains ___.

___ is the only legal form of marriage allowed in Britain. In modern Britain, most of Western Europe and the United States there are high rates of divorce and remarriage, and some people keep marrying and divorcing a series of different partners. The term ___ ___ is sometimes used to describe these marriage patterns.

This type of marriage pattern has been described as 'one at a time, one after the other and they don't last long'.

___ ___ are those where parents organize the marriages of their children to try and ensure a good match with partners of a similar background and status. They are typically found among Muslim, Sikh and Hindu minority ethnic groups. However, this custom is coming under pressure in Britain as younger people in these groups demand greater freedom to choose their own marriage partner in the same way as in wider society.

While marrying a second partner without divorcing the first is a crime in Britain, in many societies it is perfectly acceptable to have more than one marriage partner at the same time. ___ is a general term used to describe this form of marriage.

DEMOGRAPHIC CHANGE AND FAMILIES

Demography is the term used for the study of the characteristics of human populations, such as their size and structure and how these change over time. There have been a number of demographic changes in the population of Britain which have had a number of effects on the family. These include declining birth rates, fertility rates, infant mortality rates, death rates, and increased life expectancy. These changes have had an impact on family size, but also have increased pressures on families and individuals today as a result of an ageing population.

The decline in the death rate and infant mortality rate

In 1902 the death rate was 18 per 1,000, and this had declined to around 10 per 1,000 in 2009. The infant mortality rate has also fallen, from around 142 per 1,000 live births in 1902 to around 5 per 1,000 in 2009. Average life expectancy has consequently risen. Today, men can expect to live, on average, to around the age of 77, and women to around 82, though of course many will live beyond these average ages.

Explanations for changes in the death rate, infant mortality rate and life expectancy

Improved hygiene, sanitation and medicine   Public hygiene and sanitation have improved enormously since the early nineteenth century, with the construction of public sewer systems and the provision of clean running water. These changes, together with improved public awareness of hygiene and the causes of infection, have contributed to the elimination in Britain of the great

Demography is the term used for the study of the characteristics of human populations, such as their size and structure and how these change over time.

The **birth rate** is the number of live births per 1,000 of the population each year.

The **fertility rate** is the number of live births per 1,000 women of childbearing age (15–44) per year.

The **infant mortality rate** is the number of deaths of babies in the first year of life per 1,000 live births per year.

The **death rate** is the number of deaths per 1,000 of the population per year.

Life expectancy is an estimate of how long people can be expected to live from a certain age, usually from birth.

An **ageing population** is one in which the average age is getting higher, with a greater proportion of the population over retirement age, and a smaller proportion of young people.

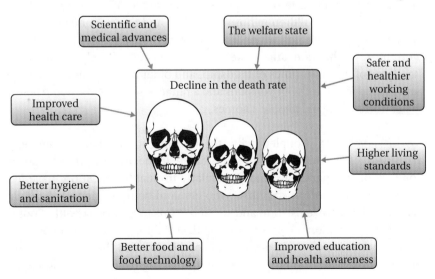

Figure 3.1 Reasons for the decline in the death rate

Scientific and medical advances

The welfare state

Safer and healthier working conditions

Decline in the death rate

Improved health care

Higher living standards

Better hygiene and sanitation

Better food and food technology

Improved education and health awareness

epidemic killer diseases of the past, such as cholera, diphtheria and typhoid, which were spread through infected water and food. These improvements in environmental conditions were more important than medical advances in wiping out these epidemic diseases. Advances in medicine and science, such as vaccines and the development of penicillin, antibiotics and other life-saving drugs, and advances in surgery and medical technology, such as transplant surgery, have further contributed to the decline in the death rate, and increased life expectancy. More sophisticated medical care means that people now survive illnesses that would have killed them even in the recent past. Before the twentieth century, the highest mortality rates were among babies and young children, but today death rates rise the older you get. The major causes of death today in Britain are from the non-infectious degenerative diseases, such as cancer and heart disease.

Higher living standards   Rising standards of living have further assisted in reducing death rates. Higher wages, better food, more amenities and appliances in the home, and greatly improved housing conditions, with less damp, inside toilets and running hot water, have all assisted in improving the health and life expectancy of the population. Because of improved transportation and food technology, a wider range of more nutritious food is available, with improved storage techniques (such as freezing) making possible the import of a range of foodstuffs, providing more affordable fresh fruit and vegetables all the year round.

Public health and welfare   There has been a steep rise in state intervention in public welfare, particularly since the establishment of the welfare state in 1945. The NHS has provided free and comprehensive healthcare, and there is much better ante-natal and post-natal care for mothers and babies. More women have children in hospitals today, and there are health visitors to check on young babies, which helps to explain the decrease in the infant mortality rate. The wide range of welfare benefits available helps to maintain standards of health in times of hardship, and older people in particular are better cared for today, with pensions and a range of services like home helps, social workers and old people's homes.

Health education   Coupled with these changes has been a growing awareness of nutrition and its importance to health. Improved educational standards generally, and particularly in health education, have led to a much-better-informed public, who demand better hygiene and public health, and welfare legislation and social reforms to improve health. Bodies like NICE (the National Institute for Health and Clinical Excellence) provide national guidance on the promotion of good health and the prevention and treatment of ill health. NICE seeks to improve the health of the public by education, such as emphasizing the benefits of exercise, giving up smoking and eating a balanced diet. Websites like NHS Direct (www.nhsdirect.nhs.uk) and Netdoctor (www.netdoctor.co.uk) provide on-line advice on health matters, enabling people to take more control of their own health. Evidence of this growing health awareness includes the public outcries in the 1980s and 1990s over risks of food poisoning – such as salmonella in eggs, 'mad cow disease' in beef, listeria in cook-chill foods, and the *E. coli* food poisoning outbreak in 1996–7 (which killed twenty people) – the public's rejection of genetically modified crops and foods in the early 2000s, and the decline in the numbers of people smoking cigarettes.

Improved working conditions Working conditions improved dramatically in the twentieth century. Technology has taken over some of the more arduous, health-damaging tasks, and factory machinery is often safer than it was 100 years ago. Higher standards of health and safety at work, shorter working hours and more leisure time have all made work physically less demanding, and therefore have reduced risks to health.

The ageing population

The decline in the death rate and increased life expectancy have meant that more people are living longer. Britain, like most Western industrialized countries, today has an ageing population. This means that the average age of the population is getting higher, with a greater proportion of the population over retirement age, and a smaller proportion of young people. However, the decline in the birth rate has meant that fewer children are being born as well, and this has changed the overall age structure of the population. For example, in 1901, about 33 per cent of the population were under age 15, 63 per cent were between the ages of 15 and 65, and only about 4 per cent were over age 65. By 2009, the proportion over 65 had risen to about 16 per cent. Figure 3.2 on page 100 shows this ageing population between 1901 and what it is projected to be in 2033. The changing shape shows that in 1901 there was quite a rapid decline in the proportion of people over the age of 50 in the population as a whole, as they began to die. By 2001 there is more of a bulge in the middle age groups, and by 2033 the older age groups make up a much larger proportion of the population, with most age groups taking up similar proportions. A quick glance at the proportion of over 70s in 1901 compared to 2033 shows this clearly.

The consequences of an ageing population

There is in many cases a long gap between people retiring from work and becoming dependent on others. Men currently retire at age 65, and women at between 60 and 65, though all women will retire at 65 by 2020, and the

Britain has an ageing population. What advantages and disadvantages might there be for families with older, retired relatives?

retirement ages for both men and women look set to rise in the future, possibly to age 68. Many people in their sixties and seventies remain very healthy, active, self-supporting and involved in the lives of their families and communities. However, the growing proportion of elderly people and a relatively smaller proportion of young people have a number of potential effects on the family, and individuals:

- There are more lone person households, as partners die.
- Elderly relatives can help with childcare and babysitting, and maybe financially (especially in the middle class). With many families in contemporary Britain having both parents in paid employment, grandparents now often play an important role in providing unpaid childcare, such as babysitting services and taking small children to school and collecting them afterwards.
- If elderly relatives are poor due to inadequate pensions and savings, their family may have to support them. This may lead to financial hardship, as

people face having to support not just themselves and their children, but also their parents and possibly grandparents too. This financial hardship can be made worse if one partner has to give up paid work to care for elderly dependants.

- The growing isolation and loneliness of older people, as friends and partners die and health deteriorates, may lead to growing dependence on their children to visit and support them. This can create problems for planning family holidays and moving for work or promotion.
- There may be emotional strain and overcrowding if an elderly, and possibly infirm, relative moves in with his or her child's family. This might cause conflict between couples, or between children and grandparents, as well as increasing costs to the family.
- There could be a return of the classic extended family. This will be considered later.
- There may be extra work for fully adult children, and particularly women. The practical burdens of caring for the elderly tend to fall mainly on their fully adult children. Increasingly, with longer life expectancy, many of these adult children are themselves elderly and facing more infirmity; for example, 65-year-olds caring for their 90-year-old parents. This responsibility falls particularly to women in the family, even though they already carry most of the burden of housework and childcare in their own homes, as discussed later in this chapter.
- There may well be increased stress and ill health for relatives who have to devote large amounts of time to caring for infirm or disabled elderly relatives.
- Young people may have difficulty in finding affordable homes of their own, as older people occupy their homes for longer. They may find they have to live with their parents longer than they would otherwise choose.

Activity

1 If you have, or were to have, an elderly parent, grandparent or great-grandparent living with you, what advantages and problems are or might be created for family life? Discuss these with others if you are in a group.
2 Go to www.statistics.gov.uk/cci/nugget.asp?id=1336 and identify three features of those who typically provide unpaid care for the dependent elderly.
3 Go to www.ageuk.org.uk (Age UK) and identify five issues of concern to older person households, and what this organization suggests should be done to resolve them.
4 Suggest three possible consequences for society as a whole of a growing proportion of older people in society.

Activity

Look at figure 3.2 and answer the following questions:
1 Approximately what percentage of females were over the age of 70 in 1981?
2 Approximately what percentage of males were aged over 70 in 1981?
3 By approximately how much did the percentage of females in the 70–9 age group increase between 1901 and 2001?
4 About what percentage of females are expected to be over the age of 80 by 2033?
5 Comparing 1901 with 2033, by how much is the percentage of (a) men and (b) women over the age of 60 estimated to increase by 2033?
6 Explain briefly how figure 3.2 shows that Britain has an ageing population.

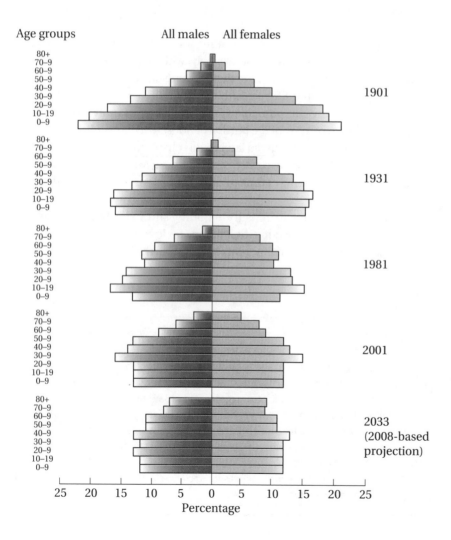

Age groups   All males   All females

1901

1931

1981

2001

2033
(2008-based
projection)

25   20   15   10   5   0   5   10   15   20   25
Percentage

Figure 3.2 The ageing population: United Kingdom, 1901–2033
Source: Office for National Stastics

The decline in the birth rate, fertility rate and average family size

Over the last century, the birth rate has been declining in Britain, from 28 per 1,000 in 1902 to about 12 per 1,000 in 2009. The fertility rate has also been declining. There was an average number of 2.77 children per woman in 1961, but this had reduced to about 1.97 by 2008. This has meant that average family and household size have been dropping, from around 6 children per family in the 1870s to an average of around 1.7 children per family in 2008. The average household size in Britain has also almost halved in the last 100 years, from around 4.6 people to around 2.4 people per household in 2009. The trend towards smaller families, and more people living alone, explains this reduction in average household size.

Reasons for the decline in the birth rate and smaller families

Contraception More effective, safer and cheaper methods of birth control have been developed over the last century, and society's attitudes to the use of contraception have changed from disapproval to acceptance. This is partly because of growing **secularization**, and the declining influence of the church and religion on people's behaviour and morality.

The availability of safe and legal abortion since 1967 has also helped in terminating unwanted pregnancies. Family planning is therefore easier.

The compulsory education of children Since children were barred from employment in the nineteenth century, and education became compulsory

> **Secularization** is the process whereby religious thinking, practice and institutions decline and lose influence in society.

Figure 3.3 Reasons for the decline in the birth rate, fertility rate and average family size

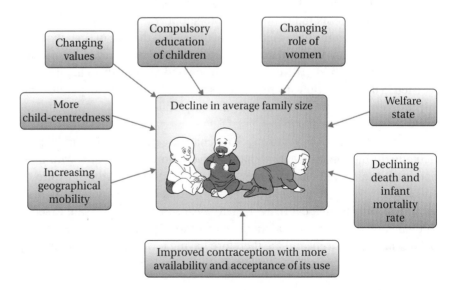

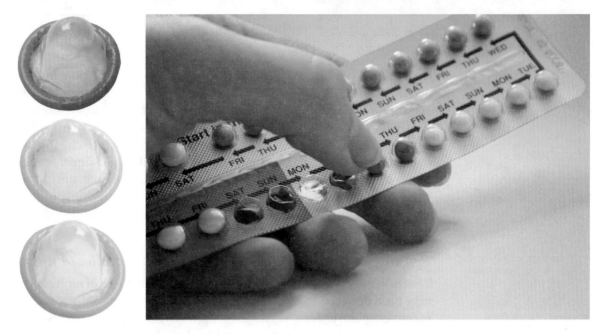

More effective methods of birth control, combined with changing attitudes to the use of contraception, have contributed to the decline in the birth rate and smaller families

in 1880, they have ceased to be an economic asset making a contribution to family income through working at an early age. Children have therefore become an economic liability and a drain on the resources of parents, because they have to be supported for a long period in compulsory education, and often in post-16 education and training, including university and college years. Parents today often have to support their children well into their twenties. Parents have therefore begun to limit the size of their families to secure for themselves and their children a higher standard of living. The move to a more child-centred society (discussed later in this chapter) has assisted in this restriction of family size, as smaller families mean parents can spend more money and time on and with each child.

The changing position of women   The changing position of women, particularly during the last century, has involved more equal status with men and greater employment opportunities. Women today have less desire to spend long years of their lives bearing and rearing children, and many wish to, and do, pursue their own careers. This means many women want to settle in their careers, pay back student loans, save for a house deposit and so on before having children, and are therefore having fewer children and having them later in life than previously.

While most women do eventually have children, there is a growing proportion who are choosing not to do so. For example, around 20 per cent of women born in the early 1960s (aged in their forties in 2007) were childless in 2007, compared to about 10 per cent of those born in the 1940s by the time they had reached their forties; and nearly 25 per cent of women born in 1973 are expected to be still childless at age 45. This trend towards childlessness can be expected to continue with women's growing position in paid employment.

The declining infant mortality rate   Until the 1940s, the absence of a welfare state meant that many parents relied on their children to care for them in old age. However, although more babies were beginning to survive infancy, it was still often uncertain whether children would outlive their parents. Parents therefore often had many children as a safeguard against some of them dying. The decline in the infant mortality rate and the death rate has meant that fewer people die before adulthood and old age, so parents no longer have more children as security against only a few surviving. In addition, the range of agencies which exist to help the elderly today means that people are less reliant on care from their children when they reach old age.

A geographically mobile labour force   Contemporary societies generally require a geographically mobile workforce – that is, a workforce that can easily move to other areas for work or promotion. This may have been a

Most women in the UK work in paid employment today, and many will combine this with childcare responsibilities. Many wish to pursue careers and will therefore either limit the number of children they have, often putting off having them until their careers are established, or choose to have none at all

factor in encouraging smaller families, because they can more easily pack up and move elsewhere.

Changing values   Parenthood involves greater pressure on couples, a life-long commitment, a loss of freedom and independence, and sacrifices like cuts in money to spend on consumer goods and the loss of time for leisure and pleasure. Not having children is becoming a positive life choice for many couples, and in a society where people seek to develop their identities through their consumer spending and leisure choices, couples are becoming more reluctant to have children.

OTHER CHANGES IN FAMILIES AND HOUSEHOLDS IN BRITAIN

In addition to the demographic changes discussed above, the family in Britain has gone through a number of other changes over the last 100 years or so, and it continues to change today. The extent of some of these changes thought to have occurred in the family has often been exaggerated, and misleading conclusions have been drawn. Each of these changes will be examined in turn. The key changes which have commonly been thought to have occurred are summarized in figure 3.4.

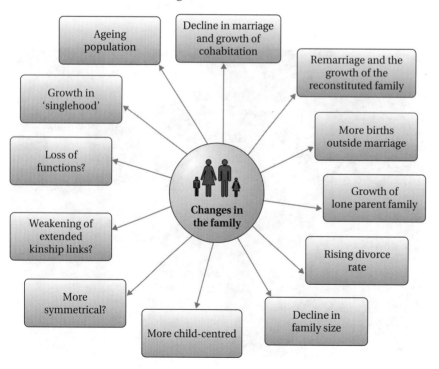

Figure 3.4 Changes in the family

The changing role of the family in society

The family in Britain and most other societies has traditionally had a number of responsibilities placed upon it (its functions), primarily connected with its role in the preparation of children to fit into adult society. These tasks of the family, and how they've changed over time are described below.

TRADITIONAL RESPONSIBILITIES (OR FUNCTIONS) OF THE FAMILY	HOW THEY HAVE CHANGED
• *Reproduction of the population* – the reproduction and nurturing of children. Having children was often seen as the main reason for marriage, as a means of passing on family property and providing a future workforce.	• In Britain since the 1970s, there has been a steady increase in the birth of children and sexual relations before and outside of marriage. In 2009, for example, nearly half (46 per cent) of children were born outside marriage. These changes are explained later in this chapter.
• The family and kinship network traditionally played a major role in *maintaining and caring for dependent children* – housing, clothing and feeding those children who were still unable to look after themselves.	• The modern nuclear family is less dependent on relatives for help and assistance in maintaining and caring for children. Welfare benefits like social security and child tax credits, and the social services, including social workers working with families, all help parents to maintain their children.
• The family provided most of the *help and care for the young, the old, the sick and the poor* during periods of illness, unemployment and other crises. Poverty often meant poor health and poor healthcare.	• This has become shared with the state through the NHS and the social services. Homes for the elderly, hospitals, welfare clinics, GPs, retirement pensions, and a range of state-provided welfare benefits reduce the dependence on kin for money and support.
• The *primary socialization and social control of children*. The family is where society's new recruits first learn the basic values and norms of the culture of the society they will grow up in. For example, it is in the family that children first learn the difference between what is seen as right and wrong, good and bad behaviour, and the acceptance of parental and other adult authority.	• The family still retains the major responsibility for the socialization of very young children, but the increase in the number of Sure Start children's centres, childminders, pre-schools and playgroups, and free nursery education for several hours a week for 3- and 4-year-olds has meant this is no longer restricted to the family. The state educational system now helps the family with the socialization of school-age children, and the mass media also play an important role.
• The family used to be one of the only sources of *education* for young people in Britain. Before compulsory schooling was provided by the state in Britain from 1880, many children from working-class families were very poorly educated by today's standards, and illiteracy rates were extremely high.	• The education of children has been mainly taken over by the state, and is now primarily the responsibility of professional teachers rather than parents. All young people between the ages of 5 and 16 (age 17 from 2013) now have to attend school by law. However, the family continues to play an important socializing and supporting role in preparing a child for school, and encouraging and supporting her or him during school years. The family still has a major effect on a child's level of educational achievement.

Activity

1 Go carefully through the section above on the traditional functions or responsibilities of the family and how they have changed. Make a list summarizing these changes under two main headings: (a) the tasks traditionally performed by the family, and (b) who performs these functions today: family, or government and state, or shared between them.

2 Identify two ways in which the family provides for the well-being of its members.

3 Do you think the changes that have occurred in the family's functions have made it more or less important in society today? Back up your viewpoint with evidence.

4 Imagine all families were banned by law tomorrow. What tasks currently carried out in your own family would someone else have to perform? Who would do these tasks, do you think?

5 Consider all the ways you can think of in which the family a child is born into might affect the chances she or he gets in life, such as in health, education and job opportunities. Be sure you explain the connection between family background and the life chances you identify.

The emergence of the privatized nuclear family, the modified extended family and the beanpole family

Over about the last 100 years, classic extended families have become much less common, and, in contemporary Britain, the **privatized nuclear family** is the most common form of family in which people live.

The privatized nuclear family is where the nuclear family is separated and isolated from its extended kin, and has become a self-contained, self-reliant, home-centred unit. Life for the modern privatized nuclear family is largely centred on the home – free time is spent doing jobs around the house and leisure is mainly home- and family-centred. DIY, gardening, watching television, or going out as a family to leisure attractions like Alton Towers are typical family activities. The contemporary nuclear family has thus become a very private institution, isolated from wider kin and often from neighbours and local community life as well.

The following explanations have been offered for this decline of extended family life and the process of privatization.

- Contemporary societies require a geographically mobile labour force, with people able and willing to move to other areas of the country to find work, improve their education or gain promotion. This often involves leaving relatives behind, thus weakening and breaking up traditional extended family life. The small size of the modern isolated nuclear family and its lack of permanent roots in an area (such as wider kin) mean that

> The **privatized nuclear family** is a self-contained, self-reliant and home-centred nuclear family unit that is largely separated and isolated from its extended kin, neighbours and local community life.

it is geographically mobile, which some sociologists argue makes it ideally suited for life in contemporary society.

- Contemporary Britain is a more **meritocratic society** – the jobs people get are mainly achieved on the basis of talent, skill and educational qualifications, rather than of whom they know. Extended kin therefore have less to offer family members – such as job opportunities – reducing reliance on kin.
- Educational success and promotion often involve upward **social mobility** and this leads to differences in income, status, lifestyle, and attitudes and values between kin. Kin have less in common, and this contributes to the weakening of extended family ties.
- With the development of higher standards of living and the provision of welfare services by the state for security against ill-health, unemployment and poverty, people have become less dependent on kin for help in times of distress. This further weakens the extended family.

> A **meritocratic society** is one in which social and occupational positions (jobs) and pay are allocated on the basis purely of people's individual experience, talents, abilities, qualifications and skills – their individual merits. **Social mobility** refers to the movement of groups or individuals up or down the social hierarchy.

The modified extended family

While there is evidence that nuclear families have become the most common form of the family in contemporary society, geographical separation does not necessarily mean all links with kin are severed. Often, in the age of mass communications and easy transportation, the closeness and mutual support between kin, typical of classic extended family life, are retained by letter writing, telephone, email and social networking and photo sharing sites like Facebook and Flickr, or through visiting. It has therefore been suggested that the typical family today in Britain is not simply the isolated nuclear family, but this modified form of the extended family.

The continued existence of the classic extended family

While the most common type of family found in modern Britain is the nuclear family or the modified extended family, there is evidence that the classic extended family still survives today in modern Britain in two types of community:

- *Traditional working-class communities.* These are long-established communities dominated by one industry, like fishing and mining, in the traditional working-class industrial centres of the north of England, and in inner-city working-class areas. In such communities, there is little geographical or social mobility, and children usually remain in the same area when they form their own families. People stay in the same community for several generations, and this creates a close-knit community life – it is the type of community shown in TV soaps such as *Coronation Street* or *EastEnders*. Members of the extended family live close together and meet frequently, and there is a constant exchange of services between extended family members – such as washing, shopping and babysitting between female kin, and shared work and leisure activities between male relatives. Such extended family life declined in the 1990s, as traditional industries closed down and people were forced to move away in search of new employment.

- *The Asian community.* There is evidence that the extended family is still very common among those who came to Britain in the 1960s and 1970s from India, Pakistan and Bangladesh. The extended family usually centres on the male side of the family, with grandfathers, sons, grandsons and their wives, and unmarried daughters. Such a family life continues to be an important source of strength and support in such communities.

The Beanpole family: the return of the extended family?

As discussed earlier in this chapter, Britain's ageing population means that a growing number of people are reaching old age, and often living well into their eighties and nineties, and 2008 estimates suggest there will be 80,000 people aged 100 and over by 2033. At the same time, couples are having fewer children and nuclear families are getting smaller. This means that there is an increase in the number of extended four- and five-generation families, with more children growing up in extended families alongside several of their grandparents and even great-grandparents. This new shape of the extended family is sometimes called the **Beanpole family**. This is because the family tree is 'thinner' and less 'bushy': fewer brothers and sisters in one generation leads to fewer aunts and uncles and cousins in the next. It is also longer, with several generations of older relatives, as people live longer. This trend towards a new emerging beanpole form of the extended family can only be

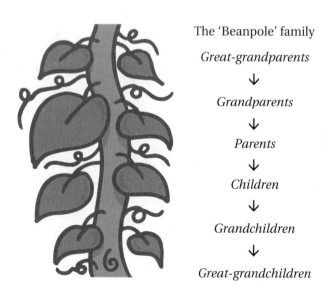

The 'Beanpole' family

Great-grandparents

↓

Grandparents

↓

Parents

↓

Children

↓

Grandchildren

↓

Great-grandchildren

Declining numbers of children in each generation and greater life expectancy mean the family tree has become thinner and less bushy – more beanpole-like – with fewer brothers and sisters, cousins, aunts and uncles, but more grandparents and great-grandparents

expected to increase with the growing numbers of the elderly, and fewer children being born.

Activity

1 Describe *two* characteristics of the privatized nuclear family.
2 Give *two* reasons for the decline of the classic extended family.
3 Explain what is meant by the modified extended family.
4 Suggest *two* advantages and *two* disadvantages of living in a beanpole family.

The emergence of the symmetrical family?

Since the 1980s there has been a debate about the emergence of a so-called 'New Man'. This New Man is allegedly more caring, sharing, gentle, emotional and sensitive in his attitudes to women, children and his own emotional needs, sharing decision-making with his partner and willing to do his fair share of housework and childcare. There is a common belief that the relations between male and female partners in the family in Britain have therefore become more equal since the second half of the twentieth century. The assumption has been that there has been a change from segregated to integrated conjugal roles, and the emergence of a more 'symmetrical' or equally balanced family.

> **Conjugal roles** are the roles played by partners in marriage / civil partnership or in a cohabiting couple.

- **Segregated conjugal roles** are those where partners have very different tasks in the family, with a clear division and separation between the male's role and the female's role.
- **Integrated** (or joint) **conjugal roles** are those where there are few divisions in the jobs done by male and female partners.

Some of these differences are identified below.

SEGREGATED CONJUGAL ROLES	**INTEGRATED CONJUGAL ROLES**
• Partners in a married or cohabiting relationship have clearly separated roles.	• Partners in a married or cohabiting relationship have interchangeable and flexible roles.
• Men take responsibility for bringing in money, major decisions, and doing the heavier and more technical jobs around the home, such as fixing household equipment and doing repairs. Women are mainly housewives, with responsibility for housework, shopping, cooking, childcare etc. They are unlikely to have full-time paid employment.	• Both partners are likely to be either in paid employment or looking for a job. Household chores and childcare are shared, with males taking on traditional female jobs like housework, cooking, shopping, etc., and female partners taking on traditional male jobs, such as household repairs, looking after the car, etc.
• Partners are likely to have separate friends and different leisure activities.	• Partners share common friends, leisure activities and decision-making.

It has been suggested that the emergence of the so-called New Man has been accompanied by a change from segregated to integrated roles. This is thought to have occurred for a number of reasons.

- The improved status and rights of women have forced men to accept women more as equals and not simply as housewives and mothers.
- The increase in the number of working women has increased women's independence and authority in the family – where the female partner has her own income, she is less dependent on her male partner, and she has more power and authority. Decision-making is therefore more likely to be shared.
- Women are now outperforming men in education and are therefore often earning the same as, or sometimes more than, their male partners. The importance of female partners' earnings in maintaining the family's standard of living, and women's growing equality in the workplace, may have encouraged men to help more with **domestic labour** (housework and childcare) – a recognition that the women cannot be expected to do two jobs at once.
- Improved living standards in the home, such as central heating, TV, DVDs, broadband Internet, music systems and a whole host of other domestic and leisure technology, have encouraged men to spend more time at home, and share home-centred leisure with their female partners.
- The decline of the close-knit extended family and greater geographical mobility in contemporary society have meant there is less pressure from kin on newly married or cohabiting couples to retain traditional roles – it is therefore easier to adopt new roles in a relationship. There are often no longer the separate male and female networks (of friends and especially kin) for male and female partners to mix with. This increases their dependence upon each other, and may mean men and women who adopt new roles avoid being teased by friends who knew them before they got married or began cohabiting.

> **Domestic labour** is the term sometimes used to refer to unpaid work in the home, such as cooking, cleaning, childcare, and looking after the sick and the elderly.

Criticisms of the view that modern marriages and cohabiting relationships are really more equal: the myth of integrated roles

The Office for National Statistics suggested in the late 1990s that rising numbers of men were choosing to become 'house-husbands', and raise children rather than work, leaving their partner to become the family breadwinner. This reversal of traditional roles reflects the growing earning power of women at work, and provides some evidence of changing attitudes among some men towards childcare and housework. However, this trend appears to be mainly happening only in those relatively few families where the woman earns more than the man and it is financially practical to swap roles. Researchers also suggest that working fathers are spending more time

Have conjugal roles really changed?

each day with their children (around an hour) compared to the 1980s (40 minutes). However, women spend two and a half times as long with their children. Evidence from a number of surveys shows that, in most cases, traditional segregated roles still remain – review the evidence yourself by studying the data presented on pages 114–16, and doing the related activity on page 117.

- Women still perform the majority of domestic and childcare tasks around the home, even when they have paid jobs themselves. They spend on average nearly twice as long as men each day on household and childcare tasks, such as household shopping, cooking the evening meal, cleaning, washing and ironing, looking after the children and caring for sick family members. The 2008 British Social Attitudes Survey reported that 80 per cent of women with partners said that they 'always or usually did the laundry'. A 2008 mumsnet.com survey found 75 per cent of mothers do most of the cooking for their children, compared to just 7 per cent of fathers. The 2007 European Social Reality Report found 85 per cent of women in the European Union did the ironing (79 per cent in the UK). Housework is the second largest cause of domestic rows, after money.
- It is women who are most likely to have to make sacrifices, if needed, to buy the children clothes, and to make sure other family members are properly fed.
- Power and authority are not equally distributed in marriage and cohabiting relationships. Women are less likely than men to have the final say on the most important decisions in the family. Research in this area suggests most decisions which couples think of as 'very important', such as moving house or taking out loans, are finally taken by men alone.

While some decisions are taken jointly, very few are taken by women alone, and those decisions that are taken by women alone are often only in relatively unimportant areas like home decoration and furnishing, children's clothes, food and other domestic spending. This was confirmed by a MORI survey conducted for Direct Line Financial Services in June 2000. This found that decisions on major spending (over £1,000) were only made jointly between men and women in 53 per cent of cases. Women made only one in ten of the decisions. In many households, men still hold the purse strings.

- Men are still often the major or sole earners, and this puts men in a stronger bargaining position than women, and often puts their female partners in a position of economic dependence.
- Women's continuing responsibility for housework and childcare often means women's careers suffer. Surveys suggest many working women are limited in the jobs they can do and the hours they can work because they are still expected to take the main responsibility for housework and childcare, and to be at home for the children leaving for and returning from school. It is often women, rather than men, who have to leave work early to pick up children, and it is mothers, rather than fathers, who are most likely to take time off work to look after children who can't attend school or nursery because they are sick. Women consequently have less pay, less security of employment, and poorer promotion prospects than men, and this reinforces men's economic superiority and greater authority in the family.
- It is mainly women who give up paid work (or suffer from lost/ restricted job opportunities) to look after children, the elderly or the sick.
- Women still take the major responsibility for managing the emotional side of family life. This refers to things like the emotional aspects of childcare, such as talking to, listening to, understanding and supporting children, including older children. It also involves liaising between family members when there are rows, and acting as the family mediator.
- There is evidence of widespread male violence in relationships, often resorted to when men are drunk and use their power to try to get women to submit to their wishes. Such violence is all too often not taken seriously by the police or courts, being dismissed as a 'domestic dispute'. This might be interpreted as a view that such violence is almost seen as a normal part of a relationship. Violence in the family is discussed later in this chapter.

While there does seem to be evidence of more role integration in leisure activities and decision-making, housework and childcare remain predominantly

WOMEN'S TRIPLE SHIFT

The points discussed in this section mean many female partners now often have three jobs – paid work, domestic labour and childcare, and emotional work – to their male partner's one job. This has sometimes been referred to as women's 'triple shift'.

women's work. While men are perhaps more involved in childcare than they used to be, this would appear to be in the more enjoyable activities like playing with the children and taking them out. The more routine jobs such as bathing and feeding and taking children to the doctor are still done predominantly by women, and it is still mostly women who get the blame if the house is untidy or children are dirty or badly dressed.

Some confirmation of the huge exaggeration of the apparent emergence of 'new men' was found in a June 2009 survey by cleaning firm Vileda. This found that four out of ten British men still thought that housework was a woman's job, with one in five men admitting that they did absolutely no cleaning around the home (and 78 per cent of those doing no cleaning were married and/or fathers). One in three men said they had never tackled the bathroom with a mop, bucket or cloth.

While men might be doing marginally more around the home in recent years, this change would appear to have been massively exaggerated. In a majority of marriages and cohabiting relationships, the traditional roles of women and men remain.

Activity

How far is there equality between partners in a household you know well? It could be your own home, or any household where there are children. Put the following questions (or some of your own) to the male partner of the household, or adapt it so both partners answer (there is some evidence men exaggerate in surveys how much work they do in the home, and asking their partners may help to overcome this).

1 Have you ever ironed your partner's blouse?
2 What foods do your children refuse to eat?
3 What do the following cost: a loaf, a jar of instant coffee, a packet of tea, a packet of butter, a tin of baked beans, a packet of washing-powder/liquid, and a packet of toilet rolls?
4 How does the washing machine work?
5 What would you use to clean the kitchen floor?
6 How do you empty the vacuum cleaner?
7 What days are the bins emptied?
8 What brand of washing powder/liquid do you use?
9 When did you last do the family shopping alone?
10 When did you last draw up the shopping list alone?
11 When did you last clean the loo?
12 What is the children's favourite meal?
13 How many hours a week do you spend on housework?
14 When did you last clean the bathroom or kitchen taps?
15 When did you last clean the bath or shower, or the kitchen/bathroom sinks?

Compare your findings with others in your group. What conclusions do your findings suggest about the apparent change towards growing equality between men and women in the family?

Twenty years of research on domestic labour – are families becoming more partnerships of equals?

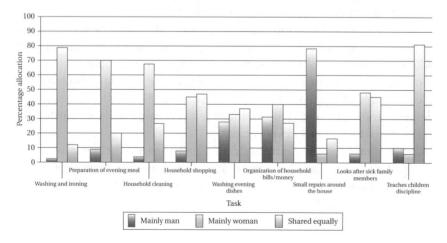

Item A Household division of labour among married and cohabiting couples: Great Britain, 1990s

Item B Percentage who never do selected household tasks: United Kingdom, 2001

Activity	Does not do activity	
	Men	Women
Cooking a meal	15	3
DIY repair work	16	46
Gardening	20	22
Non-food shopping	7	3
Food shopping	12	5
Cooking a meal (special occasion)	33	10
Decorating	8	27
Tidying the house	13	4
Helping children with homework	66	60
Washing clothes	39	5
Ironing clothes	42	8

Source: Adapted from UK Time Use Survey, Office for National Statistics

Item C Time spent on housework each day: full-time workers

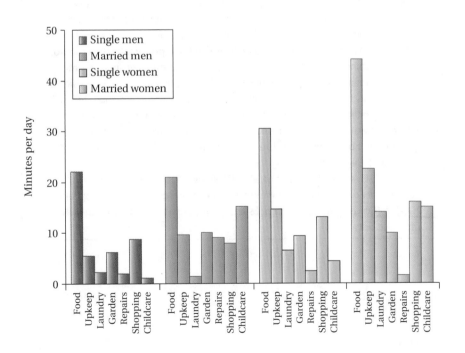

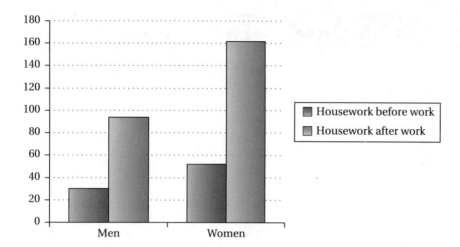

Item D Time spent on housework before and after work: full-time workers

ITEM E

Housework may affect wages because it reduces the amount of energy and flexibility that can be brought to the labour market. Individuals who go to work tired after doing the housework are likely to perform less well than others with no housework commitments; similarly, having the responsibility of organizing domestic activities may make it more difficult to concentrate at work. Furthermore, those who need to do housework at certain times (for example cooking meals) cannot be as flexible in their working hours as those with no commitments and so may be more restricted in the types of jobs they can do. As well as doing more total hours of housework than men (or single women), married women specialize in routine tasks (like cooking and laundry) which are done at times that may interfere with paid employment. In particular there is evidence that married women's housework may limit their paid employment activities towards the end of the working day. Married men, by contrast, tend to specialize in housework tasks, like gardening and household repairs, that can be put off to the weekend.

Items C, D, and E adapted from M. L. Bryan and A. Sevilla Sanz, *Does Housework Lower Wages and Why? Evidence for Britain*, ISER Working Paper 2008–3 (Colchester: University of Essex, 2008), based on data from the UK Time Use Survey

Activity

Refer to items A–E. These show the results of surveys which were conducted between 1992 and 2008. Then answer the following questions:

1. Which three household tasks were the most likely to be performed mainly by women? (Item A)
2. Which two household tasks were the most likely to be performed mainly by men? (Item A)
3. Who is most likely to look after sick family members? (Item A)
4. Which household task is the least likely to be performed mainly by men? (Item A)
5. Which three household tasks are most likely to be shared equally? (Item A)
6. Who is most likely to prepare the evening meal, and either to be solely responsible for washing evening dishes or to share it with their partners? (Item A)
7. What percentage of men never iron clothes? (Item B)
8. What percentage of women never do DIY repair work? (Item B)
9. According to Item C, which two groups spend the most time each day on food-related housework?
10. According to Item C, which activity do married men and women seem to spend roughly equal amounts of time on each day?
11. Refer to Items D and E. (a) Identify two differences between the housework done by men and that done by women; and (b) suggest how these differences might make paid work more difficult for women.
12. Reviewing the evidence in Items A–E, suggest three pieces of evidence that might be used to show family relationships are becoming more equal, and three pieces showing that they are not.
13. Drawing on all the work you have done on the issue, to what extent do you agree with the view that it is largely a myth that the contemporary family is a partnership of equals? How would you explain any differences between what women and men do in the home?

The changing position of children in the family

During the course of the twentieth century and in the early twenty-first, families have become more child-centred, with family activities and outings often focused on the interests of the children. The amount of time parents spend with their children has more than doubled since the 1960s, and parents are more involved with their children, taking an interest in their activities, discussing decisions with them, and treating them more as equals. Often, the children's welfare is seen as the major family priority, frequently involving the parents in considerable financial sacrifice and cost.

Families have become more child-centred over the past sixty years

Children today are often at the centre of family life, with the lives of parents dominated by the demands and needs of their children

The causes of child-centredness

- Families have got smaller over the last century, and this means more individual care and attention can be devoted to each child.
- The typical working week has got shorter. This means parents have more time to spend with their children.
- Increasing affluence, with higher wages and a higher standard of living, has benefited children, as more money can be spent on them and their activities.
- The welfare state provides a wide range of benefits designed to help parents care for their children, but also a range of measures, such as Sure

Figure 3.5 Reasons why families have become more child-centred

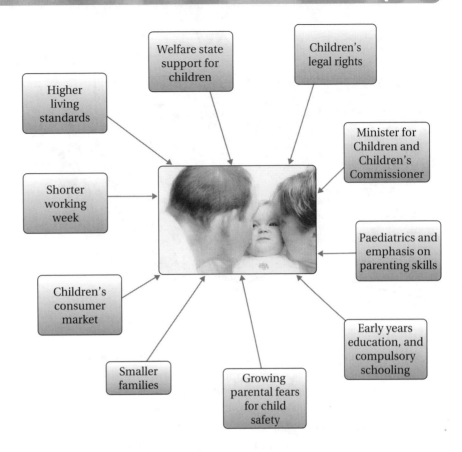

Welfare state support for children

Children's legal rights

Higher living standards

Minister for Children and Children's Commissioner

Shorter working week

Paediatrics and emphasis on parenting skills

Children's consumer market

Early years education, and compulsory schooling

Smaller families

Growing parental fears for child safety

Start, to give children a good start in life through early years education. There are now increased demands on parents to look after their children properly. Social workers, for example, have a wide range of powers to intervene in families on behalf of children who are at risk, and have the ultimate power to remove children from families if parents fail to look after them properly. The United Nations Convention on the Rights of the Child (1989) and the Children Acts of 1989 and 2004 established children's legal rights, and there is now a Minister for Children and a Children's Commissioner to champion the views of children and protect and promote their interests.

- Paediatrics, or the science of childhood, has developed rapidly over the last 100 years or so, with a wide range of research and popular books suggesting how parents should bring up their children to encourage their full development. The nurturing, protection and education of children are now seen as a vital and central part of family life, with parenting skills and early years education now recognized as an important aspect of children's educational and social development. In particular, in recent years there has been renewed emphasis on parenting skills, with a range

of websites, TV programmes like *Supernanny*, charities and government agencies providing advice and support for parents bringing up children, and suggesting ways parents can avoid having, or learn to cope with, 'problem children' (see the websites, for example, referred to on page 85 at the beginning of this chapter).

- Compulsory education and more time spent in further education and training have meant young people are dependent on their parents for longer periods of time. Tuition fees for higher education and the abolition of student grants have in recent years extended this period of dependency of young people on their parents. In this respect, childhood, including the dependency on adults it involves, has itself become extended.

- Children's lives have become more complex, with more educational, medical and leisure services for them. This frequently involves parents in ferrying children to schools, cinemas, friends, and so on.

- Growing traffic dangers and parental fears (largely unjustified) of assaults upon their children have meant that children now travel more with parents rather than being left to roam about on their own as much as they used to.

- Large businesses have encouraged a specific childhood consumer market. Businesses like Mothercare, Toys"R"Us, Nike, publishers, clothing manufacturers and the music industry aim at the childhood consumer market, encouraging children to consume – and parents to spend to satisfy their children's demands. Even top fashion designers like Stella

McCartney are now designing children's clothes. 'Pester power', the principle behind advertisers targeting children to pester their parents into buying them CDs, clothes, toys and so on, is now an important feature of the advertising business.

> ### Activity
>
> Drawing on your own experience, how far do you think advertisers target young people to encourage them to consume things? How does advertising influence you and the things you buy, and how far does it encourage you to badger your parents into buying them for you?

The rising divorce rate

The **divorce rate** is the number of people getting divorced per 1,000 married people per year.

One of the most startling changes in the family in Britain over the last century has been the general and dramatic increase in the number of marriages ending in divorce, as shown in figure 3.6. Figure 3.7 shows the changes in the **divorce rate** (the number divorcing per 1,000 married people per year) between 1971 and 2008.

The number of divorces in England and Wales rose from 29,000 in 1951 to 122,000 in 2008, with the number of divorces doubling during the 1970s. A similar pattern is shown in the divorce rate. The number of divorces is now declining, with 2008 having the lowest number of divorces since 1975, with the divorce rate the lowest since 1979. This decline is not because fewer relationships are breaking up. Fewer people are marrying and so there is a declining number of married couples to get divorced. Britain is in the top third of countries with the highest divorce rates in the European Union, and estimates have suggested more than 40 per cent of new marriages are likely to end in divorce. The average length of marriages ending in divorce was between eleven and twelve years in 2008.

> **DIVORCE AND 'BROKEN HOMES'**
>
> Divorce is the legal termination of a marriage, but this is not the only way that marriages and homes can be 'broken'. Homes and marriages may be broken in 'empty shell' marriages, where the marital relationship has broken down, but no divorce has taken place. Separation – through either choice or necessity (as in working abroad or imprisonment) – may also cause a broken home, as may the death of a partner. So homes may be broken for reasons other than divorce, and divorce itself is often only the end result of a marriage which broke down long before.

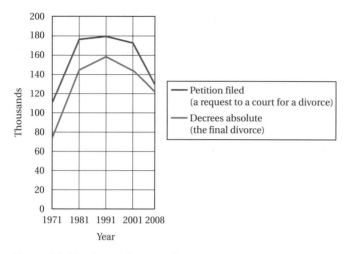

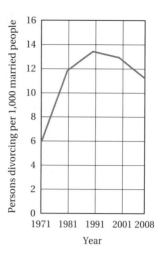

Figure 3.6 Number of divorces: England and Wales, 1971–2008

Source: Ministry of Justice and Office for National Statistics

Figure 3.7 Divorce rate: England and Wales, 1971–2008

Source: Population Trends, Office for National Statistics

Activity

Study figures 3.6 and 3.7 and answer the following questions:

1 Approximately how many divorce petitions were filed in 1971?
2 How many decrees absolute were there in 2001?
3 In what year was there the highest number of decrees absolute?
4 About how many more decrees absolute were there in 2008 than in 1971?
5 What was the divorce rate in 1971?
6 Between what years was there the largest increase in the divorce rate?
7 Explain the difference between the number of divorces and the divorce rate.
8 Between 1971 and 1981 there was a very large increase in the number of divorces and the divorce rate. Suggest possible explanations for this.
9 Figure 3.6 shows there is quite a large difference between the number of divorce petitions (requests to a court to grant a divorce) and the number of decrees absolute (the final divorce) granted. Suggest explanations for this.

Who gets divorced?

While divorce affects all groups in the population, there are some groups whose divorce rates are higher than the average. Teenage marriages are twice as likely to end in divorce as those of couples overall, and there is a high incidence of divorce in the first five to seven years of marriage and after about ten to fourteen years (when the children are older or have left home). The working class, particularly semi-skilled and unskilled, has a higher rate of divorce than the middle class. Childless couples and partners from different

Around four in every ten new marriages today are likely to end in divorce, with teenage marriages having about twice the risk of probable divorce compared to couples overall

social class or religious backgrounds also face a higher risk of divorce, as do couples whose work separates them for long periods. The rising divorce rate therefore does not affect all groups of married people equally, and some face higher risks of divorce than others.

> **Activity**
>
> Go through the groups above, and suggest explanations for why each of them is more at risk of divorce than most of the rest of the population. Can you think of other groups who might have a higher risk of divorce than most people?

Explanations for the rising divorce rate

Rising divorce rates must be treated with considerable caution, and assessed against changing legal, financial and social circumstances, if misleading conclusions about the declining importance of marriage and the family are to be avoided. The increase may simply reflect easier and cheaper divorce procedures enabling the legal termination of already unhappy empty shell marriages rather than a real increase in marriage breakdowns. It could be that people who in previous years could only separate are now divorcing as legal and financial obstacles are removed.

There are two broad groups of reasons for the increase in the divorce rate: changes in the law which have gradually made divorce easier and cheaper to get, and changes in society which have made divorce a more practical and socially acceptable way of terminating a broken marriage. These are discussed in the next sections, and figure 3.8 summarizes these changes.

Changes in the law as a reason for the rising divorce rate   Changes in the law over the last century have made divorce easier and cheaper to get, and have given men and women equal rights in divorce. This partly accounts for the steep rise in the divorce rate over the last fifty years, particularly in the 1970s and 1980s. These changes in the law are listed in the box below. However, changes in the law reflect changing social attitudes and norms, and there are a number of wider social explanations that must also be considered.

SOME RECENT CHANGES IN THE DIVORCE LAWS

The Divorce Law Reform Act of 1969

This came into effect in 1971, and was a major change. Before the 1969 Act, a person wanting a divorce had to prove before a court that his or her spouse had committed a 'matrimonial offence', like adultery, cruelty or desertion. This frequently led to major public scandals, as all the details of unhappy marriages were aired in a public law court. This may have deterred many people whose marriage had broken down from seeking a divorce. Also, marriages may have broken down – become empty shell marriages – without any matrimonial offence being committed.

The 1969 Act changed all this, and made 'irretrievable breakdown' of a marriage the only grounds for divorce. It is now no longer necessary to prove one partner guilty of a matrimonial offence, but simply to demonstrate that a marriage has broken down beyond repair. After 1971, one way of demonstrating irretrievable breakdown of a marriage was by two years of separation. This change in the law led to a massive increase in the number of divorces after 1971.

The Matrimonial and Family Proceedings Act of 1984 allowed couples to petition for divorce after only one year of marriage, whereas previously couples could normally divorce only after three years of marriage. This led to a record increase in the number of divorces in 1984 and 1985.

The Family Law Act of 1996 came into effect in 1999. This increased the amount of time before a divorce could be granted to eighteen months, introduced compulsory marriage counselling for a 'period of reflection', and required children's wishes to be considered and financial arrangements to be agreed before a divorce was granted. This was an attempt to stem the rising number of divorces by increasing the time for 'cooling off'. The compulsory counselling sessions were later abandoned because it was found they were more likely to encourage people to go through with a divorce, even when they were initially uncertain about whether they really wanted to.

Figure 3.8 Causes of the rising divorce rate

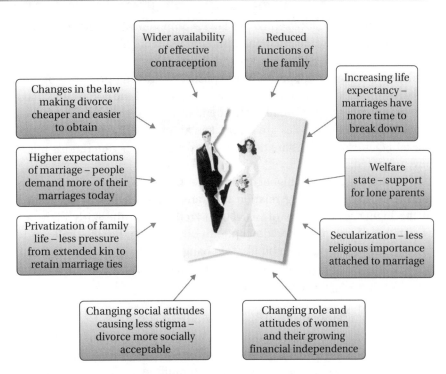

Wider availability of effective contraception

Reduced functions of the family

Increasing life expectancy – marriages have more time to break down

Changes in the law making divorce cheaper and easier to obtain

Welfare state – support for lone parents

Higher expectations of marriage – people demand more of their marriages today

Privatization of family life – less pressure from extended kin to retain marriage ties

Secularization – less religious importance attached to marriage

Changing social attitudes causing less stigma – divorce more socially acceptable

Changing role and attitudes of women and their growing financial independence

Changes in society as a reason for the rising divorce rate

THE CHANGING ROLE OF WOMEN

This is a very important explanation for the rising divorce rate. Around three-quarters of divorce petitions (requests to a court for a divorce) are initiated by women, and around seven out of ten of all divorces are granted to women. This suggests more women than men are unhappy with the state of their marriages, as women are more likely to take the first steps in ending them. This may well be because women's expectations of life and marriage have risen during the course of the last century, and they are less willing to accept a traditional housewife/mother role, with the sacrifices of their own leisure activities, careers and independence this involves.

The employment of married women has increased over the last century. For example, in 1931 only 10 per cent of married women were employed, but this had gradually risen to about 75 per cent by the beginning of this century. This has increased their financial independence, and reduced the extent of dependence on their husbands. There is also a range of welfare state benefits to help divorced women, particularly those with children. Marriage has therefore become less of a financial necessity for women, and this makes it easier for women to escape from unhappy marriages.

RISING EXPECTATIONS OF MARRIAGE

The divorce rate may have risen because couples (especially women) expect and demand more in their relationships today than their parents or grandparents might have settled for. Love, companionship, understanding, sexual compatibility and personal fulfilment are more likely to be the main ingredients of a successful marriage today, rather than the financial security which seemed more important in the past. The growing privatization and isolation of the nuclear family from extended kin and the community have also meant that couples are likely to spend more time together. The higher expectations mean couples are more likely to end a relationship in which these higher expectations are not met, but which earlier generations might have tolerated.

This view suggests that higher divorce rates therefore reflect better-quality marriages, as unsatisfying relationships are abandoned. This suggestion of the higher expectations of marriage is reflected in the fairly high rate of remarriage among divorced people. In other words, families split up to re-form happier families – a bit like 'old banger' cars failing their MOT test, being taken to the scrapyard and being replaced with a better-quality car, thereby improving the general quality of cars on the road.

GROWING SECULARIZATION

Secularization – the declining influence in society of religious beliefs and institutions – has resulted in marriage becoming less of a sacred, spiritual union and more a personal and practical commitment which can be abandoned if it fails. Evidence for this lies in the fact that around two-thirds (67 per cent in 2008) of marriages today no longer involve a religious ceremony. The church now takes a much less rigid view of divorce, and many people today probably do not attach much religious significance to their marriages.

CHANGING SOCIAL ATTITUDES

Divorce has become more socially acceptable, and there is less social disapproval and condemnation (stigmatizing) of divorcees. Divorce no longer hinders careers through a public sense of scandal and outrage. As a result, people are less afraid of the consequences of divorce, and are more likely to seek a legal end to an unhappy marriage rather than simply separating or carrying on in an empty shell marriage.

THE GREATER AVAILABILITY OF – AND MORE EFFECTIVE – CONTRACEPTION

The greater availability of – and more effective – contraception has made it safer to have sex outside the marital relationship, and with more than one person during marriage. This weakens traditional constraints on fidelity to a marriage partner, and potentially exposes relationships to greater instability.

THE GROWTH OF THE PRIVATIZED NUCLEAR FAMILY

The growing privatization and isolation of the nuclear family from extended kin and the community in contemporary society has meant it is no longer so easy for marriage partners to seek advice from or temporary refuge with relatives. This isolation can increase the demands on and expectations of each partner in a marriage. There is also less social control from extended kin pressuring couples to retain marriage ties. In this sense, there is both more pressure on marriage relationships arising from the points above, and fewer constraints preventing people abandoning marriage, and increasingly the decision whether to divorce or not lies with the married couple alone.

THE REDUCED FUNCTIONS OF THE FAMILY

As we saw earlier in this chapter, over time a number of family functions have been transferred to other social institutions. This has perhaps meant that marriage has become less of a practical necessity, and there are fewer bonds linking marriage partners. Love and companionship and personal compatibility are the important dimensions of contemporary marriages, and if some or all of these disappear, there may be nothing much left to hold marriages together.

INCREASING LIFE EXPECTANCY

People live to a greater age today than they did in the early years of the last century, and this means the potential number of years a couple may be together, before one of them dies, has increased, and is continuing to increase as life expectancy lengthens. This gives more time for marriages to go wrong and for divorces to occur. Some suggest that the divorce courts have taken on the role in finishing unhappy marriages once performed by the undertaker.

Activity

1   Go through all the reasons suggested above for the rising divorce rate, putting them in what you think is their order of importance.
2   Study television advertisements or television soaps for a few days. What kind of overall impressions are given of married life today? Refer to particular advertisements or soaps as evidence for your findings. Do you agree or disagree with the view that these create higher expectations of marriage today? Explain the reasons for your answer.
3   Of men and women marrying today, around 80 per cent lived with their partners beforehand, and living together before marriage was seen as one of the major social changes of the late twentieth century. However, many of these people eventually marry. What social pressures are there that push people towards conforming to the norm of marriage? Write down all the reasons you can think of why so many people continue to marry eventually, despite the high divorce rate and previous experience of living together outside marriage. Discuss your reasons with others in your class.

The consequences of divorce

The ending of marriages (or any relationship) is often a very painful process, and the high proportion of marriages today ending in divorce has a number of consequences, for individuals, families and society.

Consequences for children   Couples divorcing in 2008 had between them around 107,000 children under the age of 16, and it is often such dependent children who live with their parents who face the greatest difficulties when their parents divorce. Apart from the personal distress, they often face conflicts over which parent they should live with, though in practice most courts award custody to the mother.

Children often suffer great personal distress when their parents divorce, difficulties moving between different households, and conflicts in loyalty to both parents. In most cases, the courts award custody of children after divorce to mothers rather than fathers. Why do you think this is?

Even then, they face the difficulty of moving between two different households, as they visit the parent they don't live with. In the event of one or both of their parents remarrying, they may then face having to cope and adapt to living with various combinations of stepmothers and stepfathers, and stepbrothers and stepsisters. They may also risk losing contact with their fathers altogether, as after divorce around 40 per cent of fathers lose contact with their children within two years. Research reported by the *Guardian* newspaper in November 2009 found more than half of divorcing and separating parents went to court in 2008 to challenge issues relating to their children, causing great distress to the children involved. The research showed that, as a result of family conflict fought through the courts, some of these children were playing truant from school, committing crime, and turning to alcohol and drug abuse.

Consequences for adults Divorce not only involves the legal ending of a marriage, it also involves dividing up property and savings, and there are often serious legal disputes fought through the courts between divorcing partners over the division of money and property, and also over who has custody of the children and visiting rights. Divorce nearly always means a decline in income, as running two households costs a lot more than one.

Consequences for society Rising divorce has meant a growing range of different household and family structures. There is an increase in lone-parent and reconstituted families, more single person households, more cohabiting couples and births outside marriage, and higher levels of remarriage. In 2008, for example, around 40 per cent of all marriages were remarriages for one or both partners. These issues are discussed below.

Remarriage and the growth of reconstituted families

While marriage is still the usual form of partnership between men and women, marriages in which it is the first time for both partners are declining substantially. The number of these has more than halved since 1970. About two-fifths of marriages now involve a remarriage for one or both partners, mainly reflecting the increase in the divorce rate. A lot more divorced men remarry than divorced women, reflecting women's greater dissatisfaction or disillusionment with marriage. This is perhaps not surprising, given the way women often have to balance the triple and competing demands of paid employment, domestic labour and childcare, and emotional management of the family.

These trends have meant that there are more reconstituted families (sometimes called stepfamilies or blended families) with stepparents, stepchildren, and stepbrothers and stepsisters arising from previous relationships of one or both partners. Stepfamilies are the fastest-growing family type. Stepfathers are more common than stepmothers, since most children remain with the natural mother after a break-up, and in 2008 more than eight out of ten stepfamilies with dependent children consisted of a couple with at least one child from a previous relationship of the woman. This reflects the fact that it is nearly always women who gain custody of children in the event of a relationship breakdown. One in six men in their thirties are now stepfathers, raising other men's children – nearly double the proportion in the mid-1990s. Official estimates suggest there are around three-quarters of a million stepfamilies with dependent stepchildren in the UK – 10 per cent of all families with dependent children.

The growth of the lone-parent family

One of the biggest changes in the family has been the growth of the lone-parent family (also known as the single-parent or one-parent family). The percentage of lone-parent families has tripled since 1971, and Britain has one of the highest proportions of lone-parent families in Europe. Around one in four of all families with dependent children were lone-parent families in 2008 – nine out of ten of them headed by women. Over one in five (23 per cent in 2008) of dependent children now live in such families, compared to just 7 per cent in 1972.

Why are there more lone-parent families?

The rapid growth in the number of lone-parent families can be explained by a number of factors, some of which have already been discussed earlier in explaining the rising divorce rate. These include:

- *The greater economic independence of women.* Women have greater economic independence today, both through more job opportunities and through support from the welfare state. This means marriage, and support by a husband, is less of an economic necessity today compared to the past.
- *Improved contraception, changing male attitudes and fewer 'shotgun weddings'.* With the wider availability and approval of safe and effective contraception, and easier access to safe and legal abortion, men may feel less responsibility to marry women should they become unintentionally pregnant, and women may feel under less pressure to marry the future father. There are therefore fewer 'shotgun weddings' (where reluctant couples are forced into marriage by the father of the pregnant women wielding an imaginary shotgun to ensure that the man marries his daughter).
- *Reproductive technology is available to women,* enabling them to bear children without a male partner, through surrogate motherhood and fertility treatments like IVF (in vitro fertilization).

● *Changing social attitudes.* There is less social stigma (or social disapproval and condemnation) attached to lone parenthood today. Women are therefore less afraid of the social consequences of becoming lone parents.

The growth in lone parenthood has been seen by some as one of the major signs of the decline of conventional family life and marriage. Lone-parent families – and particularly lone never-married mothers – have been portrayed by some of the media and conservative politicians as promiscuous parasites, blamed for everything from rising juvenile crime through to housing shortages, rising drug abuse, educational failure of children and the general breakdown of society. The problems created by lone parenthood, particularly for boys, are usually explained by the lack of a male role model in the home, and consequently inadequate socialization.

Lone parenthood has therefore been presented as a major social problem, and the mass media have periodically, by their exaggerated and sensationalized reporting, stirred up waves of public concern about lone parents, and presented them as threats to society and the stability of family life. These waves of unjustified public concern stirred up by exaggerated and sensationalized reporting in the mass media are known as **moral panics**.

In an effort to cut the welfare costs to the state of lone parents, the Child Support Agency (www.csa.gov.uk/) was established in 1993. This was designed to encourage absent fathers to take financial responsibility for their children, thereby reducing benefit costs to the state. There have been a number of attempts to encourage lone parents to support themselves through paid employment. For example, since 1997 child tax credits to help with the costs of childcare have been introduced, along with a national childcare strategy to ensure good-quality affordable childcare, the expansion of nursery places for children aged 3 and 4, and more pre- and after-school clubs. These policies arise from the fact that it is the lack of affordable childcare that is the major deterrent to lone parents working. The national minimum wage helps to avoid the exploitation of lone parents, who are mainly women, by unscrupulous employers, and the New Deal for Lone Parents helped many lone parents to find paid employment. In 2009, about 57 per cent of lone parents were in employment.

A **moral panic** is a wave of public concern about some exaggerated or imaginary threat to society, stirred up by overblown and sensationalized reporting in the mass media.

Nailing the myths

Never-married lone mothers only account for about half of all lone parents with dependent children, with the remainder arising from divorce and separation, and occasionally widowhood, as figure 3.9 shows. Even among never-married lone mothers, the vast majority cohabit with the father and have registered his name on the child's birth certificate.

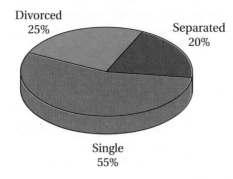

Divorced
25%

Separated
20%

Single
55%

Figure 3.9 Lone-mother families with dependent children, by marital status: Great Britain, 2008.

Source: data from *General Lifestyle Survey*, Office for National Statistics

The problems allegedly created by absent fathers have been questioned on the grounds that it is not the presence or absence of a father that is important, but whether fathers actually involve themselves in the children's upbringing. There are probably many fathers in two-parent families as well who fail to involve themselves in the care and discipline of their children, and problems like juvenile delinquency are likely to arise in any household where children are inadequately supervised and disciplined. This problem, often blamed on lone parenthood, is therefore just as likely to occur among two-parent families. A Home Office report has found no difference in the crime rates between youngsters from lone-parent and those from two-parent families. Even if there were such a link, it is likely to be caused by poverty rather than lone parenthood – because lack of childcare facilities means many lone parents have to depend on inadequate state benefits to live, and lone parents are more likely to live in overcrowded or poor-quality housing. This probably explains other factors linked in the popular imagination to lone parenthood, such as lower educational achievement.

A misleading myth is that of lone teenage mothers getting pregnant to jump the queue for social (council and housing association) housing. There is very little evidence for this. Gingerbread (www.gingerbread.org.uk) pointed out that in 2007 the average age of a lone parent was 36, with just 13 per cent of all lone parents aged under 25, and at any one time, less than 3 per cent of all lone parents are teenagers. Research in 1996 commissioned by the Economic and Social Research Council found that only 10 per cent of the small minority of women who were not in a regular relationship with the father when they became mothers were living alone with their child in social (council) housing six months after the birth. Many live with their parents, and many single, never-married parents have been in cohabiting relationships which break down. In effect, this is no different from marriages that break down.

Activity

1 Suggest reasons why, in the event of divorce, women are more likely than men to be given custody of the children.
2 Suggest explanations why most lone-parent families are headed by women.
3 To what extent do you agree with the following statements, and why?
   - 'A lone mother can bring up her child as well as a married or cohabiting couple.'
   - 'People who want children ought to get married.'
   - 'To grow up happily, children need a home with both their mother and father.'
4 Suggest and explain two advantages and two disadvantages of lone parenthood compared to two-parent families?
5 Visit the following websites, and identify five issues that seem to be of particular concern to lone parents. Describe each issue briefly, and outline any solutions that are suggested.
www.gingerbread.org.uk
www.lone-parents.org.uk
www.oneparentfamilies.org.uk

The decline in marriage and the growing incidence and acceptance of cohabitation

The decline of marriage and the growth of living together before or outside marriage were two of the major social changes at the turn of the twenty-first century. Marriage rates are declining in Britain, and there are more and more couples cohabiting rather than seeking official recognition of their relationships through marriage or, more recently through civil partnerships.

In 2008, there were 232,990 marriages in England and Wales, with first-time marriages for both parties falling by 37 per cent since 1981, whilst remarriages for both parties fell by just over a quarter (28 per cent). The number of marriages in 2008 was the lowest since 1895, with marriage rates in England and Wales at the lowest level since records began.

Over a quarter of non-married males and females in Britain under age 60 were cohabiting in 2006, twice the proportion recorded around twenty years ago. Of all men and women aged 16 to 59, 13 per cent were cohabiting, including people who were separated but not divorced. By the 2000s, the majority of people in first marriages had lived with their partner beforehand, and cohabitation is now the norm rather than the exception. Eight in every ten couples married in 2006 gave identical addresses, and this 'living in sin' included 65 per cent of those getting married in a religious ceremony. More than one in ten of all couples are now cohabiting, and around 13 per cent of dependent children are now being brought up by unmarried, cohabiting

> The **marriage rate** is the number of marriages per 1,000 single people aged 16 and over per year.

couples. Many cohabiting relationships eventually end up in marriage – about 60 per cent of first-time cohabitations turn into marriages.

The reasons for the decline of marriage and growing cohabitation have been considered earlier, including:

- the changing role of women, whose growing economic independence has given them more freedom to choose their relationships
- the growing divorce rate, and the message it is sending out to potential marriage partners
- growing secularization
- changing social attitudes and reduced social stigma: young people are more likely to cohabit than older people, and this may in part reflect the evidence that older people compared to younger people, are more likely to think that 'living together outside marriage is always wrong'; this reveals more easy-going attitudes to cohabitation among the young, showing the reduced social stigma attached to cohabitation
- the greater availability of – and more effective – contraception
- higher expectations of marriage.

More births outside marriage

Nearly half of all births (46 per cent in 2009) are now outside marriage – about five times more than the proportion in 1971. Despite the record numbers of children being born outside marriage, nearly nine out of ten of those births in 2009 were registered jointly by the parents. Both parents in two out of three

Cohabitation and giving birth to children outside marriage are both rising rapidly, and younger people are more likely to do both, though many cohabiting couples do eventually get married

of these cases gave the same address. This suggests the parents were cohabiting, and that children are still being born into a stable couple relationship, even if the partners are not legally married.

The explanations for the increase of births outside marriage are very similar to those for the increase in the divorce rate, the decline in the marriage rate and the increase in cohabitation, which were discussed above.

> **Activity**
>
> Read the sections above, and explain carefully four reasons why there are more births outside marriage today.

Living alone: the growth in singlehood – one person households

About one in three households today contains only one person, compared to one in twenty in 1901. Around half of these households are over pensionable age (age 60–5 for women, 65 for men) in 2011, compared to two-thirds in 1971.This means there is a growth in the number of younger people living alone. This trend can be explained by the decline in marriage, the rise in divorce and separation, and the fact that people are delaying marriage or cohabitation until they are older. There are nearly twice as many men as women living alone in the 25–44 age group, but there are twice as many women as men aged 65 and over, because women tend to live longer than men. Longer lives, particularly for women, explain the increase in the number of pensioner one person households.

FAMILY DIVERSITY AND THE MYTH OF 'CEREAL PACKET' FAMILIES

The **cereal packet family** refers to the stereotype of the ideal family found in the mass media and advertising. It is generally seen as involving first-time married parents and their own natural children, living together, with the father as the primary breadwinner and the mother as primarily concerned with the home and children.

The popular impression that many people have of the family in Britain at the beginning of the twenty-first century has been described as the 'cereal packet family'.

This is the stereotype often promoted in advertising and other parts of the mass media, with 'family size' breakfast cereals, toothpaste and a wide range of other consumer goods. This popular happy family image often gives the impression that most people live in a typical family with the following features.

● It is a privatized, nuclear family unit consisting of two parents living with one or two of their own natural dependent children.

- These parents are married to one another, and neither of them has been married before.
- The husband is the breadwinner and responsible for family discipline, with the wife staying at home and primarily concerned with housework and childcare (expressing herself through maternal love), or perhaps doing some part-time paid employment to supplement the family income.

This image also often includes ideas that this family is based on romantic love, as well as love of children (particularly maternal love), and that it is a nurturing, caring and loving institution – a safe and harmonious refuge from an uncaring outside world.

This stereotype of the typical family is very mistaken, because there are a wide range of households and family types in contemporary Britain. This is known as family diversity.

Why is the cereal packet stereotype misleading?

This image of the cereal packet stereotyped conventional or typical family is very misleading because, as discussed earlier in this chapter, there have been and continue to be important changes in family patterns, and there is a wide range of family types and household arrangements in modern Britain. This growing diversity of relationships that people live in shows that traditional family life is being eroded as people constantly develop new forms of relationship and choose to live in different ways. The meaning of 'family' and 'family life' is therefore changing for a substantial number of parents and children.

Households and families

Figure 3.10 shows the different types of household in Britain in 2008, and what percentages of people were living in them. In 2008, only 22 per cent of households contained a married or cohabiting couple with dependent children, and only 37 per cent of people lived in such a household; 30 per cent of households consisted of one person living alone, and at least 70 per cent of households had no dependent children in them; 10 per cent of people lived in lone-parent families, and 9 per cent of households were lone-parent families. This alone shows that the cereal packet image of the nuclear family does not represent the arrangement in which most people in Britain live.

Families with dependent children

Figure 3.11 examines families with dependent children. This shows that in 2008, about 23 per cent of such families were lone-parent families, with nearly nine out of ten of them headed by women. Although a married or cohabiting couple headed 77 per cent of families with dependent children, this doesn't mean that most of these families conformed to the cereal packet image.

- A number of these families involved a cohabiting rather than a married relationship. In 2008, around one in five households consisting of a couple with dependent children involved a cohabiting rather than a married relationship. Such arrangements do not conform to the cereal packet stereotype.
- A number were reconstituted families, in which one or both partners were previously married. More than two in five marriages currently taking place will end in divorce, and more than 40 per cent of all marriages now involve remarriage for one or both partners. About 10 per cent of all families with dependent children were stepfamilies in the early 2000s, and the stepfamily is today the most rapidly growing family type, along with cohabitation.
- Most of these families were dual-worker families, in which both parents were working. In 2009, around 80 per cent of couples with dependent children were both either in or looking for paid employment. As figure 3.12 shows, large numbers of mothers with dependent children work in paid employment, with the numbers increasing as children get older. In 2008, more than two-thirds of working-age women with dependent children (68 per cent) were in employment. This often involves complex and costly alternative arrangements for childcare while both parents are working.

The cereal packet happy family stereotype of a working father in a first-time marriage to a home-based mother caring for their two small children now makes up only about 5 per cent of all households.

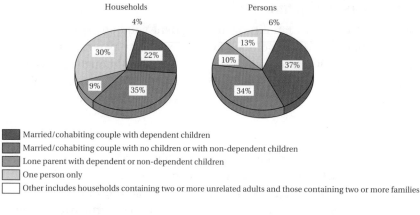

Figure 3.10 Households and people, by type of household: Great Britain, 2008

Source: data from *General Lifestyle Survey*, Office for National Statistics

■ Married/cohabiting couple with dependent children
■ Married/cohabiting couple with no children or with non-dependent children
■ Lone parent with dependent or non-dependent children
□ One person only
□ Other includes households containing two or more unrelated adults and those containing two or more families

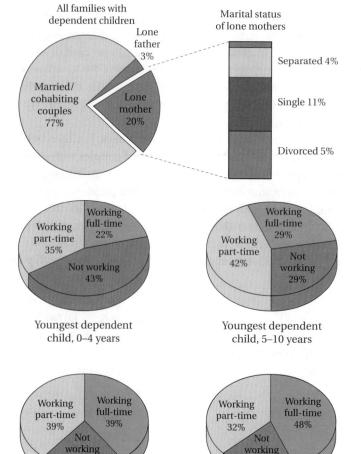

Figure 3.11 Families with dependent children, by family type and, for lone mothers, by marital status: Great Britain, 2008

Source: data from *General Lifestyle Survey*, Office for National Statistics

Figure 3.12 Working patterns (in paid employment) of women with dependent children: United Kingdom, 2008

Source: data from Labour Force Survey

Activity

Refer to figure 3.10.

1. What percentage of households in 2008 consisted of one person only?
2. What percentage of people in 2008 were living in households consisting of a married or cohabiting couple with no children or with non-dependent children?

Refer to figure 3.11.

3. In 2008, what percentage of all families with dependent children were lone-parent families?
4. What percentage of families with dependent children were headed by a lone mother who was separated?
5. What was the main cause of lone motherhood?

Refer to figure 3.12.

6. What percentage of mothers whose youngest child was aged 0–4 years were not working in paid employment in 2008?
7. Identify two trends which occur as the youngest dependent child gets older.
8. What does figure 3.12 suggest might be the main restriction on mothers with young children working in paid employment? Suggest ways this restriction might be overcome.
9. How do you think having young dependent children might affect the working lives of fathers? Give reasons for your answer.
10. Suggest reasons why many people seem to believe that the cereal packet family is the most common type of family.

The cereal packet stereotype of the family is very misleading, and conceals the wide diversity, or range, of family types and household arrangements in contemporary Britain

OTHER FORMS OF FAMILY AND HOUSEHOLD DIVERSITY

Cultural diversity

Cultural diversity refers to differences in family structure and lifestyles between ethnic and religious groups.

South Asian families

Extended family relationships are more common in minority ethnic groups originating in South Asia, from Pakistan, Bangladesh and India. Such families are commonly patriarchal in structure, with seniority going to the eldest male, and males in general. Pakistani and Bangladeshi women have the highest rates of marriage in the UK, and a very high proportion of South Asians with a partner are in a formal marriage. In a 2000 survey, a majority of Bangladeshi and Pakistani women reported their primary activity to be looking after the house and family. In many ways, the traditional British cereal packet family stereotype of a working male married to a home-based female is more likely to be found among Pakistanis and Bangladeshis than any other ethnic group. Divorce rates are low in such families because of strong social disapproval and a wide support network of kin for families under stress. Arranged marriages are still common in such communities.

African-Caribbean families

Black African and Black Caribbean families are often centred on the mother, who is in many cases the main breadwinner. Lone parenthood is higher among African-Caribbean mothers than any other ethnic group – over half of African-Caribbean families with children have lone parents, and there are low marriage rates. This partly reflects a cultural tradition, but also high rates of black male unemployment and men's inability and reluctance to support families. African-Caribbean families often have a female network of friends and kin to support women with children.

Social class diversity

Social class diversity refers to differences between upper-class, middle-class and working-class families. Classic extended families – where they still exist – are more likely to be found in what remains of traditional working-class communities, although such families are disappearing everywhere. For example, in a study of Swansea, Nicola Charles (N. Charles, *Families in Transition: Social Change, Family Formation and Kin Relationships*, Bristol, The Policy Press, 2008; full research report available for download at www.esrcsocietytoday.ac.uk) found that classic extended families were practically extinct, even in the working class, and the only group in which such families remained was the ethnic minority population. Classic extended families in the working class have been largely replaced by modified extended or privatized nuclear families. Modified extended families tend to be more common, in the working class, and privatized nuclear families more common in the middle class. Differences in income and wealth will also lead to differences in lifestyle between families from different social classes.

Life cycle diversity

Life cycle diversity refers to the way families may change through life, for example as partners have children, as the children grow older and eventually leave home, as partners separate and form new relationships, as people retire, grow older and have grandchildren. All these factors mean the family will be constantly changing. For instance, levels of family income will change as children move from dependence to independence, levels of domestic labour and childcare will differ, and levels of participation in paid employment will alter, particularly for women, depending on the absence or presence of children and their age. This means there will always be a diversity of family and household types at different stages of the family life cycle. Figure 3.13 shows an example of a family life cycle.

Regional diversity

Regional diversity refers to the way family life varies in different geographical locations around the country. There are distinctive patterns of family life in different areas of Britain. For example, on the south coast, there is a high proportion of elderly couples; older industrial areas and very traditional rural communities tend to have more extended families; and the inner cities have a higher proportion of families in poverty and lone-parent families.

Adult-kids, kippers, shared households and 'families of choice'

Young people are now less likely to follow the traditional route of living at home, leaving school, going into a job or higher education, and then settling down into an adult role of living alone or a married or cohabiting couple relationship. Increasingly, they are adopting a wider range of living arrangements before forming couple relationships later in life.

In 2009, one in four men, and one in eight women, aged 25 to 29 were still living with their parents. Some of these 'adult-kids' live with their parents because they can't afford to rent or buy their own homes. But others are staying through choice. This group is sometimes referred to as 'kippers' – 'kids in parents' pockets' – as it's cheaper, easier and often more comfortable to live at home. Even by their early thirties, one in ten men and one in twenty women are still living with their parents.

For those who have left the family home, shared households are becoming much more common, particularly among young people. This transitional period between youth and adult roles has been described as 'kidulthood' or 'adultescence'. These transitional living arrangements might include moving between living alone, going back to live with their parents, and living in shared households with their peers. There may often be a greater loyalty among young people to their friends than to their family. Such shared households, where people choose to live and form relationships with a group of people with whom they have closer relations than with their families of birth, have therefore sometimes been called 'families of choice' (although they are not strictly speaking families as they are not based on kinship relations). Such households may involve shared domestic life (cooking, eating and socializing together), and shared leisure, sporting activities and holidays. Such households are on the increase because of the high costs of buying or renting houses, the growing numbers of young people entering higher education, and the desire of young people to explore alternative living arrangements rather than simply settling down into a conventional couple household.

Figure 3.14 summarizes the range of family and household diversity in contemporary Britain.

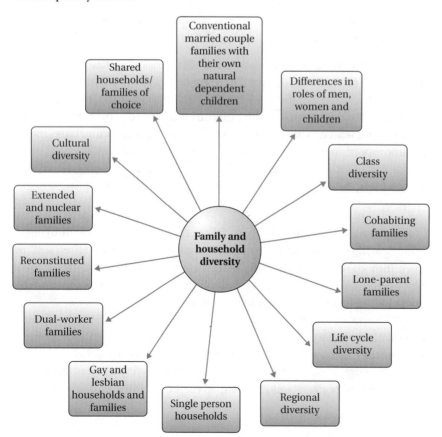

Figure 3.14 Family and household diversity

Figure 3.13 A family life cycle

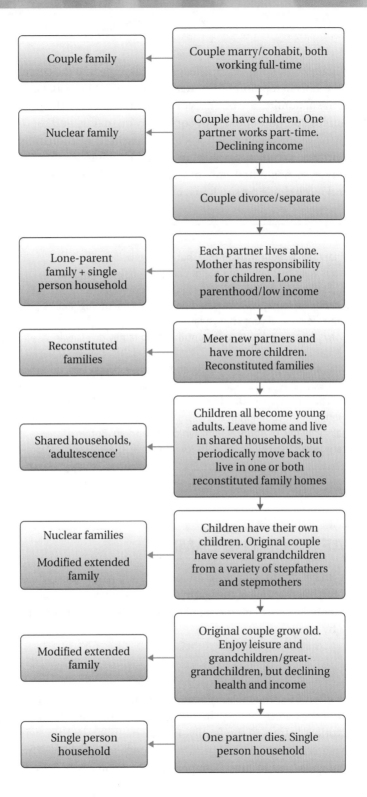

Conclusion

This section has suggested that it is very misleading to assume that the cereal packet image of the family represents the reality of family life in Britain. Only a small minority of families are of this type. It is much more realistic to recognize that families and households are constantly changing, and there is a wide diversity, or variety, of family types and household relationships in contemporary Britain. Trends suggest there will be growing numbers of extended, dual-worker, reconstituted, cohabiting, gay and lesbian, and lone-parent families, and more single person households.

Activity

1 Using an imaginary family, your own, or one that you know, describe and explain the various ways that family life might change during its life cycle. Think about issues like how housework and childcare (domestic labour), conjugal roles, caring for family members and paid employment might all change during the life cycle of your chosen family.
2 Suggest *three* ways the rising divorce rate contributes to family diversity in contemporary Britain.
3 Suggest ways that the lifestyles of upper-class and lower-working-class families might differ.
4 Suggest reasons why the cereal packet family is most likely to be found in the Pakistani and Bangladeshi communities.
5 How far is it realistic to talk of a typical family in contemporary Britain? Suggest some arguments and evidence both for and against.

CRITICAL VIEWS OF THE FAMILY

The cereal packet image of the typical family has already been questioned earlier in this chapter, but the view of the warm and supportive happy family which is often presented in the mass media has been questioned on a more fundamental level by many writers.

The 'darker side' of family life

While the family is often a warm and supportive unit for its members, it can also be a hostile and dangerous place. The growing privatization of family life can lead to emotional stress in the family. Family members are thrown together, often isolated from and lacking the support of extended kin, neighbours and the wider community. Tempers can become easily frayed, emotional temperatures and stress levels rise, and – as in an overloaded electrical circuit – fuses blow, and family conflict is the result. This may lead to violence, divorce, psychological damage to children, perhaps even mental illness and crime.

The breakdown of marriages which leads to divorce is often the end result of long-running and bitter disputes between partners. The intense emotions involved in family life often mean that incidents that would appear trivial in other situations take on the proportion of major confrontations inside the family. The extent of violence in the family is coming increasingly to public attention, with rising reports of the physical and sexual abuse of children, the rape of women by their husbands or partners, and wife- and baby-battering. One in four murders takes place in the family. This is the darker side of family life.

Because of the private nature of the family, accurate evidence on the extent of violence and abuse inside the family is difficult to obtain, and fear or shame means that it is almost certain that most of such incidents are covered up.

The abuse of children

The abuse of children is increasingly brought to everyone's attention through the mass media, though much child abuse is likely to remain undiscovered and hidden behind the closed doors of family life. There are several different types of abuse of children, as figure 3.15 shows. *Sexual abuse* refers to adults using their power to perform sex acts with children below the age of consent (age 16). *Physical abuse* refers to non-sexual violence. *Emotional abuse* refers to persistent or severe emotional ill-treatment or rejection of children, which has severe effects on their emotional development and behaviour. *Neglect* refers to the failure to protect children from exposure to danger, including cold and starvation, and failing to care for them properly, so that their health or development is affected.

A report in 2000 from the NSPCC (the National Society for the Prevention of Cruelty to Children), *Child Maltreatment in the United Kingdom*, found that around 10 per cent of children suffered serious abuse or neglect at home, with most of it committed by natural parents. In 2005, the most comprehensive survey ever of teenagers and domestic abuse, conducted by the teen magazine *Sugar* in association with the NSPCC, found one-fifth of teenage girls were hit by parents – a quarter of them regularly. In 2009, statistics from the Department for Children, Schools and Families (DCSF) showed there were 34,100 children and young people under the age of 18 who were the subject of a Child Protection Plan (CPP) in England because of various forms of abuse, including physical injury, sexual abuse, neglect and emotional abuse, with some children suffering more than one type of abuse. This was just for England, and only for abuse which was brought to the attention of social services departments. It is very likely that much abuse

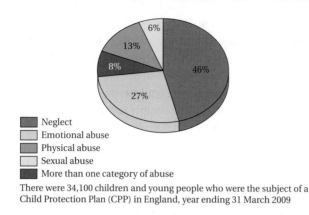

There were 34,100 children and young people who were the subject of a Child Protection Plan (CPP) in England, year ending 31 March 2009

Figure 3.15 Children and young people who were the subject of a Child Protection Plan (CPP), by category of abuse: England, year ending 31 March 2009

Source: Department for Children, Schools and Families (DCSF) (now, Department for Education)

goes on without being discovered. Some indication of this is shown by statistics from ChildLine, the free confidential counselling service for children, established in 1986. ChildLine has counselled well over a million children and young people, and almost one in five of the calls received in 2008–9 was about sexual and physical abuse.

> **Activity**
>
> Suggest reasons why the number of child abuse cases recorded in the Department for Children, Families and Schools statistics in 2009 might not give a true picture of the extent of child abuse. Do you think the increase in the number of reported cases of child abuse means the problem is growing? What other explanations might there be for the increasing reporting or discovery of child abuse?

Domestic violence

There is widespread evidence of violence by men and women against their partners. It is estimated that one in four women, and one in six men, will suffer some form of domestic violence at some point in their relationships. Most of the assaults and physically most violent incidents – 89 per cent – are committed by men against their female partners. Each year about 150 people are killed by a current or former partner, and 80 per cent of them are women. Domestic violence accounted for around 14 per cent of all violent crime in 2008–9, and between 300,000 and 400,000 incidents are recorded by the police each year, with around four out of five of the victims being women. Around 45 per cent of all violent crime experienced by women is domestic, and estimates suggest there may be as many as 6.5 million violent incidents each year.

It is women who are most likely to experience domestic violence, to experience repeated violence and to sustain injuries requiring medical treatment. Female victims of domestic violence will suffer an average of 35–7 assaults for an average period of seven years before informing any agency. Every year

Each year about 150 people are killed by a current or former partner, and 80 per cent of them are women. Most of the assaults and physically most violent incidents are committed by men against their female partners. Why do you think domestic violence is overwhelmingly committed by men against their female partners?

Every week 2 women die due to domestic violence. Don't let your friend be 1 of them.

ENOUGH If you know your friend's being hit, it's time to put a stop to her abuse, before the abuser puts a stop to her. Help her take the first step; call the National Domestic Violence Helpline for support. 0808 2000 247

Free helpline run by Refuge and Women's Aid. Open 24 hours.

in England and Wales, approximately 63,000 women and children spend at least one night in a refuge for battered women. For many women, home is neither a secure nor a safe place to be.

Statistics such as those discussed above reflect the extent and seriousness of the problem of violence in the home, particularly against women, much of which goes unreported and undiscovered. The type of physical violence carried out in the family, mainly by male partners, would quite probably result in prosecution and imprisonment if it was carried out against a stranger outside the family. Nonetheless, an estimated two-thirds of victims of domestic violence do not seek help because they are afraid the violence will get worse, are ashamed, or see it as a private matter, and only about a quarter of all domestic violence incidents are reported to the police – but they still receive one domestic violence call every minute in the UK. However, only around one in twenty of those that are reported result in a conviction.

In the past, domestic violence was often not taken very seriously by the police or courts: it was often dismissed as a 'domestic' which they did not see as their responsibility but, rather, as a private family or personal matter. However, in recent years the police and courts have been beginning to treat domestic violence more seriously, with domestic violence units, rape suites and specially trained officers in many police stations.

Despite the high level of violence against women in married and cohabiting relationships, many women do not leave their violent partners. This is often because of fear, shame and embarrassment, financial insecurity, lack of alternative housing and concerns about disruption to their children's lives.

SIBLING ABUSE

While most people think of domestic violence as occurring between adult partners, it can also occur between brothers and sisters, and may take similar forms to that between adults, or that of adults who abuse children. Sibling abuse may involve emotional, physical and sexually aggressive behaviour, like name calling, ridiculing, put-downs, hitting, slapping and punching, and unwelcome sexual touching (or worse). While most of us will probably have hit, or been hit, by our brothers or sisters as part of normal sibling rivalry, if it gets out of hand it can have very damaging consequences on the development of young people, and may even establish a pattern of abuse which resurfaces in their own adult relationships.

Disturbingly, many young women today still seem to believe that violence and aggression are acceptable parts of relationships. The 2005 survey conducted by *Sugar* magazine, referred to above, found that 16 per cent of teenage girls had been hit by a boyfriend – a quarter of them regularly. Yet over two-thirds of the girls who had been hit then stayed with their boyfriends. Of all the teenage girls who replied to the survey, 43 per cent thought it acceptable for a boyfriend to get aggressive, and 6 per cent thought it was OK for a boy to hit his girlfriend, for reasons such as cheating on him, flirting with someone else or if she was 'dressing outrageously'. Over 40 per cent of all the girls said they would 'consider giving a boy a second chance if he hit them'. A 2009 survey by the NSPCC and the University of Bristol found a third of teenage girls suffered sexual abuse by their boyfriends, with a quarter suffering physical violence, including being slapped, punched or beaten.

Rape in marriage

Rape is when someone is forced to have sex against her or his will, often accompanied by the actual or threatened use of violence. Estimates suggest more than one in four women has been raped, with over half of rapes being committed by men on their female partners, yet government estimates suggest that as many as 95 per cent of rapes are never reported to the police at all. About three-quarters of rapes, according to the British Crime Survey, take place in the home of the victim or offender. Nearly half of rapes within marriage are accompanied by the actual or threatened use of violence, and one in five women suffer physical injury. Such sexual violence in the family, then, would appear to be disturbingly common, but it was only as recently as 1991 that rape within marriage was confirmed as a criminal offence by the Court of Appeal. Nonetheless, in 2008, only about 6 per cent of all reported rapes led to a rapist being convicted, and rape in marriage or cohabiting relationships are the most difficult cases to prove in court that there was no consent.

Activity

1 Suggest three reasons why domestic violence statistics are likely to understate the extent of this social problem.
2 Do you think domestic violence by women against men is more or less likely to be reported than domestic violence by men against women? Give reasons for your answer.
3 Suggest two problems or difficulties sociologists might face in trying to research the areas of child abuse and domestic violence.
4 Go to www.womensaid.org.uk (the Women's Aid site), or www. crimereduction.homeoffice.gov.uk/violentcrime and find out the extent of domestic violence and the policy measures being taken to combat it.

This cartoon from 1896 shows domestic violence was the norm then, but are things really much better today?

'Can I have a black eye, too, Ma?' asks the little girl. 'Wait till you're old enough to get married, pet,' says her mother.

Feminist criticisms of the family

Feminist writers – those concerned with establishing equal rights for women – have been responsible for highlighting much of the violence against women in the family. However, they also have a range of other criticisms of the family, arguing that it is an institution that serves men's needs better than women's, and that it particularly oppresses and exploits women. Many of these criticisms are covered earlier in this chapter and in other chapters, and the following is simply a brief summary of them.

- Far from the popular impression of growing equality between male and female partners in the family being correct, inequalities continue. As seen earlier in this chapter, women still have most of the responsibility for housework and childcare, even when they are in full-time employment. Most women work both outside the home in paid employment and inside the home as housewives and mothers, and take the major

Look at the cartoon, and write a short explanation of how *each* of the balls and chains on the left might be seen as keeping women in shackles. Do you agree or disagree with the view suggested in the cartoon? Give your reasons

responsibility for managing family emotions and conflicts. They have three jobs (the 'triple shift') to the man's one.

- Feminists emphasize that housework is, in fact, unpaid labour. Legal and General's 2009 *Value of a Mum* survey found that the value of the work that mums do around the home is £32,812 – that's £631 a week.
- It is still mainly women who give up paid work (or suffer from lost/restricted job opportunities) to look after children, the old, the sick and male partners. Women still take most of the responsibility for childcare and child rearing, and are most likely to get the blame from society if these tasks are not performed properly.
- Women's position in the family remains a primary source of discrimination and disadvantage in the labour market. Employers are often unwilling to employ or promote married women, particularly in jobs with high levels of pay and responsibility. Marriage poses no such problem for men.
- The family is a major source of gender role socialization, which causes women to underachieve (do less well than they are able) in a wide range of areas, and keeps women in a secondary position to men in many areas of social life.

Looked at from these points of view, women have much to lose from the present organization of the family.

Activity

Discuss the view that men have much to gain, and women much to lose, from marriage and family life.

ALTERNATIVES TO THE FAMILY

Most societies in the world have some established arrangements for the production, rearing and socialization of children, and the nuclear family is probably the most common arrangement for this. However, it would be wrong to assume that the conventional nuclear family is a universal institution, and that arrangements for bringing up children always or necessarily involve the prime responsibility resting on the family or both biological parents. This is particularly the case today, when new forms of relationship are developing, and when the idea of a lifetime relationship is increasingly disappearing as people have a series of partners during their lifetimes, and abandon traditional styles of family living.

The following examples illustrate some alternative arrangements which suggest the family is not always the main way of bringing up children, nor does it necessarily have to be the family that does this.

The Nayar

Among the Nayar of south-west India before the nineteenth century, there was no nuclear family. A woman could have sexual relations with any man she wished (up to a maximum of twelve) and the biological father of children was therefore uncertain. The mother's brother, rather than the biological father, was responsible for looking after the mother and her children. Unlike in our society – where in most cases the biological parents marry and/or live together and are responsible for rearing their children – among the Nayar there was no direct link between having sexual relations, childbearing, child rearing and cohabitation.

Foster care and children's homes

It is worth remembering that a considerable number of 'looked after' children – over 87,000 in the UK in 2010 – are brought up by foster parents, with a few in children's homes. This does demonstrate that the link between natural parents and the rearing of children can be, and sometimes is, broken.

Communes

Communes are self-contained and self-supporting communities. They developed in Western Europe, the UK and the USA in the 1960s, among groups of people wanting to develop alternative lifestyles to conventional society because of the political or religious beliefs they held.

Communes often try to develop an alternative style of living and a kind of alternative household, with the emphasis on collective living rather than individual family units. A number of adults and children all aim to live and work together, with children being seen as the responsibility of the group as a whole rather than of natural parents. Many communes tended to be very short-lived, and only a few remain in Britain today.

The kibbutz

The Israeli **kibbutz** is a form of commune, and is one of the most famous and successful attempts to establish an alternative to the family. Here, the original emphasis was on collective child rearing, with the community as a whole taking over the tasks of the family. In the early kibbutzim, children were kept apart from their natural parents for much of the time and brought up in the Children's House by metapelets – a kind of 'professional parent' combining the roles of nurse, housemother and educator. Children were seen as the 'children of the kibbutz' – they were the responsibility of the community as a whole, which met all of their needs.

In Israeli kibbutzim, children from various couples are raised together as the shared responsibility of the whole community

In recent years, the more traditional family unit has re-emerged in the kibbutzim, with natural parents and children sharing the same accommodation, but the kibbutz remains one of the most important attempts to find an alternative to conventional family structures.

Shared households and 'families of choice'

As discussed earlier (see pages 141–3) households shared with peers are becoming much more common, particularly among young people. Such shared households, in which people choose to live and form relationships with a group of people with whom they may have closer relations than with their families of birth, might be regarded as a 'family of choice' and an alternative to the conventional idea of what a family is. However, there is not much evidence as yet of such arrangements providing a secure alternative means of bringing up children, though the potential is there for them to do so.

POLITICS, SOCIAL POLICY AND FAMILIES

Debates over family life have become a major feature of politics in Britain, and have had important consequences for government social policies on the family. Politicians of all the major parties have expressed similar views on the importance of the family, seeing it as one of society's central and most important institutions, and encouraging support for and strengthening of family units. They often blame family breakdown for wider social problems, such as teenage pregnancies, sexual promiscuity, educational failure, welfare dependency, poverty, drug abuse, and crime and delinquency. How these problems are linked to the family will affect the kind of social policies that are adopted to solve them. For example, if the blame is placed on the inadequate socialization and supervision of children by parents, then policies might involve either greater pressure on parents to discipline their children properly or, perhaps, support in developing parenting skills. If the blame is placed on the lack of a male role model for boys in mother-headed lone-parent families, or on the welfare state for providing so much support for families that family members fail to take responsibility themselves, then policies might involve promoting traditional married-couple families, and cutting welfare benefits to encourage families to become more self-reliant.

This chapter has referred to a range of changes and trends in families, such as rising divorce, cohabitation, lone parenthood, and births outside marriage. Governments face the dilemma of whether they accept these trends, support all those raising children in whatever family shape, size or other form that might take, and therefore adapt social policies to a changing world, or adopt policies which try to stop these changes and even reverse them.

So although there may be a whole range of policies affecting families, there is often no agreement on what the best policies and solutions to problems are.

WHAT THE POLITICAL PARTIES SAY ABOUT THE FAMILY

Conservative Party
'Strong families are the bedrock of a strong society. They provide the stability and love we need to flourish as human beings, and the relationships they foster are the foundation on which society is built...'
'we will make Britain the most family-friendly country in Europe.'
(*Source*: Conservative Party General Election Manifesto, 2010)

Labour Party
'We are committed to supporting all families, whatever their shape or size...'
(*Source*: Labour Party website, November 2009)
'Strong families are the bedrock of our society. Secure and stable relationships between parents, their children, grandparents and other family members are the foundation on which strong communities are built ... Children thrive best in families in which relationships are stable, loving and strong. We support couples who want to get married ... Marriage is fundamental to our society...'.
(*Source*: Labour General Election Manifesto, 2010)

Liberal Democrats
'Helping families stay strong'.
'... families come in all shapes and sizes. Liberal Democrats believe every family should get the support it needs to thrive, from help with childcare through to better support for carers and elderly parents.'
(*Source*: Liberal Democrats General Election Manifesto, 2010)

The Conservative–Liberal Democrat coalition government formed in May 2010
'The Government believes that strong and stable families of all kinds are the bedrock of a strong and stable society. That is why we need to make our society more family friendly...'
(*Source: The Coalition: Our Programme for Government*, by Prime Minister and Conservative leader David Cameron and Deputy Prime Minister and Liberal Democrat leader Nick Clegg, 2010)

Laws and social policies affecting the family and households

Practically all government policies affect families in some way. This chapter, for example, has mentioned a range of laws and social policies affecting the family. These include compulsory education and the welfare state – which have affected family size and divorce, and enabled both partners in a relationship to undertake paid employment – and laws protecting children and promoting women's rights, and the right of gays and lesbians to form civil partnerships; the law also defines rules and procedures for marriage / civil partnership, adoption and divorce, and establishes monogamy as the only legal form of marriage.

SOCIAL POLICY AND SOCIOLOGY

Social policy refers to the packages of plans and actions adopted by national and local government or various voluntary agencies to solve social problems or achieve other goals that are seen as important. Research by sociologists has often provided evidence to show what the problems are, and which social policies might work to resolve them, and to assess social policies to see if they are working as intended.

> **Social policy**
> refers to the packages of plans and actions adopted by national and local government or various voluntary agencies to solve social problems or achieve other goals that are seen as important.

There are two main types of social policies specifically aimed at families:

- Those aimed at providing direct material support for families, such as cash benefits like tax credits and child benefit to increase family prosperity and reduce adult and child poverty, and the Child Support Agency to ensure absent fathers contribute to the costs of bringing up their children.
- Those to help parents balance the demands of paid employment and family life, and support children, such as maternity and paternity leave, early years childcare and support through nursery education and schemes like Sure Start Children's Centres, advice services to improve parenting skills, child protection policies, and supporting lone parents into paid employment.

The activity below is designed to encourage you to examine and think about some social policies and laws that affect families and households.

Activity

1 The column on the left in the table below lists a range of issues, social policies and laws that might be considered to have an effect on families and households. The column on the right is left blank, for you to explain what social policies or laws there are on the issues, to describe what these social policies are, and how they might affect families and households, and roles and relationships within them. Take two of them (or if you're in a class, several could be shared out) or suggest ones of your own choosing. You can probably find a lot of references to these issues by searching on the Internet, but the following sites might be useful:
   - www.dwp.gov.uk (Department for Work and Pensions)
   - www.familyandparenting.org (the National Family and Parenting Institute)
   - www.gingerbread.org.uk
   - www.lone-parents.org.uk } three sites concerned with issues around lone parenthood
   - www.oneparentfamilies.org.uk
   - www.crae.org.uk (Children's Rights Alliance for England)
   - www.everychildmatters.gov.uk (Every Child Matters)

- www.surestart.gov.uk (Sure Start – help for the early years)
- www.homeoffice.gov.uk (the Home Office – useful for investigating family or child-related crimes, including forced marriage)
- www.csa.gov.uk (the Child Support Agency)
- www.ondivorce.co.uk (providing advice and support for those getting divorced)
- www.childrenscommissioner.org (the Children's Commissioner)
- www.education.gov.uk (Department for Education).
- www.parentscentre.gov.uk (a site providing advice and information to parents on a wide range of matters, including how to deal with children of all ages).

Issue, law or social policy	Description of issue, law or policy, and effects on families and households, and relationships within them
Child benefit Child protection policies Child Support Agency Children Act (2004) Civil Partnership Act 2005 Compulsory education Divorce laws (including custody of and access to children) Domestic violence laws/policies Eradicating child poverty Forced marriage Free early years education for all 3- and 4-year-olds Laws and policies on adoption and fostering of children Maternity and paternity leave National Minimum Wage New Deal for Lone Parents (Support for lone parents) Parenting skills Sure Start programmes	

2 Take any *one* trend in families in Britain today, such as births outside marriage, cohabitation, divorce or lone parenthood, and suggest: (a) two social policies you might adopt to support families through these changes; (b) two social policies you might adopt to try and stop or reverse these changes.

3   What are the main political parties currently saying about family policies, roles and relationships? Go to the websites of the political parties below, and briefly outline two policies on the family and family roles and relationships. Identify any differences between them, particularly whether they seem to be accepting the current trends in family life or seeking to stop and reverse these trends. Look for a 'policy' heading or button, but be prepared to search (try 'policy', 'manifesto' or 'family' first).
   ● www.labour.org.uk (the Labour Party)
   ● www.libdems.org.uk (the Liberal Democrats)
   ● www.conservatives.com (the Conservative Party)

ARE MARRIAGE AND FAMILIES DECLINING SOCIAL INSTITUTIONS?

ARGUMENTS THAT FAMILIES ARE IN DECLINE	ARGUMENTS THAT THEY AREN'T
● Around 40 per cent of marriages in Britain today will end in divorce, and about one in four children will experience a parental divorce by their sixteenth birthday.	● The rising divorce rate is caused by easier divorce laws, reduced social stigma and more sympathetic public attitudes, rather than more marriage breakdowns. In the past, many couples may have been condemned, by legal and financial obstacles and social intolerance, to suffer unhappy empty shell marriages or to separate without divorcing. Making divorce harder to get would simply mean couples would separate without divorcing, or live in marriages riddled with conflict and unhappiness. Marriages today are more likely to be based on love and companionship rather than the custom and financial necessity of the past. Of all divorced people, around 75 per cent remarry, about a third of them within a year of getting divorced, and half within five years. This shows that what they are rejecting is not the institution of marriage itself, but a particular marriage partner – they divorce hoping to turn an unhappy marriage into a new, happier one. The marriages that exist today are therefore probably much stronger and happier than ever, since unhappy relationships are easily ended by divorce.

ARGUMENTS THAT FAMILIES ARE IN DECLINE

- In Britain today, about a quarter of families with dependent children have just one parent.

- About 46 per cent of births are outside marriage, and the proportion is growing every year.

- There are well over a million cohabiting couples who have refused to tie the marriage knot – one in ten of all couples. This figure is expected to rise to 1.7 million by 2020, making up around one in seven of all couple households.

- Rising rates of divorce, cohabitation, lone parenthood, and reconstituted families show a picture of the family in decline. This has been blamed for a wide range of social ills, such as declining moral standards, social disorder, drug abuse, crime, vandalism, anti-social behaviour, football hooliganism, and increasing levels of violence in society.

ARGUMENTS THAT THEY AREN'T

- Lone parenthood arises from a variety of reasons (see earlier in this chapter) and lone parents are as able to provide care and security for children as two-parent families, and probably better able if the two parents don't get on.

- Despite the record numbers of children being born outside marriage, nearly nine out of ten of those births are registered jointly by the parents, with the same address given by both parents in two out of three of these cases. This suggests they are cohabiting, and that most children are still being born into a stable relationship, and live in families with concerned parents who are simply reluctant to tie the legal marriage knot. Most dependent children still live in families headed by a married or cohabiting couple.

- Many of those who cohabit eventually marry – about 60 per cent of first-time cohabitations turn into marriages – and about 54 per cent of the population over age 16 consists of married people. It would appear that marriage remains an important social institution, even in the light of the high divorce rate and previous experience of living together outside marriage.

- The causes of these social problems, all too often blamed on the family, are complex, and those who blame the family are often searching for simple solutions to difficult and complicated problems.

What really seems to be happening is not so much that the family and marriage are in decline as that they are changing. There are more lone-parent families, more reconstituted families, more gay and lesbian families, more experiments in living together before marriage, and fewer people prepared to marry simply to bring up children. Nevertheless, marriage remains an important social norm, and strong pressures from parents, peer groups, and the responsibilities brought about by the birth of children continue to propel most people into marriage sooner or later.

The important thing is that families, whatever their size or shape, should provide children with a stable environment, with good relationships between parents and children anchored in love and warmth, and without stressful lifestyles arising from things like hostility and anger, poverty, ill-health, domestic violence, poor housing and drug abuse. If this can be achieved, perhaps it doesn't really matter whether or not couples are married or have been married before, whether there is one parent or two, or whether couples are of the same or opposite sexes. Though the form of the family will keep on changing, the importance of the family lies in its role as a stable and supportive unit for one or two adults and their dependent children. In that sense, the ideal of the family perhaps still remains intact.

Activity

Is the family of less importance in society today than it used to be? Do you think the family is in decline?

CHAPTER SUMMARY

After studying this chapter, you should be able to:

- describe some social issues and social problems linked to families

- describe consensus and conflict approaches to the family, and explain the differences between them

- describe the different forms of marriage, families and households

- explain why demographic changes – like the decline in the birth rate, fertility rate, death rate and infant mortality rate and increasing life expectancy and the ageing population – have occurred, and how these changes have affected families, including family size

- describe how the role of the family in society has changed

- explain why the privatized nuclear family, or modified extended family, became the most common form of families; provide evidence for the continued existence of the classic extended family; and explain what is meant by the beanpole family and why it has developed

- explain the links between the privatized nuclear family and features of contemporary society

- critically examine the view that roles in marriage and cohabiting couples have become more equal, with an apparent change from segregated to integrated conjugal roles, and a growing partnership of equals

- explain why families have become more child-centred

- explain why families and households have become smaller

- explain the reasons for the rising divorce rate, identify the groups most at risk of divorce, and describe some consequences of divorce for individuals, families and society

- explain why there has been a large increase in the number of lone-parent families

- explain why there has been a decline in the numbers of people getting married, and increased cohabitation

- explain why remarriage and reconstituted families have become more common
- explain why there are now more births outside marriage
- explain why there are now more one person households
- explain why the cereal packet image of the family is an inaccurate stereotype of the family in modern Britain
- describe the diversity of families and households in contemporary Britain

- explain, with examples, what is meant by the darker side of family life
- outline feminist criticisms of the family
- describe alternatives to the family
- outline political views of the family, and describe some social policies and laws affecting families, including how governments seek to assist families
- identify some arguments and evidence for and against the view that the family and marriage are of declining social importance.

KEY TERMS

ageing population
arranged marriage
beanpole family
bigamy
birth rate
cereal packet family
classic extended family
communes
conjugal roles
death rate

demography
divorce rate
domestic labour
extended family
feminist
fertility rate
household
infant mortality rate
integrated conjugal roles
kibbutz
kinship

life expectancy
marriage rate
matriarchy
meritocratic society
modified extended family
monogamy
moral panic
nuclear family
polyandry
polygamy
polygyny

privatized nuclear family
reconstituted or stepfamily
secularization
segregated conjugal roles
serial monogamy
social mobility
social policy
symmetrical family
value consensus

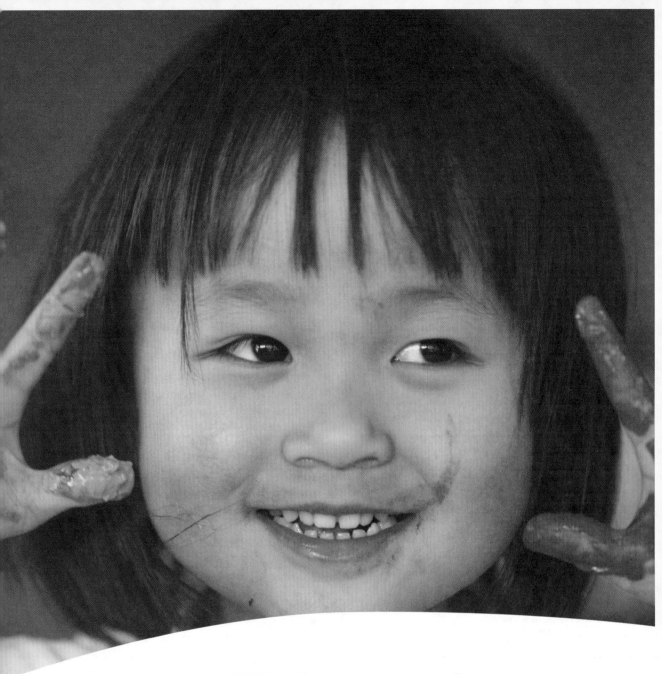

CHAPTER
4

Education

Contents

Education

KEY ISSUES

- Education as a social and political issue
- The role of education in society
- Education in Britain before the 1970s
- Comprehensive schools and selection
- Education from 1988 onwards: the free market in education
- School diversity
- Vocational education
- Equality of educational opportunity and helping the most disadvantaged groups
- Inequality in education
- Private education: the independent schools
- Is equality of educational opportunity possible to achieve?

The sociology of education covers a vast area, and it is impossible in this book to cover all aspects. This chapter therefore takes as its main focus the school system, rather than further and higher education, and concentrates on three main aspects of this: what the purposes of education are; the main features and changes which have occurred in the school system since around the 1970s; and the continuing inequalities in education, including the factors that influence whether students succeed or fail in education.

EDUCATION AS A SOCIAL AND POLITICAL ISSUE

One of the reasons education is an important political issue is that providing education is a government responsibility, and governments make laws about what age children should start school, for how long and what they should learn there. It is also an incredibly expensive business, eating up around

£84 billion a year in Britain in 2010 – about 13 per cent of total national and local government spending. It is perhaps not surprising then that politicians spend a lot of time discussing what the education system is for.

The aims and purposes of education, and what the education system should provide and how it should be run, are also political issues. Examples of these political issues include the questions below.

- What are the aims and purposes of education? For example, should schools be concerned with serving the needs of the economy, and providing the skills that employers want? Or should education be particularly to give a helping hand up to the most disadvantaged? Or stimulating the interests and creativity of children?
- Should children be selected for particular schools by ability?
- Should children be tested to measure their achievements, and how and when?
- Are educational standards high enough, and how can they be improved?
- Should parents be given the opportunity to choose any school they like for their children, and should the government provide schools for every kind of interest group, such as every religious faith?
- Who should run schools? Should they be run by local authorities (local councils) as most currently are? Or should they be run by private businesses, or groups of parents?

The on-going uncertainty among politicians about whether the education system is doing what it should is shown by the pace of change, and every year since at least 1988 there has been some new reform of the education system, and every new government or new education minister seems to have different ideas about what the education system should do and how it should be working.

Education is an important social issue in contemporary society as well. Parents want the best for their children, yet there are huge inequalities in educational opportunities and in attainment between the richest and poorest social groups, and not all children of the same ability have the same chance of succeeding in education. Yet education is still, for most people, the key and only means to a healthy, comfortable and secure adult life, and a poor-quality education can have damaging and lasting consequences throughout a person's life.

THE ROLE OF EDUCATION IN SOCIETY

Education is a major social institution, and schools in Britain command a captive audience of virtually all children between the ages of 5 and 16 (age 17 from 2013). During this period of compulsory schooling, children spend

Full-time education is compulsory in the UK from ages 5 to 16 (age 17 from 2013), though many children start younger in reception classes at primary and infant schools, at pre-schools, nurseries and playgroups. About 13 per cent of everything national and local government spends goes on education. Why do you think such importance is attached to education?

about half of the time they are awake at school during term time – about 15,000 hours of their lives.

Why is such importance attached to the provision of education in contemporary society? What does education contribute to society? Why are schools necessary in industrial societies and why is education to the age of 16/17 compulsory?

The answer to these questions lies in the *functions* that education performs in society.

Activity

1 List all the reasons you go/went to school. What benefits (if any) do you think going to school has brought you?
2 How do you think your life would differ if you didn't have / hadn't had to go to school?
3 Now read to the end of this section (on the role that education plays in society), and compare the reasons given for going to school with your own reasons. Which do you think are the more important, from your point of view?
4 What problems might there be for individuals and society if compulsory education were to be abolished tomorrow?

Socialization and social cohesion: preparation for adulthood and citizenship

The school is an important agency of secondary socialization, continuing the process of primary socialization in the family. You can read more about this in chapter 1 (see pages 11–19).

Consensus theorists argue that schools transmit from one generation to the next the culture and shared values of a society, though *conflict theorists* argue this is the culture and values of the dominant and most powerful groups in society. For example, the school curriculum hands on knowledge about history, geography, science, English language and literature, and so on. Children also learn how to develop relationships with others, including sex education, and to adopt many of the norms of the society to which they belong. Citizenship and Personal and Social Education courses are concerned with the rights and responsibilities, and duties and freedoms, of people living in a democratic society. They aim to develop knowledge, skills and understanding about laws and justice, and encourage respect for different national, religious and ethnic identities, and thereby build **social cohesion** – the bonds that bring people together and integrate individuals into a united society.

Citizenship is now part of the National Curriculum in England for 11- to 16-year-olds (Key Stages 3 and 4), with the aim of encouraging and equipping young people to play a full, active and responsible role in public life and in running the society to which they belong. Citizenship in England also involves some understanding of what it means to be British, with awareness of the history, beliefs, values and other features making up

Social cohesion refers to the bonds or 'glue' that bring people together and integrate them into a united society.

the British way of life. In Wales, citizenship is included as part of PSE (Personal and Social Education), with the teaching of Welsh to foster a sense of Welsh national identity. In Scotland, similar aims are met through the Social Studies curriculum area, and in Northern Ireland by Personal Development & Mutual Understanding (PDMU) and Learning for Life and Work (LLW).

As children move from primary school to the end of secondary schooling, they are gradually encouraged to take on more responsibilities, to become more independent and to stand on their own two feet, as they will have to when they leave school. Much of this preparation for adult life takes place through the **hidden curriculum**, which is discussed below. As a result of schooling, society is reproduced and each new generation is integrated into society.

> The **hidden curriculum** is the teaching of values, attitudes and behaviour through the school's organization and teachers' attitudes, but which is not part of the formal timetable.

What are the things that make up Britishness (or substitute any other national identity you have)? Is it traditional British food? Symbols like flags and Big Ben? Our beliefs and values? What do you think makes you British?

Activity

In this activity, if you see yourself as having some other national identity, such as being Welsh, Scottish, Irish and so on, answer these questions, where appropriate, by replacing your own national identity.

1 Suggest three ceremonies, three symbols and three values which you think might show a *British* identity, and which make the British in some ways different from people of other nations.
2 Drawing on your citizenship education, discuss what rights and responsibilities you have as a British citizen.
3 To what extent do you think the education system helps to build social cohesion? Give examples to illustrate your answer.

Education and the economy: preparation for working life

In a complex industrial society, the education system plays an important role in developing the knowledge and skills in the workforce that are needed to enable the economy to prosper. The education system carries out preparation for working life in two respects:

- *Producing a labour force with the skills needed for working life.* A literate and numerate workforce is more or less essential in an industrial society, and the key skills of use and application of number, communication and information technology are much in demand by employers. There is also the need for specific skills related to particular jobs, such as computing, engineering, CAD and science. The things learnt at school will generally affect the kind of job and training opportunities open to people after school.
- *Selecting people for different occupations. Consensus theorists* see modern industrial societies as generally meritocratic – a **meritocracy** in which most social positions are achieved by merit, such as experience, talent, skill and exam qualifications.

Social mobility

One of the most important consequences of education is the influence it has on people's life chances. These are the chances of obtaining those things defined as desirable – such as secure, well-paid jobs, good housing and health – and of avoiding those things defined as undesirable in a society, such as poverty and unemployment.

For most people, education affects in a very direct way their job opportunities – and social class position – as adults. This important result of education has been reflected in the attempts to establish **equality of educational**

A **meritocracy** (or meritocratic society) is a society in which social and occupational positions (jobs) and pay are allocated on the basis purely of people's individual experience, talents, abilities, qualifications and skills – their individual merits. In Britain today, this nearly always means educational qualifications.

**Equality
of educational
opportunity** is the
idea that every child,
regardless of his
or her social class
background, ability
to pay school fees,
ethnic origin, gender
or disability, should
have an equal chance
of doing as well in
education as his or her
ability will allow.
Social mobility refers
to the movement of
groups or individuals
up or down the social
hierarchy.

opportunity, so that all children can have the same educational opportunities in life, regardless of their social class background, ability to pay school fees, ethnic origin, gender or disability. However, despite these attempts, inequality in educational opportunity remains, as will be considered later.

In schools and colleges, people are graded and receive different qualifications, which are used by employers and other educational institutions to select suitable people for work and further courses.

Through exams, schools sort pupils out, and decide the kinds of occupation they will eventually get – for example, who will become middle-class professionals or skilled or unskilled workers. Education will therefore influence the individual's eventual social class position and the life chances they will have as an adult. In a few cases, education can be a means of upward **social mobility** into the middle class for children from a working-class family. Figure 4.1 illustrates this link between education and the class structure.

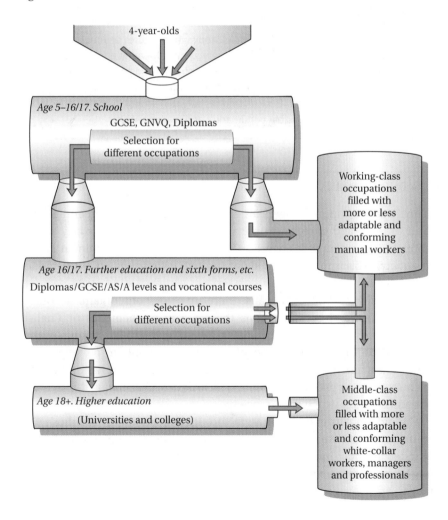

Figure 4.1 Education and the class structure

Conflict theorists question whether society is really meritocratic at all as, in most cases, the education system is not a means of upward social mobility, but seems to be sending children from working-class homes into working-class jobs as adults, and children from middle-class homes into middle-class jobs. The education system, from this point of view, is simply reproducing and justifying the inequalities that already exist in society. Exam results and qualifications give the impression that those who fail in the education system do so because of their lack of ability and effort, and have only themselves to blame. In this way, people are encouraged to accept the positions they find themselves in after schooling. However, in most cases it is not lack of ability and effort, but disadvantages arising from social class and family background that cause failure. This continuing inequality is considered later in this chapter.

Activity

1 Drawing on your own experiences at school, what features of your education do you think prepared you / will prepare you most for adult and working life after school? Think of the particular subjects studied and activities undertaken. To what extent do you think these were successful?
2 What other things do you think should be taught at school to enable people to play a full and responsible part in adult and working life?

Social control

Schools act as important agencies of social control, which encourage children to learn and conform to the values and norms expected by society (though the *conflict view* suggests these are those of the dominant groups in society). This is mainly carried out through what is known as the hidden curriculum.

This teaching is 'hidden' because there are no obvious, organized courses in 'obedience and conformity' as there are in mathematics or English, though Citizenship courses may be an exception. Citizenship courses may carry out social control, by encouraging young people to be responsible conformists and not 'rock the boat' as adults; on the other hand, they may encourage young people to become critical adults, challenging the inequalities and conflicts which divide society.

The hidden curriculum is present throughout schooling, and those who conform to it are likely to be rewarded, while those who don't are likely to be branded as non-conformists by the school and may find themselves getting into trouble. Some features of this hidden curriculum, and what is being taught, are shown below.

THE HIDDEN CURRICULUM

Features of the hidden curriculum	What is being taught
● Privileges and responsibilities given to older pupils	● Respect for elders, and acceptance of adult responsibilities
● School rules, detentions and suspensions, rewards like merit badges, prizes, good marks, etc.	● Conformity to society's rules and laws, whether you agree with them or not
● School assemblies	● Respect for religious beliefs and the dominant moral values
● Pupils' lack of power and control about the subjects taught, how the school is run or the school day organized	● Workers' lack of power and control at work
● The authority hierarchy of the school involving pupils fitting into a complex organization of heads, deputies, heads of department, year heads, etc.	● Learning about their place in the hierarchies of power and control in society and accepting it – for example, in the authority hierarchy at work
● Males and females often having different dress rules, being expected to conform to different standards of behaviour, and being counselled into different subjects, further education courses, and careers	● Males and females being expected to conform to gender stereotypes
● Respecting authority of teachers regardless of what they say or do	● Respect for those in authority, such as bosses at work and the police
● Punctuality / being on time	● Good time-keeping at work
● Streaming and setting by ability, with rewards and prizes given for hard work and exam success	● Accepting that the different levels of the job market, such as professional, managerial, skilled, semi-skilled and unskilled manual occupations, and the differences in power, status and pay between social classes, are natural and justified, as those higher up have worked harder, are more intelligent and better qualified

Activity

1 Describe in detail three features of the hidden curriculum found in your school, or the one you once attended, which reflect the values of society outside school.

2 Identify three features of the hidden curriculum in your school, or the one you once attended, which might be regarded as discriminating against students from minority ethnic groups or either boys or girls.

3 Are/were there any features of the hidden curriculum in your school which you think might encourage students to take more power and control in schools, such as democratic decision-making, free choice of dress or school councils? Explain your answer.

Implementing government policy

Schools have often been used as a means of carrying out government policies. For example, comprehensive schools were originally established by a Labour government in an attempt to create both more equal opportunities in society and greater social equality. Some schools in areas where there is widespread poverty have been given extra teachers and more resources than other schools in an attempt to relieve the disadvantages faced by the poor in education. Multicultural courses are also organized in many schools in an attempt to stop the spread of racist ideas, and to encourage respect for people from different cultural backgrounds. Equal opportunities policies have been adopted to reduce the effects of gender stereotyping, by encouraging girls to go into subjects like science and computing, which have been traditionally dominated by boys. Citizenship and the idea of Britishness are also promoted by governments wishing to encourage people to participate more in democratic society, for example by voting, and to preserve a British national identity.

Preparing for social change

As well as encouraging people to accept traditional ideas which will lead to order and stability in society, schools and colleges also prepare students for a rapidly changing industrial society. Since the 1970s there has been a massive expansion of computer courses and the use of computers in schools and colleges, in an attempt to prepare young people for a world after school in which

Schools have played a key role in making young people computer-literate in a society in which information and communication technology is increasingly dominant in all spheres of life

information and communication technology (ICT) plays a central role. ICT is now a compulsory National Curriculum subject at all key stages. Attempts to make pupils more adaptable and aware of the world of work, and to make schools more closely related to the needs of the economy, are partly due to the demands of a rapidly changing economy.

EDUCATION IN BRITAIN BEFORE THE 1970s

Until the 1960s, all children went first to primary schools (as they do now) but then were selected at age 11 by whether they passed or failed a special intelligence quotient (IQ) test (the 11+ examination) to go to one of three types of secondary school – grammar, technical, and secondary modern schools. These three types of secondary school became known as the **tripartite system**.

The 15–20 per cent of children with the best 11+ exam results went to grammar schools, with most children going to secondary modern schools. There were hardly any technical schools established. Figure 4.2 illustrates the tripartite system, and the social classes young people were being prepared for as adults.

During the 1960s, the tripartite system came increasingly under attack. The 11+ exam was seen as an unfair and inaccurate selection test, which damaged the self-esteem and educational opportunities of children who failed to win a place at a grammar school. Secondary modern schools became seen as inferior, second-rate schools, compared to higher-status grammar schools which offered better life chances to their pupils. Research suggested that the talent, ability and potential of many children in the secondary modern schools were being wasted, and could be better developed in comprehensive schools. As a result, the tripartite system was abolished in

> The **tripartite system** was the system of secondary education in which pupils were selected for one of three types of secondary school according to their performance in the 11+ exam.

Figure 4.2 The tripartite system after the 1944 Education Act

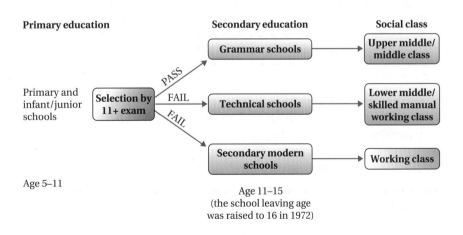

most of the country, and by the 1970s most children attended comprehensive schools.

COMPREHENSIVE SCHOOLS AND SELECTION

Comprehensive education abolished both selection at age 11 by the 11+ exam and the three types of secondary school. Children in most areas now, regardless of their ability, generally transfer to the same type of school at the age of 11, with no selection by examination. Around nine out of ten young people in the UK now attend some form of comprehensive school, with only about 230 state grammar schools remaining.

True comprehensive schools have no selection by ability at all, and children of all abilities are admitted to the same types of school and taught in mixed-ability classes. While most schools are now comprehensive schools in that they do not select by ability the majority of the pupils they admit, there are different types of comprehensive school, and some selection by ability does continue in the education system – and, through **streaming** and **setting**, in many comprehensive schools as well.

> **Streaming** involves putting students into the same group for all subjects according to their ability, while **setting** is where pupils are put into different groups or sets for a particular subject according to their ability in that subject.

SELECTION REMAINS AN ISSUE TODAY

The issue of selection by ability for secondary education, and whether this is necessary to give young people the most suitable form of secondary education, are still hotly disputed matters. Many specialist schools, including trust schools and academies (discussed below) are allowed to select up to 10 per cent of their pupils by ability, and there has been a return to streaming and a move away from mixed-ability teaching. Policy-makers in all political parties in the first ten years of the twenty-first century were increasingly talking of a return to selection for secondary education, based on student attitudes, aptitudes, interests, capabilities and skills. School and college league tables and the judging of schools and colleges on their results (see later in this chapter) constantly raise the issue of whether students should be selected by ability so some schools get the best, most able students in an area, though this of course disadvantages other schools.

The case against selection: the advantages of comprehensive schools

Opportunities remain open

In comprehensive schools, the possibility of educational success and obtaining qualifications remains open throughout a child's school career, since moving between streams and classes within one school is easier and more likely to happen than moving between different types of school in a selective system.

Late developers benefit

Late developers, whose intelligence and ability improve later in life, can be catered for better in the comprehensive system, rather than having their opportunities limited at an early age.

Middle-class parents are generally better placed to coach a less bright child – who might therefore have once got a grammar school place at age 11 – than parents from a less well-off background with a late-developing bright child, who might have failed to get a grammar school place. Comprehensives cater for both, and disadvantage neither.

More get better qualifications

Fewer students leave school without any qualifications in the comprehensive system, and more obtain higher standards than under selective systems, such as where grammar schools continue to exist or where there are other forms of selection by ability.

More social mixing and fewer social divisions

As all children attend the same type of school, there is more social mixing between students from homes of different social class and ethnic backgrounds, and this helps to overcome divisions between different social groups and build social cohesion. Selection by ability in education often benefits the middle class, which dominates selective schools and the top streams in streamed comprehensive schools. The reasons for this are discussed later in this chapter.

Reduced risk of the self-fulfilling prophecy

Children are less likely to be branded as failures at an early age – lowering their self-esteem (how they feel about themselves and their ability) – and thus avoiding the damaging effects of the **self-fulfilling prophecy**. This is the process whereby the prediction that children won't do well as a result of testing and selection by ability, actually comes true, due to the low expectations of teachers, and the consequent poor image students have of their own ability. This is discussed further later in the chapter.

> The **self-fulfilling prophecy** is the process in which people act in response to a prediction of their behaviour, thereby making the prediction come true.

Benefits of mixed-ability teaching

Where all pupils of the same age, regardless of their ability, are taught in the same type of school and in the same classroom (mixed-ability teaching), the more intelligent pupils can have a stimulating influence on the less able, and the problems created by the self-fulfilling prophecy are easier to avoid. Research has shown that mixed-ability teaching has no negative effect on

Selection by ability can have harmful effects on the self-esteem of students, and create a self-fulfilling prophecy

the 'high flyers', improves the performance of the less able, and makes no difference to a school's overall examination performance.

More choice and opportunity

The large size of many comprehensive schools, designed to contain all pupils in an area, means there are more teachers teaching a wider range of subjects to meet the needs of pupils of all abilities, with a great variety of equipment and facilities. This benefits all pupils and gives them greater choices and opportunities to develop their talents, to reach their full potential and to gain some educational qualifications.

Benefits for working-class students

Selective schools and streamed comprehensives can be much like the tripartite system, with working-class students less likely to gain places in selective schools, and more likely to be placed in the bottom streams. True comprehensive education avoids this.

The case for selection: criticisms of comprehensive education

The lack of selection by ability is not without its critics.

'High flyers' are held back

Because comprehensive schools contain pupils of all abilities, brighter children are held back by the slower pace of learning of the less able. Critics argue this wouldn't happen with selection, as 'high flyers' are taught in the same school or streams within a school.

Overlooked talents and discipline problems

The large size of some comprehensives, containing all students in an area, may make it impossible for staff to know all pupils personally, and this may create discipline problems and the talents of individuals may not be noticed and developed.

Stretching the most able

Selection by ability through streaming or setting (rather than mixed-ability teaching) in the same school means brighter students can be 'stretched', rather than being held back by slower learners who take up the teacher's time, and who may be disruptive because they are unable to cope with the work. Many so-called comprehensive schools are not true comprehensives, as they stream or set pupils, and this is really a form of selection in the same school.

Table 4.1 The effects of streaming on children's recorded ability between the ages of 8 and 11 years

Measured ability at 8 years of age – test scores	Children in an *upper* stream	Children in a *lower* stream
	Average change in test scores between 8 and 11 years	Average change in test scores between 8 and 11 years
41–5	+5.67	−0.95
46–8	+3.70	−0.62
49–51	+4.44	−1.60
52–4	+0.71	−1.46
55–7	+2.23	−1.94
58–60	+0.86	−6.34

+ indicates improvements in score, − indicates deterioration in score.

Source: adapted from J. W. B. Douglas, *The Home and the School* (Panther / Grafton Books)

Activity

Study table 4.1 and answer the following questions.
1 What average change occurred in the test scores of children in a lower stream whose test score at 8 years of age was 55–7?
2 What average change occurred in the test scores of children in an upper stream whose test score at 8 years of age was 46–8?
3 Which ability group in which stream showed (i) the greatest deterioration in test scores, and (ii) the greatest improvement in test scores?

4 What does table 4.1 suggest about the effects of streaming on children's educational performance? List all the factors you can think of which might explain this, drawing on your own experiences at school.

5 With reference to table 4.1 and the arguments above over selection, outline the arguments for and against selection by ability in education, drawing on examples from your own experiences at school.

6 Do you think streaming and setting or mixed-ability teaching is better for pupils' progress? Give some evidence to back up your view from your own experiences at school.

7 Have you had any experience of the self-fulfilling prophecy in your own schooling? How do you know whether teachers think/thought you are 'bright' or not, and how do you think this has affected your progress?

8 Suggest measures that could be taken to make comprehensive schools better for all pupils.

EDUCATION FROM 1988 ONWARDS: THE FREE MARKET IN EDUCATION

While the comprehensive system has succeeded in improving overall educational standards, the system came under increasing criticism in the 1980s and 1990s for not meeting the needs of employers and industry closely enough, for not reaching high enough standards, and for failing to benefit the most disadvantaged, poorest groups in society. As a result, attempts have been made to tie all parts of the education system more closely to the needs of industry and business, to raise standards, and to improve the educational achievement of the most disadvantaged groups.

Activity

Go to www.standards.dcsf.gov.uk and find measures that the government is taking to tackle educational underachievement by more deprived social groups, minority ethnic groups and males. Find three actions for each group, and explain how each measure might raise standards and improve levels of achievement.

The key aims of educational change

The move to comprehensive schooling, and more recent changes in the education system, have been driven by four main aims:

- raising educational standards, partly by providing more parental choice in schooling, and by creating competition between schools and colleges
- creating a more diverse school system, promoting different types of school to give parents more choice in the type of school their children go to
- economic efficiency: developing the talents of young people to improve the skills of the labour force so Britain maintains a successful position in the world economy, and making the education system meet the needs of industry and employers through more emphasis on vocational education
- creating equality of educational opportunity in a meritocratic society, and establishing a fairer society by opening up opportunities for secondary and further/higher education to the working-class and other disadvantaged groups.

The marketization of education

The 1988 Education Reform Act was the most important piece of educational legislation since the 1944 Education Act. It reduced local control of the education system, for example by teachers and local authorities (councils). At the same time, it increased control by the central government over some aspects of schools, like the National Curriculum, testing and the inspection of schools, but it also handed over more control to school governors, headteachers and the consumers of education – parents and students – in the running of schools. These changes were based on the ideas of schools having control over their own activities and competing with each other for students, with parents having the right to choose whatever school they thought best for their children (as long as there were enough school places). This process has become known as the **marketization** of education.

Since 1988, schools and colleges have gained a lot more control over how they run their institutions, and they compete with each other for students. Parents and students now have a wider choice of which schools or colleges to attend, instead of being obliged to go to their local one. It was thought that by increasing parental choice and competition for students, schools and colleges would become more efficient and accountable to parents and students. Giving parents a choice as consumers of education in a free market – rejecting some schools or colleges in favour of others, in the same way that people choose between competing supermarkets or products – was expected to drive up education standards. Poorly performing schools or colleges would risk losing money as student numbers fell, and might face closure, while those that performed well would grow and improve even more.

Table 4.2 illustrates some of the main features and policies linked to the marketization of education since 1988, and a number of these are explained and discussed in the pages that follow.

> **Marketization**
> in education is the process whereby schools and colleges become more independent, compete with one another for students, and become subject to the free market forces of supply and demand, based on competition and parental choice.

The free market in education has made schooling a bit like supermarket shopping, where parents can 'read the labels' and pick and choose the type and quality of school they want. However, the more better-off and educated middle-class parents and young people have gained the most benefits from the marketization of education. Why do you think this is?

Table 4.2 The marketization of education

Policy	Aims
Target setting *National testing* (SATs, GCSEs, GCEs and other exams) with publication of results *National league tables* of school performance, including exam results *Office for Standards in Education, Children's Services and Skills (Ofsted)* – inspecting and publishing reports on the strengths and weaknesses of schools	• to identify the best schools, and shame the worst into improving their standards or face closure • to give parents and students the information to choose the best schools • to encourage schools to compete for students and money
More independence for schools (with less control by local councils)	• to give schools the control to make changes to compete and attract students by improving quality and standards
Formula funding (money allocated per student)	• to enable popular schools that attract students to get the most money so they can expand and improve. Those that don't attract students will risk being closed
Parental choice *Open enrolment* *A diversity of school types*, like specialist and faith schools	• to enable parents to choose the schools they consider best for their children, rather than just having to go to the local one

Raising standards: competition, diversity and choice in schooling

More money for schools, more nursery education and smaller primary school classes

The Labour government, first elected in 1997, established a national maximum class size of thirty for all 5-, 6- and 7-year-olds, and allocated huge amounts of extra money to schools to enable them to provide the staff, materials, buildings and facilities necessary to provide a high-quality learning environment for children, and thereby improve standards. All children aged 3 and 4 now get a guarantee of five half-days of nursery education a week.

Activity-based learning

Teaching has become more student-centred and activity based, with the aim of developing students' skills and understanding. GCSEs, AS- and A-levels, GNVQs and Applied GCEs have become more activity- and skills-based exams. This has led to much better exam results among 16- to 18-year-olds. Modular exams (which students can take in parts) aim to ensure that all students can obtain some qualifications by allowing them to resit parts of a course. AS-levels aim to encourage 16- to 18-year-olds to study a broader range of subjects, and to make them more flexible and less specialized. In 2008, coursework assessment was dropped from most AS- & A-level courses, as it was thought there was too much assessment and that the courses were not demanding enough, or stretching the most able students.

The National Curriculum, national testing, target-setting and an emphasis on literacy and numeracy

To improve standards across the country, and ensure all students had access to the same high-quality curriculum, the 1988 Education Reform Act set up the National Curriculum, a range of subjects and set programmes of study that must be followed by all school students in England (there are different requirements in Scotland, Wales and Northern Ireland). There are attainment targets (goals which all teachers are expected to enable students to reach), with formal teacher assessment at the end of Key Stages 1–3, and national tests (SATs) in English, maths and science at the end of Key Stages 2 and 3 (ages 11 and 14) to ensure these targets are met. In addition, all primary schools (Key Stages 1 and 2) must have a stronger emphasis on literacy and numeracy each day, to improve basic skills in these areas.

National 'league tables'

Schools and colleges are now required to publish tables of testing (SATs) and exam results (GCSEs, AS-levels, A-levels, Applied GCEs and GNVQs). These

The National Curriculum England (2010)

Key Stage	Ages / Year group	Compulsory ('statutory') subjects
1	5–7 (Years 1–2)	English, Mathematics, Science, History, Geography, Art and design, Music, Information and communication technology (ICT), Design and technology, Physical education, Religious education
2	7–11 (Years 3–6)	Same as Key Stage 1 plus a Modern foreign language
3	11–14 (Years 7–9)	Art and design, Citizenship, Design and technology, English, Geography, History, ICT, Mathematics, Science, Modern foreign language, Music, Physical education, Religious education
4	14–16 (Years 10–11)	English, Mathematics, Citizenship, ICT, Science, Physical education, Religious education

Source: The Qualifications and Curriculum Development Agency (QCDA)

National testing through SATs, exams and formal teacher assessment have been used to improve, check and measure the quality and standards of education

have become known as 'league tables', as like league tables in football, they are designed to give parents and students an idea of how well schools and colleges are doing so they can choose the best. By encouraging competition for students between schools and colleges, these league tables aim to raise overall standards.

Local management of schools (LMS)

Local management of schools (LMS) gives schools (rather than local authorities – county and city councils in most areas) much greater control of their budgets, and of a wide range of other aspects of the school. This is designed to make schools more responsive to local needs and the wishes of parents. These changes aimed to encourage schools to run on market principles, where they compete with one another for students and therefore funds.

Formula funding

Schools and colleges are funded by a formula which is largely based on the number of students they attract. It was thought this would drive up standards by rewarding successful schools and colleges that attracted students (and hence money), giving less successful schools and colleges the incentive to improve.

Open enrolment and parental choice

Parents are now allowed to express a preference for the school of their choice, and a school cannot refuse a pupil a place if it has vacancies. This was designed to raise the quality of teaching and exam results by encouraging competition between schools. Unpopular schools run the risk of losing pupils and therefore money, and the government has taken steps to close what it sees as 'failing' schools which are unpopular with parents and where exam and test results, and standards of behaviour, are poor. In most cases, parents don't really have much choice of school, as places are usually filled up by those living in the school's 'priority area' (the area from which children are admitted first).

More information for parents

To help parents to choose the best schools and encourage schools to improve their standards and performance, schools now have to provide, by law, a school profile containing a wide range of information for parents, including their successes, areas for improvement, and progress on Ofsted reports. These school profiles can be found at http://schoolsfinder.direct.gov.uk.

Specialist schools and selection by ability

Since the early 2000s there has been a huge growth in the number of specialist schools of various types, often including specialist faith schools, trust schools and academies, which are discussed later in the chapter. These schools have a special focus on their chosen subject area, such as technology, languages, business and enterprise, or music. These are an attempt to move away from what were called 'bog standard' comprehensives. These schools have to raise money from private business, but they then get extra money from the government and are allowed to select up to 10 per cent of their pupils by 'aptitude' (ability) in the specialist subject. It is thought that by specializing these schools will raise standards in their specialist subjects, and that selection by ability will raise standards, not just in the specialist subjects, but across the whole school curriculum.

The Office for Standards in Education, Children's Services and Skills (Ofsted)*

The Office for Standards in Education, Children's Services and Skills (Ofsted) was established to conduct inspections of all state schools and sixth-form and further education colleges in England to ensure schools and colleges were doing a good job, by publishing their inspection reports and requiring action to be taken on any weaknesses identified.

Activity

1 Identify and explain two ways in which the educational reforms from the late 1980s to the present have introduced market forces into the education system.
2 Is competition between schools a good thing? Identify and explain its advantages and disadvantages.
3 Do you think the recent changes in education will succeed in raising standards? Go through each of the changes since the 1980s, and explain why they might or might not improve standards.
4 Do you think schools alone can be held responsible for exam results and truancy rates? What other factors might influence how good a school's exam results are, and whether pupils play truant or not?

Criticisms of the free market in education and other recent changes

While the changes in education may have given individual schools more control of their affairs, and made them more responsive to parents, this has been at the expense of greater central government control, such as through the National Curriculum (or Welsh, Scottish and Northern Ireland equivalents), and cooperation between schools has been replaced with

---

* Ofsted only applies in England. Similar functions are carried out in Wales by Estyn (Her Majesty's Inspectorate for Education and Training in Wales), in Scotland by HMIE (Her Majesty's Inspectorate of Education) and in Northern Ireland by ETI (the Education and Training Inspectorate).

competition. The development of the free market in education, increased intervention by central government, the attempt to raise standards and the more vocational emphasis in education have been very controversial, and these changes have been criticized in a number of ways. The main criticisms are outlined below.

The middle class has gained the most

Middle-class parents have been able to make the greatest use of parental choice and open enrolment, and it is they who are better placed to make the most effective use of the education system to their children's advantage. The educational system remains socially selective, and the higher the social class of the parents, the better are the schools to which they send their children. For example, research in 2009 from Bristol University and the London Institute of Education found that many middle-class parents choose schools for their academic record, while many poor parents pick the school nearest to their home, regardless of the quality of education on offer. The reasons why the middle class are able to take more advantage of the education system than the working class are considered later in this chapter, but include the fact that their own higher levels of income and education means they are better placed than many working-class parents to:

- shop around and find the best schools
- understand and compare schools in the league tables
- know more about how to assess school Ofsted inspection reports and what constitutes a good school
- afford more easily to move into the priority areas of the best schools
- afford higher transport costs, giving their children a wider choice of schools
- make more effective use of appeals procedures should they be refused a place at their chosen school.

This means that those who have already benefited from education the most will gain more, while those who are more disadvantaged may become further disadvantaged.

Activity

To understand the difficulties involved in choosing a school, and why the more educated middle-class are most successful at it, examine the advice given on the following government website on how to choose a school. Draw up a list of what steps parents are expected to take, and how difficult you think this might be.
www.direct.gov.uk/en/Parents/Schoolslearninganddevelopment/ChoosingASchool/index.htm

Student needs at risk and social divisions increased

The needs of students have been replaced by the need of the school or college to achieve a good position in the league tables of results. Brighter students, or those, for example, on the C/D grade borderline at GCSE, are likely to get more resources spent on them, disadvantaging weaker students who are less likely to deliver the prestige results, such as grades A*–C at GCSE and AS/A-level, necessary to gain or maintain for parents the image of a good school or college. Evidence suggests hundreds of teenagers who achieve less than a B grade in their AS-level exams are forced out of school halfway through their A-level courses because of fears their grades would lower the school's league table ranking. Weaker students, who are more likely to come from working-class backgrounds (for reasons discussed later in this chapter), may find their needs are neglected because the risk of them getting poorer results might undermine the league table position of the school or college. As a result, social divisions between the middle class and the working class are widened.

Specialist schools and selection by ability

As seen earlier, and later in this chapter, selection by ability can lead to a lowering of the self-esteem of those not selected, and may lead to lower expectations by teachers, and the self-fulfilling prophecy. Specialist schools, and some of the other schools mentioned later in the school diversity section, are often seen as being better schools, and therefore given higher status by parents and pupils than other schools, and are given extra resources. As pupils compete for places, specialist schools may increasingly select their pupils by aptitude/ability (up to 10 per cent of their intake). This will create unfair competition between schools, and increase inequality between them. Middle-class parents are likely to gain most from this, and the working-class to lose out, adding further to divisions between social classes.

The unfairness of league tables

League tables of test and exam results don't really reveal how well a school or college is doing. This is because, as later parts of this chapter show, the social class and ethnic backgrounds and gender of students can affect how well they perform in education. Schools and colleges in more deprived working-class areas may produce results which are not as good as those in middle-class areas, yet their students may have actually made much more progress than middle-class students compared to what they started school with. For example, a sixth form or college where students enter with four GCSEs of grade C cannot normally be expected to get results at AS- and A-level as good as one where students enter with seven GCSEs of grades A*, A and B. The latter sixth form or college might get better results and a higher league table position than the first one, but the scale of achievement of the students in the first one might in reality have been greater.

League tables therefore do not show how much value has been added by the educational institution (the 'value-added' approach). They may conceal underperforming schools or colleges in advantaged middle-class areas, where results should be much better given their social class intake, and successful schools and colleges in more deprived working-class areas.

Difficulties in improving schools and colleges

Competition between schools and colleges for students, and therefore for money, the emphasis on exam results, and the need to present a good image to parents in the free market may make it harder for poorer schools and colleges to improve, as students go elsewhere. Such schools and colleges may therefore lack the resources to improve their performance – the opposite of what was intended by the reforms.

'Dumbing down'

As school students, and particularly post-16 further education and sixth-form students, now have a choice of institutions, this may lead to a 'dumbing down' of teaching and subject content. The need for schools and colleges to retain students – and the money they bring with them – means that, if students have too much work to do or find the work difficult, they may go to another course or educational institution where things seem easier and less demanding. Retaining (keeping) students may mean not pushing students too hard for fear of losing them.

Problems with the National Curriculum and testing

The National Curriculum in England (and possibly Welsh, Scottish and Northern Ireland equivalents) has been criticized for not giving teachers enough opportunity to respond to the needs of their pupils, as teachers are told what they have to teach and when they have to teach it. Testing (the SATs) has been criticized for putting too much pressure on young children, and possibly giving them a sense of failure early in their schooling. More generally, teaching may become too focused on the content of the tests as a way to get the good test results needed for a high position in the league tables, at the expense of the wider school curriculum.

Activity

1 Identify and explain *three* educational policies that have attempted to improve standards in education in about the last twenty years.
2 Identify and explain *two* reasons why league tables of test and exam results may not give a fair impression of how effective a school or college is.
3 Explain what is meant by the self-fulfilling prophecy.

4 Explain *two* reasons why middle-class parents might be more effective in achieving better schooling for their children than those from working-class backgrounds.

5 Suggest *two* reasons why selection by ability in education may have harmful effects on some children.

SCHOOL DIVERSITY

Part of the process of promoting greater parental choice in schooling has meant that there is now a greater diversity (or range of different types) of state-funded schools than ever before. This chapter has already referred to grammar schools, general comprehensive schools, and specialist schools (a form of comprehensive). This section will outline some of the other state-funded types of school, and some of the debates surrounding them. Private (independent) schools are discussed at the end of this chapter, and these do provide a further choice for those parents who are sufficiently well off to afford the high fees required to enjoy the privileges gained by private education.

The government is promoting diversity in schools by encouraging 'partners' like private businesses, universities and colleges, community groups and educational charities to become more involved in running schools, and to help to raise standards by using their expert knowledge. The schools mentioned below often do not exist in a pure form, but may involve elements of different types. For example, a trust school may also be a faith school and a specialist school.

Trust schools

These are state-funded schools which receive extra support from a charitable trust made up of the partners referred to above, working together for the benefit of the school. They remain under local authority (council) control.

Academies and free schools

These are independently run schools, found only in England, that are funded by central government and manage their own affairs, rather than being funded and controlled by local authorities (local councils). Although they involve no fees and are part of the state system of education, they operate like independent schools in the state system.

Academies

Academies were originally set up in 2000 in England as new schools to replace those which were seen to be giving poor education to their students, particularly in the most deprived areas. It was thought that more independence, more control by headteachers, and links with sponsors like private businesses could bring more power and new expertise (like that in business) to improve educational standards. Parents often get the impression through publicity and new buildings and equipment that academies are the best schools in an area. This means there often aren't enough places in academies for all those who want them.

In 2010, the focus of academies changed from improving education in deprived areas to giving more independence to schools in the most advantaged areas. While all state schools in England were encouraged to consider opting out of council control to become independent academies, those which were seen as providing the highest educational standards and were rated as 'outstanding' by Ofsted school inspectors were given top priority. Such schools are most likely to be found in advantaged areas where well-off middle-class parents live. Academies are the fastest-growing type of school.

Free schools

Plans for free schools were first announced in 2010, and at the time of writing they appeared similar to academies, but were to be established and controlled by local groups, such as by parents or teachers concerned about poor educational standards. Early plans suggested they would only be set up when parents demanded them, and with the support of groups of parents. They might be smaller schools than academies and other state schools, with smaller budgets, fewer facilities and established in more modest buildings like converted warehouses and similar commercial and residential property, to meet the demands of small local communities. Free schools seemed to be primarily aimed at meeting the wishes of parents and raising educational standards in the poorest, most disadvantaged areas.

Academies (and possibly, in future, free schools) have been very controversial because:

- they only have to follow, in England, minimum parts of the National Curriculum, so all pupils will not necessarily be getting a similar standard of education.
- their success record in disadvantaged areas before 2010 was not very good, and some did not improve education standards compared to the schools they replaced.
- they control their own admissions policies, and those that have improved standards have often done so by being more selective in the students they choose. They select students who are the best behaved and likely to do well – students more likely to be from middle-class homes and those without special educational needs – and are more likely to exclude 'difficult' pupils than other schools. Some academies are therefore denying educational help to those students who most need it, and

other schools in the area have an unfair proportion of lower-ability, more disruptive and special educational needs students who have been rejected by the academies.

- they don't offer parents more choice of schools for their children: academies are selecting parents and children, rather than parents selecting schools.
- they weaken a planned state system of schooling, breaking it up into independent, competing schools, with the most favoured schools now likely to be those in the most advantaged middle-class areas.
- free schools, which are potentially smaller schools with smaller budgets in more modest buildings, may lack the range of facilities, subject choices and experiences children in most other schools have, disadvantaging rather than helping those in the poorest areas.
- interested and motivated groups of parents setting up free schools may hold extremist beliefs of one form or another, creating a curriculum and a school ethos (or character) that denies children exposure to the wide range of opinions, experiences and cultural lifestyles available in most schools.

Many of the points above suggest the development of academies and free schools will widen existing inequalities in education (discussed later in this chapter), with the most advantaged in society having even more access to the best schools than they do already, and the most disadvantaged losing out even more.

Faith schools

Faith schools are schools with a religious character. Around one-third of state schools are faith schools, and around one-quarter of pupils attend them. Faith schools make up 40 per cent of independent schools (fee-paying private schools). They have existed a very long time in the UK. Well before state education began in 1870, there were a range of Church of England, Catholic, Methodist, Jewish and Quaker schools. Although faith schools have been overwhelmingly Christian, in recent years there has been a drive to create more to meet the faith needs of minority ethnic groups, including Muslim, Hindu and Sikh schools.

Strengths of faith schools

- They enable parents to choose an education for their children in accordance with their religious beliefs.
- They often have a character and ethos (attitudes and beliefs) which many parents, even if they are not religious, think will be good for their children's moral and social development.

Faith schools are those with a religious character. Although faith schools have been overwhelmingly Christian, in recent years there has been a drive to create more to meet the faith needs of minority ethnic groups, including Muslim and Sikh schools

Problems of faith schools

- *They discriminate on religious and ethnic grounds.* If the school has too many applications, they are allowed to give priority to children on the basis of religious belief and factors like attendance at church/mosque/temple/synagogue, baptism, knowledge of holy texts or religious lifestyle aspects, like eating Halal meat at home.
- *They could damage a multicultural society and social cohesion,* as children are being divided and educated on the basis of what separates them from other children, and they won't grow up with the same understanding of a variety of faiths as they might in a non-faith school. This could breed intolerance, divide communities and cause religious hatred.
- *They encourage parents to lie about their faith* or pretend to be religious for a while, just to get into their chosen school and avoid what they regard as the worst schools.
- *Religious institutions and religious leaders are choosing parents,* not parents choosing schools. This gives them too much power in a society where the vast majority of the population never attend any religious ceremonies nor claim to hold religious beliefs.

EDUCATION OTHERWISE – HOME SCHOOLING

While education is compulsory in the UK until age 16 (age 17 from 2013), school is not, and some parents decide to educate their children otherwise – at home. There are often a variety of reasons for this. For example, parents may feel that the local schools aren't any good and they can do a better job themselves, or that their children have been bullied, have special needs, found it hard to fit in, suffer anxiety, or haven't made progress at school.

Some see home schooling as disadvantageous for children, as they miss out on the social aspects of schooling, like making new friends and mixing with others, and the resources, specialist teachers and range of subjects available in schools.

You can read more about home schooling at www.education-otherwise.org.

Special schools

Special schools cater for those who have special educational needs (SEN), ranging from mild to severe learning difficulties, which may sometimes be combined with physical disabilities. They have specialized facilities (like soft play areas, low-level benches, wheelchair access and sensory rooms), specially trained teachers and higher levels of staffing than mainstream schools, and very small groups or one-to-one teaching to cater for the often complex learning difficulties of pupils.

More and more children with special needs are now being taught in mainstream schools. This has the advantage of enabling students with SEN to grow up alongside other children without SEN, rather than them becoming marked out as different from an early age. However, some students require the specialized education, specially trained and experienced teachers, one-to-one support and resources that only special schools can provide. There is also a potential risk of bullying and ridiculing in mainstream schools that is rarely found in special schools. One way around this has been for children to spend time in both types of school, for example attending mainstream schools only for some subjects and activities.

Activity

1 Suggest two arguments for and two against the view that children with special educational needs are best taught in mainstream schools.
2 Suggest two arguments for and two against educating children at home rather than at school.
3 Surveys suggest that a majority of the population are opposed to the state funding any faith schools. Many are particularly concerned about the growth of separate faith schools for minority ethnic groups as a threat to social cohesion. Suggest some arguments and evidence for and against faith schools (if you're in a group, you could divide into two groups for and against, and debate the issue).

VOCATIONAL EDUCATION

The emphasis on making education meet the needs of industry, and preparing young people for work, is known as vocational education. A key feature of this has been improving the quality of the basic skills of the workforce, with a particular focus on the 14–18 age group. The aim has been to develop the talents of young people to improve the skills of the labour force so Britain maintains a successful position in the world economy, and to produce a more flexible labour force, fitting education more to the needs of employers. Measures to achieve this have included:

- work experience programmes for pupils in school years 10 and 11 to ease the transition from school to work, and help/encourage them to get jobs successfully and carry them out well, with a better understanding of work and the economy
- more educational courses, and government training schemes for those leaving school, which are more closely related to the world of work, and concerned more with learning work-related skills. For example,

Do you think work experience programmes at school are useful? Do you think vocational courses are more or less valuable to students compared to doing more academic courses like traditional GCSEs and AS- and A-levels?

work-based NVQs (National Vocational Qualifications) and school/college-based GNVQs (General National Vocational Qualifications) were developed to provide nationally approved and recognized qualifications for vocational courses. Vocational GCSEs and Applied GCEs (vocational A-levels) were intended as vocational alternatives to academic GCSEs and A-levels

- an expansion of post-16 education and training
- a stronger emphasis on key skills in the use and application of number, and in communication and information technology. These are the skills that most employers find that school leavers lack.

All these changes were designed to produce a more flexible labour force, fitting education to the needs of employers.

Criticisms

Work experience is often seen by school students as boring and repetitive, involving little development of their skills and little to do with their future ambitions.

Post-school training schemes are often similarly criticized for providing little development of skills, for being used as a source of cheap labour by employers, and for not leading to 'proper' jobs at the end of the training.

Vocational education and qualifications are often seen as having lower status than more traditional academic subjects and courses. Vocational qualifications are, in general, less likely to lead to university entry, and are more likely to lead to lower-status, lower-paid jobs as adults.

Activity

1 Should schools be concerned mainly with meeting the needs of business and industry, and fitting people into the job market? Or should they be concerned with the development of individuals, allowing them to pursue and develop their interests? Suggest two advantages and two disadvantages of each view.

2 Think about your school work experience programmes. Were/are they very useful to you? Give reasons for your answer.

3 Do you think AS- and A-levels have the same status as vocational qualifications, such as NVQs, GNVQs and Applied GCEs? Explain your answer.

EQUALITY OF EDUCATIONAL OPPORTUNITY AND HELPING THE MOST DISADVANTAGED GROUPS

The Labour government of 1997–2010 emphasized the need to create equality of educational opportunity for all, particularly focusing on the most deprived and most disadvantaged areas where educational results were poor. This was carried out by a number of measures referred to earlier to raise standards, plus schemes such as Sure Start to ensure children in disadvantaged areas had the best start in life, and more money and better-paid teachers were provided for schools in the poorest areas through schemes such as Excellence in Cities and Education Action Zones.

Despite the period of frenzied change in education over the last thirty years or so, aimed at improving standards, giving parents more choice and helping the disadvantaged, equality of educational opportunity has not been established, and there remain very wide differences between the achievements of pupils of similar ability who come from different social class and ethnic backgrounds or are of different genders. It is to this continuing inequality that we now turn.

INEQUALITY IN EDUCATION

Underachievement is the failure of people to fulfil their full potential – they do not do as well in education (or other areas) as their talents and abilities suggest they should.

The development of the education system in Britain aimed to secure equality of educational opportunity for all children, regardless of their social class, ethnic background, or sex. However, despite these efforts, sociological evidence has made it clear that not all children of the same ability achieve the same success in education, and inequalities in educational opportunity remain. The failure of pupils to do as well in education as they should, given their ability, is called **underachievement**.

The evidence suggests that social class origins (the social class of a child's parents), ethnicity and gender continue to have an influence on how well people do in education, even when they are of the same ability, and these factors appear to be more important than innate (inborn) ability in affecting the level of educational achievement or success. This section will look at the patterns of inequality remaining in education, and some of the explanations for them.

Social class and underachievement

The facts

Social class is one of the key factors that determine whether a child does well or badly at school. There are major differences between the levels of achievement of the working class and the middle class and, in general, the higher the social class of the parents, the more successful a child will be in education. Social class inequality in education begins even before children start in primary school and the gap between the classes becomes wider as children move through the education system, with the higher levels of the system dominated by middle-class students.

Lower-working-class children, compared to middle-class children of the same ability:

- are already well behind in their educational development *even before they get to school*
- are more likely to start school unable to read
- do less well in National Curriculum SATs (Standard Assessment Tests)

Inequality in education begins even before children start primary school, with those from disadvantaged backgrounds up to a year behind more privileged youngsters educationally by the age of 3

- are less likely to get places in the best state schools
- are more likely to be placed in lower streams
- generally get poorer exam results. For example, around three-quarters of young people from upper-middle-class backgrounds get five or more GCSEs A*–C, compared to less than a third from lower-working-class backgrounds
- are more likely to leave school at the minimum leaving age of 16 (rising to age 17 from 2013), many of them with few or no qualifications of any kind. Only about half of young people from unskilled manual families stay on in post-16 full-time education, compared to about nine in every ten from managerial and professional families
- are more likely to undertake vocational or training courses if they stay in education after age 16/17, rather than the more academic AS- and A-level courses which are more likely to be taken by middle-class students and which are more likely to lead to university education
- are less likely to go into higher education. Young people from unskilled lower-working-class families make up only around 5 per cent of those accepted into higher education.

Explaining working-class underachievement

There is a range of factors that explain social class differences in educational achievement, which can be grouped into three main categories:

- material explanations, which put the emphasis on social and economic conditions
- cultural explanations, which focus on values, attitudes and lifestyles
- factors within the school itself.

Material explanations Although schooling is free, material factors like poverty and low wages, diet, health and housing can all have important direct effects on how well individuals do at school, and after leaving school.

POVERTY AND HOME CIRCUMSTANCES

- Poor housing conditions such as overcrowding and insufficient space and quiet can make study at home difficult.
- Higher levels of sickness in poorer homes may mean more absence from school and falling behind with lessons.
- Low income or unemployment may mean that educational books and toys are not bought, and computers are not available in the home. This may affect a child's educational progress before or during her or his time at school. There may also be a lack of money for out-of-school trips, sports equipment, calculators and other hidden costs of free state education (see box).

THE HIDDEN COSTS OF 'FREE' STATE SCHOOLING

The hidden costs of sending a child to a state school now amount to nearly £700 a year for a primary school child, and £1200 for a secondary school child. These are the costs parents are expected to pay for things like school uniform, PE kit, school trips, class materials, stationery, swimming lessons, school lunches, travel, photographs, charity contributions and other school activities. Even when these costs are voluntary, some schools still pressure parents to pay up, even if they have difficulty in affording them.

Source: *The Cost of Schooling* (British Market Research Bureau, for the Department of Children, Schools and Families, 2009)

- It may be financially difficult for parents on a low income to support students in education after school leaving age, no matter how bright their prospects might be. This is particularly the case in further education, where the Education Maintenance Allowance (EMA) is low, and there may be travel costs involved. In higher education, student grants have been replaced by student loans, and tuition fees are payable, and the debts arising from student loans are likely to be a source of anxiety to those from poorer backgrounds, deterring them from going to university.

- Young people from poorer families are more likely to have part-time jobs, such as paper rounds, babysitting or shop work. This becomes more pronounced after the age of 16, when students may be combining part- or full-time work with school or college work. This may create a conflict between the competing demands of study and paid work.

The effects of these material factors tend to be cumulative, in the sense that one aspect of social deprivation can lead to others. For example, poverty

Explain in your own words, with examples, how this cartoon shows that the effects of social deprivation on educational achievement are cumulative

Figure 4.3 Social class and educational underachievement

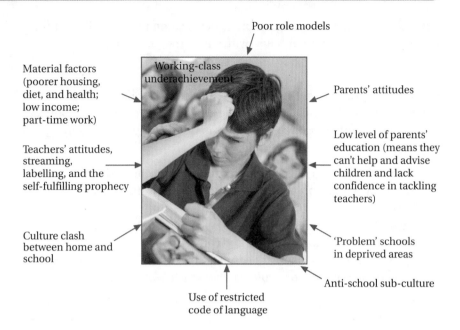

Poor role models

Working-class underachievement

Material factors (poorer housing, diet, and health; low income; part-time work)

Parents' attitudes

Low level of parents' education (means they can't help and advise children and lack confidence in tackling teachers)

Teachers' attitudes, streaming, labelling, and the self-fulfilling prophecy

Culture clash between home and school

'Problem' schools in deprived areas

Anti-school sub-culture

Use of restricted code of language

may mean overcrowding at home *and* ill-health *and* having to find part-time work, making all the problems worse.

THE CATCHMENT AREA AND ROLE MODELS

Catchment areas (or priority areas) are the areas from which primary and secondary schools draw their pupils. In deprived areas, where there may be a range of social problems such as high unemployment, poor housing, poverty, juvenile delinquency, crime and drug abuse, there are often poor role models for young people to imitate. The accumulated effects of the environment on children's behaviour mean schools in such areas are more likely to have discipline problems and hence a higher turnover of teachers. This may mean that children from the most disadvantaged backgrounds have the worst schools. In contrast, schools in middle-class neighbourhoods will probably have stronger and more conformist role models for young people, fewer discipline problems, and therefore have a better learning environment. Additionally, schools in middle-class areas will have more active and wealthy parent–teacher associations able to provide extra resources for the school. Parents in poorer areas may find it difficult to make financial contributions to school funds, and therefore the schools in such areas may lack the extras found in schools in wealthier, middle-class areas.

Cultural explanations   Cultural explanations suggest that the values, attitudes, language and other aspects of the life of working-class groups act as a barrier to success in education. The blame for underachievement in education is placed on young people's socialization in the family and community, and on the cultural values with which they are raised.

PARENTS' ATTITUDES TO EDUCATION

Middle-class parents on the whole seem to place a higher value on their children's education and take more interest in their progress at school than working-class parents. Evidence suggests middle-class parents, compared to working-class parents, on the whole:

- take more interest in their children's progress at school, shown by them visiting the school more frequently to discuss how their children are getting on
- become more interested and encouraging as their children grow older, when exam options are selected and career choices loom
- are more likely to want their children to stay at school beyond the minimum leaving age and to encourage them to do so.

These differences between working-class and middle-class parents, however, do not necessarily indicate that working-class parents have a poor attitude to education, or that they don't care about their children's progress. Working-class parents are more likely to work longer hours, doing shiftwork and overtime, and are less likely than the middle class to get paid for time off work. This may mean it is more difficult for working-class parents to visit schools, rather than that they don't care about their children's progress. Middle-class parents also, of course, can more easily afford to continue to support their children in education after the age of 16/17. The interest shown by middle-class parents may be due to the importance of educational qualifications in obtaining their own middle-class occupations. By contrast, working-class parents may see education as of less importance because they may have found their own education had little relevance to their working-class jobs. This may lead to poor motivation of some working-class children in school and therefore lower levels of achievement, regardless of ability. Parental attitudes can also affect the child's learning by the lower value placed on books or educational toys in many lower-working-class homes.

PARENTS' LEVEL OF EDUCATION

Because they are generally themselves better educated, middle-class parents tend to understand the school system better than working-class parents. Lower-working-class parents may feel less confident in dealing with teachers at parents' evenings, and in dealing with subject options and exam choices. Middle-class parents know more about schools, the examination system and careers and so are more able to advise and counsel their children on getting onto the most appropriate subjects and courses. They can hold their own

In what ways might parents influence success or failure in their children's education?

more in disagreements with teachers (who are also middle-class) about the treatment and education of their child. They know what games and books to buy to stimulate their children's educational development both before and during schooling (and have the money to buy them) and can help their children with school work generally. As a consequence, even before they get to school, middle-class children may have learned more as a result of their socialization in the family. These advantages of a middle-class home may be reinforced throughout a child's career at school. By contrast, these same reasons for middle-class success may also explain why many of the poorest working-class children are well behind their middle-class peers even before they start school.

LANGUAGE USE: THE RESTRICTED AND ELABORATED CODES

Success at school depends very heavily on language – for reading, writing, speaking and understanding. Bernstein argues that there is a relationship between language use and social class, and that the language used by the middle class is a better instrument for success at school than the language used by the working class. His view is that the language used by the lower working class has a restricted code while the language used by the middle class has an elaborated code.

- The **restricted code** of language is used by both middle-class and working-class people, but is more characteristic of working-class people. It is the sort of language which is used between friends or family members – informal, simple, everyday language (such as slang), with limited explanation, sometimes ungrammatical and limited in vocabulary. This form of language is quite adequate for everyday use with friends because they know what the speaker is referring to – the context is understood by both speakers and so detailed explanation is not required. Bernstein argues that lower-working-class people are mainly limited to this form of language use.

- The **elaborated code** of language is used mainly by middle-class people. It is the language of strangers and individuals in some formal context, where explanation and detail are required – like an interview for a job, writing a business letter, writing an essay or examination answer, or in a school lesson or textbook. It has a much wider vocabulary than the restricted code.

Bernstein argues that the language used in schools is the elaborated code of the middle class, and that it is the middle-class child's ability to use the elaborated code that gives her or him an advantage at school over working-class children. The elaborated code of the middle class is more suited to the demands of school work, since understanding textbooks and writing essays and answers to examination questions require the detail and explanation which is found mainly in the formal language of the elaborated code. Middle-class children who are used to using the elaborated code at home will therefore find school work much easier and learn more in school than those working-class children whose language is limited only to the restricted code. In addition, the teacher may mistake the working-class child's restricted use of language for lack of ability, and therefore expect less from the child. The self-fulfilling prophecy (discussed later in this chapter) may then come into effect.

THE CULTURE CLASH

Schools are mainly middle-class institutions, and they stress the value of many features of the middle-class way of life, such as the importance of hard work and study, making sacrifices now for future rewards, the right form of dress, behaviour, manners and language use, good books, good TV programmes, quality newspapers, and so on. This means that middle-class children may find that school greets them almost as an extension of their

The **restricted code** is the informal, simple, everyday language, sometimes ungrammatical and with limited explanations and vocabulary, which is used between friends or family members.

The **elaborated code** is the sort of formal language used by strangers and individuals in some formal contexts where explanation and detail are required, and uses a much wider vocabulary than the restricted code.

Activity

1 With reference to the cartoon above, explain the difference between the elaborated and restricted codes of language use.
2 Explain *two* ways that having access to the elaborated code might provide advantages in education.

home life, and they may start school already familiar with and tuned in to the atmosphere of the school – such as the subjects that will be explored there, seeking good marks, doing homework, good behaviour, a cooperative attitude to teachers, and other features of middle-class culture. Consequently, they may appear to the teacher as fairly intelligent and sophisticated.

For the working-class child, the atmosphere and values of the school may be quite unfamiliar and different from those of his or her home. This is likely to result in a culture clash between her or his home and social class background and the middle-class culture of the school. This culture clash may partly explain working-class underachievement.

Factors inside the school

The material and cultural explanations discussed so far are mainly concerned with factors outside the school that influence children's education. However, there is also a range of factors in the school itself that can affect how well children perform in education. See, for example, Rutter et al.'s work – Item A in the box below.

ITEM A
DO SCHOOLS MAKE A DIFFERENCE?

Rutter et al., in their book *Fifteen Thousand Hours: Secondary Schools and their Effects on Children*, reported research they had carried out in twelve schools. This study attempted to show, in the face of much previous research suggesting the opposite, that good schools can make a difference to the life chances of all pupils. Rutter et al. suggest that it is features of the school's organization which make this difference. These features are summarized below.

- Teachers are well prepared for lessons.
- Teachers have high expectations of pupils' academic performance, and set and mark classwork and homework regularly.
- Teachers set examples of behaviour – for example, they are on time and they use only officially approved forms of discipline.
- Teachers place more emphasis on praise and reward than on blame and punishment.
- Teachers treat pupils as responsible people, for example by giving them positions of responsibility looking after school books and property.
- Teachers show an interest in the pupils and encourage them to do well.
- There is an atmosphere or ethos in the school which reflects the above points, with all teachers sharing a commitment to the aims and values of the school.
- There is a mixture of abilities in the school, as the presence of high-ability pupils benefits the academic performance and behaviour of pupils of all abilities.

ITEM B
THE BRUTAL TRUTH

. . . but what do we mean by a good school? Examination results are the only criteria we accept, and politicians imply these have something to do with quality of teaching, sound leadership, strong discipline, clarity of aims and so on. And these can all make a difference. The brutal truth, however, is that the surest way to turn a bad school into a good one is to change the pupils who attend it . . . Parents, particularly middle-class parents, look at exam results and choose [schools] accordingly. Some don't bother with the results: they see well-scrubbed, nicely dressed and well-behaved pupils, and say that's the one for their child. They are right: home background, as you'd expect when you think how much more time children spend at home than at school, is another guide to attainment . . . A school can change the head, sack teachers, crack down on truancy and bad behaviour . . . these things may make the school happier, more peaceful, more businesslike. They may even improve exam results. They will make no long-term difference at all unless the intake changes . . . Rebranding the school may make a difference . . . a bright new wrapper always helps, for schools as well as chocolate bars, . . . but as long as schools have differing pupil intakes, some will be deemed 'good' and some 'bad'.

Source: adapted from Peter Wilby, 'Parents' admissions trauma is down to gross inequality outside school gates', *Guardian*, 5 March 2009

Teachers' attitudes, streaming and setting, labelling and the self-fulfilling prophecy Evidence suggests that teachers' judgements of pupils' ability are influenced by factors other than ability alone. For example, teachers seem to take into account things like standards of behaviour, dress, speech and the types of home children come from, including the social class background of

Activity

Refer to item A opposite, 'Do schools make a difference?'

1 Explain how you think each of the features of a 'good' school which Rutter et al. describe might help pupils of all backgrounds and abilities to make more progress.

2 Are there any other features that you would expect to find in a good school?

3 List at least three characteristics, based on your own opinions, of a good teacher. How important do you think the role of the teacher is in the educational progress of pupils, compared to the home, the neighbourhood, and the pressures of friends?

Refer to item B opposite, 'The brutal truth'

4 Describe in your own words what the 'brutal truth' in item B is.

5 How do you think Peter Wilby (item B) might respond to Rutter et al.'s view that good schools can make a difference to the life chances of all pupils?

6 Suggest what Wilby seems to think are the main factors that affect whether or not a school is judged good or bad?

7 What does item B suggest might be the main factor influencing educational achievement?

pupils. Teachers are middle-class, and children from middle-class homes who share the same standards and values as the teacher are often likely to be seen by teachers as brighter and more cooperative than those from working-class homes.

Streaming and setting are systems used in schools to separate pupils into different groups according to their assumed ability. Even if children are really of equal ability, teachers are more likely to think working-class children are less intelligent because of the assumptions they hold about their home backgrounds. This may explain why working-class children tend to be found more in the lower streams of streamed comprehensive schools. Streaming therefore seems to divide pupils along social class lines, and reflects the class divisions in society, with many children from lower-working-class homes placed in lower streams. This is illustrated in figure 4.4.

Figure 4.4 Social class divisions and streaming

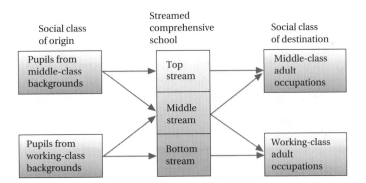

In what ways might the attitudes and behaviour of teachers affect a student's progress?

Streaming has been shown to be unfair and harmful to the self-esteem and educational performance of bottom-stream pupils, as teachers expect less from children in lower streams and give them less encouragement than those in higher streams.

Much research has suggested that predicting whether a child will be a success or failure through testing, teachers' judgements and streaming or setting, and **labelling** him or her as bright or slow, can actually make that child a success or failure. Such predictions and labelling can affect an individual's view of himself or herself – their self-esteem – and the individual may act in accordance with the prediction made and the label attached. This process of predicting that something will happen, and of pupils acting in the way teachers expect them to act in accordance with the label they have been given, is known as the self-fulfilling prophecy. Figure 4.5 illustrates this process.

Once placed in bottom streams, pupils may become victims of the self-fulfilling prophecy – those pupils labelled as 'bottom-stream material' may take on the characteristics expected of them by teachers. Because more working-class children tend to be put into bottom streams by teachers, and middle-class children continue to dominate the higher streams, streamed comprehensive schools may actually create working-class underachievement in education, adding to the material and cultural difficulties working-class children already face in education.

> **Labelling** is defining a person or group in a certain way – as a particular type of person.

Figure 4.5 The self-fulfilling prophecy: two examples

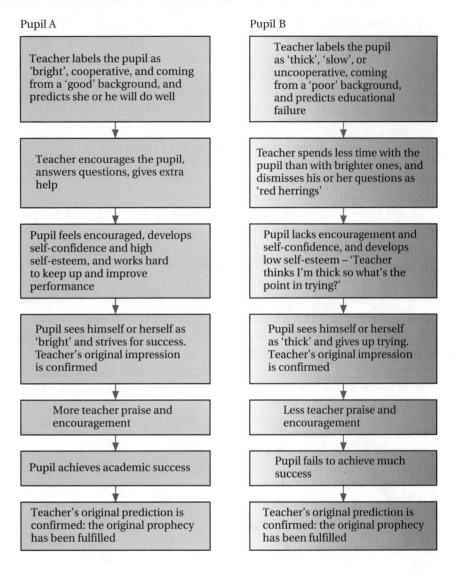

Pupil A

Teacher labels the pupil as 'bright', cooperative, and coming from a 'good' background, and predicts she or he will do well

Teacher encourages the pupil, answers questions, gives extra help

Pupil feels encouraged, develops self-confidence and high self-esteem, and works hard to keep up and improve performance

Pupil sees himself or herself as 'bright' and strives for success. Teacher's original impression is confirmed

More teacher praise and encouragement

Pupil achieves academic success

Teacher's original prediction is confirmed: the original prophecy has been fulfilled

Pupil B

Teacher labels the pupil as 'thick', 'slow', or uncooperative, coming from a 'poor' background, and predicts educational failure

Teacher spends less time with the pupil than with brighter ones, and dismisses his or her questions as 'red herrings'

Pupil lacks encouragement and self-confidence, and develops low self-esteem – 'Teacher thinks I'm thick so what's the point in trying?'

Pupil sees himself or herself as 'thick' and gives up trying. Teacher's original impression is confirmed

Less teacher praise and encouragement

Pupil fails to achieve much success

Teacher's original prediction is confirmed: the original prophecy has been fulfilled

Activity

1 In a streamed school, the best and most qualified teachers are often kept for the upper-stream classes. Why do you think this is the case? How might it affect the progress of those facing the greatest difficulties in the lower streams?

2 List all the reasons you can think of to explain why pupils from lower-working-class homes are more likely to be placed in lower streams than those from middle-class homes.

The anti-school sub-culture   Most schools generally place a high value on things such as hard work, good behaviour and exam success. One of the effects of streaming and labelling is to divide pupils into those in the top streams who more or less conform to these aims and therefore achieve high status, and those in the bottom streams who are labelled as failures by the school and are therefore deprived of status. In response to this, bottom-stream pupils often rebel against the school and develop a **sub-culture**. This consists of an alternative set of values, attitudes and behaviour in opposition to the aims of the school. This is called an **anti-school (or counter-school) sub-culture**, and provides a means for bottom-stream pupils to achieve some success and status in their peer group.

Among such pupils, truancy, playing up teachers, messing about, breaking the school rules, and generally disrupting the smooth running of the school become a way of getting back at the system and resisting a schooling which has labelled them as 'failures' and denied them status.

Because of all the factors discussed above causing the underachievement of working-class pupils in schools, bottom-stream pupils are very often working-class and such pupils will often be found in this anti-school sub-culture. They then themselves reject the school which has already rejected them by labelling them as failures and 'thick'. This almost guarantees their failure in education, as they look forward to leaving school at the earliest possible opportunity, often before taking any GCSEs or other formal qualifications.

> A **sub-culture** is a smaller culture shared by a group of people within the main culture of a sociiety, in some ways different from the main culture, but with many aspects in common.
> An **anti-school (or counter-school) sub-culture** is a set of values, attitudes, and behaviour in opposition to the main aims of a school.

The cartoon shows some forms that the anti-school (or counter-school) sub-culture might take. Do you have evidence from your own schooling of the anti-school sub-culture?

The 'double test' for working-class children

Taken together, the factors in the home, social class background and the school help to explain why working-class students do less well at school than middle-class students of the same ability. Schools test all pupils when doing subjects like mathematics, English or science. However, for the working-class student there is a double test. At the same time as coping with the academic difficulties of school work which all students face, working-class youngsters must also cope with a wide range of other disadvantages and difficulties.

These problems on top of the demands of academic work explain working-class underachievement in schools. These disadvantages start even before primary school entry and become more and more emphasized as children grow older, as they fall further and further behind and become more disillusioned with school. In this context, it is perhaps not surprising that a large majority of those who leave school at the minimum leaving age of 16 (rising to age 17 in 2013) every year, with few or no qualifications, come from lower-working-class backgrounds.

Activity

1   Put the following explanations for working-class underachievement in what you think is their order of importance: home circumstances; parents' attitudes to education; parents' level of education; the catchment area; language use; the culture clash; teachers' attitudes, streaming and setting, labelling and the self-fulfilling prophecy; the anti-school sub-culture.
2   In the light of your list, suggest ways that schools and teachers might improve the performance of pupils who face social class disadvantages in education.
3   Do you think schools can make up for problems that begin outside school, such as in the home and the neighbourhood? Give reasons for your answer.

Compensatory education is extra educational help for those coming from disadvantaged groups to help them overcome the obstacles they face in the education system and the wider society.
Positive discrimination involves giving disadvantaged groups more favourable treatment than others to make up for the disadvantages they face.

Compensatory education

In order for all young people to have an equal chance in the education system, those coming from deprived backgrounds need extra help and resources to enable them to compete on equal terms with other children, and help them overcome the disadvantages in education arising from their deprived social class backgrounds. This idea of extra help is known as **compensatory education**, and involves **positive discrimination** as an attempt to overcome working-class underachievement.

Schools in disadvantaged areas, where home and social class background are seen as obstacles to success in education, are singled out for extra favourable treatment, such as more, and better-paid, teachers and more money to spend on buildings and equipment, to help the most disadvantaged succeed in education.

The idea of positive discrimination is based on the idea of equality of educational opportunity. In this view, children from disadvantaged backgrounds and poor homes can only get an opportunity in education equal to those who come from non-disadvantaged backgrounds if they get unequal and more generous treatment to compensate (hence the term *compensatory education*).

Education Action Zones and Excellence in Cities Action Zones

In Britain, attempts at compensatory education were made with the setting-up in the late 1990s of Education Action Zones in socially disadvantaged areas, which later became Excellence in Cities Action Zones. Schools in these areas were given extra money to help them improve the educational performance of the most disadvantaged young people. However, there is little evidence that these managed to improve much on student achievements, and schools have, so far, not been able to overcome or compensate for the disadvantages arising from home and social class background.

Activity

1 Suggest *three* material factors in pupils' home and family backgrounds that may affect how successful they are in education. Be sure to explain how the factors you identify affect their education.
2 Explain, with examples, what is meant by a 'culture clash' between the home and the school.
3 Suggest *three* cultural factors that may affect pupils' educational achievements.
4 Identify *two* ways in which a school's catchment area might influence the education of pupils from the area.
5 Identify and explain *three* factors inside schools which may explain the underachievement of pupils from disadvantaged backgrounds.
6 Explain what is meant by 'labelling' and how it might influence the educational achievements of pupils.
7 In the light of your answers to questions 1–4, suggest *four* policies you might adopt to overcome the obstacles to success in education facing the most disadvantaged.

Ethnicity and underachievement

The facts

Many children from ethnic minority backgrounds tend to do as well as and often better than many white children. For example, Indian Asians – particularly girls – are more likely to get better GCSE and A-level results than white students, to stay in education post-16/17, and to enter university. However, those of Pakistani and Bangladeshi origin, and particularly males from African-Caribbean homes, tend to do less well than they should given their ability. There is some evidence that African-Caribbean males may actually be falling farther behind, and they are at the bottom of the heap by the time they reach GCSE. Most of what follows focuses mainly on the African-Caribbean group, though some of the points also apply to the Pakistani and Bangladeshi minority ethnic groups as well.

- Taken overall, they appear to have below-average reading skills.
- African-Caribbean, Pakistani and Bangladeshi pupils consistently have lower levels of attainment than other ethnic groups across all National Curriculum key stages, and are less likely to attain higher grade (A*–C) GCSE results than children of white or Indian origin.
- Male African-Caribbeans are over-represented (that is, there are more than there should be given their numbers in the population as a whole) in special schools for those with learning difficulties and in special units for children with emotional, behavioural and social difficulties.
- African-Caribbean pupils are between three and six times more likely to be permanently excluded from schools than white students of the same sex, and to be excluded for longer periods for the same offences.
- Where schools are streamed by ability, they are over-represented in lower streams. Evidence suggests they are put in lower streams even when they get better results than pupils placed in higher streams.
- They are more likely than other groups to leave school without any qualifications.
- They are less likely to stay on in education post-16/17, and when they do, they are more likely to follow vocational courses rather than the higher-status academic courses, like AS- and A-levels.
- Relatively fewer obtain AS- and A-levels and go on to higher education at universities (though African-Caribbean females do better than both African-Caribbean and white males).
- In the population as a whole, they are generally less qualified than those of white or Indian origin.

Explaining the underachievement of some ethnic minorities

There is no single factor that explains the differences between ethnic groups – a range of factors work together to produce the lower levels of achievement of Pakistani, Bangladeshi and African-Caribbean school students. The following sections identify some of these explanations.

Social conditions   Young people from minority ethnic backgrounds often face a series of disadvantages in social conditions, such as poor-quality housing, overcrowding and higher rates of unemployment in their homes, which contribute to difficulties in coping with school work. Around one-fifth of white households lived below the poverty line in 2008–9, compared to about two-fifths of African-Caribbean households, and three-fifths of Pakistani and Bangladeshi households. Such material disadvantages are a major obstacle to success in education, and many of the factors discussed above explaining working-class underachievement also affect some minority ethnic groups, as they tend to be mainly working-class.

Racism   Although all schools are now legally obliged to have an anti-racist policy, and teachers are trained in equality legislation and equal opportunities, research in primary and secondary schools has found an unusually high degree of conflict between white teachers and African-Caribbean pupils. Teachers often hold stereotypes, with more positive expectations of Asians, particularly Asian girls (as relatively quiet, well-behaved and highly motivated), than of African-Caribbeans, whom they often have low expectations

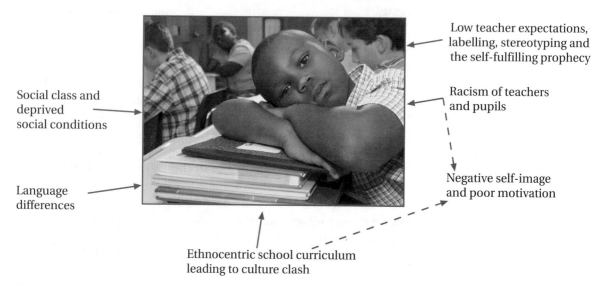

Low teacher expectations, labelling, stereotyping and the self-fulfilling prophecy

Social class and deprived social conditions

Racism of teachers and pupils

Language differences

Negative self-image and poor motivation

Ethnocentric school curriculum leading to culture clash

Figure 4.6 Ethnicity and educational underachievement

of and expect to be trouble-makers. This may mean teachers label African-Caribbeans and take swift action against them. African-Caribbean students, unlike whites and Asians, are often punished not for any particular offence but because they have the 'wrong attitude'. Such stereotyping and labelling may lead to the self-fulfilling prophecy of failure.

Although racism is not as widespread in teaching as in some professions, like the police and legal professions, and teachers have often been, and are, among the first to tackle racism, there is racism among teachers and pupils, as there is in the rest of society. African-Caribbean male pupils, in particular, are more likely to fight racism and form anti-school peer groups, and there is some evidence they go to school with negative attitudes, reinforcing their labelling by teachers as trouble-makers. This might explain the high level of black exclusions from school, since most permanent exclusions are for disobedience of various kinds, such as refusing to comply with school rules, verbal abuse or insolence to teachers.

An ethnocentric curriculum   Because of racism in both the school and the wider society, minority ethnic group children in Britain, particularly African-Caribbeans, may grow up with a negative self-image – a lack of self-respect and confidence because they feel they are in some ways rejected. The school curriculum tends to be ethnocentric, which may contribute to this low self-esteem.

Ethnocentrism means that school subjects concentrate on a particular society and culture – in this case white British society and culture – rather than recognizing and fully taking into account the cultures of different ethnic communities. This may cause a culture clash between home and school for African-Caribbean pupils and those from other under-achieving minority ethnic groups, and may lead to low motivation in school and poor educational achievement. However, a lot of work has been done in schools

> **Ethnocentrism** is a view of the world in which other cultures are seen through the eyes of one's own culture, with a devaluing of the others.

Activity

1 What evidence can you think of, if any, from your own experiences at school, which suggests that the cultures of minority ethnic groups are either ignored or treated in a degrading way? Think about the subjects you studied, the textbooks you used, and the kinds of activity you undertook.

2 Many schools today are trying to include the cultures of minority ethnic groups in school subjects and activities. What evidence is there of this happening in your experience? Give examples.

3 Discuss the following statements: (a) 'Cultural differences between people of different ethnic groups are very important and should be recognized and welcomed in schools', and (b) 'Anti-racism should only be discussed in schools which have a mix of different ethnic groups.'

> **Activity**
>
> Refer to figure 4.6 (on p. 214) and the sections above.
> 1 Go through the explanations for the underachievement of some ethnic minorities, putting them in what you think is their order of importance. Give reasons why you have put them in that order.
> 2 For each of the explanations, suggest changes that could be made in both school and society which might help to improve the educational achievements of minority ethnic groups.
> 3 Explain how the factors identified in figure 4.6 might combine to create low self-esteem in some minority ethnic group students, and how this might affect their progress in the education system.

in recent years to promote equality and understanding between different ethnic groups, and to tackle racism and discrimination, and to reduce ethnocentric biases in teaching and textbooks, so this may be an explanation of declining significance.

Language In some Asian households, English is not the main language used, and some Asian pupils may speak English as a second or additional language rather than as their first. In some black (African-Caribbean) households, Caribbean English is used – a form of non-standard English. Pupils for whom English is an additional language tend to have lower attainment than pupils whose first language is English. This language difference may cause difficulties in doing some school work and communicating with the teacher, and it may be unconsciously penalized in the classroom, because most teachers are white and middle-class. Teachers may mistake language difficulties for lack of ability, possibly leading to the self-fulfilling prophecy, and such cultural difficulties may therefore present obstacles to motivation and progress at school.

Gender differences in education: the underachievement of boys

While the educational achievements of both males and females have improved in recent years, there are still big differences between them. Until the 1980s, the major concern was with the underachievement of girls. This was because, while girls used to perform better than boys in the earlier stages of their education, up to GCSE, after this they tended to fall behind, being less likely than boys to get the three A-levels required for university entry, and less likely to go into higher education. However, in the early 1990s girls began to outperform boys, particularly working-class boys, in all areas and at all levels of the education system. The main problem today is with the underachievement of boys.

Girls now outperform boys in all areas and at all levels of the education system, and the main problem today is with the underachievement of boys

The facts

- Girls do better than boys at every stage in National Curriculum SAT (Standard Assessment Test) results in English, maths and science.
- Girls are now more successful than boys at every level in GCSE, and in every major subject (including traditional boys' subjects like design, technology, maths and chemistry) except physics. In 2008–9, 74 per cent of girls got five or more GCSEs (grades A*–C) compared to 66 per cent of boys (see figure 4.7). In English at GCSE, the gender gap is huge, with 72 per cent of girls getting a grade A*–C, compared to 58 per cent of boys in 2010.
- A higher proportion of females stay on in post-16 sixth-form and further education, and post-18 higher education.
- Female school leavers are now more likely than males to get two or more A-level passes (or equivalent) (see figure 4.7).
- More females than males now get accepted for full-time university degree courses.

Problems still remaining for females

The attention given to girls outperforming boys and the underachievement of boys can draw attention away from the fact that large numbers of girls are also low attainers and are underachieving, and other problems do still remain for girls.

- Females and males still tend to do different subjects, which influences future career choices. Broadly, arts subjects are female, science and

Table 4.3 GCSE, AS- and A-level achievements of males and females in all subjects: UK, 2010

	Male entries	Pass rate [a] (%)	Female entries	Pass rate [a] (%)
GCSE (full course)	2,651,002	65	2,723,488	73
Applied GCSE (Double award)	30,844	49	45,475	56
Applied GCSE (Single award)	9,500	68	9,163	77
A-level	393,642	97	460,291	98
Applied A-level (Double award)	3,060	92	6,516	96
Applied A-level (Single award)	15,494	94	21,316	97
AS-level	557,196	86	640,294	90
Applied AS-level (Double award)	2,566	82	5,999	89
Applied AS-level (Single award)	21,474	81	29,292	89

[a] Passes are grades A*–C for GCSE, and grades A*–E at AS- and A-level. Pass rates are rounded up or down to nearest whole number.

Source: Joint Council for Qualifications, 2010

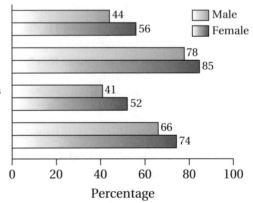

Accepted to university degree courses (UK, 2009): Male 44, Female 56

16-year-olds in post-16 full-time education (England, 2008): Male 78, Female 85

17-year-olds achieving two or more GCE AS/A-levels (or equivalent) grades A–E (UK, 2007–8): Male 41, Female 52

15-year-olds achieving five or more GCSE grades A*–C (England, 2008–9): Male 66, Female 74

Figure 4.7 Some male and female differences in education achievement: 2007–9

Source: data from Department for Children, Schools and Families; UCAS; Joint Council for General Qualifications

Figure 4.8 Percentage of entries by subject and sex, GCSE and A-level: United Kingdom, 2010

Source: Joint Council for Qualifications, 2010

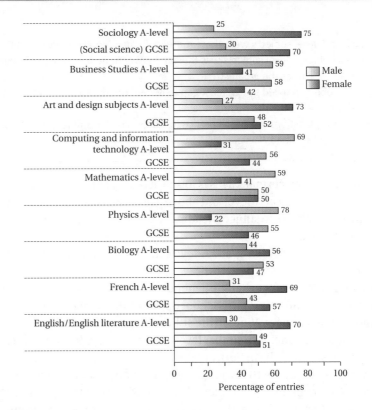

Activity

Refer to table 4.3.

1 In which qualification was there the largest gap between the pass rates of males and females?
2 In which qualification was there the largest gap between male and female entries?
3 In which qualification did females achieve the best pass rate?
4 In which qualification did males and females achieve the most similar pass rates?

Refer to figure 4.7:

5 What difference was there between the percentage of female and male students obtaining five or more GCSE grades A*–C in England in 2008–9?
6 What percentage of 17-year-old males achieved two or more GCE A-levels (or equivalent) in 2007–8?
7 Which difference showed the largest gap in the achievements of males and females.

Refer to figure 4.8:

8 In which GCSE subjects were there more female than male entries in 2010?
9 In which three GCSE subjects was the gap between the percentage of male and female entries the greatest?

10 In which A-level subjects were there more male than female entries in 2009?

11 In which three A-level subjects was the gap between the percentage of male and female entries the greatest?

12 Which subject showed the greatest gap between the percentage of male and female entries at *both* GCSE and A-level?

13 Suggest explanations for the difference in subjects males and females choose to study at GCSE and A-level.

technology subjects male. This is found at GCSE, and becomes even more pronounced at A-level and above. Girls are therefore less likely to participate after 16 in subjects leading to careers in science, engineering and technology.

● Girls achieve fewer high-grade A-levels than boys with the same GCSE results.

● There is little evidence that the generally better results of girls at 16 and above lead to improved post-school opportunities in terms of training and employment. Women are still less likely than men with similar qualifications to achieve similar levels of success in paid employment, and men still hold the majority of the positions of power in society.

● Among people in the 16–59 age group in the population as a whole who are in employment or unemployed, men tend to be better qualified than women. However, this gap has decreased among younger age groups, and can be expected to disappear if females keep on outperforming males in education.

Explaining gender differences in education

What follows are some explanations for the huge improvement in the performance of girls since the late 1980s, the underachievement of boys and the subject choices that continue to separate males and females.

Why do females now do better than males?

EQUAL OPPORTUNITIES

The work of sociologists in highlighting the educational underperformance of girls in the past led to a greater emphasis in schools on equal opportunities. This was to enable girls to fulfil their potential more easily. These policies included things like monitoring teaching and teaching materials for gender bias to help schools promote 'girl-friendliness', not only in male-dominated subjects but across the whole range of the experience of girls in schools. Teachers are now much more sensitive about avoiding gender stereotyping in the classroom, and this may have overcome many of the former academic problems which girls faced in schools.

GROWING AMBITION, MORE POSITIVE ROLE MODELS AND MORE EMPLOYMENT OPPORTUNITIES

The number of male jobs has declined in recent years, while there are growing employment opportunities for women. As a consequence, girls have become more ambitious and they are less likely to see having a home and family as their main role in life. Many girls growing up today have mothers working in paid employment, who provide positive role models for them. Many girls now recognize that the future involves paid employment, often combined with family responsibilities. Sue Sharpe found in *Just like a Girl* in 1976 that girls' priorities were 'love, marriage, husbands, children, jobs, and careers, more or less in that order'. When she repeated her research in 1994, she found these priorities had changed to 'job, career and being able to support themselves'. These factors may all have provided more incentives for girls to gain qualifications.

THE WOMEN'S MOVEMENT AND FEMINISM

The women's movement and feminism have achieved considerable success in improving the rights and raising the expectations and self-esteem of women. They have challenged the traditional stereotype of women's roles as housewives and mothers, and this means many women now look beyond being a housewife/mother as their main role in life.

GIRLS WORK HARDER

There is mounting evidence that girls work harder and are better motivated than boys:

- They put more effort into their work.
- They spend more time on doing their homework properly.
- They take more care with the way their work is presented.
- They concentrate more in class (research shows the typical 14-year-old girl can concentrate for about three or four times as long as her fellow male students).
- They are generally better organized – for example, they are more likely to bring the right equipment to school and meet deadlines for handing in work.

GIRLS MATURE EARLIER THAN BOYS

By the age of 16, girls are estimated to be more mature than boys by up to two years. Put simply, this means girls are more likely to view exams in a far more responsible way, and recognize their seriousness and the importance of the academic and career choices that lie ahead of them.

Why do boys underachieve?

Many of the reasons given above also suggest why boys may be underachieving. However, there are some possible additional explanations. These are summarized in figure 4.9.

LOWER TEACHER EXPECTATIONS

There is some evidence that staff are not as strict with boys as with girls. They are more likely to extend deadlines for work from them; have lower expectations of boys; are more tolerant of disruptive, unruly behaviour from boys in the classroom; and accept more poorly presented work from them. This will mean boys perform less well than they otherwise might.

POORER BEHAVIOUR

Boys are generally more disruptive in classrooms than girls. They may lose more classroom time learning things because they are sent out of the room or sent home. The exclusion rate for boys is at least three times higher than that for girls, and four out of every five permanent exclusions and three out of four fixed period exclusions from schools were of boys; most of these are for disobedience of various kinds, and usually come at the end of a series of incidents.

LACK OF POSITIVE ROLE MODELS

Teaching is often seen as a mainly female profession, and there is a lack of male role models, especially in primary schools. Learning has therefore come to be seen as a feminine and 'girly' activity, contributing to a negative attitude among boys to schools and schooling.

PEER PRESSURE

Boys appear to gain 'street cred' and peer group status by not working, and some develop almost an anti-education, anti-learning laddish sub-culture, in

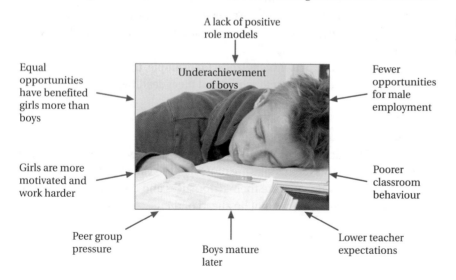

Figure 4.9 Gender and educational underachievement

A lack of positive role models

Equal opportunities have benefited girls more than boys

Underachievement of boys

Fewer opportunities for male employment

Girls are more motivated and work harder

Poorer classroom behaviour

Peer group pressure

Boys mature later

Lower teacher expectations

which schoolwork is seen as girly and unmacho. Some boys achieve peer group 'macho' status by resisting teachers and schools, through laddish behaviour like messing about in class and not getting on with their work. This may explain why they are less conscientious, and lack the persistence and application required for exam success, contributing to their underachievement.

THE DECLINE IN MALE EMPLOYMENT

The decline in traditional male jobs may be a factor in explaining why many boys are underperforming in education. They may lack motivation and ambition because they may feel that they have limited prospects, and getting qualifications won't get them anywhere anyway, so what's the point in bothering?

Activity

1 Go through the reasons suggested above for why girls outperform boys in education. List the explanations in what you think is their order of importance and, drawing on your own experiences at school or college, try to think of any other explanations for the underachievement of boys.

2 Discuss the steps that might be taken in schools to improve the performance of boys.

3 Go to www.nationalstrategies.standards.dcsf.gov.uk/genderandachievement and identify three measures that are being taken to reduce gender differences in educational achievement.

Why do males and females still tend to do different subjects?

There is still a difference between the subjects that males and females do at GCSE and above, as figure 4.8 on page 219 shows. Females are still more likely to take arts, humanities and social science subjects, like English literature, history, foreign languages, psychology and sociology, and males are more likely to take scientific and technological subjects, particularly at A-level and above (even though girls generally get better results when they do take them). This is despite the National Curriculum (or Welsh, Scottish and Northern Ireland equivalents), which makes maths, English and science compulsory for all students. However, even within the National Curriculum, there are gender differences in option choices. For example, girls are more likely to take home economics, textiles and food technology, while boys are more likely to opt for electronics, woodwork or graphics.

These differences might be explained as follows:

GENDER SOCIALIZATION

Gender socialization (discussed in chapter 1, see pages 19–35) means that, for example, from an early age boys and girls are encouraged to play with different toys and do different activities at home, and they very often grow up seeing their parents playing different roles around the house. This socialization may encourage boys to develop more interest in technical and scientific subjects, and discourage girls from taking them.

SUBJECT AND CAREER ADVICE

In giving subject and career advice, teachers may be reflecting their own socialization and expectations, and reinforcing the different experiences of boys and girls by counselling them into different subject options, according to their own gender stereotypes of suitable subjects.

SCIENCE AND THE SCIENCE CLASSROOM ARE STILL SEEN AS MAINLY MASCULINE

Boys tend to dominate science classrooms – grabbing apparatus first, answering questions aimed at girls and so on, which all undermine girls' confidence and intimidate them from taking up these subjects. Gender stereotyping is still found in science, with the invisibility of females particularly obvious in maths and science textbooks, where examples are often more relevant to the experience of males than females. This reinforces the view that these are 'male' subjects.

Activity

Read the following comments from year 11 boys talking about doing English and science, and then answer the questions beneath:

'I hate it! I don't want to read books.'

'Science is straightforward. You don't have to think about it. There are definite answers. There are no shades to it.'

'In science, everything is set out as a formula, and you have the facts. All you have to do is apply them to the situation.'

'When you read a book, it's like delving into people's lives. It's being nosy.'

'English is about understanding, interpreting . . . you have to think more. There's no definite answer . . . the answer depends on your view of things.'

'I don't like having discussions – I feel wrong . . . I think that people will jump down my throat.'

'That's why girls do English, because they don't mind getting something wrong. They're more open about issues, they're more understanding . . . they find it easier to comprehend other people's views and feelings.'

'You feel safe in science.'

Source: adapted from Eirene Mitsos, 'Boys and English: Classroom Voices', *English and Media Magazine*, 33, Autumn 1995

1 What are the main points being made about the differences between English and science, and explain whether or not you agree with them and why.

2 Suggest three reasons why males and females tend to do different subjects.
3 Why do you think that even when girls take traditional boys' subjects like technology, physics and computing, they still often get higher grades than boys?
4 Nearly three-quarters of students taking GCSE and A-level Social Science and Sociology exams are girls. How would you explain this?
5 Suggest any links there might be between subject choices at school and gender role socialization in society as a whole (see pages 19–35 for some discussion of gender role socialization).
6 Applying the research methods you studied in chapter 2, carry out a small survey among male and female students to discover what influenced them in making subject and exam choices.

PRIVATE EDUCATION: THE INDEPENDENT SCHOOLS

A continuing obstacle to the establishment of equality of educational opportunity in Britain is the continued existence of a fee-paying private sector of education – the independent schools.

There are many poor-quality schools in the private sector of education, but most research and discussion has been about what are known as the 'public schools', which, despite their name, are not in fact 'public' at all, but very expensive private schools. The public schools are a small group of independent schools belonging to what is called the 'Headmasters' and Headmistresses' Conference' (HMC). Pupils at these schools are largely the children of wealthier upper-middle- and upper-class parents who have decided to opt out of free, state-run schooling and can afford to pay for a private education.

The public schools are long-established private schools, many dating back hundreds of years, which charge fees running into thousands of pounds a year. For secondary age students in 2009–10, annual fees for day students averaged around £11,500, and for boarders (living in) £24,000. The two most famous boys' public schools are probably Eton and Harrow (boarding fees around £30,000 a year, plus extras, in 2010–11), and many of the 'top people' in this country have attended these or other public schools. A public school education means parents can almost guarantee their children will have well-paid future careers bringing them power and status in society.

Eton College, one of Britain's most famous public schools, with fees of £29,862 a year plus extras in 2010–11, counts among its former students nineteen British prime ministers, numerous princes, kings, archbishops, judges, generals, admirals and other members of Britain's elite

The case for independent schools

The defenders of private education point to the smaller class sizes and better facilities of the public schools compared to those found in the state system, which mean children have a much better chance of educational success. Many teachers are paid more, examination results are often better, and pupils have a much higher chance of getting into university. Many defend private education on the grounds that parents should have the right to spend their money as they wish, and improving their children's life chances is a sensible way of doing so.

The case against independent schools

Many remain opposed to private education, arguing that most people do not have the money to purchase a private education for their children, and it is wrong that the children of the well-off should be given more advantages in education than the poor. Despite many of the schools catering only for the well-off, they have traditionally had the same tax subsidies and benefits through charitable status as charities helping those in poverty or need. As well as these tax subsidies through charitable status, the taxpayer also pays the cost of training the teachers in these schools, since they attend state-run universities and colleges. This means public schools are effectively subsidized by the taxpayers, the vast majority of whom can't afford for their children to attend them.

The quality of teaching in independent schools is often no better than in state-run schools. However, their pupils may obtain better results because classes tend to be smaller than in state schools, allowing more individual attention, and the schools often have better resources and facilities. For example, Eton College in 2009 had assets estimated at £194 million, with the added advantage of charitable status. These investments and fee income allow Eton to spend around £20,000 per year on each student, compared to about £5,500 for the average state school student in 2009–10. The opponents of private education argue more money should be spent on improving the state system so everyone has an equal chance in education.

Research has shown that even when children who go to private schools, especially the public schools, get worse examination results than children who go to state comprehensive schools, they still get better jobs in the end. This suggests that the fact of attending a public school is itself enough to secure them good jobs, even if their qualifications are not quite as good as those of pupils from comprehensives.

Activity

Go to the websites of either Eton College (www.etoncollege.com), or Harrow School (www.harrowschool.org.uk), and explore how the educational facilities and lifestyle of these schools differ from the school you went to. Do you think those attending such schools have unfair advantages in education compared to the typical student?

Elite education and elite jobs

A public school education remains a prime qualification for the **elite** jobs in society – that small number of jobs in the country which involve holding a great deal of power and privilege.

An **elite** is a small group holding great power and privilege in society.

Although only about 7 per cent of the population have attended independent schools (and public schools are only a proportion of these schools), many of the top positions in the civil service, medicine, the law, the media, the Church of England, the armed forces, industry, banking and commerce are held by ex-public-school pupils.

In many cases, even well-qualified candidates from state schools will stand a poor chance of getting such jobs if competing with public school pupils. The route into the elite jobs is basically through a public school and Oxford and Cambridge universities (where nearly half of students come from public schools). This establishes the 'old boys' network', illustrated in figure 4.10, through which those in positions of power recruit others who come from the same social class background and who have been to the same public schools

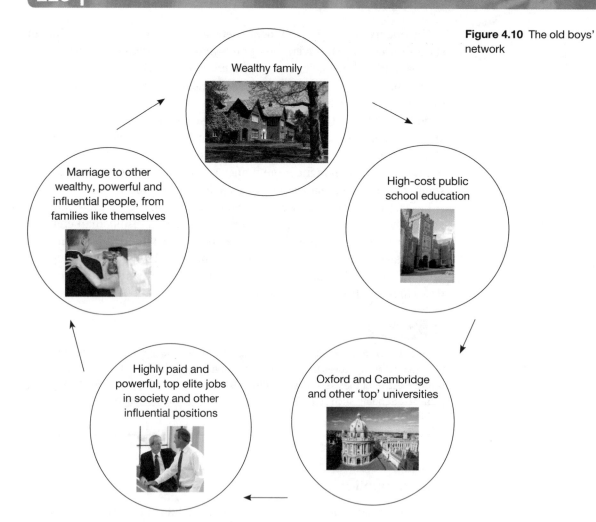

Figure 4.10 The old boys' network

and universities as themselves. This shows one aspect of the clear relationship which exists between wealth and power in modern Britain, and how being able to afford a public school education can lead to a position of power and influence in society.

A public school education therefore means well-off parents can almost guarantee their children will have well-paid future careers bringing them similar levels of power and status in society to their parents. This undermines the principle of equality of educational opportunity, and any idea that Britain might be a meritocracy. This is because social class background and the ability to pay school fees, rather than simply academic ability, become the key to success in education. Not all children of the same ability have the same chance of having parents able to afford this route to educational success.

Activity

Should private education be abolished? List the arguments for and against. If you are in a group, debate this issue.

IS EQUALITY OF EDUCATIONAL OPPORTUNITY POSSIBLE TO ACHIEVE?

Despite attempts to secure equality of educational opportunity, children of equal ability but from different social classes, from different ethnic backgrounds, and of different sexes are still not achieving the same success in education. Compensatory education has not overcome the disadvantages faced by many pupils.

We live in an unequal society, where different groups and classes do not start the educational race on equal terms. In such a society, the combined effects of socialization, home and social class background, teachers' attitudes, the white, middle-class language and culture of the school, and the continued existence of a privileged private sector of education will mean the realization of the ideal of equality of educational opportunity will remain an impossible dream.

It has been suggested that reforming schools is about as worthwhile an exercise as rearranging the furniture on the Titanic – the luxury liner that sank on its first voyage. This is because, in terms of improving life chances, schools often do not make much difference to social class, gender or ethnic inequalities in society as a whole, so reforming schools is basically a pointless exercise. Do you agree?

CHAPTER SUMMARY

After studying this chapter, you should be able to:

- explain why education is a social and political issue
- describe and explain the role of education in society, including consensus and conflict approaches
- describe how education seeks to build social cohesion and citizenship
- explain what is meant by the 'hidden curriculum', and how it reflects the values of society outside school
- outline briefly the education system before the 1970s
- outline the main arguments for and against comprehensive schools and selection in education
- explain what is meant by streaming, setting and mixed-ability teaching, and the problems associated with each of them
- explain what is meant by a meritocracy and equality of educational opportunity
- describe, explain and criticize the various changes in education from 1988 onwards, including attempts to improve standards, the marketization of education, parental choice and the growing diversity of schools
- explain how the government has tried in recent years to improve standards in schools

and make them more aware of the needs of industry and business

- describe and explain some of the advantages and disadvantages of academies, free schools and faith schools
- suggest some arguments for and against educating children outside schools at home
- suggest some advantages and disadvantages of children with special educational needs being educated in either special or mainstream schools
- describe what is meant by vocational education, and suggest some criticisms of it
- explain what is meant by positive discrimination and compensatory education.
- explain what is meant by educational underachievement
- describe, and give a range of explanations for, the differences in achievement in relation to social class, ethnicity and gender
- explain what is meant by the self-fulfilling prophecy, and the problems associated with streaming and labelling in education
- discuss the arguments for and against the existence of the private sector of education
- explain the obstacles to the achievement of equality of educational opportunity

KEY TERMS

anti-school (counter-school) sub-culture
compensatory education
elaborated code
elite
equality of educational opportunity
ethnocentrism
hidden curriculum
marketization
meritocracy
positive discrimination
restricted code
self-fulfilling prophecy
setting
social cohesion
social mobility
streaming
sub-culture
tripartite system
underachievement

Crime and Deviance

Contents

Crime and Deviance

KEY ISSUES

- Social control, deviance and crime
- The difficulty of defining deviance
- Why are some deviant acts defined as criminal while others are not?
- Crime as a social issue: the social significance of criminal and deviant behaviour
- The pattern of crime
- What's wrong with official crime statistics?
- Is the crime rate increasing?
- Explaining crime and deviance
- The victims of crime
- Government initiatives and policy solutions to crime
- Deviance, crime and social change

SOCIAL CONTROL, DEVIANCE AND CRIME

Deviance is the failure to conform to social norms.
Crime is behaviour which is against the law – law-breaking.
A **law** is an official legal rule, formally enforced by the police, courts and prison, involving legal punishments if it is broken.

As discussed in chapter 1, norms and values are learnt through socialization, and these provide the social rules that enable people to know how to behave in society and to live together in some orderly way. Knowing what norms and values are though does not necessarily mean that people will conform to them, so formal and informal agencies of social control seek to persuade or force individuals to conform to those social values and norms which have been learnt through socialization, and to prevent **deviance** (a failure to conform to social norms) and **crime** (behaviour which is against the **law** – law-breaking).

These agencies of social control include formal agencies specifically set up to carry out social control, such as the police, courts, the probation service and prisons making up the criminal justice system, and informal agencies like the family, the peer group, education, the mass media, religion and the workplace. These all seek to encourage conformity by a range of positive and negative sanctions (rewards and punishments). These issues were discussed more fully in chapter 1, and you may wish to refresh your memory by referring to pages 15–19. Check your understanding by completing the activity below.

Activity

1 Describe, with examples, two *formal* ways in which individuals are encouraged to conform to social rules. Be sure to give examples of two particular ways and two particular social rules.
2 Identify three *informal* agencies of social control that encourage individuals to conform to social rules, and give an example in each case of how they do this.
3 Describe two positive and two negative sanctions that people may face to encourage them to conform to social rules.

THE DIFFERENCE BETWEEN CRIME AND DEVIANCE

Deviance is any non-conformist behaviour which is disapproved of by society or a social group, whether it is illegal or not. It is norm-breaking behaviour, and can range from being eccentric to criminal activity. Crime is the term used to describe behaviour which is against the law – law-breaking. As shown below, while a lot of crime is also seen as deviant, this isn't always the case, and there are many acts people regard as deviant which are not criminal (see below).

Juvenile delinquency is crime committed by those between the ages of 10 and 17, though the term *delinquency* is often used to describe any anti-social or deviant behaviour by young people, even if it isn't criminal.

> **Juvenile delinquency** is crime committed by those between the ages of 10 and 17, though the term *delinquency* is often used to describe any anti-social or deviant behaviour by young people, even if it isn't criminal.

THE DIFFICULTY OF DEFINING DEVIANCE

Crime is easy to define, as the law states what a criminal act is. However, while deviance appears to be easy to define as any non-conformist behaviour, it is, in fact, quite difficult to pin down what members of any society or group actually regard as deviant behaviour. Deviance covers a very wide range of behaviour, and what is regarded as deviant will depend on the norms of a group or society. These norms differ between societies and between groups within the same society, and they change over time. Whether or not an act is defined as deviant will therefore depend on the time, the place, the society and the attitudes of those who view the act. The following examples illustrate how definitions of deviance can vary according to a range of circumstances.

What is deviant? In Ancient Greece, homosexual relationships were not prohibited, though they were governed by social codes. Only since 1967, however, has homosexuality been made legal in the UK after centuries of condemnation and it is now accepted by most of the general public. As another example, in the seventeenth century, elaborate wigs were an accepted part of high-society fashion. Nowadays, wearing such a wig would be seen as deviant, though the practice still persists in the traditional robes of lawyers and judges

Non-deviant crime?

Most people commit deviant and even illegal acts at some stage in their lives, and there are many illegal acts which most people don't regard as particularly deviant. For example, parking and speeding offences, under-age drinking, use of soft drugs like cannabis, pinching office stationery, or making unauthorized personal calls on the office phone are all illegal but extremely common, so it is difficult to see them as deviant. Some offences, like under-age drinking, are often seen as expected behaviour, and those who don't commit the offence may even be seen as deviant by those around them.

The time

Deviance can only be defined in relation to particular norms, and norms change over time. For example, cigarette smoking used to be a very popular and socially acceptable activity, but is increasingly becoming branded as deviant. Since July 2007, it has been illegal in the UK (and also in a number of other European countries) to smoke indoors in workplaces and buildings open to the public, and smokers are now unwelcome in many places. Attitudes to homosexuality have also changed dramatically. Homosexuality was illegal in the UK before 1967, but since then has become legal and widely accepted; it is now possible to have an officially approved gay marriage in the form of a civil partnership. Fashion is an obvious example of changing norms – people today would generally be regarded as deviant were they to wear the fashions of seventeenth-century England, or even those of a few years ago (but not if they come into fashion again).

The society or culture

Deviance is culturally relative – what is regarded as deviance in one society or group is not necessarily so in another. For example, consumption of alcohol is often seen as deviant and illegal in many Islamic countries, but is seen as normal in Britain.

Attitudes to smoking have changed

The social group

What may be acceptable in a particular group may be regarded as deviant in the wider society. Norms can vary between social groups in the same society. For example, smoking cannabis is perfectly acceptable behaviour among Rastafarians in Britain, and among many young people who are not Rastafarians, although it is regarded as deviant by many adults, and it is illegal.

The place or context

The place where an act takes place may influence whether it is regarded as deviant or not. For example, it is seen as deviant if people have sex in the street, but not if it takes place between a consenting couple in a bedroom. Fighting in the street is seen as deviant, but not if it takes place in a boxing ring. The sale of prescription drugs in a local chemist is not regarded as deviant, but selling them at a club would be. Killing someone may be interpreted as heroic, manslaughter, self-defence, murder, a 'crime of passion', justifiable homicide or euthanasia (mercy killing). So it is not the act itself that is deviant but the place or context in which it takes place.

What counts as deviance varies between social groups and places, and sometimes acts are so common it is difficult to see them as deviant at all. For example, smoking cannabis is often regarded as deviant in Britain, and it is a criminal offence. Yet around one in five 16- to 24-year-olds use it each year, and one in ten of 16- to 59-year-olds. This is about half the proportion who smoke cigarettes. In the Netherlands, cannabis use is accepted, and there are officially approved premises (coffeeshops) for its sale and consumption. The photo on the right shows one of Amsterdam's oldest coffeeshops

Activity

Apart from the examples given above:

1 Identify and explain two examples of acts which are against the law but are not usually regarded as deviant by most people.
2 Give three examples of deviant acts which are not against the law.
3 Identify and explain two examples of acts which are generally accepted by the majority of people in Britain, but which might be regarded as deviant in some social groups there – for example minority ethnic or religious groups.
4 Explain the circumstances in which the following acts might *not* be regarded as deviant or illegal:
   - two men having sex together
   - killing ten people
   - driving through red traffic lights
   - deliberately breaking someone's arm
   - punching someone in the face
   - breaking into someone's house and removing her or his possessions
   - taking children away from their parents by force.

WHY ARE SOME DEVIANT ACTS DEFINED AS CRIMINAL WHILE OTHERS ARE NOT?

Cannabis use in some countries of the Middle East is a common practice, with few laws enforced to control its use, and yet alcohol consumption is strictly banned by laws which are vigorously enforced. In Britain, the opposite is more or less the case, despite the massive social cost caused by alcoholism in terms of family breakdown, days off work, acts of violence and costs to the NHS, and little evidence that cannabis has any addictive properties. Why are there such differences in the way some acts are defined as criminal while other, similar acts are not? There are two broad competing views on this.

The consensus approach

The consensus approach suggests that social rules are made and enforced for the benefit of everyone. The law and the definition of crime represent a consensus – a widespread agreement among most people – that some deviant acts are so serious that they require legal punishments to prevent them occurring. This may seem fairly clear in cases such as murder, rape and armed robbery, but it is not so clear on other issues, like those of alcohol and soft drug abuse. From the consensus view, this would be explained by the varying norms found in different societies, which mean alcohol and drugs are viewed differently.

Illegal

Legal

The conflict approach: inequalities in power

The conflict approach suggests that the law reflects the interests of the richest and most powerful groups in society, who have managed to impose their ideas and way of thinking on the rest of the population through the agencies of social control. Those in positions of influence in society, such as newspaper editors, politicians, owners of industry, powerful pressure groups, judges and the police, are much better placed to make their definition of a crime stick than the ordinary person in the street. They also have the power to define some acts as criminal through newspaper campaigns, by passing laws in Parliament, or by treating some offences more seriously than others.

In this way the powerful are able to maintain their own position of power and influence by defining those activities which are against their interests as deviant or criminal. The issue of alcohol raised above could well be explained by the power of the wealthy large brewers and distillers. A further example is the way laws against picketing by trade unionists are much stronger and more rigidly enforced than those imposing health and safety standards on

employers. Middle-class crimes such as tax evasion are often neither prosecuted, nor pursued as vigorously, nor punished as severely as a working-
class offence such as benefit fraud, which is much more likely to result in
prosecution and a prison sentence.

Activity

1 Which view explaining why some deviant acts are defined as criminal while
   others are not do you find most convincing? Give reasons for your answer.
2 Do you think the law is biased in deciding both which acts are defined as
   criminal, and which ones get pursued by the police and the courts? Give
   reasons for your view.

CRIME AS A SOCIAL ISSUE – THE SOCIAL SIGNIFICANCE OF CRIMINAL AND DEVIANT BEHAVIOUR

Social issues tend to be matters that people worry about, and crime worries
many people, and in some cases can cause misery and anxiety to individuals
and cast a blight over entire neighbourhoods. Victims of crime may experience stress and insecurity, physical injury, personal loss, a sense of having
their homes violated after burglaries, and a lasting fear of being victimized
again, leading to a heightened sense of personal insecurity and a fear of
leaving their homes. For some crimes, such as domestic violence, child abuse
and racial harassment, there may be a prolonged pattern of repeat victimization having lifetime consequences for those victimized.

Even though crime rates have been falling in recent years, fear of crime
remains persistently higher than the real risk of being a victim of crime. For
example, the 2009–10 British Crime Survey showed 15 per cent of people
thought they were fairly or very likely to be a victim of burglary in the next
year, whereas the actual risk was just 2 per cent. Older people have particularly high levels of fear of crime, as they tend to be more home-centred
and dependent on the media for information. The media tend to generate
public debates and fuel popular fears with their focus on bad news and
exaggerated reporting of crime to sell papers and attract viewers. This
can create quite unnecessary levels of anxiety, with exaggerated reports
of exceptional crimes of violence and suggestions of crime 'spiralling out
of control'. For example, the extent of violent crime is widely exaggerated
by the media, with reports of robbery with violence (mugging) and knife
and gun crime given very high prominence. Yet around half of all violent

Do you think the media give a false impression of most young people, such as in stories about knife and gun crime, and anti-social behaviour?

crime involves no injury whatsoever, and occurrences of both knife and gun crimes are falling.

Teenage crime

The media often give the impression that most young people are frightening and threatening binge-drinking, drug-crazed, anti-social young tearaways, turning town centres and local neighbourhoods into war zones ravaged by gun- and knife-carrying gangs of young thugs.

A survey commissioned by Women in Journalism in 2009 found that teenage boys most frequently appeared in the media in stories about crime, and were most commonly described using terms like *yobs, thugs, sick, feral* (wild), *hoodie, lout, heartless, evil, frightening* and *scum*. While it is true that young males are the largest group of criminals, as discussed later in this chapter, and that anti-social behaviour by young people is a common problem, it is certainly not true that most young people are criminals or anti-social. A survey for the *Guardian* newspaper in 2009 found that in fact the vast majority of teenage boys were conformist and law-abiding, and happy with their family, school and social lives. Young people are far more likely to be the victims of violent crime than any other social group, and adults pose far more of a risk to the safety of young people than young people do to adults. Anti-social behaviour, which includes much behaviour often linked to young people, such as teenagers hanging around on the streets, vandalism, graffiti and other deliberate damage to property, being drunk or rowdy in public places, also includes leaving rubbish or litter lying around, people using or dealing drugs, noisy neighbours or loud parties, and abandoning old or burnt-out cars, which are probably as much linked to adults as young people.

There is more discussion on the mass media and crime and deviance, and the way the media exaggerate these, on pages 327–9 in chapter 6.

Racism and other 'hate crime'

A **hate crime** is any criminal offence that is motivated by hostility or prejudice based upon a victim's identity. This may include features like their physical or mental disabilities, their age, their race, religion or beliefs, and their **sexual orientation** (such as whether they are lesbian/gay or heterosexual).

Any hate crime can have serious consequences for victims, including anger, fear of further attacks, depression, personal expense (through damaged property or time off work), and injury and poor health.

One of the most common forms of hate crime is racism. Black and minority ethnic communities are most at risk of being victims of many types of crime, but they are particularly vulnerable to hate crimes of racist violence and harassment, most of which are not reported to the police.

The British Crime Survey (BCS) estimated that there were around 207,000 racially motivated incidents in 2008–9, including harassment, abuse, threats, intimidation and violence – more than 560 incidents every day of the year. Both black people (African-Caribbeans) and Asians are around fourteen times more likely to be the victim of a racially motivated incident than white people, and black and Asian people often live with the threat of being attacked in the streets or in their homes. Such incidents can affect not only the individual victim, but also the victim's family, and create a climate of insecurity and fear that spreads throughout minority ethnic communities.

> A **hate crime** is any crime that is motivated by hostility and prejudice based upon a victim's identity, such as their race, disability, religion, beliefs or sexual orientation.
> **Sexual orientation** refers to the type of people that individuals are either physically or romantically attracted to, such as those of the same or opposite sex.

AND YOU GET ANNOYED ABOUT JUNK MAIL.

COMMISSION FOR RACIAL EQUALITY

And you get annoyed about junk mail

Such racist incidents have been formally recognized in law since the 1998 Crime and Disorder Act, with new offences of racially aggravated assault, harassment and criminal damage carrying higher penalties than similar offences without a racist motivation. For example, the maximum sentence for common assault in 2009 was 6 months in prison and/or a £5,000 fine, while the penalty for racially aggravated common assault was 2 years and/or an unlimited fine.

Activity

1 Suggest two reasons why young people are often stereotyped in the mass media as criminal and anti-social.
2 Suggest two reasons in each case, with examples of particular crimes, why exaggerated media reporting of crime might cause unnecessary fears among: (a) older people; (b) women.
3 Suggest two consequences for individuals that might follow from being a victim of crime. Illustrate your answer with examples of particular crimes.
4 Suggest and explain two ways in which high levels of crime in a neighbourhood might affect communities beyond the actual victims of crime.
5 Suggest and explain two ways in which racially motivated incidents might undermine social cohesion in contemporary Britain.
6 Suggest two measures governments might take to prevent racism and racially motivated crime.
7 Go to www.homeoffice.gov.uk/crime-victims/reducing-crime/hate-crime and identify:
   (a) three types of hate crime
   (b) three steps the government is taking to tackle hate crimes
   (c) two reasons why victims of hate crimes might wish to report them anonymously (without their identity being known).

THE PATTERN OF CRIME

Information on the pattern of crime is obtained from official crime statistics, which are compiled from several main sources:

1 *Police-recorded crime.* These are offences either detected by or reported to and recorded by the police.
2 *Victim surveys.* These survey the victims of crime and include crimes not reported to, or recorded by, the police. They therefore give a more accurate picture than police-recorded crime. An example is the British Crime Survey (BCS).

3 *Self-report surveys.* These consist of anonymous questionnaires in which people are asked to own up to committing crimes, whether or not they have been discovered. They include the Home Office's *Offending, Crime and Justice Survey.*

4 *Court and prison records, and records on police cautions.* These reveal the characteristics of offenders who have been caught.

Self-report and victim surveys are discussed later in this chapter.

The use of crime statistics

Crime statistics are used for a variety of purposes:

- for comparison with previous years to discover trends in crime
- to look at the police detection rate (the number of crimes cleared up by the police, with an offender identified and action taken against them – sometimes called the 'clear-up rate') to measure police efficiency
- to show where the police should concentrate resources to reduce crime;
- to provide the public (often via the media) with information on crime patterns
- to provide a basis for sociologists to explain crime, including what is and what is not shown in the statistics
- to reveal police assumptions and stereotyping, as the statistics are in part created by the activities of the police themselves and the offenders they choose to pursue and the offences they choose to record.

Figure 5.1 shows a breakdown of the main types of offence recorded by the police in 2009–10, and those revealed by the British Crime Survey (BCS) victim survey.

It is notable that, despite wide media coverage of dramatic incidents such as attacks on the elderly, violence against the person made up only about one in five of both police-recorded and BCS offences in 2009–10. Most crimes of

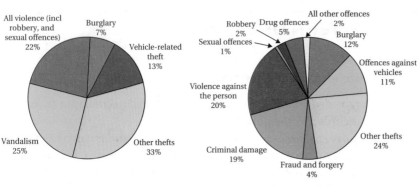

Figure 5.1 The pattern of crime in official statistics: police-recorded crime and British Crime Survey (BCS) crime, England and Wales, 2009–10

Source: Crime in England and Wales 2009/10 (Home Office, 2010)

violence against the person do not result in any serious physical injury, and over a half (54 per cent) of all violent crime reported to the police in 2009–10 did not result in *any* physical injury to the victim. Only a small proportion of such cases call for professional medical attention, and in only a few of such cases is the victim admitted to hospital. In fact, as figure 5.1 shows, most crime is fairly small-scale property and vehicle-related crime, and vandalism (criminal damage).

Criminal statistics are notoriously unreliable, so the pattern of crime shown in them must be treated with considerable caution. The problem of the crime statistics will be discussed shortly, but for the moment our concern will be with explaining the pattern shown in the official statistics.

The pattern of offending

The pattern of crime revealed by the various statistical sources mentioned above shows that most crime is committed:

- in urban areas (towns and cities)
- against property (80 per cent of all crime)
- by young people (roughly half of all those convicted are 21 or under, with the peak age for crime being 18 for males, and 14 for females), particularly working-class males.

For some offences, such as street crime and some drug offences, there is – according to official statistics – an over-representation of some minority ethnic groups, particularly black (African-Caribbean) minority ethnic groups.

Why is the crime rate higher in urban areas?

The official crime rate is significantly higher in urban areas than in rural areas. There are four main reasons for this.

More opportunity for crime

Large urban areas provide greater opportunities for crime: there are more and larger shops, warehouses and business premises, cars, houses and other typical targets of crime.

Policing

There is a greater police presence in urban areas, so more crime is likely to be detected. Different policing methods also mean the police are more likely to take formal action (arrest and prosecution) in urban areas. In rural areas they are less likely to arrest offenders for minor offences, preferring merely to issue more informal warnings, or in the case of young people perhaps visiting the offender's parents or her or his school.

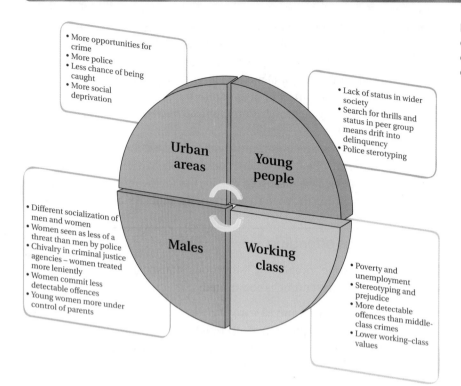

Figure 5.2 Some explanations for the pattern of crime shown in official crime statistics

- More opportunities for crime
- More police
- Less chance of being caught
- More social deprivation

Urban areas

- Lack of status in wider society
- Search for thrills and status in peer group means drift into delinquency
- Police sterotyping

Young people

- Different socialization of men and women
- Women seen as less of a threat than men by police
- Chivalry in criminal justice agencies – women treated more leniently
- Women commit less detectable offences
- Young women more under control of parents

Males

Working class

- Poverty and unemployment
- Stereotyping and prejudice
- More detectable offences than middle-class crimes
- Lower working–class values

Less chance of being caught

In the large cities, life is more impersonal and people do not know each other so well. Strangers are more likely to go unrecognized, and are therefore more able to get away with offences. Potential criminals are less likely to steal within a small rural community where everyone knows almost everybody else and suspicious strangers in the community are likely to be noticed. Any local offenders are quite likely to be known in the community.

Social deprivation

Social deprivation and social problems, such as poor housing, unemployment and poverty, are at their worst in the inner cities. These have been linked to crime, as people try to resolve their desperate situations through illegal means.

Why are most convicted criminals young?

Official statistics show that roughly half of all those convicted are aged 21 or under, and a 2002 survey found that almost half of Britain's secondary school students admitted to breaking the law. There are several explanations for this.

Status frustration and the influence of the peer group

Status frustration means young people are frustrated at their lack of an independent status in society.

Young people are caught in the transition between child and adult status: they are no longer expected to behave as children, but are denied the full rights and responsibilities of adults. They therefore often feel deprived of status in society and suffer from status frustration. The period of status frustration weakens young people's sense of identity – of who they are. This means that young people often lack a sense of identity and direction, and they are therefore in a state of drift. In this period of drift, the peer group can provide some support for an identity and status independent of school or family, and therefore takes on a greater importance among young people than at any other age.

Many young people also lack the responsibilities involved in having children, in paying rent or mortgage repayments, and often in keeping down a job. This lack of responsibilities, combined with the search for excitement and peer group status, means many young people drift into minor acts of delinquency and clashes with the law. Peer group pressure may also give young people the confidence and encouragement to involve themselves in minor acts of delinquency which they would not engage in on their own. The idea of status frustration helps to explain why many young people give up crime as they grow older. Adulthood, marriage or cohabitation, parenthood, their own home and employment give them a more clearly defined, independent status in society, and the peer group becomes less important for achieving status.

While most young people will break the law at some time, the kinds of offence they commit are usually fairly trivial and peer group related. For example, under-age drinking, vandalism and shoplifting are the most common offences committed by young people. The reasons most often given for their law-breaking are to impress others, and boredom. Research conducted at the Centre of Criminology at Edinburgh University found that about half the offences committed by 11- to 15-year-olds involved rowdiness and fighting in the street, with the rest consisting mainly of shoplifting (usually sweets) and vandalism (usually graffiti).

Police stereotyping

Young people tend to commit more visible types of crime than older people, such as vandalism, violent offences like brawls in the street after drinking sessions, anti-social behaviour, street crime and shoplifting. The police are therefore more likely to see young people as the source of problems, and this stereotype means the police spend more time observing and checking youths. As a result, more get caught, get defined as offenders, and appear in

How does this picture help to explain why young people are in a state of drift? Using the explanations in this section, suggest how the peer group might help to overcome the types of problem identified in the picture, and how this might be linked to delinquency

Reproduced by permission of David Haldone

the statistics. In fact, the Edinburgh research referred to above found that young people were far more likely to be the victims of crime than to commit crimes, and these crimes were often committed by adults. The young complained of being followed by 'weirdos', bothered by 'flashers', alcoholics and junkies, and in fear of rape and other sexual assaults. Children of school age were around five times more likely to become victims of mobile phone theft than adults. However, the Edinburgh research found that the police often didn't take the complaints of the young seriously, seeing them primarily as trouble-makers. More than half had been moved on, told off, stopped and questioned, or stopped and searched during the previous nine months. This situation discourages young people from reporting offences against them, and reinforces the impression of young people as delinquents rather than as the victims of crime.

Activity

1 What evidence, if any, do you have from your own experience that the police stereotype young people, and unfairly make them out to be trouble-makers?
2 Suggest reasons why the police might hold such stereotypes.

Why are most convicted criminals male?

Men are responsible for about four *known* offences for every one committed by women, they are more likely to be repeat offenders, and in general they commit more serious offences. Only about 5 per cent of the prison population are women. Why is this?

Why do males commit more crime than women?

- Owing to gender role socialization, the tough and dominant behaviour expected of men is more likely to lead to more serious and detectable criminal behaviour, and men are more likely than women to carry out crimes of violence and other serious offences.
- The police see men as more likely to be criminals than women, and they are more likely to press charges in the case of men.
- Men have more independence and opportunities to commit crime – they are less restricted by the demands of housework and childcare.

Why do females appear to commit less crime than men?

1. The chivalry thesis

The **chivalry thesis** suggests that more paternalism or **sexism** on the part of the police and courts means they regard female offenders as a less serious threat than men, particularly for minor offences. They therefore adopt more informal approaches to their offences, such as unrecorded cautions or simply letting them off. According to the Home Office, women are consistently treated more leniently by the law, with women first offenders about half as likely to be given a sentence of immediate imprisonment as their male counterparts.

> The **chivalry thesis** is the suggestion that paternalism or sexism on the part of the police and the courts means they regard female offenders as a less serious threat than men, particularly for minor offences, and treat women more leniently than men. **Sexism** is prejudice or discrimination against people (especially women) because of their sex.

Evidence against the chivalry thesis   While women are far less likely to commit serious offences than men, those who do are likely to face more severe punishment than men, particularly for violent crime, as it violates socially acceptable patterns of feminine behaviour. Women offenders are more likely to be remanded in custody (put in prison) than men while awaiting trial for serious offences, but in three-quarters of cases, women do not actually receive a prison sentence when they come to trial. Women are about twice as likely as men to be denied bail when charged with drug offences, and three times as likely for offences involving dishonesty. Many women in prison appear to have been sentenced more severely than men in similar circumstances – for example, by being imprisoned rather than given Community Payback (formerly Community Service and then Community Punishment). Many women prisoners are there for not paying fines, for drug offences (around 35 per cent of all women prisoners) or for committing theft, fraud and robbery trying to feed themselves or their children. More than half of women prisoners have children under age 16. Women are over twice as likely as men to be imprisoned for theft, and, in effect, many women are sent to jail for being poor.

Women generally commit less crime than men, and only about 5 per cent of the prison population is female, but the female crime rate is slowly rising. How might you explain this?

In general, then, women might commit less crime, and fewer serious offences, than men, but appear to suffer more serious consequences when they do. This may well be because in our society women are expected to be good – acting in a feminine and conformist manner – and punished if they're not, but men are expected to be a bit tough and aggressive and periodically go off the rails and so are punished less severely when they do so.

2. *Police stereotyping* means women who commit crimes may benefit from the police stereotype that they are less likely than men to be criminals, and so are less likely to have their behaviour watched and get caught. Those that do get caught are also more likely than men to benefit from more informal approaches to their offences – particularly for minor offences – such as cautions or warnings rather than being charged.

3. *More social control* means teenage girls are likely to be more closely supervised by their parents, reducing the chances of their getting into trouble in the first place.

4. The demands of the *housewife/mother role* – caring for husbands, partners, children and dependent elderly relatives – means adult females may be less likely to get involved in crime as they have less opportunity to do so.

5. Women's offences are more likely to be *less detectable offences*, such as sexual offences like prostitution, or petty theft, like shoplifting.

Growing female criminality

Although men still commit a lot more crime than women, that pattern is slowly changing in the UK and other European countries, and there is a growing increase in the proportion of crime committed by females, most noticeably by young women. In 1957, for example, men were responsible for 11 times as many offences as women, but by 2009 that ratio had narrowed to 4 times as many. The number of crimes committed by girls (aged 10–17) in England and Wales went up by 25 per cent between 2004 and 2007, with significant increases in minor assaults, robberies, public order offences and criminal damage.

Changing gender roles and 'ladette' culture Growing female crime may be due to changing gender roles. Women in contemporary Britain have more independence than in the past, and they are becoming more successful than men in both education and the labour market, and some of the traditional forms of control on women, like the housewife/mother role and parental supervision mentioned above, are weakening, particularly among younger women. There's a lot more of a masculinized 'ladette' culture, in which young women are adopting behaviour traditionally associated with young men, as they assert their identity through binge drinking, gang culture, risk-taking, being hard and in control, and peer-related violence. There is some evidence that the police are now reacting in a more serious way, taking more action and prosecuting girls involved in such behaviour rather than dealing with it informally by other means, which would increase the statistics for such offences.

Why are most convicted criminals working-class?

According to official statistics, working-class people are more likely to be arrested and charged with crimes than those of other social classes. There are a number of possible explanations for this.

Poverty and unemployment

There is a link between the level of crime and the state of the economy. Property crime in particular seems to rise when people are hard up, when poverty is on the increase and people need to provide for their families. Such hardship provides an obvious explanation for the most common offences of property crime, and would account for the high proportion of working-class criminals. In a society where there are wide inequalities in wealth and income, some level of crime is to be expected from those who live a more deprived life than others.

Stereotyping and prejudice

Working-class youth fit more closely the police stereotype of the 'typical criminal', and there is therefore a greater police presence in working-class areas than in middle-class ones. This means there is a greater likelihood of offenders being seen and arrested by the police when committing an offence than in middle-class areas. Crime rates will therefore be higher in working-class areas simply because there are more police to notice or respond quickly to criminal acts.

The activities of working-class youth are more likely to be defined by the police as criminal than the same behaviour in the middle class. For example, a case of university students getting drunk and wrecking a restaurant might result in their having to pay for the damage and be dismissed by the police as a foolish escapade that got out of control – a temporary lapse in otherwise conformist behaviour – but the same behaviour by working-class football supporters would be more likely to be seen as hooliganism, with resulting prosecutions for criminal damage. The prejudices of middle-class judges and magistrates may mean that, when working-class people appear in court, they are more likely to be seen as typical criminals and found guilty. The middle-class are more likely to be found not guilty. Their offences may be seen more as a temporary lapse in otherwise good behaviour, and so are punished less severely than those of the working class.

Informal social control

Working-class youth are also more likely to be prosecuted if they are caught than the middle-class. This is perhaps because they are less likely to benefit from informal processes of social control. For petty offences, middle-class youth are more likely to be dealt with by parents and teachers than by the law, with the police perhaps visiting the parents to give them a warning.

Lower-working-class values

Some have suggested that the values of the lower working class often carry with them risks of brushes with the law. These values are discussed later in this chapter.

> **White-collar crimes** are offences committed by individuals who abuse their positions in middle-class jobs for personal gain at the expense of the organization or clients of the organization.

Activity

Most judges and magistrates come from white, upper-middle-class or middle-class backgrounds.

1 Suggest ways this might influence judges and magistrates to give more favourable and sympathetic treatment to some groups and less favourable and unsympathetic treatment to others. Give examples of particular groups.
2 Imagine you are to appear in court on a shoplifting charge. You desperately want to get off lightly. Identify and explain four ways you might try to give a good impression to the judge or magistrate.
3 What might this activity suggest about the real pattern of crime in society?

White-collar and corporate crime

White-collar crimes are offences committed for personal gain by people in the course of their middle-class jobs. These include offences such as bribery and corruption in government and business, fiddling expenses, professional misconduct, fraud and embezzlement. Examples include doctors, pharmacists and dentists who defraud the NHS by falsifying prescriptions and patient records to claim more from the NHS than that to which they are entitled, such as one GP who made £700,000 over five years writing fake prescriptions. The millionaire press baron Lord Conrad Black, former owner of the *Daily* and *Sunday Telegraph*, was in 2007 convicted and jailed for six and a half years in the United States for misusing his position as Chair of Hollinger International to defraud shareholders of millions of dollars for private gain. A spectacular example of white-collar crime was the case of Nick Leeson, who bankrupted Barings Bank in 1995 after losing the bank £830 million.

Corporate crimes are offences committed by large companies which directly profit the company rather than individuals. These include offences like misrepresentation of products, industrial espionage, breaches of health and safety regulations, environmental pollution and price fixing.

Examples of corporate crimes

- *Manufacturing offences and dangerous products*: the rigging of test results on the morning-sickness drug Thalidomide in the 1960s led to birth defects in thousands of babies. See also the box below on the Ford Pinto.

> **Corporate crimes** are offences committed by large companies, or by individuals on behalf of large companies, which directly profit the company rather than individuals.

PROFITS VERSUS SAFETY

The Ford Pinto car, advertised in the 1970s as the car that gave you a warm feeling, was found to have a fault that meant the car tended to erupt in flames in rear-end collisions. The car – which became known as 'the barbecue that seats four' – continued in production for eight years before the safety faults were corrected, in which period between 500 and 900 people were thought to have died in burn deaths after accidents. The failure to rectify the fault followed the notorious 'Ford Pinto memo' which showed it was cheaper to pay out to victims ($50 million) than to rectify the safety problems ($121 million).

- *Dangerous plant and environmental pollution*: in 1984, the Union Carbide chemical plant leaked poisonous gas in Bhopal in India. This affected half a million people, and by 2010 an estimated 35,000 had died, with a further 120,000 suffering severe symptoms like blindness and birth defects in children. The pollution continues today. (See www.bhopal.org for more information.)
- *Breaches of health and safety*: in 1987 the *Herald of Free Enterprise* cross-Channel ferry capsized in a calm sea just outside Zeebrugge harbour; 193 people died, as rules governing the closing of the bow doors of the ship had not been complied with.
- *Computer hacking*: in the early 1990s, British Airways illegally hacked into computers to obtain confidential information about its rival Virgin Atlantic.
- *Financial offences – ENRON*: in the USA in 2001, ENRON concealed large debts of around $50 billion, eventually causing the company to collapse, many people to lose large amounts of their investments, and thousands of employees to lose their jobs.
- *Unfair trade practices – cheating the consumer*: in 2007 UK supermarkets and dairy companies were fined £116 million for fixing the price of milk and cheese so that prices (and profits) were kept artificially high, costing consumers £270m more than they would have paid without price fixing.

Although white-collar and corporate crimes often have no individual victim, as in a household burglary or a violent street attack, the examples above do point to the widespread harm that these offences can cause to the public – through dangerous and faulty goods, foods and medicines – and the lasting and long-term effects of environmental pollution can affect thousands of people for generations to come. All too often the people who suffer the most harm from white-collar and corporate crimes are the poor, who are most likely to buy the cheapest and unsafe products, to be employed in more dangerous workplaces with poor enforcement of health and safety regulations, and to be at risk of being defrauded by middle-class professionals.

The under-representation of white-collar and corporate crime White-collar and corporate crimes are substantially under-represented (there appear to be fewer than there really are) in official statistics, giving the impression that the middle-class commit fewer offences. However, there may be many companies and white-collar criminals who simply don't get caught or even have their crimes detected. The impression gained from the official statistics that most crime is committed by the working-class may therefore be quite misleading.

There are several reasons why white-collar and corporate crimes are under-represented in the official statistics.

- *They are hard to detect and investigate*, as the offences often involve some form of technical or insider knowledge, with investigation requiring a lot of skill and expert knowledge which local police forces often lack. In offences like bribery and corruption both parties stand to gain something. Both face trouble if discovered, and so seek to conceal the offence.

- *Institutional protection means they are often not reported and prosecuted, even if detected.* Violations of health and safety legislation by companies often lead only to a reprimand, and crimes such as professional misconduct, medical negligence, industrial espionage and computer fraud are rarely reported and prosecuted, to protect the interests or reputation of the profession or institution and avoid the loss of public confidence which the surrounding scandal might cause. A private security firm is more likely to lead any such investigation, rather than it being reported to the police, with suspected offenders dealt with by being sacked or forced to retire rather than by being prosecuted.

- *They are often without personal or individual victims.* Often the victim is impersonal, like a company or the public at large, rather than an individual, so there is no individual victim to report an offence.

- *There is often a lack of awareness that a crime has been committed* and therefore it is not reported. For example, stealing very small amounts of money from a large number of customers' accounts, leads to barely perceptible small losses to individual victims, and members of the public may lack the expertise to know if they are being misled, defrauded or sold dangerous or counterfeit goods.

- *Even if reported, offenders have a better chance than other criminals of being found not guilty*, as most juries, like the public at large, hold the stereotype that crime is a mainly working-class phenomenon, rather than being committed by wealthy, established companies and affluent, well-educated, so-called respectable middle-class people. Defendants are often of the same background as the judge, and may appear more plausible, honest and respectable to juries, and so may be less likely to be found guilty, or more likely to have their offences seen as temporary lapses in otherwise good behaviour, and to receive more lenient sentences than working-class offenders.

In general, the higher up you are in the social class hierarchy:
- the less likely are your crimes to be detected
- the less likely are your crimes, if detected, to result in your arrest
- the less likely you are, if arrested, to be prosecuted
- the less likely you are, if prosecuted, to be found guilty
- the less likely you are, if found guilty, to be given a prison sentence.

> **Activity**
>
> 1 With reference to particular offences, suggest two reasons why white-collar crimes may not result in a criminal conviction.
> 2 What are the implications of the under-representation of white-collar and corporate crimes in official statistics for the view that most criminals are working-class?

Why are some minority ethnic groups over-represented in the crime statistics?

The evidence on ethnicity and crime

At first glance, official statistics appear to suggest that some minority ethnic groups, particularly black people (African-Caribbeans), are more likely to commit crime than white people. Minority ethnic groups, particularly the black population, are over-represented in the criminal population – that is, there are more than there should be given their proportions in the population as a whole. Table 5.1 shows they have a much higher involvement than white people at various stages of the criminal justice system, and in 2010, the Ministry of Justice reported that, given their proportions in the population, Black and Asian people were more likely than white people:

- to be stopped and searched by the police
- to be arrested
- to be charged and face court proceedings
- to receive a custodial sentence if found guilty
- to be in prison. In 2009, around 27 per cent of male prisoners and 30 per cent of females were from black and minority ethnic groups, even though they make up only about 9 per cent of the general population.

Sociological explanations for the over-representation of black and minority ethnic groups in crime statistics

1. Age, social class and location Compared to white people, minority ethnic groups are more likely to be working-class, and tend to have higher proportions of young people and those suffering social deprivation, higher rates of unemployment, lower pay and to live in deprived urban communities. The higher official crime rates therefore might be because of the same factors discussed earlier as affecting white people, but a higher proportion of minority ethnic groups are affected by them. This explanation suggests that ethnic origin in itself has nothing to do with higher crime rates.

Table 5.1 Proportion (%) at different stages of the criminal justice system compared with ethnic breakdown of general population, England and Wales, 2008–9

	Ethnicity						
	White	Mixed	Black	Asian	Other	Not stated / Unknown	Total
General population (aged 10 & over) @ 2001 Census	89.4	1.3	2.6	5.2	1.5	0.0	100
Stops and searches	67.0	2.8	14.8	8.8	1.3	5.4	100
Arrests	80.6	2.8	7.6	5.4	1.4	2.2	100
Cautions[a]	82.6		6.7	4.9	1.5	4.3	100
Court ordered supervision by probation service	82.0	2.7	6.0	4.7	1.2	3.4	100
Prison population	72.8	3.4	14.4	7.2	1.7	0.5	100

[a]Separate Mixed ethnicity category not available here, and included in other categories

Source: adapted from *Statistics on Race and the Criminal Justice System – 2008/09* (Ministry of Justice, 2010)

Activity

Refer to table 5.1.
1   What percentage of those stopped and searched by the police in 2008–9 were black?
2   What percentage of those in prison were black?
3   Which ethnic group shows the highest risk of being arrested compared to its proportion in the population as a whole?
4   Using examples, how might the information in table 5.1 be used to show that minority ethnic groups are more likely to be criminal than the white population?

2. Labelling, stereotyping and racism in the criminal justice system   Many sociologists have argued that the criminal statistics showing higher crime rates by some minority ethnic groups are a **social construction**. This means they are socially constructed or created by people's interpretations and actions, rather than simply being out there waiting to be collected.

Official statistics do not give a valid (or true) record of ethnicity and offending, but are created as a result of discrimination towards blacks and Asians by the police and other criminal justice agencies. It is this that creates the

A **social construction** is something, like official statistics or the definitions of crime and deviance, that is created by people's interpretations and actions, and only exists because people have constructed it by giving it a particular meaning, interpretation and label.

Criminal Isn't it?

misleading impression that blacks and Asians are more likely to be offenders than whites.

How the police go about their work – what they look out for – is guided by their ideas about who the typical trouble-makers and criminals are. Black and Asian people (especially youths) fit this police stereotype, and they are therefore more likely to be labelled as untrustworthy, trouble-makers and potential criminals and subjected to heavier policing than white people. Many judges and magistrates hold similar stereotypes, and the evidence suggests that they crack down harder on black and Asian people than on white people, giving them heavier fines and sentences than white offenders committing similar offences.

That this is an inaccurate and unfair stereotype is shown by self-report surveys, in which people own up to offences they've committed (these are discussed later in this chapter). While official statistics like those in table 5.1 above suggest black people have the highest rate of offending, the self-reported *Offending, Crime and Justice Survey* in figure 5.3 shows that official statistics do not merely exaggerate the extent of offending among ethnic minorities to an alarming degree, but present a wholly incorrect picture of who the main offenders really are. As figure 5.3 shows, black people are significantly less likely to offend than white people, and it is white people who have the highest rate of offending overall and the second highest for serious offences.

Evidence on discrimination in the criminal justice system shows that, compared to white people, black and Asian people, even though they are less likely to be offenders, are:

- up to 26 times (black people) and 6 times (Asians) more likely to be stopped and searched by the police in England and Wales (*source*: the *Observer*, 17 October 2010)
- more likely to be arrested for similar offences
- more likely to be charged where white offenders are cautioned for similar offences
- more likely to be remanded in custody than released on bail
- more likely to be given prison sentences rather than probation or Community Payback.

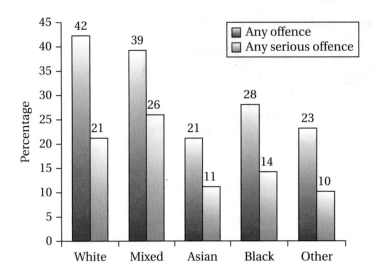

Figure 5.3 Self-reported lifetime offending (%)

Source: C. Sharp and T. Budd, *Minority Ethnic Groups and Crime: Findings from the Offending, Crime and Justice Survey 2003*, On-line Report 33/05, Home Office, 2005

Activity

Refer to figure 5.3.
1 Which ethnic group has the highest proportion of self-reported lifetime offenders of any offence?
2 What percentage of black people admitted committing any serious offence?
3 Which ethnic group is the least likely to commit any offence?
4 Suggest two reasons why the information from the self-report survey in figure 5.3 might be inaccurate, and suggest what steps you might take to overcome them.

This pattern whereby official statistics suggest that the highest levels of criminality are found among black people, while self-report surveys show white people to have the highest proportion of offenders, points to racism in the criminal justice system. This is also reflected in table 5.2, which shows that minority ethnic groups are under-represented, or not represented at all, in some of the most powerful positions in the criminal justice system.

3. Institutional racism The Macpherson Report of 1999 into the murder of Stephen Lawrence (see box) suggests that the view of labelling, stereotyping and racism as an explanation for the links between ethnicity and crime shown in official statistics is a persuasive one, as Macpherson identified **institutional racism** in the police and the criminal justice system. The persistence of such racism led the Metropolitan Black Police Association, in 2008, to warn people from minority ethnic groups not to join the force, because of 'a hostile atmosphere where racism is allowed to spread'.

Institutional racism is 'the collective failure of an organization to provide an appropriate and professional service to people because of their culture, colour or ethnic origin. It can be seen or detected in processes, attitudes and behaviour which amount to discrimination through unwitting prejudice, ignorance, thoughtless and racist stereotyping which disadvantages minority ethnic people' (Macpherson Report, 1999).

Table 5.2 Ethnic minorities and the criminal justice system, 2008–9

Position	Ethnic minority %
Whole population aged 10 and over (2007)	10.6
Law Lord	0.0
Crown Prosecution Service	11.6
Probation Service (2008)	17
High Court judge	3.5
Circuit judge	3
Recorder	7
Magistrates	8
District judges	4
Barristers	11
Solicitors (in private practice)	20
Prison officers	5
Community Support Officers	12
Police officers	4.4

Source: *Statistics on Race and the Criminal Justice System – 2008/09* (Ministry of Justice, 2010); *Annual Staff Diversity Review, 2008/09* (Her Majesty's Prison Service, 2009); Judicial Database, Judiciary of England and Wales

Activity

Refer to table 5.2.
1 To what extent does table 5.2 suggest that minority ethnic groups are unequally represented in the staff of the criminal justice system? Give evidence from the table to back up your view.
2 Suggest reasons why minority ethnic groups might be poorly represented, or not represented at all, in some parts of the criminal justice system.
3 What difficulties do you think people from minority ethnic groups might face in joining or staying in the police force?
4 Suggest how the information in table 5.2 might be used to suggest that institutional racism exists not just in the police force but in the criminal justice system as a whole.
5 Explain carefully, with examples, how the evidence in table 5.2 and the sections above might be used to explain the unequal treatment of black and Asian people by the law, and the high proportion of black and Asian people among those in prison.

THE STEPHEN LAWRENCE INQUIRY AND THE MACPHERSON REPORT (1999)

The investigation into the police handling of the murder of 18-year-old Stephen Lawrence by five white youths in 1993 led to the Macpherson Report in 1999. This was highly critical of London's Metropolitan Police, pointing to a series of mistakes and a 'lack of urgency' and mishandling of the police investigation, including their assumption that Stephen Lawrence was involved in a street brawl rather than being the victim of an unprovoked racist attack. It pointed to the existence of *institutional racism* in the police force, and recommended a series of improvements. These included race-awareness training, more minority ethnic police officers and stronger disciplinary action to get rid of racist police officers. The Macpherson Report established an official view of the widespread existence of institutional racism in many areas, including policing, the health services and education, and led to a campaign to stamp out racism in a wide range of public and private organizations.

WHAT'S WRONG WITH OFFICIAL CRIME STATISTICS?

The previous sections outlined some explanations of the pattern of crime as revealed in official crime statistics. However, sociologists are very critical of these statistics, arguing that they are unreliable and inadequate as sources of evidence about the nature and extent of crime and the social characteristics of criminals. Many crimes go undiscovered, unreported or unrecorded, and, in 2008–9, of those that were reported to the police and recorded by them, only about a quarter were detected or cleared up, with an offender identified and action taken against them. Estimates suggest only about 3 per cent of all crime in England and Wales ends with a conviction.

This means those appearing in official statistics are an unrepresentative sample of officially classified criminals who happen to have been caught, and we don't really have very reliable evidence about who is committing the majority of offences. This leaves open the possibility that the high proportion of young, urban, working-class males in official statistics may give a misleading impression of the criminal population as a whole. Self-report and victim surveys are the two main sources of evidence showing the inadequacy of official crime statistics.

Self-report and victim surveys

Sociologists know that the number of crimes is far higher than the official statistics suggest, because of the use of self-report and victim surveys.

Why might victims keep quiet about crime? Imagine each of the people in this picture is a victim of crime (for example, the child perhaps is suffering physical or sexual abuse, or the father could be a victim of blackmail or violent threats to his family), and consider why they might not report the crime

Self-report surveys are anonymous questionnaires where people are asked to own up to committing crimes, whether they have been discovered or not (the box on p. 265 shows the kind of questions that might be asked in a self-report survey). An example is the Home Office's *Offending, Crime and Justice Survey*, which collects information about offending by, particularly, young people.

Victim surveys involve people reporting on being the victim of a crime, whether or not they reported it to the police. An example is the British Crime Survey (BCS), carried out every year by the Home Office. This tries to discover how much crime goes unreported by victims and unrecorded by the police.

These surveys mean it is possible to estimate how much crime there really is in society. However, they are only estimates, and even self-report and victim surveys do not give a full picture of the real levels of crime in society. For example, not everyone will admit to being a victim or an offender, and around a fifth of people approached refuse to cooperate with victim surveys. As with all surveys, there is the issue of the extent to which the findings are representative, and can be generalized to the whole population. Some other strengths and weaknesses of these surveys are shown in table 5.3 below.

The dark figure of unrecorded and unreported crime

Official crime statistics only show crimes which are known to the police and are recorded by them, or reported in victim surveys like the British Crime Survey. Many offences go unreported and undiscovered. Figure 5.4, derived

Table 5.3 Strengths and weaknesses of self-report and victim surveys

Self-report surveys

Strengths/advantages	Weaknesses/disadvantages
• They provide information uncovering some of the dark figure of unrecorded and unreported crime. • They may provide information on offenders not caught by the police. • They help to find out about victimless crimes like fraud, bribery and corruption or illegal drug use.	• Offenders may exaggerate, understate or lie about the number of crimes they've committed. • Offenders may not admit to some offences, particularly more serious ones. This means such surveys tend to over-emphasize more minor or trivial offences, like petty theft, or vandalism/criminal damage. • Those who are persistent, prolific and serious offenders are the least likely to participate in such surveys.

Victim surveys

Strengths/advantages	Weaknesses/disadvantages
• They provide information uncovering some of the dark figure of crimes not reported to or recorded by the police. • They provide insights into the victims of crime, like their perceptions of the police, and attitudes to crime and anti-social behaviour.	• People may forget they were victimized, particularly the more trivial incidents, or forget whether they were victimized in the period covered by the survey (for example, the British Crime Survey (BCS) covers the last twelve months). This may make results inaccurate. • They may not realize they have been the victims of a crime – particularly white-collar and corporate crimes, where they may not realize that they have been duped, 'conned' or, for example, sold dangerous products. • Victims may feel embarrassment or guilt at admitting to being a victim, such as in the case of sexual offences or domestic violence. • They often don't include all crimes. • Crimes without victims, like drug offences or white-collar crimes like bribery and corruption and fraud, where both parties have something to lose, are not likely to be recorded.

from the 2005–6 British Crime Survey (the last year the data was collected in this form), shows a large gap for many offences between the amount of crime committed and that finally recorded by the police. This figure, that could be as much as 80 per cent or more for some crimes, is known as the 'dark figure' of unrecorded and unreported crime. The British Crime Survey estimates that, overall, about four times as many offences are committed

(*cont.* on p. 267)

EXAMPLE OF A SELF-REPORT SURVEY

1   I have stolen or driven a vehicle without permission, even if the owner got it back.
2   I have stolen or tried to steal parts off the outside, or things from inside, of a vehicle.
3   I have deliberately damaged things that didn't belong to me, for example by scratching, burning, smashing, or breaking them, including things like vehicles, trains, rubbish bins, skips, windows, bus shelters, etc.
4   I have gone into someone's home, or buildings like a factory, office, shop, hospital, or school without permission, because I wanted to steal or damage something.
5   I have used force, violence or threats against someone in order to steal from them, or from a shop, petrol station, bank or any other business.
6   I have, without using force, violence or threats, stolen things, like something someone was carrying or wearing, for example by taking something from their hand, pocket or bag, or stolen things from a shop, the school or college I attend or used to attend, or where I work, or used to work.
7   I have deliberately used force or violence on someone, whether they were injured or not, for example, by scratching, hitting, kicking or throwing things.
8   I have sold illegal drugs, such as heroin, cocaine, crack, ecstasy, and cannabis to people, including friends.
9   I have had in my possession, or taken, illegal drugs, such as marijuana/cannabis, heroin, crack, cocaine, speed, ecstasy, or magic mushrooms.
10 I have travelled on a train or bus without a ticket or deliberately paid the wrong fare.
11 I have taken a weapon, like a knife, out with me in case I needed it in a fight.
12 I have bought something cheap or accepted as a present something I knew was stolen.
13 I have struggled or fought with a police officer to get away from them or to stop them trying to arrest someone.
14 I have written things or sprayed paint on a building, fence, train or somewhere else where I shouldn't have.
15 I have been noisy or rude or acted in such a way in a public place or in or near my home so that someone complained or got me into trouble.
16 I have threatened or been rude to someone because of their skin colour, race or religion.

Source: Adapted from the 2003 Crime and Justice Survey and the 2005 Offending, Crime and Justice Survey, Home Office, 2005, 2006; A. Campbell, Girl Delinquents (Blackwell, 1981)

Activity

1   Work through the self-report survey questions in the box above. List any offences you and/or your friends have committed, whether or not you've been caught, no matter how trivial or whether they're on the list or not. Include your family and people you know, as well as strangers. What conclusions might you draw from your findings about the levels of undiscovered crime in society?
2   List three crimes which a victim might choose not to report to the police, and explain why in each case.
3   Have you or any of your friends ever been a victim (or suspected you might have been a victim) of a crime that you didn't report to the police? Explain the reasons why you didn't report it. What does this tell you about the real extent of crime in society?

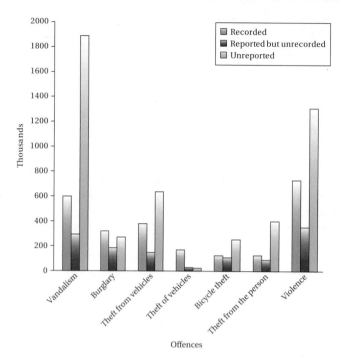

Figure 5.4 Levels of recorded, unrecorded, and unreported crime: England and Wales 2005–6 (BCS comparable crimes)

Source: adapted from *Crime in England and Wales 2005/06* (Home Office / Office for National Statistics, 2006)

Activity

Study figure 5.4 and answer the following questions.

1 Approximately how many crimes of vandalism were recorded by the police?
2 Approximately how many thefts from vehicles were recorded?
3 In which offence category was crime most likely to be recorded in 2005–6?
4 In which offence category was crime most likely to be reported?
5 About how many thefts from vehicles were there in total in 2005–6?
6 Approximately how many bicycle thefts were reported but unrecorded?
7 According to the statistics in figure 5.4, a high proportion of crimes of vandalism, thefts from vehicles, violence, and thefts from the person went unreported. Suggest reasons for this for each offence.
8 Suggest, with examples, reasons why the police may decide not to record a crime: (a) which has been reported to them, and (b) which the police themselves have detected.
9 Explain how the information given in figure 5.4 might be used to show that official crime statistics give a misleading impression of the extent of crime in society. Is there any evidence for the opposite view for particular types of crime? Be sure to give statistical evidence from figure 5.4.

Like an iceberg, where most of the ice is hidden beneath the surface, so it is with crime, with a hidden 'dark figure' of undiscovered, unreported or unrecorded crime

as the number recorded by the police, though for some categories of crime, such as vandalism, theft from the person, and theft from motor vehicles, the number is much higher. Many burglaries, rapes, crimes of domestic violence, woundings and common assaults go unreported.

The failure to report crimes to the police

As table 5.4 and figure 5.5 suggest, a large number of people who are victims of crime don't bother to report it to the police. There are a number of reasons for this, which you may wish to compare with your own findings from the activity on page 265.

- *Victims may think that the incident is too trivial to report;* for example, where the incident involved no loss or damage, or the loss was too small, such as losing a small amount of money, garden tools or bottles of milk.
- *Victims may think there is little point in reporting the incident as they feel the police could not do anything about it,* by either recovering their property or catching the offenders; for example, cases of shoplifting or being pickpocketed.
- *Victims may fear embarrassment or humiliation at the hands of the police or in court.* Researchers at Surrey University in 2009 estimated between 70 per cent and 90 per cent of rapes were unreported, with rape victims not reporting the crime because of embarrassment, because they think the police won't believe them or take them seriously, because they are made to feel it is their own fault they were raped, or because of not wanting to get their attacker – who is often known to them – into trouble. Recent rises in the number of reported rapes and crimes of domestic violence are often explained by changing police practice, and their growing willingness to treat such offences in a more serious way and to be more sympathetic to the victim. However, victims may still feel there is little point in reporting a rape, as of those reported in 2007–8 around 50 to 66 per cent were dropped by the police, and only about one in fifteen women reporting a rape saw the rapist convicted.
- *People may not report offences because they will themselves be in trouble.* Some crimes benefit both parties, and there is no obvious victim. The consequences of reporting such offences will harm all concerned. For example, offences such as the illegal supplying of drugs, consensual under-age sex, or giving and accepting bribes involve an agreement between both parties, and both will lose out if the police find out. Similarly, the illegal drug user who gets ripped off is more likely to be charged with an offence than shown sympathy by the police, and is therefore extremely unlikely to report the incident.

Table 5.4 Reasons for not reporting incidents to the police: by type of offence

Reason for not reporting	Vandalism	Burglary	Thefts & attempted thefts from vehicles	Other household theft	Other personal theft	Violence	All offences
Percentages							
Too trivial / no loss / police could do nothing	85	67	88	84	67	52	75
Private matter / dealt with ourselves	8	14	8	8	10	36	15
Inconvenient to report	4	7	6	7	9	4	6
Reported to other authorities	3	4	1	2	17	9	6
Common occurrence	2	1	1	2	1	3	2
Fear of reprisal	2	6	0	3	1	4	2
Police related reasons[a]	2	2	1	1	1	2	2
Other reasons[b]	4	10	5	3	9	8	6

[a] Police related reasons include dislike or fear of the police and previous bad experiences with the police or courts.

[b] This category includes: something that happens as part of job; partly my/friend's/relative's fault; offender not responsible for actions; thought someone else had reported incident / similar incidents; tried to report but was not able to contact the police / police not interested; other.

Source: adapted from *Crime in England and Wales 2009/10* (Home Office, 2010)

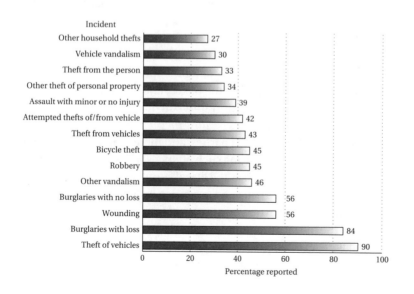

Figure 5.5 Percentage of incidents reported to the police: 2009–10

Source: Adapted from *Crime in England and Wales 2009/10*, Home Office, 2010

Activity

Refer to figure 5.5.

1 Which offence was (a) most likely, (b) least likely, to be reported to the police? Suggest reasons for this in each case.
2 What percentage of the following offences were reported to the police in 2009–10?
    (a) thefts from the person
    (b) bicycle thefts
    (c) thefts of vehicles
3 With reference to figure 5.5 suggest reasons, with examples, why some offences are reported to the police much more than others.

Refer to table 5.4.

4 Which offence did 88 per cent of people say they didn't report because they thought it was too trivial, involved no loss or the police couldn't do anything?
5 Which offence did most people say they didn't report because they saw it as a private matter or dealt with it themselves?
6 For all offences, what were the two most common reasons given for not reporting crime to the police?
7 Suggest examples of offences and/or the circumstances for victims not reporting crimes to the police in each of the following cases:
    (a) they sympathize with the offender;
    (b) they wish to protect the institution in which the offence occurs.
8 How do you think the evidence in figure 5.5 and table 5.4 might be used to challenge the view that most criminals are young, male, and working-class?

- The *victim may fear reprisals if the crime is reported*, for example the blackmail victim afraid of the consequences of reporting the blackmailer, or a burglary victim fearing repeat victimization.
- *Victims may feel it is a private matter they would rather deal with themselves.* Examples might include offences such as theft or assault between friends.
- *Victims may not be aware an offence has been committed.* 'Lost' property may have been stolen, and while the media often report cases of hoax gas-meter readers, cowboy builders, and so on, there may be many people who never actually realize they have been the victims of such a hoax or been conned.

The failure of the police to record a crime

The police may decide not to record an offence that has been reported to or observed by them because:

- they may regard the matter as too trivial to waste their time on, such as the theft of a very small sum of money.

- it has already been satisfactorily resolved, or because the victim does not wish to proceed with the complaint.
- they may regard the person complaining as too unreliable to take his or her account of the incident seriously, as in the case of complaints made by a tramp, a drug addict or someone who is drunk.
- they may think that a report of an incident is mistaken, or that there is simply insufficient evidence to show that a crime has been committed
- they may interpret the law in such a way that what is reported is not regarded as an offence.
- they may regard an incident as nothing to do with them, even though an offence has been committed. This has traditionally been true in cases of domestic violence, such as rape and other violence within marriage or cohabiting relationships.

Activity

The police often have a great deal of work to do, and every arrest they make involves considerable paper work. The police also have discretion over whether to arrest and charge someone for some offences. For example, when people are clubbing and pubbing in town centres, there may be lots of trouble, but the police can choose to move people along rather than arrest them.

1 Suggest two examples of crimes which the police might turn a blind eye to. Give reasons for your answer.
2 Suggest two crimes the police would be forced to record and investigate. Give reasons for your answer.
3 Sometimes the police seem to take some offences more seriously than at other times, and this results in increasing numbers of arrests and prosecutions for these offences, for example drink-driving at Christmas. List, with examples, all the factors you can think of which might make the police occasionally increase their levels of activity against some offences.

IS THE CRIME RATE INCREASING?

Much of what was said in the previous section suggests that official crime statistics provide no real guide to the type or extent of crime, and that they must therefore be used with great care. Such care must also be applied to statistics which show increases (or decreases) in the amounts of recorded crime.

Much public and media concern is always expressed at any increase in recorded crime, but such increases need not necessarily mean there are really more crimes being committed, or that people are at greater risk of being victims of crime. The increases could be explained by a wide range of

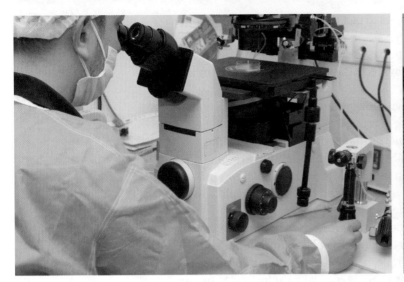

Forensic science and other sophisticated scientific techniques, together with schemes like Neighbourhood Watch, increase the reporting, recording and detection of crime – but this doesn't necessarily mean there are more crimes being committed

factors, which suggest more offences are being discovered, reported to and recorded by the police, but not necessarily that more offences are actually being committed. These factors include:

- *The mass media.* The mass media may exaggerate and distort the fear of crime, and make problems seem worse than they are. This sensitizes people and groups to particular offences or groups of people, and therefore raise demands for police action against the perceived (often imaginary) threats to law and order.
- *Changing counting rules.* Changing rules for counting crimes can lead to higher numbers of offences being recorded, but this does not necessarily mean there is more crime. For example, since April 2002, a person vandalizing six cars in a street has been counted as committing six separate offences, whereas before this would have counted as one.
- *More sophisticated police training, communication and equipment,* such as the use of computers, CCTV, forensic science and DNA testing, and higher policing levels all lead to increasing detection rates. Neighbourhood Watch schemes may also lead to more crimes being reported and detected.
- *Changing police attitudes and policies* – a stronger desire by the police to prosecute certain offenders due to changing police attitudes and policies towards some offences, such as a crack-down on prostitution, drug-dealing or drink-driving. This may give the impression of an increase in crimes of that type, when it is simply that the police are making extra

efforts and allocating more officers to tackle such crimes, and therefore catching more offenders.

- *Changes in the law* make more things illegal, such as rape in marriage, forced marriage or racially aggravated assault, harassment and criminal damage.
- *Easier communications*, such as mobile phones, email and police community websites make reporting of crime easier.
- *Changing social norms and public attitudes* – for example, changing attitudes to rape among the police and the public may have resulted in more rapes being reported, even though no more have been committed. The same might apply to crimes like domestic violence and child abuse, which are also statistically on the increase.
- *People have more to lose today* and more have household contents insurance cover. Insurance claims for theft need a police crime number, so more crime is reported. For example, nearly all thefts of cars and burglaries with loss are reported today so people can claim the insurance money.
- *People may be bringing to the attention of the police less serious incidents, which they may not have reported in the past.* For example, they may have become less tolerant of vandalism and anti-social behaviour, particularly by nuisance youth, and expect the police to take action and stop it.

It is an irony of the official statistics that attempts to defeat crime by increased levels of policing, more police pay and resources, and a determination to crack down on offences can actually increase the levels of recorded crime. The more you search for crime, the more you find; and the official crime rate rises.

Figure 5.6 People are now becoming more intolerant of some incidents, such as anti-social behaviour and vandalism, and reporting them to the police for action, though this doesn't necessarily mean there are more incidents than in the past

> **Activity**
>
> Go to either the Home Office (www.homeoffice.gov.uk) or the Office for National Statistics (www.statistics.gov.uk) and, searching for 'crime statistics':
> 1 Identify the three most common crimes recorded by the police in England and Wales, or Scotland or Northern Ireland, in the latest year for which statistics are available.
> 2 Identify what percentage of all crimes in England and Wales (or Scotland or Northern Ireland) were not detected or cleared up, with an offender identified by the police and action taken against them. Try to find the latest detection or clear-up rate for your local police force.
> 3 Find the latest British Crime Survey, and identify the two offences that are least likely to be reported to the police.
> 4 On the Home Office site, find out two measures that the Home Office is taking to try to reduce crime.

EXPLAINING CRIME AND DEVIANCE

Deviance covers very wide and varied forms of behaviour, and definitions of deviance and crime vary widely between societies, and change over time. There have been a huge number of attempts to explain the causes of deviance, and particularly crime, and why some people commit crime while the majority appear not to. No single explanation can possibly provide an adequate account of all forms of deviance – premeditated murder, armed robbery, causing death by dangerous driving, domestic violence, making a fraudulent home or car insurance claim, anti-social behaviour, pilfering from a local shop, and just being rude and obnoxious are such widely differing acts that no single explanation can cover them all. The following sections briefly cover some of the major explanations which have been offered by sociologists for deviance, particularly criminal deviance.

Biological and psychological theories

These theories suggest that deviant/criminal behaviour is caused by something in people's biological or psychological make-up, which prevents them from conforming to conventional norms and legal rules. Crime is put down to there being something wrong with criminals, rather than with society.

Sociologists generally reject these explanations, as it is impossible to be born a criminal or a deviant, because crime and deviance involve legal and social rules, and what counts as deviant or criminal will depend on how society defines these rules, and these change between societies and over time, and there is no act that in itself is ever always regarded as criminal or deviant. To suggest that criminals are different from normal people also fails to recognize that many people will commit acts of deviance and crime, albeit trivial offences, at some time in their lives, and many criminals are never detected.

Such explanations are based on an unrepresentative group of criminals or deviants who have been caught and labelled as such, and this is a problem for many explanations of crime and deviance, including those below.

Inadequate socialization

Some suggest that the reason people commit crime and other forms of deviance is because of poor socialization and lack of control by families and communities. Young people are brought up in families and communities that fail to provide proper guidelines on right and wrong, which leads to people either choosing deviance and crime over conformity, becoming anti-social or being indifferent to whether the law is broken or not in their peer group and community. This might help to explain some forms of deviance, like anti-social behaviour among young people, but crime and deviance are so widespread through all social groups in society that it is difficult to put it all down to poor parenting and inadequate socialization.

Anomie

An American sociologist, Robert Merton, suggests that all societies set goals which people are encouraged to achieve, such as making money, career success, and buying consumer goods and their own home. Norms or social rules define the socially approved ways of achieving these goals, such as hard work and educational qualifications. Most people are what Merton calls *conformists* – they try to achieve society's goals in approved ways.

Merton argues deviance arises when the approved ways of achieving society's goals don't correspond with the actual situation individuals are in. In these circumstances, **anomie** results.

> **Anomie** refers to a state of confusion and uncertainty over social norms.

This is a situation in which people face confusion and uncertainty over what the social norms are, as these no longer help them to cope with the conditions they find themselves in. For example, many disadvantaged groups such as the poor and the lower-working-class, have little chance of achieving society's goals by acceptable means; they lack opportunities because they face disadvantages in education, or are unemployed or stuck in dead-end jobs with no promotion prospects. A strain is therefore placed on these individuals – they want to achieve the same goals as everyone else, but lack the opportunities for doing so by conventional means. Merton suggests people may respond to these difficulties in achieving society's goals by

Merton's rule-breakers

breaking the rules, for example turning to crime or other deviant behaviour. He identifies four different types of rule-breaking: innovation, ritualism, retreatism and rebellion. Innovators, for example, break the accepted rules for achieving success and turn to deviant or illegal means of achieving society's goals, such as theft. The cartoon below illustrates these four types of deviance.

INNOVATORS

Try to achieve the society's success goals by illegitimate means, such as theft or fraud.

RITUALISTS

Continue to work within the system but give up trying for success, for example office workers stuck in dead-end jobs and simply going through the motions, with little interest in their work and no career ambition.

RETREATISTS

Abandon both the goals and the approved means of achieving them, and become drop-outs, turning to drink, drugs, or some other deviant behaviour.

REBELS

Reject society's goals and the accepted means of achieving them, and replace them with their own, for example revolutionaries.

Activity

Look at the cartoon on Merton's rule-breakers.
1 Which one of the four types of rule-breaker would those who fiddled their income tax normally be considered as?
2 Explain in what way each of Merton's rule-breakers is deviant, and how each would have to change to become conformist.
3 Classify each of the following acts/groups according to Merton's ideas:
   ● someone cheating in exams.
   ● a teacher who has lost interest in the job, but carries on teaching.
   ● a heroin addict.
   ● a terrorist.
   ● a tramp.
   ● a lazy student who only pretends to do any work.
4 Suggest two examples of your own for each type of rule-breaking (or deviance), and explain how your examples show each type of deviance.

Sub-cultural explanations

A **sub-culture** is a smaller culture shared by a group of people within the main culture of a society, in some ways different from the dominant culture, but with many aspects in common. Figure 5.6 illustrates, with examples, this idea of a sub-culture. Sub-cultural explanations of crime and deviance suggest that those who commit crime share some values which are to some extent different from the main values of society as a whole.

Status frustration and the deviant sub-culture

While most lower-working-class young people accept the main goals of society, like gaining wealth and achieving educational success, they have little chance of attaining them. This is because they live in deprived areas, with many social problems and the worst chances in the job market. They therefore develop status frustration. This simply means they lack status in society, and feel frustration at being unable to achieve such status by accepted means.

Their response to this sense of status frustration is to develop a set of alternative, deviant values which provides them with alternative ways of gaining status – a deviant sub-culture. Delinquent acts are based on a deliberate reversal of accepted norms. At school, playing truant, messing about in class and destroying school property may replace the values of studying and exam success. Stealing becomes a means of getting money, replacing a job or career success, and vandalism replaces respect for property. Such acts of

> A **sub-culture** is a smaller culture shared by a group of people within the main culture of a society, in some ways different from the main culture, but with many aspects in common.

Figure 5.6 Culture and sub-cultures

The dominant culture of a society

Criminal sub-culture

Gay sub-culture

Traveller sub-culture

Youth sub-cultures

Minority ethnic group sub-cultures

Lower-working-class sub-culture

Drug sub-culture

Sub-cultures: smaller cultures which are in some ways different from the dominant culture, but have many things in common with it

delinquency enable some lower-working-class youths to gain a status in their peer group which the wider society has denied them. Delinquency also gives them a way of getting their revenge on the system which has condemned them to failure.

The lower-working-class sub-culture

Some suggest that the values of lower-working-class male sub-culture can often lead to crime among young people. This sub-culture encourages men to demonstrate their toughness, their masculinity and their 'smartness', and to pursue excitement and thrills. These features of working-class life can lead to clashes with the law. For example, the concern with 'toughness' might lead to offences like assault.

These values may become exaggerated in the lives of young males who want to achieve status in their peer group by engaging in delinquent acts to show how tough and smart they are. A 'good night out' might consist of a few drinks, a fight outside the pub, a rampage round the streets with mates, and a run-in with the police, with everyone competing to show they are more macho than the rest.

Relative deprivation, social exclusion and marginalization

Marginalization is the process whereby some people are marginalized or pushed to the margins or edges of society by poverty, ill-health, lack of education, disability, racism and so on, and face **social exclusion**. This is where people are excluded from full participation in education, work, community life and access to services and other aspects of life seen as part of being a full member of mainstream society. Those who lack the necessary resources are excluded from the opportunity to participate fully in society, and are denied the opportunities most people take for granted.

Relative deprivation is a related idea. This refers to people having a sense of deprivation because they lack things compared to the group with which they identify and compare themselves.

Those who find themselves pushed to the margins of society, excluded from the normal everyday life that most members of society enjoy, and who have a sense of relative deprivation, are vulnerable to committing crime. This is because crime offers one route to resolving the problems of relative deprivation, social exclusion and marginality that arise when people are denied things that others may take for granted.

Edgework and the seduction of crime

Some suggest that people commit crime for the excitement, thrills and buzz arising from taking the risk of getting caught. Some are seduced into crime

Marginalization is the process whereby some people are pushed to the margins or edges of society by factors such as poverty, ill-health, lack of education, disability and racism.
Social exclusion is where people are excluded from full participation in mainstream society, as they lack the resources and opportunities most people take for granted.
Relative deprivation is a sense of lacking things (deprivation) compared to the group with which people identify and compare themselves.

The excitement derived from edgework – the kicks derived from living 'on the edge' through risk-taking – may explain why already well-off people turn to crime even though they don't need the money

and other forms of deviance not necessarily for material gain, but because they are attractive as forms of 'edgework'. Committing crime is a source of pleasure derived from the kicks involved in living 'on the edge', with acts like shoplifting, vandalism, doing drugs, fighting and other fairly petty offences being adventures providing pleasure, excitement and adrenalin flows that are more important than any worry about the risk of being caught or any need for items stolen. The 'thrills and spills' of edgework as a motivation for crime may appeal to all people at various times, and would help to make sense of crime committed by richer people who don't need to turn to crime for money.

Labelling

Labelling theory is concerned with two main features:

- the process whereby some people committing some actions come to be defined or labelled as deviant, while others do not
- the consequences which follow once a deviant label has been applied, and how this may create more deviance or crime.

The first of these issues was discussed earlier in this chapter, so here the emphasis will be on the consequences which follow once a deviant label has been applied.

The deviant master status

Labelling theorists point out that most people commit crimes and other deviant acts at some time in their lives, but not everyone becomes defined as a deviant or a criminal. For labelling theorists, what is important in explaining crime is the consequences of being caught and labelled.

Once someone is caught and labelled as a criminal or deviant, the label attached may become the dominant label or **master status** which overrides all other characteristics of that person – she or he becomes not someone's partner, mother/father, friend or business associate, but an 'ex-con', a thief or a hooligan.

> A **master status** is the dominant status of an individual which overrides all other characteristics of that person, such as that of an 'ex-con' or thief.

Once a person is labelled as 'mad' (mentally ill), as a football hooligan, as a thief or as a failure at school, the label may have quite serious consequences for his or her life, as people are treated differently according to the label. Each label carries with it a range of prejudices and images – the football hooligan, for example, is often seen as irresponsible, violent, a drunkard, a racist and a serious threat to society. A person with a conviction for theft may be seen as fundamentally untrustworthy and never to be left alone with valuables, and if things go missing this may automatically reinforce suspicions that they have been stolen by the labelled thief. The bottom-stream pupil in school may be seen as a waster, and thoroughly untrustworthy and unreliable. Once labelled, a person's behaviour might be interpreted differently from that of a person not labelled as deviant. For example, teachers may treat some questions from bottom-stream 'delinquents' as red herrings, but regard the same questions from top-stream conformists as intelligent and worthy of discussion. Much the same could apply when different pupils offer excuses for not doing homework, missing games, and so on. Someone with a history of mental illness may have signs of eccentricity interpreted as evidence of his or her mental illness, but the same behaviour might pass unnoticed in a person not labelled as mentally ill.

Deviant careers

Labelling may lead to a **deviant career**, and people start acting the way they have been labelled.

> A **deviant career** is where people who have been labelled as deviant find conventional opportunities blocked to them, and so are pushed into committing further deviant acts.

For example, a man caught in an isolated act of stealing may be prosecuted, imprisoned and labelled as a 'criminal' and later as an 'ex-con' – friends desert him, employers refuse to offer him jobs, and the man may then begin to see himself primarily as a criminal. Since alternative opportunities are closed off to him, and everyone treats him as a criminal anyway, he may then turn to crime as a way of life and follow a deviant career of crime.

In this way, labelling theory suggests that the attachment of a label can actually generate more deviance. For example, adult prisons and Young Offenders Institutions play a key role in making the labels of 'criminal' and, later, 'ex-con' stick. They immerse offenders in a criminal sub-culture, increase the opportunities to learn about crime, and make it extremely hard for them to go back to living a normal life when they are released. More crime may therefore result as alternative opportunities are limited. An example of a deviant career is shown in figure 5.7.

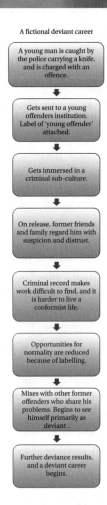

A fictional deviant career

A young man is caught by the police carrying a knife, and is charged with an offence.

⬇

Gets sent to a young offenders institution. Label of 'young offender' attached.

⬇

Gets immersed in a criminal sub-culture.

⬇

On release, former friends and family regard him with suspicion and distrust.

⬇

Criminal record makes work difficult to find, and it is harder to live a conformist life.

⬇

Opportunities for normality are reduced because of labelling.

⬇

Mixes with other former offenders who share his problems. Begins to see himself primarily as deviant.

⬇

Further deviance results, and a deviant career begins.

Figure 5.7 The development of a deviant career

Activity

In each of the cases listed below:
1 Identify a possible label which may be attached to the person concerned as a result of her or his deviant behaviour.
2 Outline how a deviant career might develop by describing the possible consequences of the labelling for the person's future life and relationships.
3 Suggest ways that a person might avoid being labelled even after she or he has committed the deviant act.
  - a young woman caught shoplifting
  - a male teacher who publicly declares himself to be gay
  - a person who is temporarily admitted to a mental hospital as a result of a nervous breakdown
  - an 18-year-old man who gets arrested during a fight at a football match
  - a school student caught cheating in exams

THE VICTIMS OF CRIME

Since the 1980s, there has been a rapid growth in victim surveys like the British Crime Survey, and studies of the impact of crime on victims and their needs and rights. All sections of the criminal justice system, like the police and courts, are increasingly paying attention to the interests of victims and the impact of crime on local communities. For example, the police are making greater efforts to engage with the community and keep victims informed about progress in catching offenders, and victims of sexual assault are getting more specialist help and more sympathetic and specially trained police to deal with them. Victim Support schemes are now an integral part of the criminal justice system.

It has been increasingly recognized that if the victims of crime do not have confidence in the criminal justice system to support them and catch and punish offenders, then most crime will remain unreported, victims will be unwilling to give evidence and offenders will go unpunished.

Who are the victims of crime?

- The poor are, overall, the most likely victims of crime: the unemployed, the long-term sick, low-income families, those living in rented accommodation and in areas with high levels of deprivation. The poorest fifth of people in Britain, compared to the richest fifth, face around twice the risk of being victims of burglary and vehicle-related thefts, as well as higher risks of vandalism, and overall household crime.

> Those who have the fewest and least valuable material possessions are those most likely to have them stolen or vandalized, while those who have the most, and most valuable, material possessions are the least likely to have them stolen or vandalized. Those who steal from the poor and vandalize their property are mainly other poor people.

- Young men (aged 16–24) have about twice the risk of young women of being a victim of a violent crime, most of it committed by other young people. Older men and women are the least likely to be victims of violent crime.
- Women are far more likely than men to be victims of crimes like sexual assault, rape and domestic violence. Every week two women die due to domestic violence.
- Black (African-Caribbeans) and Asian people are up to fourteen times more likely to be victims of racially motivated incidents than white people, and face between two and six times the risk of being murdered, in comparison to white people.

Activity

Explore the Home Office website on victims of crime (www.homeoffice.gov.uk/crime-victims/victims, www.homeoffice.gov.uk/crime-victims/how-you-can-prevent-crime) and www.homeoffice.gov.uk/crime-victims/reducing-crime.

1 Identify and explain two government suggestions on how people might take action themselves to avoid becoming victims of crime.
2 Identify and explain two policies for reducing the number of victims of crime which focus on stopping offending, such as community safety or youth crime strategies.

GOVERNMENT INITIATIVES AND POLICY SOLUTIONS TO CRIME

Over the years, governments have taken a range of measures to tackle crime, but with mixed success. The main deterrent to crime seems to be not the severity of the sentence or punishment, but the risk of getting caught in the first place. However, the police are detecting a smaller proportion of crimes than ever, with estimates suggesting only about 3 per cent of all crime results in a conviction. Table 5.5 outlines some of the measures that have been, and are being, tried to tackle crime.

Activity

1 Look at the range of policies in table 5.5 that have been used to tackle crime. Which three policies do you think are likely to be the most effective in tackling crime? Give reasons for your answer.
2 Discuss your answer with others in your group, and see if there is any agreement on the most effective measures to take.
3 Go to the Victims for Restorative Justice website (www.why-me.org) and suggest two ways in which restorative justice might help the victims of crime, and two reasons why it might encourage offenders not to re-offend.
4 Using Google, or the Home Office website (www.homeoffice.gov.uk), investigate how effective the policies you identified in question 1 are in stopping criminal and deviant behaviour.

Table 5.5 Policies to tackle crime

Policy	Description/comment
Electronic tagging	Electronic tag is fitted to ankle of offenders to monitor and control their movements.
Community Payback	Instead of prison, offenders do work in the community, like cleaning off graffiti, painting community centres or digging pensioners' gardens.
Restorative justice	Where offenders and victims meet face-to-face, and offenders attempt to restore or repair the harm and damage they caused to their victims.
Curfew schemes and Anti-Social Behaviour Orders (ASBOs)[a]	To ban people from specific areas and to keep young tearaways off the streets.
More police on the streets, and more efficient policing	Recruiting more police officers, cutting paperwork so officers have more time patrolling, monitoring police performance, and taking action where results are poor.
Zero tolerance policing	Tackling *all* crime, including low-level crimes like vandalism, petty theft and criminal (and even non-criminal) anti-social behaviour, where police tolerance and inaction can create an 'anything goes' culture in some communities, leading to more crime.
More community involvement in policing	More community policing and schemes like Neighbourhood Watch, to promote public confidence in the police, and encourage people to report crime and to volunteer evidence that might help to secure convictions.
Fast-track justice for young offenders	So punishment follows quickly on the crime.
Crime diversion	Divert young offenders from crime, through projects like sport, arts and car maintenance projects.
Rehabilitation of offenders to stop them reoffending	Rehabilitate criminals, through education and skills training, and help with finding jobs when they leave prison – 39 per cent of criminals released in 2007 reoffended and were convicted within one year. Others may have reoffended but not been caught. The present prison regime is not working for many prisoners.
Better use of technology	More closed-circuit television cameras, more DNA testing, photos on credit cards, more alarms and better locks on homes and cars, etc., to deter and catch criminals.
Tougher sentencing	Heavier sentences for offenders, particularly persistent (repeat) offenders.
Decriminalizing drug offences (i.e. stopping treating drug abuse as a criminal offence) and treating drug addicts	Drug abuse is the single largest cause of crime. Decriminalization and treatment programmes to cure addiction would reduce crime.

[a] These were proposed to be phased out in 2010–11.

DEVIANCE, CRIME AND SOCIAL CHANGE

This chapter has shown that the definition and explanation of deviance and crime are no simple matters. This is hardly surprising given the very wide range of behaviour that the term 'deviance' covers.

We must recognize that deviance, and even crime, are not by any means always harmful to society. Much crime remains fairly trivial, and the wide range of non-conformist behaviour, its quirks and oddities, add a richness of colour and variety to what might otherwise be a drab existence.

Without deviance, even without crime, there would be no possibility of innovation and change. The rebels and the reformers, the heretics and the inventors, and campaigners for peace and justice have all been labelled as deviants or criminals at one time or another. For example, Jesus Christ was seen as a rebel in his time, and crucified for it. Nelson Mandela was imprisoned in South Africa for thirty years for alleged terrorist offences in fighting a white racist society; his role in changing South African society led him later to become president of South Africa and an internationally respected world leader and celebrity. Che Guevara fought in the 1950s against a corrupt and repressive regime in Cuba, later to become Minister of Industry and National Bank President in a new socialist Cuba, as well as the global icon, shown in the picture, which persists to this day. Martin McGuinness is a former commander of the Derry Brigade of the IRA (Irish Republican Army), and was imprisoned in the 1970s for his role in fighting against discrimination and violent attacks against Catholics, and British rule and the presence of British troops in Ireland. His early battles, once defined as deviant and criminal, so changed Northern Ireland that he is, at the time of writing, a British MP, a member of the Northern Ireland Assembly and the Deputy First Minister of Northern Ireland, and is pictured opposite with US Secretary of State Hillary Clinton in 2009.

Nelson Mandela

Che Guevara

It is often the non-conformists and law-breakers who have contributed to changes which many would regard as of benefit to all. Deviance should be treated with an open mind, for what is regarded as deviant today is often the accepted behaviour of tomorrow.

Martin McGuinness with Hillary Clinton

CHAPTER SUMMARY

After studying this chapter, you should be able to:

- define social control and explain how it is carried out formally and informally through agencies of social control

- explain the difference between crime and deviance

- explain how and why definitions of deviance vary

- explain the link between deviance and power

- explain why crime is a social issue and a source of public debate, and describe the significance of criminal and deviant behaviour for victims, communities and society in general

- describe and explain the pattern of crime shown in official crime statistics, including class, age, gender, ethnicity and locality

- explain why white-collar and corporate crimes often go undetected or unrecorded

- explain a range of reasons why official crime statistics provide no accurate record of the full extent of crime in society

- describe some strengths and weaknesses of self-report and victim surveys

- explain why an increase in the official crime rate might not necessarily mean that there has been an increase in the real amount of crime

- provide a range of explanations for crime, delinquency and deviance

- describe and explain the ideas of labelling and deviant careers

- outline some policy solutions to crime

- suggest reasons why deviance and crime may not always be harmful to society.

KEY TERMS

anomie
chivalry thesis
corporate crime
crime

deviance
deviant career
hate crime
institutional racism
juvenile delinquency

law
marginalization
master status
relative deprivation
sexual orientation

social construction
social exclusion
status frustration
sub-culture
white-collar crime

The Mass Media

Contents

CHAPTER

6

The Mass Media

KEY ISSUES

- What are the mass media?
- The traditional and the new media
- Who uses the new media, and what for?
- The significance of the new media in contemporary society
- The mass media and socialization
- Media regulation: formal controls on the media
- Ownership of the mass media
- The mass media, public opinion and social control
- Bias in the media: what affects the content of the media?
- The mass media, power and democracy
- Crime, deviance and the media
- The effects of the mass media on audiences
- Violence and the media
- Into the future

WHAT ARE THE MASS MEDIA?

The term *mass media* refers to the technology, organizations and products involved with communication with large mass audiences without any face-to-face personal contact. The main media of mass communication include terrestrial (earth-based) and satellite television, radio, newspapers and magazines, books, cinema, CDs and DVDs, advertising, computers and computer games, mobile phones and the Internet.

THE TRADITIONAL AND THE NEW MEDIA

The mass media are now often divided into the traditional and the new media.

The traditional media

The traditional media refers to those media that communicated in a one-way process to very large mass audiences. This is the type of media associated with traditional broadcasting, like the terrestrial television channels (BBC 1 and 2, ITV 1, and Channels 4 and 5) and BBC radios 1 and 2, and mass circulation national and Sunday newspapers. There was little consumer choice, beyond a few TV channels, radio stations or newspapers and magazines.

The new media

The new media refers to those media using new technology which first emerged in the late twentieth and early twenty-first centuries spreading content using screen-based, digital (computer) technology. These include computers and the Internet; electronic e-books; digital cable and satellite TV; digiboxes and DVD recorders enabling customized, individualized television viewing with a choice of hundreds of television channels; digital media like CDs, DVDs and mp3; Internet downloads of films, videos and music onto mobile phones and mp3 players, user-generated media content through websites like Facebook, MySpace and YouTube; and interactive video/computer games through Play Stations and X-boxes.

While the traditional media involves different devices for different media content – like printed format for books, newspapers and magazines, radios and mp3 players to listen to music and radio programmes, televisions to watch shows, and phones to make calls – the new media technology often involves using a single device doing several things. For example, the latest media technology, like Apple's iPhone and iPad, enables users, on a single

The traditional media include separate devices like printed books, television and newspapers, and were a one-way 'take it or leave it' process of mass communication

Much new media activity, like satellite TV and Internet access, is via communication satellites in space, rather than land-based cables, pylons and transmitters

The new media involves digital (computer) screen-based technology, often integrating many uses into a single device, as in Apple's iPhone and iPad shown here. Traditional print and TV are also now competing with the Internet, as shown by the BBC website pictured here

device, to make phone calls, read books, send text messages and emails, take photos and record videos and send them to friends and upload them to Internet sites, browse the Internet, play music, watch films and TV, consult maps, and hundreds of other applications. Likewise, businesses and advertisers are able to communicate with millions of people at the same time through a single device.

Differences between the traditional and new media

The new media differs from traditional forms of the mass media in several ways:

It is digital

Essentially, this means 'using computers', whereby all data (text, sound and pictures) are converted into computer code which can then be stored, distributed and picked up via screen-based devices, like mobile phones, DVDs, digital TVs and computers.

It is interactive

This means consumers have an opportunity to engage or interact with the media, creating their own material, and customizing the media to their own wishes, with much greater choice compared with the passive consumption and 'take it or leave it' features of the traditional media. For example, people don't just have to watch the news or other content that media professionals provide: they can actually create it themselves, by uploading videos to YouTube, posting items on the Internet, 'blogging' – writing Internet diaries – for all to see and spreading their ideas on Facebook and Twitter; they can press the red button on their digital TV handsets to explore issues more and vote people on or off reality TV shows like *Big Brother*, buy things from advertising programmes and rent films to view, and they can set their own TV schedules, using DVD recorders, digiboxes and BBC's iPlayer.

It is dispersed

This means it is less centralized and controlled than traditional media, and more adapted to individual choices. There is a huge growth of media products of all kinds, which are more outside the control of large organizations. The routine use of the Internet for information, shopping and entertainment, email, laptop computers, interactive digital TV, social networking sites like Facebook, downloadable content onto mobile phones, and podcasts to mp3 players mean the production of media content is now becoming more generally dispersed throughout the population, rather than restricted to media professionals. For example, people are now making their own videos and posting them on the Internet. In 2010, there were at least 20 hours of consumer-generated video uploaded to YouTube every minute. Internet diaries – 'blogs' – are beginning to rival traditional journalism as sources of information and news. Estimates of the number of blogs vary wildly, but a 2008 estimate suggested 184 million people globally had started a blog. There is huge scope for people to create and spread their own information outside the control of media companies and the agencies of social control.

Activity

1 Go to www.en.wikipedia.org and look up 'digital media', 'interactivity', 'hypertext' and 'virtual reality'. Follow the hypertext links given in Wikipedia and give two examples of contemporary media that use each of these.
2 Go to www.youtube.com, do a search on sociology uk, and report your findings on any two sociology videos.

3 Go to www.news.bbc.co.uk and watch the UK news headlines on Internet video, making a note of the latest headline stories. Now do the same with www.sky.com. Compare the two sets of news stories, and whether they seem to be covering the same material. What might this suggest to you about how the media influences our views of the world?

4 Discuss with others in your group, or do a small survey, and find out what people use the new media for, and whether they use them more or less than the traditional media like newspapers, books and television.

WHO USES THE NEW MEDIA, AND WHAT FOR?

The new media is rapidly catching up with, and threatening, the traditional media as a means of mass communication. Internet use across Europe is now around 14 hours a week per person compared to around 12 hours a week of TV viewing, according to a Microsoft survey. In the UK, around 75 per cent of households had Internet access in 2010, and 80 per cent of the population used the Internet; 38 per cent of all on-line users have a social networking profile, most of them on Facebook, which was the second most frequently used site after Google in 2009. People in the UK spend an average of about 33 hours a week watching TV, compared to 12 hours a week on-line, though Internet usage is higher for younger age groups. In March 2008, 3.5 billion video clips were viewed by UK web users – an average of 128 on-line video clips per viewer. Advertisers now spend more on Internet advertising than they do on TV, and newspapers also have to compete with the Internet for advertising income. Many national newspapers and TV stations now have their own websites, reaching millions more people than their own printed papers or TV channels do. The importance of advertising income means that increasingly websites have to appeal to mass audiences if advertisers are to be persuaded to advertise. Spam (unasked-for electronic bulk messages via texting or email) is becoming a cheap means for advertisers to reach masses of people.

The box below represents some of the uses of the new media. It is important to remember that, in most cases, the individual consumer is only one of millions, and those providing the service, albeit customized to individual use, are communicating with millions of people, with funding and profits provided, in most cases, by advertisers.

USES OF THE NEW MEDIA (INCLUDING THE INTERNET)

- Buying and selling products
- Education
- All kinds of research
- Finding information of all kinds, such as on health or religion
- Contacting support groups
- Finding and making friends, and building social networks, including on-line dating
- Entertainment
- Communicating with friends and family
- Banking, paying bills and other financial transactions
- Downloading, filesharing and listening to music
- Sharing and viewing photos and videos
- Reading or watching the news, including on-line newspapers, and sports results
- Creating and uploading text and photo/video content
- Writing Internet diaries (blogging)
- Viewing pornography
- Playing games, like Farmville on Facebook (which has at least 63 million users)
- Accessing information about government, local council or health services
- Buying travel services, like train and flight tickets, and booking hotels
- Watching television, including catch-up TV through applications like the BBC iPlayer, watching films and listening to the radio

---

THE SIGNIFICANCE OF THE NEW MEDIA IN CONTEMPORARY SOCIETY

There is little doubt that new media technology has made a massive impact on contemporary society. For example, six in every ten of the world's population owned a mobile phone at the end of 2008, and for a variety of uses, like those discussed above, other than making phone calls; and nearly a quarter of the world's 6.7 billion people were using the Internet.

There are very wide debates about the new media and their significance in contemporary society. Some have an optimistic view, seeing the new media as playing a positive role in society, while others are more pessimistic. The following sections summarize these two sides of the discussion.

Optimistic views of the new media

Widening consumer choice

There are now hundreds of digital cable and satellite TV channels, websites and on-line newspapers for people to choose from. People can now make their own TV schedules, for example.

More media user participation

Interactive digital TV, digiboxes, blogging and **citizen journalism** (where the public, rather than professional journalists, collect and report news), video- and photo-sharing websites like YouTube, and social networking sites like Facebook and MySpace are all giving consumers more opportunities to participate in using and producing media content.

More access to information

Everyone now has access to huge amounts of information from all over the world. This potentially gives people more power in society, as they can gain access to information for themselves rather than relying on others for it. An everyday example might be people being able to check symptoms of illness on-line, through websites like NHS Direct (www.nhsdirect.nhs.uk) and Netdoctor (www.netdoctor.co.uk), and also to check any risks associated with prescribed medicines they have been given. This gives patients more power through information rather than being solely dependent on doctors.

The Internet gives individuals more access to information than ever before, giving them more power and control over their lives rather than being dependent on others. Websites, like NHS Direct and Netdoctor shown here, enable individuals to check their symptoms on-line and receive health advice, without being obliged to visit GPs' surgeries

More democracy

There is now a far wider range of news sources, and a vast ocean of information available to all. More people, not just large media corporations, have the opportunity to communicate with vast numbers of other people. This is discussed later in this chapter.

Social life and social interaction are enhanced

The new media have opened up new channels for communication and interaction, enhancing or supplementing existing face-to-face interactions. Factors like gender, age, ethnicity and social class might once have meant some conversations in the real world might have been avoided, but alternative identities can be constructed in cyberspace or virtual worlds, and the media may become part of the means by which people express themselves. People can stay in touch via email when they are away from home, or meet anonymously in chat rooms or social networking sites which may lead to face-to-face meetings. Social networking and sharing sites like MySpace, Bebo, YouTube, Facebook and Flickr, and 'Googling' friends can enhance social networks, re-establish lost contacts between old friends, create on-line communities and bring people together. Ofcom found that in 2007 one in four Britons logged on to such websites at least twenty-three times each month, making the UK the most 'digital' nation in Europe, and second only to Canada among world users of these websites.

Pessimistic views of the new media

A threat to democracy

Transnational corporations like Microsoft, Google, Yahoo!, Vodaphone and News Corporation control the Internet technology, the satellite channels and mobile networks. This poses a threat to democracy and enhances the power of the already powerful, as more and more of what we know is dominated and controlled by global corporations.

The lack of regulation

The global nature of the new media, such as the Internet and satellite broadcasting, means there is a lack of regulation or control, by national bodies like Ofcom (see later). This means undesirable things like bias, Internet crime, paedophilia, pornography, violence and racism can thrive virtually unchecked.

There is no real increase in consumer choice

There is poorer-quality media content, with 'dumbing down' to attract large audiences, much of the same content on different TV channels, and endless

Will the new media technology lead to an increase in social isolation? What do you think?

repeats. Celebrity culture replaces serious programming, and national newspaper websites chase after large audiences, and therefore advertising, by replacing serious news reporting with 'infotainment' (information wrapped up to entertain).

The undermining of human relationships and communities

There will be an increase in social isolation, with people losing the ability to communicate in the real world as they spend less quality time with family and friends, and more wrapped up in solitary electronic media. There will consequently be a loss of **social capital** or the useful social networks which people have, as they spend less time engaging with the communities and neighbourhoods in which they live.

Social capital refers to the social networks of influence and support that people have.

The digital divide

Not everyone has access to the new media, and there is inequality, or a **digital divide**, between those who can and those who can't afford, or don't have the technology to support, access to the new media, like pay-to-view satellite channels, computers and broadband Internet access. This creates national and global inequalities, and a new digital underclass, who are excluded from the alleged benefits of the new media. For example, Europe and North America make up around 39 per cent of the world's Internet users, even though these areas comprise just 17 per cent of the world's population. Figure 6.1 illustrates this.

The **digital divide** refers to the gap between those people with effective access to the digital and information technology making up the new media and those who lack such access.

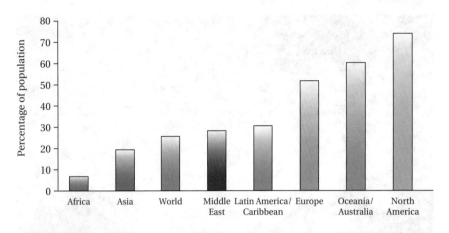

Figure 6.1 The digital divide: percentage of population using the Internet, September 2009

Source: www.Internetworldstats.com

Activity

1 Examine the arguments and evidence above and, drawing on your own experiences, try to reach a conclusion about whether the new media are, overall, having a good or bad effect on society. If you are in a group, you might divide yourselves up into two groups for and against, and debate the issue.

2 Refer to figure 6.1 and answer the following questions:

(a) What percentage of the population in which area of the world had the highest level of Internet users in 2009?

(b) In what region did approximately 20 per cent of the population use the Internet?

(c) Approximately what percentage of the world population were Internet users in 2009?

(d) Suggest three ways that not having access to the Internet, via a computer and/or a mobile, might disadvantage households in contemporary Britain.

THE MASS MEDIA AND SOCIALIZATION

The significance of the media as an agency of socialization

As considered in chapter 1, there is a wide range of agencies involved in people's socialization, and the media are only one influence on the way people might think and behave. Nonetheless, the media are now major influences in socialization, not least because they play such a central part in many people's lives. For example, there are 27 million televisions in British homes, with the typical viewer watching television for about 33 hours a week in January 2010 – around 5 hours a day. Around 90–95 percent of those over age 4 watch television. Around 10 million newspapers are sold every day. Young people

Use of the new media is now a feature of everyday life, and they play an important role in secondary socialization

between the ages of 5 and 16 spend on average nearly 6 hours a day in front of a TV, computer or games console, according to statistics by market research agency Childwise in 2009. In 2008, British people were spending just over a quarter of their total leisure time on the Internet, rising to a third for those aged 18–24, and this excludes time spent on-line at work or at school and university.

The media have therefore become a key agency of secondary socialization and informal education, as they become ever more important sources of information, entertainment and leisure activity for large numbers of people. Our view of the world, our political and social attitudes, our view of others such as political leaders are more and more formed through our impressions gained from the media rather than through personal experience. These impressions can influence how we think we should live our lives and how we should act, how we might vote in elections, and our own personal senses of identity.

The media and identity

The explosion of the new media in recent years has meant that society is becoming media-saturated and, as the figures in the previous section suggest, the media are present in very many aspects of our lives and play a growing part in shaping the world we live in.

What we see, hear or read in the media often has important influences on our identity – how we see ourselves and how others see us. People often use the media to confirm or explore their identities, values and interests, such as finding out and keeping up with the latest social attitudes, or trends in fashion, music, cooking or gardening. The media create desires and pressures to buy things, and shape our ideas about the things we should buy – our consumer choices. Many people often come to see and define their self-image and the one they want to present to other people in terms of media imagery, whether this be a gender identity, an ethnic identity, a national identity, a social class identity, a hybrid identity (mixing different identities) or any other identity they might wish to adopt. For example, people may adopt media-induced images, styles, brand names, and trends, with celebrities, fashion models, musicians, soap stars or other media figures as role models in their own lives.

Activity

1 Work out approximately how many hours in a typical week you spend watching television or DVDs, playing computer games or using the Internet, listening to the radio or music, reading newspapers and magazines, or at the cinema.

2 Work out approximately how many hours a week you spend sleeping.

3 There are 168 hours in a week. Take away the number of hours you spend sleeping from this total. Now work out what percentage of your waking life you spend under the direct influence of the mass media (you can do this by dividing the number of hours spent watching TV, etc., by the number of waking hours and multiplying by 100).

4 List all the ways you think the mass media influence you in your life, such as your lifestyle and identity, knowledge about current affairs, attitudes and opinions, tastes in music and fashion, and your views of different social groups, such as women and men, minority ethnic groups, the disabled, and the elderly.

5 Do you think the media have a large effect on your beliefs and values, your sense of identity and your consumer choices? What other influences on your beliefs and values might also be important?

Socialization and media stereotyping

As suggested above, the media can contribute to the formation of impressions about other social groups. These impressions are often created by the media presenting stereotypes of different groups, and such stereotyping is a common feature of media coverage of events. A stereotype is a generalized, oversimplified view of the features of a social group, allowing for few individual differences between its members. Stereotyping often distorts and exaggerates some characteristics of some individuals in a group, and assumes they apply to everyone in that group. There is some reference to media stereotyping of older people on page 488, of lone parents on page 131 and of the cereal packet family on pages 135–6, and you should refer to these. The following sections will review some other examples of media stereotypes.

Gender stereotyping

The section in chapter 1 on gender role socialization (see pages 19–35) considered the way that the mass media formed and reinforced gender stereotypes, and most obviously in advertising. You may wish to refer to the media section on pages 30–5 now.

When women appear in the mass media, it has traditionally been in a limited number of stereotypes, such as:

- the *sex object* – typically slim, sexy, seductive and scantily clad
- in their relationships with men, as bosses, husbands and lovers
- as emotional and unpredictable
- the housewife and mother, content, capable and caring, keeping the family together and managing its emotions.

The masculine stereotype of the physically well-built, muscular, strong, handsome, brave, independent, unemotional, assertive non-domestic male still often appears in the media, though men, in comparison to women, are presented in a wider range of roles which have no particular reference to their gender.

Harmful consequences of media stereotyping of gender The media frequently expose people to images of 'perfection' in magazines, on TV, in films, music videos and advertisements, which in most cases do not conform to the reality of their everyday lives. This may have harmful effects on their mental health, by inducing feelings of guilt, inadequacy and lack of self-confidence among the majority of women and men who don't measure up to the media stereotypes. This may partly explain why so many women are concerned with slimming and dieting, why anorexia and other eating disorders are illnesses affecting mainly teenage girls (through, increasingly, adult women as well), and why many women in this country are on tranquillizers.

Research in 2001 from Glasgow University found women were up to ten times more likely to be worried about their weight than men, even when they were not overweight. Many surveys have found teenage girls to be obsessed with body image and the desire to acquire a 'perfect' celebrity body, and expressing unhappiness and seeking continual reassurance about their face, hair, weight, skin, teeth, breasts, tummy, bottom, thighs and legs. Even girls under age 10 link happiness and self-esteem with being slim and pretty. These harmful consequences of media stereotyping are also beginning to affect men more, with evidence of them having mounting concerns over

Gender stereotypes like those shown here are very common in the media, and may have harmful consequences for the majority who fail to live up to the stereotype

their appearance and sexual attractiveness, their body size and shape, their diet, health and dress sense. The growing use by men of cosmetics and cosmetic surgery – as well as the increase in eating disorders among men – all suggest that the factors that have traditionally affected women are now also beginning to have an effect on men.

Stereotyping of the young

The mass media often create a stereotype of young people as a problem group in society – as trouble-makers, druggies, layabouts, yobs and vandals. Exaggerating the occasional deviant behaviour of a few young people out of proportion to its real significance in society can generate exciting stories and sensational headlines that help to sell newspapers and attract TV viewers.

The mass media provide for many people the only source of information about events, and therefore distort people's attitudes and give a misleading

The media frequently present young people as a trouble-making problem group, rather than as the fairly conformist future adults most are, like the students shown here

impression of young people as a whole. Old people, who tend to be more home-based, are particularly vulnerable to such stereotypes, as their impressions are formed more strongly by the media.

Folk devils and moral panics   In his book on the Mods and Rockers of the 1960s, *Folk Devils and Moral Panics*, Stan Cohen suggests that mass media stereotypes of young people, particularly where unusual or exceptional behaviour is involved, provide exciting stories and sensational headlines, and help to sell newspapers. He argues that young people have been used as **scapegoats** – blamed for things that are not their fault – to create a sense of unity in society, by uniting the public against a common enemy.

Young people are relatively powerless, and an easily identifiable group to blame for all of society's ills. Some young people who get involved in relatively trivial deviant or delinquent actions or groups, such as anti-social behaviour, hooliganism, vandalism or soft drug abuse, face **labelling** in the media as **folk devils** or groups posing a threat to society.

This causes a **moral panic** in society – an over-reaction suggesting that society itself is under threat. Editors, politicians, church people, police, magistrates and social workers then pull together to overcome this imagined threat to society.

The folk devils become visible reminders of what we should not be. In this view, young people play much the same role as witches in the past – an easy scapegoat to blame for all of society's problems. As a result of these moral panics, all young people may then get labelled and stereotyped as a potentially troublesome problem group.

Scapegoats are groups or individuals blamed for something which is not their fault.
Labelling is defining a person or group in a certain way – as a particular type of person.
Folk devils are individuals or groups posing an imaginary or exaggerated threat to society.
A **moral panic** is a wave of public concern about some exaggerated or imaginary threat to society, stirred up by overblown and sensationalized reporting in the mass media.

Activity

1 Go to http://en.wikipedia.org/wiki/Mods_and_Rockers. Read what it says about the Mods and Rockers in the 1960s, and suggest reasons, with evidence, why they might have been seen as folk devils causing a moral panic in society. Is there any evidence they posed any real threat to society?

2 Refer to the cartoon below, which suggests that social workers are often used as scapegoats, getting blamed for things that are not their fault. Can you think of any other groups in contemporary society who are often used as scapegoats? Give reasons for your answer.

'A pit bull terrier? No, they've cornered a social worker!'

Every time there is a case of serious child abuse, the mass media, particularly newspapers like the *Daily Mail*, *Daily Mirror*, *Sun* and the *Daily Express*, attack the social workers responsible for child welfare, whipping up public hostility as suggested in the cartoon. Such newspapers often use social workers as scapegoats, seeming to blame them more for not preventing child cruelty and abuse than the parents and stepparents who nearly always carry out the actual abuse. This is a bit like blaming the police, rather than criminals, for crime, or blaming doctors for disease and ill-health

Stereotyping of minority ethnic groups

The mass media frequently stereotype and use as scapegoats black and Asian people and others from minority ethnic groups. Minority ethnic groups make up only about 8 per cent of the population of Britain, yet frequently this small minority are presented in quite negative ways in the media, as if they were major causes of conflict and social problems that otherwise wouldn't exist. Minority ethnic groups often only appear in the media in the context of trouble of various kinds, and as scapegoats on which to blame social problems.

They are presented in a limited range of degrading, negative and unsympathetic stereotypes, such as:

- law breakers, such as drug dealers, welfare fraudsters and 'muggers' (committing street robbery with violence)

- low-paid workers
- people with a culture that is seen as alien and a threat to British culture – a kind of 'enemy within', with immigration seen as a threat to the British way of life and the jobs of white workers
- people causing conflict and trouble, as in stories portraying racial problems, involvement with gangs, drug, gun and knife crime, or those suggesting all Muslims are terrorists
- people causing social problems, such as asylum seekers, immigrants (whether legal or illegal), rioters, welfare scroungers, lone parents, and so on, rather than as people with social problems like persecution, poverty, racial discrimination, poor housing, and being victims of racist attacks by white people
- people who often do well in sport and music, but are rarely portrayed as academic or professional successes
- people who have problems internationally – for example, who run their own countries chaotically; who live in famine conditions (images of starving babies); who are always having tribal conflicts, military coups and so on, and who need the white Western countries to help solve their problems for them.

Degrading stereotypes of black people are still frequently found in books, films and comics. Little is heard about their successes and achievements, their history and culture, or about the discrimination and deprivation they often face in housing, employment and education (see chapters 4 and 8). Attacks on black people by white racists rarely receive media coverage, and media attacks stir up public hostility to minority ethnic asylum seekers and the Muslim community. Such stereotyping may create, confirm and reinforce racial prejudices about black and minority ethnic groups among whites, thereby reinforcing the racism which is deeply entrenched in British society, and leaving non-white minority ethnic groups to take the blame for problems that are not created by them at all.

Activity

Do you think that the media still stereotype minority ethnic groups, young people and men and women? While you are watching television, reading newspapers or magazines, or using other media, try to identify:
(a) any stereotypes that you come across;
(b) any exceptions to the stereotypes.
Make notes on these examples, and discuss them with others in your group.
What evidence, if any, can you point to that stereotyping is still occurring in the media?

MEDIA REGULATION: FORMAL CONTROLS ON THE MEDIA

Although the mass media in Britain are generally free to report whatever they like, and the state and government have no power in normal times to stop the spreading of any opinions through censorship, there are some formal limits to this freedom, and the government and the state have a number of direct and indirect controls over the mass media, particularly television and radio, and there are also other official regulators of the mass media. It should be remembered that the following media regulators operate mainly with British-based media and media-providers, and there are some forms of media, like satellite broadcasts and the Internet, that can be extremely difficult for the regulators in any single country to control. Some states, like China, have tried to control Internet access and censor Internet content, but this is often at the expense of civil liberties, and violates human rights in a way that would be unacceptable in most European countries.

The law

The law restricts the media's freedom to report anything they choose in any way they like. The principal legal limits to the media's freedom are shown in the box below.

LEGAL LIMITS TO THE MEDIA'S FREEDOM

- *The laws of libel* forbid the publication of an untrue statement about a person which might cause him or her to suffer contempt, ridicule, dislike or hostility in society.
- *The Official Secrets Acts* make it a criminal offence to report without authorization any official government activity which the government defines as an 'official secret'.
- *Defence Advisory Notices or 'DA-Notices'* are issued by the government as requests to journalists not to report national security information which the government believes might be useful to an enemy. These usually concern military secrets and similar information.
- *The Race Relations Acts* and the *Racial and Religious Hatred Act of 2006* forbid the expression of opinions which will encourage hatred or discrimination against people because of their ethnic group or religious beliefs.
- *The Obscene Publications Act* forbids the publication of anything that the High Court considers to be obscene and indecent, and likely to 'deprave and corrupt' anyone who sees, reads or hears it.
- *Contempt of Court* provisions forbid the reporting and expression of opinions about cases which are in the process of being dealt with in a court of law, or that are likely to prejudice a fair trial.

Ofcom

Ofcom (Office of Communications) is the main regulator of the mass media in the UK, with responsibilities across television, radio, telecommunications and wireless communications services. This has responsibility for:

- furthering the interests of consumers
- securing the best use of the radio spectrum
- ensuring that a wide range of television, radio, electronic media and communications services are available in the UK, with high-speed, high-quality services having a broad appeal
- protecting the public from any offensive or potentially harmful effects of broadcast media, and to safeguard people from being unfairly treated in television and radio programmes, or having their privacy invaded.

The BBC

The BBC is a largely state-funded body, which is governed by the BBC Trust, whose members are appointed by the Queen on advice from government ministers. The Trust aims to represent the interests of licence fee payers (TV viewers and radio listeners) and to ensure the BBC remains independent, and resists pressure and influence from any source. The BBC is partly regulated by Ofcom, and partly by the Trust. The BBC is financed by the state through the television licence fee, plus income from a series of private spin-off companies, which top up the licence fee income with substantial profits. The state can therefore have some control over the BBC by refusing to raise the licence fee. Although the BBC is not a private business run solely to make a profit like the independent commercial broadcasting services (independent TV and radio), and is not dependent on advertising for its income, it still has to compete with commercial broadcasting by attracting audiences large enough to justify the licence fee.

Independent broadcasting

Independent broadcasting includes all the non-BBC television and radio stations. These are regulated by Ofcom, which licenses the companies which can operate in the private sector, and is responsible for the amount, quality and standard of advertising and programmes on independent television and radio, and deals with any complaints.

The Press Complaints Commission

The Press Complaints Commission is a voluntary body appointed by the newspaper industry itself to maintain certain standards of newspaper journalism. It deals with public complaints against newspapers, but it has no real power to enforce effective sanctions as a result of these complaints.

OWNERSHIP OF THE MASS MEDIA

The mass media are very big business. The ownership of the main mass media in modern Britain is concentrated in the hands of a few large companies, which are interested in making profits (see table 6.1)

Of the total circulation of national daily and Sunday newspapers, 86 per cent is controlled by just four companies, and over half (56 per cent) by two companies (News International and the Daily Mail and General Trust). One individual, Rupert Murdoch of News International, owns the *Sun*, *News of the World*, and *The Times* and *Sunday Times*, newspapers which made up about 36 per cent of all national daily and Sunday newspaper sales in Britain in 2010. As table 6.1 shows, this concentration extends also to other areas of the media, such as TV, book and magazine publishing, and websites. The details of who owns what are continually changing, but in 2010 Rupert Murdoch, for example, also owned 40 per cent of BSkyB, all of HarperCollins – the world's largest English-language book publishers – and the networking site MySpace.

Most media conglomerates are now based in the United States, and US transnational media and communications corporations, like Microsoft, Google, Yahoo!, Vodaphone, News Corporation, AOL/CNN/Time-Warner, and Nokia dominate global communications. In Britain, two companies – BT and Virgin Media – own the cable network for delivering phone, TV and Internet, and in 2008 just six companies provided 86 per cent of Internet services, as well as phone and TV, and six companies controlled the mobile networks.

The same few companies control a wide range of different media, and therefore a large proportion of what we see and hear in the media. This concentration of ownership gives a lot of power to business people who are neither elected nor accountable to the public.

This poses a threat to democracy and enhances the power of the already powerful, as more and more of what we know is dominated and controlled by global corporations.

Activity

Explain why the concentration of ownership of the mass media might be of some concern in a democracy (refer to pages 345–6 in chapter 8 if you're not really sure what a democracy is).

Table 6.1 Who owns what: national newspaper group ownership and some of their interests in publishing, television and digital media, United Kingdom, 2010

Company	Share of UK national daily and Sunday newspaper circulation (%: August 2010)	National newspapers (all of which have related websites)	Also owns
News International (UK arm of News Corporation)	36	*Sun, The Times, News of the World, Sunday Times, Times Literary Supplement*	40% of BSkyB – Sky television, broadband and telephony; HarperCollins book publishers; wide range of websites, including MySpace and page3.com
Daily Mail and General Trust	20	*Daily Mail, Mail on Sunday*	Second-largest regional newspaper owners, with over 100 papers, including the most widely read free paper, *Metro*; 90% of Teletext; 20% of ITN; various radio stations and large range of websites
Trinity Mirror	18	*Daily Mirror, Sunday Mirror, Daily Record, People, Sunday Mail*	Over 200 local and regional newspapers; over 300 websites
Northern & Shell	12	*Daily Express, Sunday Express, Daily Star, Daily Star Sunday*	*OK!* magazine; Channel 5 TV; various soft porn TV channels
Telegraph Media Group (part of Press Holdings Limited)	6	*Daily Telegraph, Sunday Telegraph, Scotsman*	*Spectator*
Guardian Media Group	3	*Guardian, Observer*	Guardian Weekly; over 40 local newspapers; various local websites and TV Channels; Guardian Unlimited network of websites; shares in various consumer magazines, including Sainsbury's magazine
Pearson	2	*Financial Times*	Longman, Pearson and Penguin book publishers; Ft.com
Seven companies	97		

Source: data from Audit Bureau of Circulation; corporate websites

Rupert Murdoch of News Corporation is now the world's most powerful media owner, with substantial interests in TV satellite broadcasting, websites, films and newspaper, magazine and book publishing across the world

BRITAIN'S NATIONAL DAILY AND SUNDAY NEWSPAPERS

Newspapers can be separated into three main groups:

The 'quality' newspapers

These include *The Times*, *Guardian*, the *Daily Telegraph*, the *Independent* and the *Financial Times*, and on Sunday the *Sunday Times*, the *Observer*, the *Independent on Sunday* and the *Sunday Telegraph*. These are fairly serious in tone and content, and are concerned with news and features about politics, economic and financial problems, sport, literature and the arts, and give in-depth, analytical coverage in longer articles and news stories. These are more likely to have a middle-class readership.

THE TIMES

The Daily Telegraph

theguardian

The 'middle-brow' or mid-market newspapers

These are the *Daily Express* and *Daily Mail*, and the *Sunday Express* and the *Mail on Sunday*. These are in-between the qualities and the red tops, and include features of each. While they tend to have a slightly more serious tone and content than the red tops, they also cover a range of the more colourful issues found in them. They are aimed primarily at the middle-brow middle/lower-middle class, but have readers drawn from the whole social spectrum.

Daily Mail

DAILY EXPRESS

The popular or 'red-top' tabloid press

These are the mass-circulation, tabloid (small-size) daily and Sunday newspapers aimed at mass audiences. They are the *Sun*, *Daily Mirror* and *Daily Star*, and on Sunday *News of the World*, *Sunday Mirror*, *People* and *Daily Star Sunday*, and are generally referred to as 'red tops' because of the colour of their masthead logos. These aim to entertain as much as providing news, and concentrate on the sensational aspects of the news, like political scandals and crime, and human interest stories, such as sex scandals and celebrity gossip, plus entertainment, loads of sport and other light topics, written in very simple language combined with large headlines and many colour photographs. They are primarily aimed at a working-class readership.

Activity

Look at the box on Britain's national daily and Sunday newspapers.

1 Compare one quality and one red-top newspaper for the same day, by either getting hold of a copy of each or viewing them on-line on their related websites. Study the kinds of stories, advertisements, photographs and cartoons, and the language they use. List all the differences between them. In the light of your findings, suggest and explain carefully three reasons why these two types of newspapers are, in general, read by members of different social classes.

2 Carry out a small survey asking people:
   (a) What their main source of news is, such as radio, television, newspapers, Internet and so on.
   (b) Which medium they think is the most believable or reliable source of news, giving the most truthful accounts, and why.
   (c) Which medium they think is the most unbelievable source of news, least likely to give a truthful account of events, and why.
   (d) Draw up conclusions about which source of news people generally seem to use the most and which they find the most reliable/truthful, and summarize their reasons for this. Compare your results with others in your group, and try to reach an overall conclusion about what people find to be the most believable/reliable news source, and why people seem to find some news sources more reliable than others.

THE MASS MEDIA, PUBLIC OPINION AND SOCIAL CONTROL

Most people will base their opinions and attitudes not on personal experience, but on evidence and knowledge provided by newspapers, television, the Internet and other media. Indeed, if the media didn't report an event, or distorted it, or totally made it up, the only people likely to know about it would be those who were actually involved. For most of us, the mass media are our only source of evidence, and they colour, shape and even construct our view of the world.

If most of our opinions are based on knowledge obtained second-hand through the mass media, then this raises the important issue of the power of the mass media to influence our lives. Most people think and act in particular ways because of the opinions they hold and the knowledge they have, and many would agree that an 'informed' opinion – based on evidence – is the best opinion. However, do the mass media inform us about everything, and do they stress certain things in more favourable ways than others? Do they give false impressions of what is happening in society? The main mass media are privately owned and controlled, and run to make a profit. What effects does this pattern of ownership and control have on the content of the media? Does it create **bias** in them? What are the implications of this in a democracy? These are the sorts of questions which have interested sociologists and which will be explored in this section.

The mass media play a key role in providing the ideas and images which people use to interpret and understand much of their everyday experience, and they actively shape people's ideas, attitudes and actions. The mass media therefore have an important role in forming public opinion. The pressure of public opinion can be a significant source of social control, in so far as most people prefer to have their behaviour approved of by others, rather than feel isolated and condemned by them.

Most people use and believe the mass media, particularly television, as their main source of news. However, their reliance on such sources may be misguided. This is because the mass media don't simply show the facts on which people can then form opinions. They select facts and put an interpretation on them, frequently stressing the more conservative values of society. The mass media can then be said to act as an agency of social control. They carry this out in two main ways: agenda-setting and gate-keeping, and norm-setting.

> **Bias** refers to a subject being presented in a one-sided way, favouring one point of view over others, or deliberately ignoring, distorting or misrepresenting issues.

Agenda-setting and gate-keeping

Agenda-setting is the idea that, even if you don't believe the media tell us *what* to think, it does tell us what to *think about*. This is because the media have an important influence over the issues that people think about because the agenda, or list of subjects, for public discussion is laid down by the mass media.

Obviously, people can only discuss and form opinions about things they have been informed about, and it is the mass media which provide this information in most cases. This gives those who own, control and work in the mass media a great deal of power in society, for what they choose to include in or leave out of their newspapers, programmes and websites will influence the main topics of public discussion and public concern. This may mean that some subjects are never discussed by the public because they are not informed about them.

The media's refusal to cover some issues is called **gate-keeping**.

Such issues are frequently those potentially most damaging to the values and interests of the upper class. For example, strikes are widely reported (nearly always unfavourably), while industrial injuries and diseases, which lead to a much greater loss of working hours (and life), hardly ever get reported. This means that there is more public concern with tightening up trade union laws to stop strikes than there is with improving health and

> **Agenda-setting** refers to the process whereby the media selects the list of subjects to report and bring to public attention.

> **Gate-keeping** refers to the media's refusal to cover some issues.

safety laws. Similarly, crime committed by black people, migrant workers and asylum seekers gets widely covered in the media, but little attention is paid to attacks on these people by white racists. This tends to reinforce people's racial prejudices. A final example is the way welfare benefit fraud by poor people is widely reported, but not tax evasion by the rich, with the result that there are calls for tightening up benefit claim procedures and cracking down on fraud, rather than strengthening agencies concerned with chasing tax evaders.

Activity

1 Study the main newspaper, radio, television or Internet news stories for three days. Draw up a list of the top five headline stories, perhaps under headings like quality newspapers, red tops, BBC TV news, ITN news, BBC news website, Sky News, Radio 1 news and so on. This is easiest to do if a group of people divide up the work. The following websites may help in this:
www.bbc.co.uk
www.itn.co.uk
www.guardian.co.uk
www.thesun.co.uk
www.mirror.co.uk
www.sky.com/skynews

2 Compare your lists, and see if there is any evidence of agreement on the 'agenda' of news items for that week. If there are differences between the lists (check particularly the newspapers), suggest explanations for them.

Norm-setting

Norm-setting is the process whereby the mass media emphasize and reinforce conformity to social norms, and seek to isolate those who don't conform by making them the victims of unfavourable public opinion.

Norm-setting means the process whereby mass media emphasize and reinforce conformity to social norms, and seek to isolate those who do not conform by making them the victims of unfavourable public opinion. This is achieved in two main ways:

- *Encouraging conformist behaviour,* such as not going on strike, obeying the law, being brave, helping people, and so on. Advertising, for example, often reinforces the gender role stereotypes of men and women.
- *Discouraging non-conformist behaviour.* The mass media often give extensive and sensational treatment to stories about murder and other crimes of violence, riots, welfare benefit fraud, football hooliganism, animal rights and environmental protesters, and so on. Chapter 3 (see page 131) mentioned how the media have often attacked lone-parent families. Such stories, by either emphasizing the serious or undesirable consequences which follow for those who break social norms, or presenting

The mass media often give very negative or hostile treatment to groups and issues of all kinds that they regard as holding values and beliefs that are outside the boundaries of sensible society, such as stories about animal rights activists of all kinds

them in negative ways, are giving lessons in how people are expected *not* to behave. For example, the early treatment of AIDS in the mass media nearly always suggested it was a disease that only gay men could catch. This was presented as a warning to those who strayed from the paths of monogamy and heterosexuality – both at the time core values of British society.

Stan Cohen illustrates this idea of norm-setting very well in the following passage:

A large amount of space in newspapers, magazines and television and a large amount of time in daily conversation are devoted to reporting and discussing behaviour which sociologists call deviant: behaviour which somehow departs from what a group expects to be done or what it considers the desirable way of doing things. We read of murders and drug-taking, vicars eloping with members of their congregation and film stars announcing the birth of their illegitimate children, football trains being wrecked and children being stolen from their prams, drunken drivers being breathalysed and accountants fiddling the books. Sometimes the stories are tragic and arouse anger, disgust or horror; sometimes they are merely absurd. Whatever the emotions, the stories are always to be found, and, indeed, so much space in the mass media is given to deviance that some sociologists have argued that this interest functions to reassure society that the boundary lines between conformist and deviant, good and bad, healthy and sick, are still valid ones. The value of the boundary line must continually be reasserted: we can only know what it is to be saintly by being told just what the shape of the devil is. The rogues, feckless fools and villains are presented to us as if they were playing parts in some gigantic morality play.

(From Stanley Cohen, ed., introduction to *Images of Deviance* (Penguin, 1982))

Activity

1 How is deviance defined in the passage above by Stanley Cohen?
2 What does the passage suggest is one of the functions of the mass media's interest in deviance?
3 Give examples from the passage of (a) two types of deviant behaviour which are not regarded as criminal in contemporary Britain, and (b) two types of deviant behaviour which are regarded as criminal in contemporary Britain.
4 Think of one example of deviance which is currently receiving a lot of attention in the mass media and is of major public concern. Explain how this might be reasserting the value of the 'boundary lines between conformist and deviant' behaviour (highlighted in the text).
5 Look at a range of newspapers and news websites and try to find examples of norm-setting headlines and stories. Explain in each case what types of behaviour are being encouraged or discouraged.

BIAS IN THE MEDIA: WHAT AFFECTS THE CONTENT OF THE MEDIA?

Bias in the media is concerned with whether the media present subjects in a one-sided way, and favour one point of view at the expense of others.

The mass media obviously cannot report all events and issues happening in the world. Of all the happenings that occur in the world every day, how is what counts as news selected? Who decides which of these events is newsworthy? The news, like any other product for sale, is a manufactured product. What factors affect the production and packaging of this product? What decides the content of the mass media? The processes of agenda-setting, gate-keeping and norm-setting discussed above influence media content. The sections below discuss some of the other factors that influence the content of the media, and may cause bias in them. Figure 6.2 on page 320 summarizes these factors.

The owners

Sometimes the private owners of the mass media will impose their own views on their editors. However, even when the owners don't directly impose their own views, it is unlikely that those who work for them will produce stories which actively oppose their owners' prejudices and interests, if they want to keep their jobs. The political leanings of the owners and editors are overwhelmingly conservative.

Making a profit

The mass media are predominantly run by large business corporations with the aim of making money, and the source of much of this profit is advertising. It is this dependence on advertising which explains why so much concern is expressed about ratings for television programmes, the circulation figures of newspapers, and the social class of their readers, and the number of 'hits' a website gets. Advertisers will usually advertise only if they know that there is a large audience for their advertisements, or, if the audience is small, that it is well-off and likely to buy their products or services.

Advertising and media content

The importance of advertising affects the content of the media in the following ways:

- Audiences or readers must be attracted. If they are not, then circulation or viewing figures will fall, advertisers will not advertise, and the particular channel, website or newspaper may go out of business. This means that what becomes 'news' is partly a result of commercial pressures to attract audiences by selecting and presenting the more colourful and interesting events in society.
- In order to attract the widest possible audience or readership, it becomes important to appeal to everyone and offend no one. This leads to a conservatism in the media, which tries to avoid too much criticism of the way society is organized in case it offends the readers or advertisers. This may mean that minority or unpopular points of view go unrepresented in the mass media.
- It may lead to a distortion of the news by concentrating on sensational stories, conflict, celebrity gossip, and scandal, which are more likely to attract a mass audience than more serious issues are. Alternatively, for those media which aim at a 'select' readership from the upper and upper-middle classes, it is important that the news stories chosen should generally be treated in a conservative way, so as not to offend an

Activity

The popular mass media often seem obsessed with the activities and lives of celebrities, and health issues like anorexia, size zero fashion models and offering health advice of doubtful quality.

1 Study two of the red-top newspapers or popular magazines. Make a list of the types of stories and pictures they include.
2 As a sociologist and probable consumer of such material, suggest reasons why these media cover these issues, and why people buy these media in such large numbers.

audience which has little to gain (and everything to lose) by changes in the existing arrangements in society.

News values and newsworthiness

Journalists obviously play an important role in deciding the content of the mass media, as it is journalists who basically select what the news is and decide on its style of presentation. News doesn't just happen, but is made by journalists. Research has shown that journalists operate with values and assumptions about which events are 'newsworthy' – these assumptions are called **news values**. These guide journalists in deciding what to report and what to leave out, and how what they choose to report should be presented.

Issues or events that are newsworthy include:

> **News values** are the values and assumptions held by journalists which guide them in choosing what to report and what to leave out, and how what they choose to report should be presented.

- issues that are easily understood
- events that occur quickly or unexpectedly, such as disasters
- events that involve drama, conflict, excitement and action
- events that are in some way out of the ordinary
- events that have some human drama or interest to them, such as the activities of celebrities and other famous personalities, scandal or armed sieges
- events that are considered important – events in the home country are generally considered more important than those happening in the rest of the world, and national events are generally considered more important than local ones
- stories which it is assumed will be of interest to the media audiences – giving the readers and viewers what they want. This is of great importance if the audience or readership is to continue to be attracted and viewing figures kept up or papers sold.

The idea of news values means that journalists tend to play up those elements of a story which make it more newsworthy, and the stories that are most likely to be reported are those which include many newsworthy aspects. These features affecting the content of the media suggest that the mass media present, at best, only a partial, and therefore biased, view of the world.

Selection

The processes of agenda-setting, gate-keeping and norm-setting mean some events are simply not reported and brought to public attention. Some of those that are reported may be singled out for particularly unfavourable treatment. In these ways, the mass media can decide what the important issues are, what news is, what the public should and should not be concerned about, and what should or should not be regarded as normal behaviour in society.

With reference to the list of factors making issues newsworthy, explain why the news values of journalists might make them consider the story in the cartoon is worth reporting

---

Activity

1 Refer to the three news stories below, or any major news stories which are currently receiving wide coverage in the mass media. List the features of these stories which you think make them newsworthy. To find more details on any story, try a Google search on the Internet.

2 Take one contemporary big news story. Study one quality and one red-top newspaper of the same day and compare their coverage of this story. For example, do they sensationalize it and present new or different angles? What evidence is there, if any, that the news values of red tops differ from those of the quality press? Give examples to back up your answer.

3 Imagine you wanted to run a campaign to prevent a waste incinerator being built in your neighbourhood (or choose any topic of interest to you). In the light of your expert knowledge about news values, suggest ways you might get the attention of journalists, and activities you might undertake to achieve media coverage of your campaign. Explain why you think the activities you identify might be considered newsworthy.

The terrorist attack on the 'twin towers' of the World Trade Center in New York on 11 September 2001 was massive international news story. Two passenger aircraft were hijacked, and deliberately crashed into the twin towers, causing both towers to collapse, and killing around 3,000 people. This dominated world news for weeks and months afterwards, and provoked a range of conspiracy theories on the Internet.

On 3 May 2007, **3-year-old Madeleine McCann** vanished from her holiday apartment in Praia da Luz, Portugal. Thanks to a high-profile campaign run by the McCann family, Madeleine's face was rarely out of the public consciousness. At the time of writing, it was still not known what happened to Madeleine. The mystery of Madeleine's disappearance led to a feeding frenzy in the red-top tabloid press, with a mass of unsubstantiated theories and wild speculation about her disappearance. Both ITV's *Tonight with Trevor McDonald* and the BBC's *Panorama* had documentaries on her disappearance, and six months after she vanished the story was still dominating the headlines of the red-top tabloid press, and theories abounded on the Internet.

On 12 January 2010, a catastrophic earthquake struck the Caribbean island of Haiti, just 16 miles from the capital Port-au-Prince. The Haitian government reported that an estimated 230,000 people had died, 300,000 had been injured, and a million people made homeless.

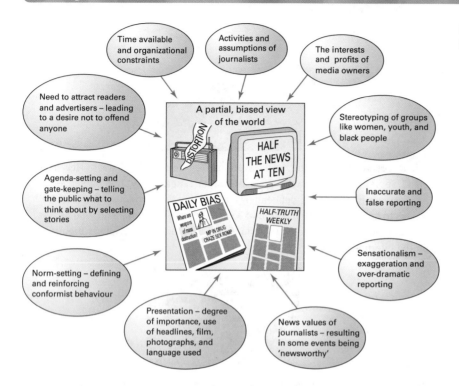

Figure 6.2 Sources of bias in the media

The presentation of news

The way news items are presented may be important in influencing the way people are encouraged to view stories. For example, the physical position of a news story in a newspaper or webpage (front page / lead story or small inside column or hyperlink), the order of importance given to stories in TV or Internet news bulletins, the choice of headlines, and whether there is accompanying film or photographs will all influence the attention given to particular items. A story may be treated sensationally, and it may even be considered of such importance as to justify a TV or radio newsflash. Where film is used, the pictures shown are always selected from the total footage shot, and may not accurately reflect the event. The actual images used in news films may themselves have a hidden bias. For example, in the reporting of industrial disputes, employers are often filmed in the peace and quiet of their offices, while workers are seen shouting on the picket lines or trying to be interviewed against a background of traffic noise. This gives the impression that employers are more calm and reasonable people and have a better case than the workers.

The media can also create false or biased impressions by the sort of language used in news reporting. This bias in the use of language in newspapers was illustrated by the survey commissioned by Women in Journalism in

2009 mentioned in chapter 5, which found teenage boys were commonly described in the media using terms like *yobs, thugs, sick, feral* (wild), *hoodie, lout, heartless, evil, frightening* and *scum*.

> **Activity**
>
> Study the language of newspaper reporting – the red-top tabloids are probably the easiest – and find some examples of language which might give a distorted or biased impression of particular individuals or groups, such as animal rights activists being described as 'nutters'.

Inaccurate and false reporting

Other influences on media content, and possible sources of bias, lie in inaccurate reporting, because important details of a story may be incorrect. Politicians are always complaining that they have been inaccurately quoted in the press. False reporting, through either completely making up stories or inventing a few details, and the media's tendency to dramatize events out of all proportion to their actual significance in society, typical of much reporting of the royal family, are devices used to make a story more interesting and sell newspapers. This is particularly common in the mass-circulation red-top press. In 2009, a number of these were fooled into publishing bogus celebrity stories in an experiment to show that the red-top editors published celebrity news stories with little regard for the truth. Further confirmation of this came in 2010, when Hollywood stars Brad Pitt and Angelina Jolie sued the *News of the World* for suggesting the couple were separating and had consulted a divorce lawyer about dividing their wealth, which the couple completely denied. This apparently false story rapidly appeared on the celebrity gossip pages of newspapers, magazines and websites across the globe. Such methods mean the media can be accused of manipulating their audiences.

Organizational constraints

Newspapers and TV programmes tend to work within very tight time schedules, and there is intense competition in news reporting. News is now rolling 24-hour news, with news channels like BBC News Channel, Sky News, CNN and newspaper-linked websites delivering breaking news and analysis all day long, every day, with constant updating of news bulletins.

This means that short-cuts to news gathering may need to be taken, that inadequate evidence is collected to justify any conclusions drawn, and that stories aren't checked as carefully as they should be. For example, the media

News reporting is highly competitive, with companies around the world all competing to get the best coverage of the very latest up-to-the-minute events. How do you think this might cause bias in news reporting?

may rely on police or government press releases for stories, but this means reporters only report what they have been told, and they often haven't done the legwork to check stories for themselves.

The assumptions and activities of journalists

The views and assumptions of journalists can have an important influence on media content – after all, they are the ones who actually write and report the news stories.

Journalists tend to be mainly white, male and middle-class, and this influences whose opinions they seek for comment, what issues they see as important, and how they think issues should be presented and explained to audiences. Journalists are likely to give greater importance to the views of powerful people, as their views appear more 'reasonable' to journalists, and they tend to ignore or treat less favourably what they regard as extremist or radical views.

Journalists are doing a job of work, and they like to keep their work as simple as possible. This means they often obtain information from news agencies, government press releases, public relations consultants and so on. This means powerful and influential groups like businesses, the government, political parties, and those with power and wealth are more likely to be able to influence journalists.

All these features discussed above, including the earlier sections on media stereotyping, suggest that the mass media generally present, at best, only a partial and biased view of the world.

THE MASS MEDIA, POWER AND DEMOCRACY

Pluralist views

Pluralism is a view that suggests that power in society is spread among a wide variety of groups and individuals, with no single one having a monopoly on power and influence. Pluralists point out that the Internet, cable, satellite and digital television, and the global reach of modern mass media technology offer such a huge range and choice of media products and access to knowledge from across the world that no single group or class can impose its views on others. The media now cover all kinds of interests and all points of view. New media technology also means ordinary people now have the opportunity to create their own media products and distribute them around the world (see below). What appears in the media therefore reflects a wide range of views, and is driven by the wishes of consumers. The fight for audiences in competition with other companies means the mass media have to cater for audience tastes – audiences will simply not watch TV programmes, view webpages or buy newspapers which do not reflect their views. If media companies do not satisfy their audiences, they'll go out of business.

Marxist views

Marxist writers disagree with the pluralists. They suggest the content of the media reflects the wishes of the media owners, and the views of the most

Pluralism is a view that sees power in society spread among a wide variety of groups and individuals, with no single one having a monopoly on power and influence.

powerful and influential members of society are given greater weight than those of less powerful groups. Not all groups in society have equal influence on editors and journalists to get their views across, and only very rich groups will have the resources required to launch major media companies or websites to get their views across independently. It is the rich, powerful and influential who are more likely to be interviewed on TV, to appear on chat shows, to be quoted in newspapers, and so on. Ideas or groups which threaten the status quo (the existing arrangements in society) are attacked, ridiculed or ignored. Marxists argue that people have been socialized by the media themselves into the belief that they are being provided with what they want. The media themselves may have created their tastes, so that what audiences want is really what the media owners want.

Power and the new media

At the beginning of this chapter, some features of the new media were discussed. Some suggest that new media technology, like the Internet and mobiles, can give more power to ordinary people. Social networking sites like Facebook, blogging, texting, taking and uploading photographs and videos on mobiles, YouTube, and other Internet sites can empower people, by enabling them to learn about, and providing information about, things they didn't know before. More people, not just large media corporations, have the opportunity to communicate with vast numbers of other people. For example, ordinary people can now publish their thoughts on Twitter (www.twitter.com), attack those in power on Blogger (www.blogger.com), and report on events excluded from other mainstream media by sending their own news stories and photos to citizen journalism sites like Demotix (www.demotix.com). Protest groups of all kinds have built websites to spread their messages across the world, including terrorist websites seeking to recruit supporters and promote their views. Protesters can now reach, in ways never before possible, a worldwide audience very rapidly. Public outrage can bring websites to their knees, by overwhelming them with emails and hits, and targeting advertisers to get them to withdraw advertising from the sites. This electronic technology of the new media can make it increasingly difficult for the mainstream media newspapers and news channels to ignore stories they might have dropped in the past, and gives more power to the once powerless. For example, video shot on a mobile phone by a protester at a London demonstration in April 2009 provided evidence that it was police brutality that caused the death of a man, which the police had tried to cover up before the video emerged. This forced the mainstream media to accept the protesters' version of events, rather than that of the police.

How might mobile phone technology be used to give more power to ordinary people, and expose wrongdoing by the already powerful?

The limitations of the new media

While there is evidence that the new electronic media can give more power to ordinary people, the new media are not public property open to all. Global corporations like Microsoft, Google, Yahoo!, Vodaphone and News Corporation control the Internet technology, the satellite channels and mobile networks, and more and more of what we know is dominated and controlled by global corporations. Google holds massive amounts of information about people's web browsing, monitors millions of webpages, and in a sense is watching everything we do on the Internet. If anyone can be said to control the Internet, it is Google.

MySpace, the second largest networking site after Facebook, is owned by News Corporation. Governments are now using electronic means for increased social control through surveillance of emails, monitoring of websites and intercepts of mobile calls. Google, for example, withdrew from China in 2010 because that government was hacking into Google to track human rights activists. Facebook has been blocked from time to time in several countries. Wealthy and powerful people, corporations and governments can still control the new media, and the same media that can give power to ordinary people simultaneously give more power to the already powerful.

Much of this chapter has suggested that the mass media act as a conservative influence in society, and give only a biased view of the world. However, some argue that the wealth of information provided by the mass media encourages and promotes a variety of opinions, and this enables the population to be informed on a wide range of issues, which is essential in a democratic society. The section below examines briefly some of the competing views on this aspect of the role of the mass media in modern Britain.

THE MEDIA PROMOTE DEMOCRACY	THE MEDIA RESTRICT DEMOCRACY
• Because the media in Britain are not controlled by the state, the risk of censorship by governments is reduced, and free speech is protected. Journalists are free to report and comment – within legal limits.	• The media (particularly newspapers) reflect the conservative views of their wealthy owners. While journalists are often critical and expose wrongdoing, they will frequently avoid issues which might cost them their jobs by upsetting newspaper owners or TV station bosses.
• The wide variety of privately owned media means a range of opinions are considered and public debates take place. By criticizing the actions of governments, the mass media can play an important 'watch-dog' role, and keep governments in touch with public opinion.	• The variety of opinion presented is limited. Working-class political views – for example, of strikes – are rarely reported. The ideas and actions of the least powerful groups are the most likely to be excluded. Those who in some way present a challenge or threat to the status quo – the existing way society is organized – are presented as irresponsible or unreasonable extremists.
• The media give an unbiased account of news. TV news has to be impartial.	• News values, agenda-setting, norm-setting and other sources of bias mean only some issues are covered, and these are not presented in neutral ways. The media choose what to report and how to report it, and therefore provide a biased view of the world.
• The media accurately reflect public opinions that already exist in society rather than creating new ones. People wouldn't read newspapers or view TV and websites unless they were providing what their audiences wanted.	• The media do not simply reflect public opinion, but actively form and manipulate it. People can only form opinions on the basis of the knowledge they have, and the media are primarily responsible for providing this knowledge. The owners of the mass media hold overwhelmingly conservative views, and their ownership gives them the power to defend their position by forming favourable public opinion.
• Anyone can put his or her views across, by setting up a website, or blog, through citizen journalism, publishing a newspaper, distributing leaflets, putting up posters, and other means of communicating ideas.	• Only the rich have the resources necessary to publish and distribute a newspaper on a large scale, or to set up a television or radio station, and it is the wealthy who own and control the main means of electronic communication. The concentration of ownership of the mass media is a threat to democracy, as a small powerful group of media owners can control access to ideas, information and knowledge. Those who wish to put forward alternative views to that presented in the mass media may not be allowed access to the media by their owners, and will therefore be denied any real opportunity to persuade public opinion of their ideas.

CRIME, DEVIANCE AND THE MEDIA

The mass media provide knowledge about crime and deviance for most people in society, including politicians, the police, social workers and the public at large. The mass media tend to be very selective in their coverage of crime, exploiting the possibilities for a 'good story' by dramatizing, exaggerating and sensationalizing some crimes out of all proportion to their actual extent in society. For example, attacks on old people and other crimes of violence – which are quite rare – are massively over-reported, giving a false and misleading impression of the real pattern and extent of such crimes. This process can create many unnecessary fears among people by suggesting that violence is a normal and common feature of everyday life. This is particularly likely in the case of the housebound elderly. A Home Office report confirmed this view, arguing that TV programmes which stage reconstructions of unsolved crimes, such as the BBC's *Crimewatch UK*, exaggerate the level of dangerous crime and unnecessarily frighten viewers.

The media, labelling and deviancy amplification

As seen earlier in this chapter, the media's pursuit of what they regard as good stories means they often distort, exaggerate and sensationalize the activities of some groups. The media have the power to label and stereotype certain groups and activities as deviant, and present them as folk devils causing some imagined threat to society. Even if much of what is reported is untrue, this may be enough to whip up a moral panic – growing public anxiety and concern about the alleged deviance.

This can raise demands for action by the agencies of social control to stop it. Often these agencies, such as schools, social services, the police and magistrates, will respond to the exaggerated threat presented in the media by taking harsher measures against the apparent trouble-makers. Such action, particularly by the police, can often make what was a minor issue much worse – for example by causing more arrests – and amplify (or make worse) the original deviance. This is known as **deviancy amplification**.

Groups which have fitted this pattern include Mods and Rockers in the 1960s and other youth sub-cultures, glue-sniffers, football hooligans, and Travellers on their way to Glastonbury or Stonehenge. Figure 6.3 illustrates the way the media can amplify deviance and generate a moral panic. Figure 6.4 shows a range of moral panics, not all of them criminal or deviant, which have arisen in Britain since the 1950s.

Deviancy amplification is the process by which the mass media, through exaggeration and distortion, actually create more crime and deviance.

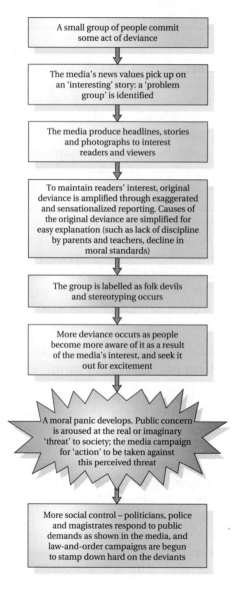

Figure 6.3 Deviancy amplification, moral panics and the media

Figure 6.4 Folk devils and moral panics: Great Britain, 1950s–2000s

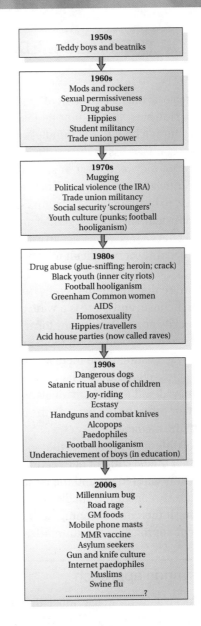

1950s
Teddy boys and beatniks

1960s
Mods and rockers
Sexual permissiveness
Drug abuse
Hippies
Student militancy
Trade union power

1970s
Mugging
Political violence (the IRA)
Trade union militancy
Social security 'scroungers'
Youth culture (punks; football hooliganism)

1980s
Drug abuse (glue-sniffing; heroin; crack)
Black youth (inner city riots)
Football hooliganism
Greenham Common women
AIDS
Homosexuality
Hippies/travellers
Acid house parties (now called raves)

1990s
Dangerous dogs
Satanic ritual abuse of children
Joy-riding
Ecstasy
Handguns and combat knives
Alcopops
Paedophiles
Football hooliganism
Underachievement of boys (in education)

2000s
Millennium bug
Road rage
GM foods
Mobile phone masts
MMR vaccine
Asylum seekers
Gun and knife culture
Internet paedophiles
Muslims
Swine flu
..................................?

Activity

Refer to figures 6.3 and 6.4.
1 Try to fill in each of the stages of any current moral panic in society.
2 Suggest ways that the presence of the mass media at events might make deviant activity worse – for example, playing up to the cameras.
3 Explain how Muslims may be seen as a source of moral panics in contemporary Britain.

THE EFFECTS OF THE MASS MEDIA ON AUDIENCES

Much of this chapter suggests that the content of the media does have some effect on the audience. However, this cannot be taken for granted. People are conscious, thinking human beings, not mindless robots. They might not swallow everything they come across in the media, and they might respond in a variety of ways to what they read, hear or see. For example, they might dismiss, reject, ignore, criticize, forget or give a different meaning to a media message, and this is likely to be influenced by factors such as their own social experiences, their ethnic origin, social class, gender and so on. For example, a black person is likely to reject a racist message in a TV broadcast or newspaper report. It therefore becomes very difficult to generalize about the effects of the media.

We also need to be aware that the media is only one influence on the way people might think and behave, and there is a wide range of other agencies involved in people's socialization. People can form their own judgements on media content, and it would be somewhat foolhardy to suggest all behaviour can be explained by exposure to the media. Families, friends, schools, workplaces and workmates, churches, social class, ethnicity, gender, disability, age and so on may all influence individual and group behaviour and attitudes. The question may then be not what do the media do to people, but what do people do with the media.

There are a number of different approaches that sociologists have adopted to the question of whether media content does actually have an influence or effect on audiences, mainly centred around the issue of whether audiences are passive dopes mindlessly consuming media content, or active interpreters of that content, giving it their own meanings and interpretations.

Some of these different approaches are summarized below.

The hypodermic syringe approach

This approach, sometimes called the 'magic bullet' theory, suggests the media act like a hypodermic syringe (or a bullet), injecting messages and content into the 'veins' of media audiences with immediate effects – for example, seeing violence on television, and then going out and attacking someone. Media audiences are seen as unthinking, passive, gullible and easily manipulated robots, who are unable to resist the 'drug' injected by the media.

Two main criticisms of this approach are:

- Audiences don't all react the same way – this will depend on their socialization, their own ideas and how they interpret what they see or hear. For example, they may reject violence they view rather than copying it.

The hypodermic syringe model suggests that the media inject messages into the 'veins' of media audiences, with an immediate effect on their behaviour

- There is little research evidence that supports this view of the effects of the media.

The two-step flow approach

This approach suggests the media influences opinion leaders (first step) – those whom others listen to and take notice of, like teachers, friends or influential members of any social group. These opinion leaders then influence audiences, passing on information and views they have picked up through the media (second step). Media audiences are seen as relatively passive, and although the media don't have a direct effect on them as in the hypodermic syringe approach, they are still influenced by the media through its effect on opinion leaders.

The main criticism of this approach is that it suggests that people are easily influenced by opinion leaders. It does not recognize that people may have views, opinions and experiences of their own on which to base their views of media content.

The uses and gratifications approach

This approach sees audiences as thinking, active and critical human beings, not passive, easily manipulated robots. The effects of the media will depend on what the audiences use the media for, and their own various pleasures and interests (*gratifications*). People use the media in different ways, such as for pleasure, information, relaxation, company, keeping up with trends, and as background 'wallpaper' while doing other things. This approach makes it difficult to generalize about the effects of the media, as these are likely to vary depending on what people use the media for.

Activity

1 Explain how the cartoon above illustrates the ways people use the media for different uses and gratifications.
2 Which individuals in the cartoon do you think the media is having the most effect and the least effect on? Give reasons for your answer.

The selective filtering or decoding approach

This suggests that people are not blank pieces of paper waiting to be written on by the media, but have choices and experiences of their own, and interpret, or decode, and filter what they read, see or hear in the media. They do this by **selective exposure**, **selective perception** and **selective retention**.

● *Selective exposure* means people may only watch or read media output that fits in with their existing views and interests.

- *Selective perception* means people will filter and interpret media output, so they only see or hear that which fits in with their own views and interests.
- *Selective retention* means people will ignore or forget media output that is not in line with their own views and interests.

This approach means that it is impossible to know what the effects of the media on audiences will be, as this will depend on the values, attitudes and beliefs of those audiences. An example of the application of these filters might be the way people respond to party political election broadcasts, depending on which political party they personally support, as suggested in the cartoon below.

Activity

Selective exposure, selective perception and selective retention

1 Explain how the cartoon above illustrates the idea that people filter what they view in the media.
2 Refer to the section above on the effects of the media on audiences. Which approach best fits your own media habits? Which do you find the most persuasive? Give reasons for your answer.
3 Suppose you wanted to study the effects of a TV programme on an audience. Suggest how you might go about researching this.
4 Carry out a short survey finding out what use people make of the mass media in their daily lives – for example, for leisure, relaxation, information, background 'wallpaper' while doing other things, exploring and confirming their identities, and so on.
5 Identify four ways that you think you are influenced by the content of what you see or read in the media.
6 Explain briefly *in your own words* what is meant by each of the hypodermic syringe, two-step flow, uses and gratifications, and selective filtering approaches to the effects of the media on audiences.

VIOLENCE AND THE MEDIA

Violence, including pornography, on the Internet, in computer games, in TV news reports and dramas, and in films, videos and DVDs, are now part of popular culture, and more people are exposed to such violence than ever before. By the time they are 18, estimates suggest American children will have seen on television around 16,000 real and fictional murders and 200,000 acts of violence.

Such media violence is often blamed for increasing crime and violence in society. An example of this view occurred after the murder in 1993 of 2 year-old James Bulger by two 10-year-old boys. The judge in the case commented: 'I suspect that exposure to violent video films may in part be an explanation.'

Assertions, like that in the Bulger murder, that media violence generates real-life violence are commonplace, and masses of research have been done to investigate whether such a link really exists, particularly in relation to children. However, despite all the research, there is little reliable and undisputed evidence about whether violence in the media leads to an increase in aggressive behaviour, though the weight of evidence suggests there is no such link. For example, a 2003 report by the Broadcasting Standards Commission found that children are fully aware that television production is a process and that they are not watching reality, with the report concluding: 'They are able to make judgements . . . they are not blank sheets of paper on whom messages can be imprinted'. Children displaying tendencies to violence may have had such tendencies regardless of television viewing.

Much media violence is fictional, and there is a problem in defining what counts as 'violence'. Boxing and wrestling, fights in TV dramas, parents hitting children, police attacking protesters, shooting, news film of warfare

Do you think watching mindless – purely for entertainment – violent media content, like horror films and violent thrillers, or playing violent computer games makes people act more violently in real life?

and many children's cartoons all depict violent scenes, but they are unlikely to have the same effects on every individual. Researchers and audiences may not all view scenes showing real-life violence, fictional violence and cartoon violence in the same way. As Tony Giddens has pointed out,

> In crime dramas featuring violence (and in many children's cartoons) there are underlying themes of justice and retribution. A far higher proportion of miscreants are brought to justice in crime dramas than happens with police investigations in real life, and in cartoons harmful or threatening characters usually tend to get their 'just desserts'. It does not necessarily follow that high levels of the portrayal of violence create directly imitative patterns among those watching . . . In general, research on the 'effects' of television on audiences has tended to treat viewers – children and adults – as passive and undiscriminating in their reactions to what they see. (Anthony Giddens, *Sociology*, 4th edition, Polity)

The box below shows some competing claims about the effects of media violence. Even if there were evidence it did have some effects, the earlier section on media effects on audiences suggests media violence is unlikely to have the same effects on everyone, and it may actually reduce, rather than increase, real-life violence.

SOME COMPETING CLAIMS ABOUT THE EFFECTS OF VIOLENCE IN THE MEDIA

Some of the different and competing claims on the effects of violence in the media on violence in real life are summarized below:

- *Copycatting:* like a hypodermic syringe injecting a drug, exposure to media violence causes children to copy what they see and behave more aggressively in the real world.
- *Catharsis:* media violence does not make viewers more aggressive, but reduces violence as it allows people to live out their violent tendencies in the fantasy world of the media rather than in the real world.
- *Desensitization:* repeated exposure of children to media violence has gradual 'drip-drip' long-term effects, with increased risk of aggressive behaviour as adults, as people tend to become less sensitive and disturbed when they witness real-world violence, have less sympathy for its victims, and become socialized into accepting violence as a normal part of life.
- *Sensitization:* exposure to violence in the media can make people more sensitive to and less tolerant of real-life violence.
- *Media violence causes psychological disturbance in some children:* watching media violence frightens young children, causing nightmares, sleeplessness, anxiety and depression, and these effects may be long-lasting.
- Media violence causes some people to have exaggerated fears about crime and the safety of their communities.

> ### Activity
>
> 1. Refer to the earlier section on the effects of the media on audiences, and suggest two possible effects on audiences of violent media content for *each* of the hypodermic syringe, two-step flow, uses and gratifications, and selective filtering approaches.
>
> 2 Refer to the box on the previous page headed *Some competing claims about the effects of violence in the media.*
>
>   (a) Suggest three different ways people might react to watching a violent movie.
>
>   (b) Look at each of the possible effects, and try to make at least one criticism of each one, as in the following example:
>
> | Effect of violent media content | Criticism |
> |---|---|
> | *Desensitization:* repeated exposure to media violence increases the risk of aggressive behaviour, as people become less sensitive and disturbed when they witness real-world violence, have less sympathy for its victims, and become socialized into accepting violence as a normal part of life. | Violent media content might so horrify and sensitize people to it that they become more opposed to it in real life. |
>
> 3 Suggest reasons why children might be more vulnerable to media violence than adults.

INTO THE FUTURE

We are living in the middle of the most dramatic communications explosion of all time. New technology is changing the mass media so rapidly that new developments are occurring almost daily. Digital broadcasting enables us to receive hundreds of cable and satellite television channels; interactive television enables audiences to participate in what they are watching; there are millions of webpages to view; and there is the possibility of doing a range of electronic-based communication tasks on single devices which slip inside a jacket pocket or a bag.

The media have become a gigantic international business, with instant news from every part of the globe. International marketing of TV programmes and films to international audiences is backed by huge investments. The Internet has millions more people going on-line every year. All-dancing, all-singing computers are already beginning to replace televisions, stereos and landline phones in our homes, with instant access to colossal amounts of information and entertainment from the entire globe. Printed newspaper sales have been steadily declining, and may well continue to do so, as more and more news services and newspapers appear in electronic form on the Internet. Printed books are facing growing competition from e-readers, like Amazon's Kindle which can hold upwards of 1,500 books, or devices like Apple's iPad.

The speed of technological change is now so great that the world is said to be rapidly becoming a 'global village'. This means that the whole world has become like one small village, with everyone (at least those who are affluent enough) exposed to the same information and messages through mass media which cut across all national frontiers. It remains to be seen how the media will develop during the twenty-first century, but it seems likely there will be an enormous increase in the power of the already powerful media companies.

CHAPTER SUMMARY

After studying this chapter, you should be able to:

- explain what is meant by the term *mass media*

- describe what is meant by the 'traditional' and the 'new' media, some of the differences between them, and a variety of purposes for which people use the new media

- describe different views on the significance of the new media in contemporary society

- describe, with examples, a variety of ways that the mass media contribute to socialization, the formation of identity, and views on gender, age and ethnicity

- describe, with examples, the role of the mass media in stereotyping and scapegoating

- describe briefly a number of formal controls on the media, including the law and bodies set up to regulate them

- describe the concentration of ownership of the mass media and explain why this might be of some concern in a democracy

- describe some differences between the quality and the red-top newspapers, and their relationship to different social classes

- describe a variety of ways in which the mass media might form public opinion and exercise social control

- explain the terms *agenda-setting*, *gate-keeping* and *norm-setting*

- explain what is meant by bias in the media, and identify a range of factors influencing the content of the mass media, including the news

- explain, with examples, what is meant by *news values*

- describe pluralist and Marxist views on the power of the mass media, and examine the extent to which the new media might give more power to ordinary people

- describe competing views of the role of the mass media in a democracy

- explain how the mass media might give false impressions of crime, amplify deviance and create moral panics

- discuss different views of the effects of the mass media on audiences, including the hypodermic syringe, the two-step flow, the uses and gratifications, and the selective filtering approaches

- describe different arguments about the effects of media violence.

KEY TERMS

agenda-setting
bias
citizen journalism
deviancy amplification

digital divide
folk devils
gate-keeping
labelling
moral panic

news values
norm-setting
pluralism
scapegoats
selective exposure

selective perception
selective retention
social capital

CHAPTER
7

Power

Contents

CHAPTER 7 Power

KEY ISSUES

- What is power? What is politics?
- Power in everyday life
- Types of political system
- Citizenship
- Political participation
- Influencing decision-making in a democracy
- Political parties in Britain
- Influences on voting behaviour
- Why do people abstain in elections?
- Opinion polls and elections
- Is Britain a democracy?
- Social problems and the role of the state
- The welfare state

WHAT IS POWER? WHAT IS POLITICS?

When most people in Britain think about politics, they usually think about voting and elections, councillors and MPs, and often boring party political broadcasts on television. This is quite a narrow view of politics, and of course in many parts of the world people are unable to vote in elections, and don't even have the right to be bored by the television broadcasts of competing political parties. However, politics is not simply about councils and governments, but more widely about the exercise of power.

Power is the ability of people or groups to exert their will over others and get their own way, even if sometimes others resist this.

Politics is concerned with the struggle to gain power and control, by getting in a position to make decisions and implement policies. This means that when partners in a personal relationship argue about decisions

> **Power** is the ability of people or groups to exert their will over others and get their own way.
> **Politics** is the struggle to gain power and control in a relationship, group or society, by getting into a position to make decisions and implement policies.

341

affecting them, we can talk about the politics of the personal. In family life, disputes between husbands and wives or cohabiting partners, and parents and children, are part of family politics. The power differences between men and women can be considered as sexual politics.

Authority and coercion

A distinction is often made between two types of power:

- **Authority** is power which is accepted and obeyed because it is seen as legitimate (fair and right) by those without power. We obey those with authority because we accept they have the right to tell us what to do.
- **Coercion** is that type of power which is not accepted as legitimate by those without power, as the power-holders rule without the consent of those they govern. People only obey because they are forced to by violence or the threat of violence.

Weber identified three main types of authority, which explain why people accept this use of power as legitimate:

- **Traditional authority** is accepted and obeyed because power is based on established traditions and customs, like that of the monarchy.
- **Charismatic authority** is based on a power-holder's charismatic personality – people accept and obey their power because of their personal charm and magnetism, like that often found in political leaders, such as US presidents Barack Obama and Bill Clinton, former South African

> **Authority** is power which is obeyed because it is accepted as fair and right. **Coercion** is rule by violence or the threat of violence.

> **Traditional authority** is power accepted and obeyed because it is based on established traditions and customs. **Charismatic authority** is power accepted and obeyed because it is based on a power-holder's personal charm and magnetism.

In what circumstances might the rational-legal authority of police officers become coercion instead?

leader Nelson Mandela, German Nazi dictator Adolf Hitler, or religious leaders like Jesus Christ.

- **Rational-legal authority** is power accepted and obeyed because it is based on formal rules and laws, like that of a police officer or a teacher.

> **Rational-legal authority** is power accepted and obeyed because it is based on formal rules and laws.

In this chapter, the focus will mainly be on power in society as a whole, and particularly the political system – the extent to which individuals can influence the decisions of governments, the policies of the political parties, and the factors which affect the way people vote. A key question will be to what extent Britain can be regarded as a democratic society.

First, however, it is worth briefly examining how power is used in everyday life.

POWER IN EVERYDAY LIFE

As suggested in the references above to personal, family and sexual politics, power relations are found in all aspects of everyday life. The basis of this power is usually because one person or group is dependent on another in some way – what they can do is limited by what the power-holder allows, though there may often be a power struggle between them. For example, employers have power over employees, as employees need work and wages to live. However, this doesn't mean employers can treat their staff in any way they wish: workers have legal employment rights, and can use trade unions and take strike action as they struggle with employers to prevent unfair treatment. In the 1960s and 1970s in Britain, there were a huge number of strikes, as workers struggled with bosses to get better pay and employment conditions. There are fewer strikes today as trade unions have become weaker, and there are more employment laws to protect workers from discrimination and exploitation. Nonetheless, in 2009–10 there were major strikes – power struggles – by British Airways cabin crew and postal workers.

Power struggles often take place between employers and employees, as in the 2010 postal strikes and struggles shown here between postal workers and the Royal Mail

Activity

1 Look at the following examples of where power is used in everyday life. In each case:

   (a) Describe with an example what the basis of the power relationship might be.

   (b) Explain whether the power used in your example is coercion or authority, and if it is authority which of the three kinds of authority it is (traditional, charismatic or rational-legal).

   (c) Describe with an example what form a power struggle might take.

Here are two examples of the power of children over other children to help you get started.

A child might have power over other children because they are physically stronger, and use *coercion* through unwanted physical bullying to dominate and control them – the resulting fight is a form of power struggle; a child might have power over others because they are an elected representative on a school council, and so have *rational-legal authority* to set the rules for other children. Children in the minority who didn't like the rules being set might struggle against the representative by organizing to get a replacement elected, while the present representative might try to whip up enough support to keep their position.

Now do the same in the following relationships:

   (i)   Parents and children
   (ii)   Teachers and students
   (iii) Police and the public
   (iv)   Prison warders (guards) and prisoners
   (v)   Landlords and tenants
   (vi)   Husbands and wives or cohabiting couples
   (vii) Doctors and patients
   (viii) MPs or councillors and the public

2 Look at the following situations where people are using their power in modern Britain. In each case, briefly explain whether they are using authority or coercion, and if authority, which type. Give reasons for your answer. Be warned – some may involve bits of both authority and coercion, and so it may be worth discussing your answers with someone else.

   (a) A white police officer who stops and searches people simply because they're black, and then arrests them for objecting.

   (b) A traffic warden who gives someone a parking ticket for illegal parking.

   (c) A school pupil who beats up other pupils if they won't give him or her money.

   (d) A teacher in a school who puts a student in detention for not doing his or her homework.

   (e) A couple who beat their children because they won't do as they're told.

   (f) A prime minister who orders his or her detectives to clear a restaurant of other customers so he or she can eat in peace.

   (g) A manager who tells workers to stop chatting and get on with their work.

(h)   A man who beats his wife because she displays too much independence.

(i)   A prison officer who puts a prisoner in solitary confinement for refusing to follow orders.

3   What do you think are the circumstances which influence whether the use of power is seen as fair or not?

TYPES OF POLITICAL SYSTEM

There are differences between societies in the amounts of power ordinary people have to influence government decisions, and these differences are shown in two opposing political systems: **totalitarianism** and **democracy**. While these two are presented as opposing systems, most political systems will fall somewhere between the two. It will be seen later, for example, that even in Britain, often seen as the 'home' of democracy, aspects of totalitarianism remain.

> **Totalitarianism** is a system of government in which society is controlled by a small powerful group or an individual, and ordinary people lack any control over government decision-making.
> **Democracy** is a form of government in which the people participate in political decision-making, usually by electing individuals to represent their views.

Totalitarianism

Totalitarianism is a system of government in which society is controlled by a small powerful group – an elite – and ordinary people lack any control over government decision-making. There are no free elections and no civil liberties, and most of the features found in a democracy do not exist. The government rules by coercion rather than consent. People are forced to obey the government because of its control of the police, the courts, and the army. All the major social institutions, like the economy, the education system, religion, the legal system, the police, and the mass media, are strictly controlled by the government. Ideas opposed to those of the government are censored, and any opposition organizations crushed by force. Examples of totalitarian societies include Hitler's Germany in the 1930s and 1940s, and the contemporary People's Republic of China ('Communist' China) and North Korea.

A **dictatorship** is a form of totalitarianism in which power tends to be concentrated in the hands of one person, such as Hitler.

Democracy

Democracy is a system of government which basically involves 'government of the people, by the people, for the people', in which ordinary people have some control over government decision-making. It is impractical for everyone in society to be permanently and directly involved in political

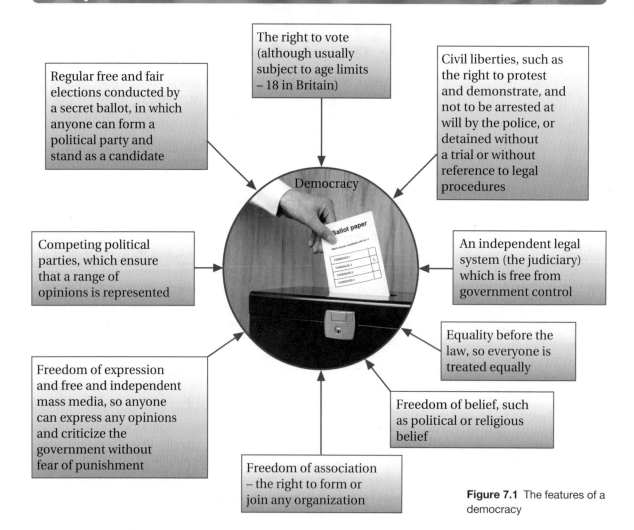

The right to vote (although usually subject to age limits – 18 in Britain)

Regular free and fair elections conducted by a secret ballot, in which anyone can form a political party and stand as a candidate

Civil liberties, such as the right to protest and demonstrate, and not to be arrested at will by the police, or detained without a trial or without reference to legal procedures

Democracy

Competing political parties, which ensure that a range of opinions is represented

An independent legal system (the judiciary) which is free from government control

Freedom of expression and free and independent mass media, so anyone can express any opinions and criticize the government without fear of punishment

Equality before the law, so everyone is treated equally

Freedom of belief, such as political or religious belief

Freedom of association – the right to form or join any organization

Figure 7.1 The features of a democracy

decision-making, so often representatives are elected to represent people's opinions – such as MPs (members of parliament) and local councillors in Britain. This is known as representative or parliamentary democracy, and is found, for example, in Britain, France, Germany, the other countries of the European Union, India and the USA. In such democracies, people use a whole range of means to put pressure on those they elect to represent them, to ensure they do what they want them to do (these are discussed through-out this chapter). There is no guarantee these elected representatives will respond, and often the only effective alternative is to try to remove them at the next elections. While electing representatives is an important part of a democracy, a democratic society usually includes many other features to ensure that representatives can be replaced if they follow unpopular policies and that people can freely express their opinions. Figure 7.1 illustrates the main features of a democracy.

CITIZENSHIP

Citizenship is about the legal, social, civil and political rights and responsibilities of individual citizens in a democratic society. Figure 7.1 and table 7.1 show what these citizenship rights and responsibilities mean.

In Britain in recent years there has been more emphasis placed on **active citizenship**, focusing on people actively taking up their citizenship responsibilities and not just passively accepting their rights, and encouraging them to get involved in the communities in which they live. This is because fewer and fewer people are turning out to vote in elections, and many people are not engaged in the lives of their communities, failing to exercise the democratic rights and responsibilities they have as citizens (this is explored further in the next section). The European Convention on Human Rights was incorporated into English law in 1998 as the Human Rights Act, and this spelt out and protected citizens' rights. Citizenship is now a compulsory part of the National Curriculum in England for secondary age students (in Wales, it is included as part of PSE (Personal and Social Education); in Scotland, similar aims are met through the Social Studies curriculum area, and in Northern Ireland by Personal Development & Mutual Understanding (PDMU) and Learning for Life and Work (LLW)), with the aim of encouraging new generations to feel more aware of their rights and responsibilities, and to encourage them to become more active citizens. This involves things like making sure they have their say and getting involved in the decision-making that affects their lives and communities, for example by voting, standing for election as councillors, getting involved in voluntary, community and protest groups, and becoming volunteers in community groups and activities and helping the disadvantaged.

Table 7.1 Citizenship

Area	Examples of rights	Examples of responsibilities
Legal	The right to a fair trial, a lawyer, freedom from police harassment and arbitrary arrest. A wide range of laws protecting consumers.	Legal responsibilities, like paying taxes, doing jury service and obeying the law.
Social	State-funded healthcare, education and other welfare-state services.	Participating in the life of the community, getting involved in local issues and protests, looking out for the interests of the most vulnerable and volunteering to help them, and taking responsibility for one's actions.
Civil and political	These include all the political and civil rights shown in figure 7.1.	Going out to vote in elections, making sure politicians do what they said they'd do when elected, and protesting if they fail to do so, or trying to stop them implementing policies for which they have no popular support.

Activity

1 With reference to figure 7.1 and table 7.1, identify three political rights that people have as citizens in contemporary Britain.

2 Identify three social responsibilities that people might have as citizens.

3 On the basis of figure 7.1 and table 7.1, write a brief description of the 'perfect' citizen.

4 Go to www.teachernet.gov.uk/teachingandlearning/subjects/citizenship/ and/or using your own knowledge from school, identify five things that students might be expected to know about as a result of following citizenship courses at school.

5 Identity the ways in which Britain might be regarded as a democratic society according to figure 7.1. To what extent do you think it is true that everyone has equal rights as citizens and the same amounts of power and influence in society?

POLITICAL PARTICIPATION

Political participation is concerned with the extent to which people are active citizens, such as actively involving themselves in the life of their communities, the decision-making processes that affect them, voting, standing as elected representatives (like councillors or MPs) and making sure those they elect represent their interests and support them.

One of the major concerns in contemporary Britain is that there are declining levels of political participation and engagement. There are declining numbers voting and standing as candidates in elections and joining political parties. Most people don't believe they have much influence on decision-making in their area or the country as a whole, and few contact elected representatives (MPs and councillors). There are declining numbers doing voluntary work in their communities, or getting involved in community or protest groups. For example, in 2009, over half the population had not been involved in any political activity in the last two to three years, such as signing a petition, contacting an MP or councillor, joining a protest march, going to a political meeting or boycotting products for environmental, ethical or political reasons. Figure 7.2 illustrates this lack of political participation and engagement for a range of factors.

Who participates?

The degree of political participation and active citizenship is influenced by four main factors: social class, gender, age and ethnicity, with the most significant factor being social class. The people most likely to be politically engaged and active citizens are older, middle-class white men.

Figure 7.2 What the public says about political engagement and active citizenship

Source: adapted from *Audit of Political Engagement 6 and 7: The 2009 and 2010 Reports* (Hansard Society, 2009 and 2010)

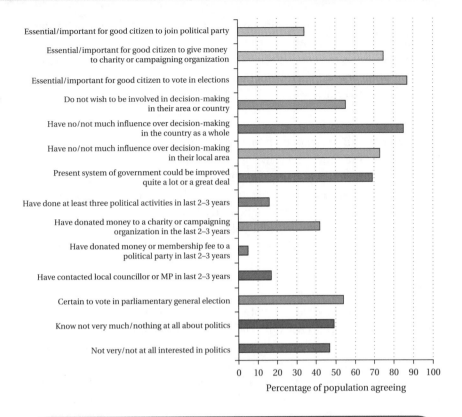

Activity

Refer to figure 7.2.

1 Approximately what percentage of the population thought that they had no or not much influence over decision-making in: (a) their local area; (b) the country as a whole?

2 About what percentage do not wish to be involved in decision-making in their area or country?

3 What percentage think the system of government could be improved quite a lot or a great deal?

4 Identify the three indicators above that people think are essential or important for being good citizens. Now compare these with what people actually do. What does this suggest to you about people's political participation and engagement in active citizenship?

Social class

Individuals from more middle-class professional and managerial backgrounds are much more likely to be involved in the aspects of political participation and active citizenship shown in figure 7.2 than those from manual working-class backgrounds. For example, they are much more likely to contact MPs and councillors, to vote, and to give money to charitable or campaigning organizations. This is linked to higher levels of education, giving individuals the confidence to know who to contact and what to say to get their point across. Their higher incomes also make donations to organizations easier to afford.

Gender

Women are less likely than men to be politically engaged. For example, they are less likely than men to know as much about politics, to vote, to discuss politics, to contact an MP or councillor, or to become a councillor or MP. This may be because women have traditionally tended to be more focused on the private world of the family and household, with men more concerned with the public world of work and politics. However, this is likely to change as females are now outperforming males in education and increasingly in the world of work.

Age

Older people are more likely to vote, as they see this as part of their responsibilities as a citizen – a civic duty; older people also make up the majority of local councillors – the average age of councillors in England was 59 in 2008.

Young people have less knowledge of politics, are less likely to vote, and are less involved in local politics and other aspects of active citizenship than older people. The 2009 British Social Attitudes survey found that, while young people have always been less likely to vote than older people, the situation is getting worse, despite citizenship education in schools, as today's young people are now less likely to vote than people of the same age twenty years ago. In 2010, the Electoral Commission estimated that 56 per cent of 17- to 25-year-olds were not on the electoral roll, on which they must be registered in order to vote.

This apparent political apathy among the young may be explained by:

- *Single issues* – they are more concerned about single issues such as animal welfare, climate change, environmental pollution and anti-war activity, and so are more likely to join pressure groups and be part of new social movements (discussed below) than to get involved with mainstream politics and political parties.
- *Lack of impact* – they feel that they have a very limited ability to influence political parties and government policies.
- *Political alienation* – they feel cut off from the world of mainstream politics, with politicians seen as out of touch with young people.

Ethnicity

Black and minority ethnic groups are much more likely than white people to think the political system works well and that they have an influence over

Young people are more likely to participate in protest movements with activities like demonstrations, than in the mainstream political parties and in voting. Why do you think this is?

decision-making in their local area or nationally. However, they are less active citizens than white people and less politically engaged. For example, they are less likely to participate in any political activity, like signing a petition, contacting councillors or MPs, or giving money to a charity or campaigning organization. They are less likely to vote than the white ethnic majority, with about a third in 2010 not even on the electoral roll which would allow them to vote.

Why don't people participate?

As shown above, some social groups participate more than others in the political process, but there seem to be some general underlying reasons why people are not engaging in the political process, and taking on some of their responsibilities as active citizens.

The Power Inquiry's report, *Power to the People* (2006), gives five main reasons why people don't get involved in the more formal aspects of politics, like voting:

- They do not feel they have enough influence over political decisions and policy making.
- The main political parties are too similar, lack principle, and require citizens to support too many policies.
- The voting system creates unequal and wasted votes.

- They lack information or knowledge about formal politics.
- Voting procedures are inconvenient and unattractive.

Activity

Refer to the sections above on political participation.

1 Describe your own levels of active citizenship and political participation, and how much influence you think you have over local and national decision-making.

2 Taking into account your social class, gender, age and ethnic characteristics, suggest reasons why you do, or do not, participate in or engage with local or national politics.

INFLUENCING DECISION-MAKING IN A DEMOCRACY

There are a number of ways individuals can influence the decision-making process in a democracy, or protest against policies adopted or proposed for implementation. Joining a political party is an obvious way, which enables them to take part in formulating the policies of that party, which may eventually become government policy if the party wins a general election.

The existence of competing political parties, combined with free elections and freedom of speech, means that parties must represent a range of interests if they are to be elected or to stay in power: the need to attract voters means parties have to respond to the wishes of the electorate. Voting is the most obvious way ordinary people can influence political decisions, and is an important part of their responsibilities, as well as their rights, as citizens. A further method is by writing to their local MP or councillor to try to have their concerns taken up, or by writing to the press and using public opinion to put pressure on elected politicians. However, individuals on their own have limited power, and the most effective way of influencing decision-making is to join together with others concerned about the same issue, by forming or joining a pressure group, or identifying themselves with a new social movement (see below).

Protest groups

Every form of government needs some level of popular support if it is to stay in power, and government policies may not succeed when people show widespread resistance to them. When governments seek to implement unpopular policies, they are likely to encounter protest groups of various kinds, as people exercise their rights as citizens to influence political decision-making. Pressure groups and new social movements are the most common means of expressing protests against particular policies, or urging governments to adopt policies the groups favour.

Pressure Groups

Pressure groups are organizations which try to put pressure on governments, councillors, and others with power to implement policies which the groups favour, or to prevent unpopular policies from being implemented.

Pressure groups, which are sometimes called interest groups, are important in a democracy as channels for the representation of a wide range of interests and opinions which might otherwise be forgotten or ignored by those with power. They therefore help to keep political parties and governments in touch with the opinions of the citizens who elected them, and are an important means for people to exercise their citizenship rights and participate in the political process.

There are two main types of pressure group, though particular groups may combine both:

- *Protective or defensive groups* are concerned with defending the shared interests of their members or of a particular social group. Examples of these include the AA (the Automobile Association), Age UK, the NSPCC (the National Society for the Prevention of Cruelty to Children), trade unions and professional associations, and employers' organizations like the CBI (the Confederation of British Industry).
- *Promotional groups* are concerned with promoting a particular cause rather than protecting the interests of a particular group. Examples include ASH (Action on Smoking and Health), the Child Poverty Action Group (concerned with eliminating child poverty), environmental action groups like Greenpeace and Friends of the Earth, and animal rights groups like the Animal Liberation Front. Some of these pressure groups, like Friends of the Earth or Greenpeace, are also likely to take part in the wider activities and actions of new social movements as well.

Pressure groups can have different impacts on power-holders depending on whether they are insider or outsider groups. Insider groups are generally more effective in getting their point of view across, as they have more direct access to and influence on those with power – particularly on government policy makers.

- **Insider groups** are those that are, in a sense, inside government – they present research evidence to governments and are consulted by them on a regular basis. Representatives are often invited to sit on government committees and working groups. Examples include the NFU (National

Farmers' Union, www.nfuon-line.com/), the NSPCC (www.nspcc.org.uk) and the BMA (British Medical Association, www.bma.org.uk).

- **Outsider groups** are those that generally operate outside the day-to-day machinery of governments. Examples include Fathers-4-Justice (www.fathers-4-justice.org) and CND (the Campaign for Nuclear Disarmament www.cnduk.org).

> **Outsider groups** are pressure groups that, for various reasons, do not have everyday active and close links with governments.

PRESSURE GROUPS AND POLITICAL PARTIES

Pressure groups differ from political parties in three main ways:

- They do not try to take power themselves by having their members elected to Parliament and forming a government.
- They do not claim to represent the interests of everyone, but only the particular concerns of some sections of the population.
- They are generally concerned with only one issue or a group of related issues rather than the wide range of issues on which political parties have to form policies.

Table 7.2 gives examples of some pressure groups in Britain and indicates what the aims of each group are.

New social movements

Another way of influencing decision-making in a democracy, exercising citizenship rights to protest, and active citizenship through social and political participation, is through individuals identifying and involving themselves with a new social movement (NSM).

A **new social movement** (NSM) is a broad movement of people who are united around the desire to promote, or block, a broad set of social changes in society. Unlike political parties or pressure groups, they are often only informally organized through a network of small, independent, locally based groups.

There are two main types of new social movements:

> A **new social movement** (NSM) is a broad movement of people who are united around the desire to promote, or block, a broad set of social changes in society.

- *Defensive NSMs* are concerned with defending a natural or social environment seen to be under threat, such as animal welfare, the environment or world peace.
- *Offensive NSMs* are concerned with establishing, defending or extending citizenship rights for those who, to some degree, are denied them through institutional discrimination and marginalization. Examples of these include the anti-racist, women's and gay movements.

New social movements often gain support from men and women of all social classes and ethnic groups, with a wide range of different beliefs and values. It has been suggested that new social movements represent political activity by the non-powerful, non-wealthy and the non-famous.

Table 7.2 Examples of pressure groups in Britain

Organization	Website	Aim
Protective or defensive groups		
National Farmers' Union	www.nfuon-line.com	To protect and promote the interests of farmers.
Age UK	www.ageuk.org	To help older people enjoy a better life by providing services, support, products, advice, information and research, and to campaign on matters of concern to the elderly.
National Society for the Prevention of Cruelty to Children (NSPCC)	www.nspcc.org.uk	To protect children who are deprived, neglected or at risk of abuse.
Confederation of British Industry (CBI)	www.cbi.org.uk	To protect and promote the interests of British business.
British Medical Association (BMA)	www.bma.org.uk	To protect and promote the interests of doctors.
Law Society	www.lawsociety.org.uk	To protect and promote the interests of lawyers.
Trades Union Congress (TUC)	www.tuc.org.uk	To protect the conditions and rights of workers, to campaign for a fair deal at work and for social justice.
National Union of Teachers (NUT)	www.teachers.org.uk	To protect and promote the interests of teachers and children in schools.
Promotional groups		
Action on Smoking and Health (ASH)	www.ash.org.uk	To promote opposition to tobacco smoking and eliminate the harm caused by tobacco.
Child Poverty Action Group (CPAG)	www.cpag.org.uk	To campaign for the abolition of child poverty in the UK and for a better deal for low-income families and children.
Electoral Reform Society	www.electoral-reform.org.uk	To ensure votes in all elections have equal value through the use of the single transferable voting system in all elections and to establish proportional representation.
Greenpeace	www.greenpeace.org.uk	To defend and protect the environment, and investigate, expose and confront environmental abuse, and promote environmentally responsible solutions.
Stonewall	www.stonewall.org.uk	To protect the interests of lesbians, gay men and bisexuals, and campaign for their equality.

Globalization
refers to the growing interdependence of societies across the world, with the spread of the same culture and economic interests across the globe.

New social movements have emerged over issues like opposition to war, damage to the environment, human rights and civil liberties, and **globalization**.

Globalization refers to the growing interdependence of societies across the world, with the spread of the same culture and economic interests across the globe. For example, media and consumer products are often produced for a world market, by the same firms running businesses all over the world. Examples of globalization might include the way call-centres for the UK are located in low-waged India, and Nike trainers are produced at low cost in the Far East and sold for huge profits across the world.

New social movements often become the focus for an individual's definition of him/herself, their self-expression and identity, for example as an environmentalist, an eco-warrior, an animal rights activist, a feminist, an anti-racist or gay. This identity may influence people's lifestyles, such as what they eat, the clothes they wear, the social activities they enjoy, and the general values they hold. The gay movement, for example, includes a whole gay lifestyle, of clothes, clubs, consumer products and music. The 'pink pound' (the spending money of gay people) is now seen as a major market for advertisers and producers of all kinds of products.

Table 7.3 shows some of the typical concerns of new social movements, and examples of them.

Methods used by pressure groups and new social movements

There is a range of methods used by pressure groups and new social movements to influence public opinion, political parties and governments. These organizations and movements, and particularly new social movements, have

Table 7.3 New social movements

Main focus	Some typical issues	Examples
Environment	Global warming / climate change; sustainable energy; genetically modified (GM) crops and foods; household waste incinerators.	The movement against GM crops and foods, including the destruction of fields where such crops are being grown.
Human and civil rights	Discrimination against minority ethnic groups, women, gays, etc.	Gay movement; women's movement; anti-racist movement.
Globalization	Concern over the way the interests of a small number of North American and European and multinational firms seem to be dominating the world's economy and culture, destroying local businesses and local culture, and exploiting cheap labour. Examples of such firms include Nike, Coca Cola and McDonalds.	Large and often violent demonstrations against gatherings of the world's richest nations, like those in Seattle (USA) in 1999, Genoa (Italy) in 2001, Evian (Switzerland) in 2003, Edinburgh, Stirling and Gleneagles (Scotland) in 2005, and London in 2009.
World peace	Maintaining world peace, stopping international conflicts, and Western countries from using their military power to bully other less developed countries.	Stop the War movement (2001 onwards), against America's 'war on terror', including the invasion of Iraq by the USA and Britain in 2003, and the war in Afghanistan.

NEW SOCIAL MOVEMENTS, POLITICAL PARTIES AND PRESSURE GROUPS

New social movements differ from political parties and pressure groups in several ways:

- They have support from a much wider social background, with greater proportions of young people. Supporters are more likely to be involved in a range of new social movements and alternative lifestyles. NSMs are often found at peace and music festivals, like Glastonbury.
- They more commonly have international connections with other movements through the Internet and other new media.
- They are more likely to operate outside the existing political framework, and use more unconventional and sometimes illegal tactics, such as civil disobedience, demonstrations (sometimes violent) and direct action, like protesters blocking roads, breaking up meetings and destroying animal testing laboratories.
- They cover a range of issues, rather than just the single issues of many pressure groups.
- They often focus on world issues, not just national ones.
- They are often an important part of an individual's identity and lifestyle, like the gay movement.
- They are less likely to have full-time staff and a formal national organization, and are more likely to work through the active involvement, commitment and participation of supporters through a network of local groups, linked through new media technology like the Internet and mobiles.
- They are generally involved in more frequent and on-going protests.
- They are more likely to use the Internet and other new media as means of communication and for rallying support and coordinating action (see 'Stop the War' box).

Activity

1 Go on the Internet, and try to find out about any one new social movement. Study the website, and see if you can guess what kind of people the site seems to be aimed at.

2 With reference to the box 'New social movements, political parties and pressure groups', describe how far the NSM you have studied fits with the features of an NSM described there.

You may find the following websites a useful *starting* point, but be prepared to explore the sites and follow any links – remember, there is not one group, but a network of many, involved in new social movements.

Environment:	www.greenpeace.org.uk
	www.foe.co.uk
Human and civil rights:	www.liberty-human-rights.org.uk
	www.equalitynow.org
	www.stonewall.org.uk
	www.uk.gay.com
Globalization / world poverty:	www.globalpolicy.org
	www.oxfam.org.uk
	www.newint.org
	www.adbusters.org/home
World peace:	www.stopwar.org.uk
	www.peacenews.info

STOP THE WAR (WWW.STOPWAR.ORG.UK/)

The 'Stop the War' coalition in 2003, against the invasion of Iraq by Britain and the USA, was the largest coordinated political protest ever seen, with over 2 million people protesting on the streets of London, and many millions more across the world. These people were drawn from all sections of society, and the Internet allowed tiny groups with virtually no resources to mobilize millions of people, through websites and emails to press and supporters, enabling protest to spread across the globe like a Mexican wave. The Internet and other new media like Facebook and mobiles have enabled such new social movements to engage with people in a way the conventional political parties have failed to do, and have proven to be a key means of mobilizing support for a social protest movement.

---

been very effective in using the new media and new media technology, and you should refer to pages 324–5 for a discussion of how the new media may influence the distribution of power in society.

Methods used include:

- contributions to the funds of political parties; for example, trade union support of the Labour Party or contributions to the Conservative Party by businesses
- lobbying MPs, government ministers and local councillors. This means going to the entrance hall or lobby of the House of Commons or local MPs' or councillors' surgeries to put the group's case
- sponsorship of MPs: paying their election and other expenses in exchange for their support in the House of Commons. Trade unions and the Police Federation both do this
- advertising in the mass media
- setting up an Internet website
- leafleting and poster campaigns
- organizing petitions, opinion polls or Facebook groups to show how much support they have. Internet petitions (e-petitions) are now very common, and these can be created and signed at the official site of the Prime Minister's Office at 10 Downing Street to lobby the government directly (http://petitions.number10.gov.uk)

- holding public meetings
- letter-writing or email campaigns to newspapers, local councillors and MPs
- demonstrations
- organizing mass campaigns, such as those against new road building, or the campaign against genetically modified crops in the 2000s
- civil disobedience – breaking the law to bring attention to their cause. This kind of tactic is used by the Animal Liberation Front when it breaks into laboratories and releases animals used for experiments in scientific research. In the late 1990s, tunnelling under new airport and road sites to stop development became a popular tactic for a time
- the use of shock tactics. These might include the use of shocking and disturbing images, like teddies covering their eyes so they cannot witness child abuse (used by the NSPCC), or images of dead animals to attract the public's attention

Shocking images are sometimes used by pressure groups to attract attention, like this one by PETA (People for the Ethical Treatment of Animals)

- strikes, to put economic pressure on the government to change its policies
- the provision of expertise. Pressure groups, particularly, often have specialized knowledge gathered through research which they can lay at the disposal of the government, giving them a direct influence on government policy. For example, the Child Poverty Action Group, Shelter and the CBI are all providers of expert knowledge to governments
- the use of the legal system to challenge or review decisions made by those with power. Examples might include the use of the Human Rights Act and the European Court of Human Rights and other legal routes to challenge and change government decisions.

> **Activity**
>
> Imagine that you wanted to campaign against something, such as the proposed closure of a local school, plans to build a new airport or road, or plans to build a waste incinerator in your area. Choose any issue you like, and plan out how you might organize a campaign to achieve your aims. Think carefully of how you might get people together and all the activities you might engage in to influence those with power. What obstacles, including money, might you find in carrying out a successful campaign?

Are all protest groups equally effective?

Pressure groups and new social movements are important in a democracy as a means of representing a wide range of interests and influencing those with power. However, there are a number of criticisms of the effectiveness of such groups in influencing power-holders, and in spreading power more evenly throughout society.

- Not all interests are represented through pressure groups and new social movements, and not all groups in the population are equally capable of forming them. Disadvantaged groups like the poor, the unemployed, some minority ethnic groups, the disabled, the mentally ill and the old often lack the resources or education to make their voices heard. Substantial wealth and education mean some groups can run more effective campaigns bring their concerns to the attention of power holders, such as employers' organizations like the CBI.
- Not everyone has the same chance of meeting top decision-makers. Insider groups are generally more successful than outsider groups. Getting to see and influence decision-makers is far easier if you are from the same social class background. 'Friends in high places' and the 'old boys' network', which is considered in the discussion of public schools

Protest groups in action, top left to bottom right: poster for green energy; a petition against Trident nuclear submarines; a publicity stunt against Sizewell B nuclear reactor; collecting signatures for a petition to save Warwick fire station from closure; and demonstrations against the 2003 invasion of Iraq

in chapter 4, mean that the interests of the upper and middle classes are generally more effectively represented than those of the working class or marginalized groups.

- Some groups holding key positions in the economy are able to bring pressure to bear on the government through strike action. For example, railway and airline workers or petrol tanker drivers can cause widespread disruption by strike action, and so are more likely to get action on their grievances than, say, pensioners or students.

These factors are of some concern in a democracy, as not all protest groups have the same amount of influence. Some interests get represented more effectively than others and some interests may not be represented at all.

POLITICAL PARTIES IN BRITAIN

A **political party** is a group of people organized with the aim of forming the government in a society.

In a democracy, the existence of a range of political parties is essential if voters are to have a choice of candidates and policies to select from. Those candidates and parties that manage to get elected to local councils, the UK, Scottish or European Parliaments, or the Welsh or Northern Ireland assemblies, are often put under pressure, by the methods discussed earlier, to implement policies which people favour.

The discussion below covers the major parties in Britain which put up candidates for election to local councils, the British Parliament at Westminster (www.parliament.uk) and the European Parliament in Strasbourg (www.europarl.europa.eu). However, **Nationalism** in Wales, Northern Ireland and Scotland has become quite strong, with growing numbers of people demanding more control over their affairs rather than everything being decided in London.

This has led to some powers being taken away from the UK Parliament and given to various bodies in these countries (this is called 'devolution'). These bodies are the National Assembly for Wales in Cardiff (www.assemblywales.org), the Scottish Parliament in Edinburgh (www.scottish.parliament.uk) and the Northern Ireland Assembly in Belfast (www.niassembly.gov.uk). There are also nationalist parties, like Plaid Cymru in Wales (www.plaid-cymru.org), the Scottish National Party in Scotland (www.snp.org) and Sinn Fein in Northern Ireland (www.sinnfein.ie) that fight for representation on these bodies, as well as the British and European Parliaments. These parties aim to promote and implement policies that build a sense of pride, commitment and national identity in their respective nations.

> A **political party** is a group of people organized with the aim of forming the government in a society.

> **Nationalism** is a sense of pride and commitment to a nation, and a very strong sense of national identity.

The Labour Party

The Labour Party was founded in 1906, and is today one of the two main political parties in Britain. Traditionally the Labour Party placed great emphasis on state ownership and workers' control of key sectors of the economy – such as the banks, insurance companies and all the major industrial companies – and a very strong commitment to the welfare state, the ending of poverty and support for trade unions. These policies traditionally meant the party was seen as the defender of working-class interests.

In the early 1990s, many of the Labour Party's traditional policies were reviewed and changed, with the party adopting policies which it was thought would have more appeal to voters. These new policies coincided with the Labour Party relaunching itself as 'New Labour', and appealing to all social classes rather than mainly the working class.

These new policies clearly succeeded with the voters. The Labour Party took power for the first time in eighteen years after winning the 1997 general election with a landslide victory, with the largest number of MPs of any party since 1945 and the largest number in the party's history. This success was repeated in the 2001 and 2005 elections, but they came second to the Conservatives in the May 2010 general election.

The centre parties

The centre parties have policies which traditionally fell between those of Labour and the Conservatives, but all the main parties seem to be increasingly sharing similar policies, differing only in detail rather than their general approach.

The *Liberal Democrats* were founded in 1988, and they are today the main 'third party' in British politics. They have considerable influence in local government (local councils), and after the May 2010 general election for the UK Parliament the fifty-seven Liberal Democrat MPs formed a coalition government with the Conservatives, giving them for the first time considerable influence in national government.

The *Green Party* mainly campaigns around environmental issues, and draws support from a wide range of people who are more concerned about this than any other political issue. There is also some evidence it attracts support from those who wish to register a protest vote against the other parties. The Green Party won their first-ever parliamentary seat at Westminster in the May 2010 general election.

The Conservative (Tory) Party

Conservatives

The Conservative Party is a very long-established political party, and is today one of the two main parties in British politics. The Conservative Party gets the bulk of its funds from big business, and draws much of its traditional support from the upper and middle classes and private business. After its crushing defeats in the 1997, 2001 and 2005 general elections, the Conservative Party began to review its policies, to try to present a more caring and compassionate image, with policies likely to have more appeal to voters of all social classes. This new approach seemed to work, as the Conservatives became the largest party, with the most MPs and the largest share of the vote, in the May 2010 general election – their best result for thirteen years.

The policies of the main political parties are constantly changing, and the best way to see what their latest policies are and what differences there are between the parties, is to find out for yourself by doing the following activity.

Activity

1 To find out about the policies of the different political parties, go to their websites below. Take one area of interest to you, such as the environment, education, poverty or the family, and see what the parties have to say. You will probably find their policies on these issues in their election manifestos. Note any differences between them, and explain which groups of people the different policies might appeal to.

2 Explore briefly some other issues, and see if you can find things that might explain why many working-class people have traditionally voted Labour, while many middle-class people have traditionally voted Conservative.

Labour Party	www.labour.org.uk
Conservative Party	www.conservatives.com
Liberal Democrats	www.libdems.org.uk
Green Party	www.greenparty.org.uk

INFLUENCES ON VOTING BEHAVIOUR

You would expect people to vote in elections purely on the issues, and on the policies held by the different parties. Some argue that 'issue-voting' has become more important in recent years, but research suggests that the political party for which people decide to vote is the result of a range of factors. Party policies are, surprisingly, a relatively minor factor among them, and the following factors all have an influence.

The family

As a major agency of socialization, the family plays an important role in political socialization or the formation of an individual's political beliefs. Political socialization in the family, along with the other factors considered below, often means an individual will have an attachment to a particular political party, making them more receptive to some views than to others. Many people tend to share the general political beliefs and attitudes of their parents, and continue to support the political party their parents did.

Age

Broadly, the older a person is, the more likely he or she is to vote – around 75 per cent of the over-55s turn out to vote in general elections, compared to around a third of 18- to 24-year-olds. Amongst the over-65s there is generally more support for the Conservative Party, reflecting a more traditional attitude on issues of personal morality and freedom, such as drugs, race relations, crime, homosexuality and the position of women in society. Young people are also more likely to involve themselves in the politics associated with the new social movements discussed earlier, rather than the traditional mainstream political parties.

Gender

Traditionally, women have been more conservative than men. In recent years women have been more pro-Labour than men, but both men and women are now displaying more **volatility** in voting. This means they are less committed to any one party, and are more willing to change the party they vote for if they believe another party offers them better personal benefits. This is discussed below.

Volatility in voting means that people have become less predictable, and are less committed to any one party, with their support swinging to and fro between different political parties.

Ethnicity

The ethnic group to which people belong appears to have some influence on their voting habits. Black and Asian people have traditionally been more inclined to support the Labour Party than other parties. This is because Labour has traditionally had more sympathetic policies on equality and race relations, and is more concerned with reducing the racial discrimination, social deprivation and unemployment which minority ethnic groups are more likely to encounter.

Region – geographical area

Voting patterns seem to be associated with the geographical area in which people live. Those in the north of England, Scotland, Wales and inner-city areas are more likely to support the Labour Party. Those in the southern parts of England and rural areas have traditionally been more likely to support the Conservative Party. This could be because of social class differences between these areas, with higher numbers of traditional working-class people, and more unemployment and social deprivation, in areas supporting Labour.

Religion

Religion is not a particularly important influence on voting in most of the United Kingdom, although members of the Church of England have traditionally been more likely to support the Conservative Party. Non-Christians (mainly members of minority ethnic groups), Roman Catholics and those without a religion have traditionally been more likely to vote Labour.

In Northern Ireland voting coincides almost exactly with the divisions between Protestants and Catholics, with Protestants supporting parties which support union with Britain (the Democratic Unionist and Ulster Unionist Parties), and Catholics supporting nationalist parties sympathetic to a united Ireland (Sinn Fein and the Social Democratic and Labour Party).

Party images and party leaders

Most people have general impressions or images of what the political parties stand for, and evidence suggests the way most people vote is influenced by this 'party image', and whether a party appears to be the best one to handle issues like health, education and the economy, rather than by knowledge of what the actual policies of the political parties are.

For example, working-class people might vote for the party that presents a more 'caring' image, supporting the NHS and education, and that appears more sympathetic to the needs of the poor and disadvantaged, rather than one that seems to support big business and the well-off, and promote self-interest over the needs of the wider community.

The personalities of party leaders often have an important role in forming these images of parties and whether people vote for them. For example, whether they come across as likeable, honest, caring, intelligent, decisive and 'attractive'. This is perhaps why political parties, during election campaigns, often concentrate more in their advertising and television broadcasts on presenting particular images or impressions of themselves and their leaders (for example, caring, efficient, and friendly) than on explaining what their actual policies are.

Political parties often try in their advertising to present particular images or impressions of their parties and leaders, rather than explaining what their actual policies are

The mass media

The mass media are major agencies of socialization, and have important influences on people's general beliefs and opinions. Chapter 6 shows how many of the mass media tend to present a very conservative view of society – generally supporting the establishment and the way things are currently organized in society. This helps to create a long-term climate of opinion that favours the mainstream political parties at the expense of smaller parties which might want to make radical changes.

Because newspapers tend to put forward a particular political opinion, many people see them as unreliable sources of evidence, and turn to the television instead. There is little evidence to suggest that party political broadcasts on television have much influence in changing people's voting habits, except in cases where people find it difficult to make up their minds which way to vote. A **floating voter** is an undecided voter with no fixed political opinion or commitment to any political party, and who therefore might regularly switch votes between parties from one election to the next. It is these voters who are most likely to be influenced by the media, and it is at these floating voters that many TV party election broadcasts are aimed.

> A **floating voter** is one who is undecided, with no fixed political opinion or committed support for any political party.

The mass media and voting: key findings

- Where people already have established political views, the mass media are more likely to reinforce those views than to change them.
- People tend to be selective in their choice of programmes and newspapers and they only see and hear what they want to. They will either choose those that present information which confirms their existing opinions and avoid those that conflict with them, or reject those aspects which do not conform with their existing ideas. For example, there are committed Labour voters who might read a Conservative-supporting newspaper like the *Daily Mail*, but ridicule Conservative election broadcasts and ignore the paper's Tory politics.
- While in general the media are unlikely to change people's voting behaviour in the short term (such as in the run-up to a general election), they might be effective in changing attitudes over a longer period of time. For example, they might gradually change people's perception of a particular party or political leader, by constantly rubbishing, day in, day out, over a long period, those it wants to lose, and similarly endlessly praising those it wants to win. The *Sun* claimed in 1997 that 'It was the Sun wot swung it' (for Labour) by rallying behind Labour leader Tony Blair. In 2009, the *Sun* changed its support, and decided to support the Conservatives (see front page below), and began a campaign against Labour. The influence of the mass-circulation red-top newspapers, like the *Sun*, is, however, declining, as people now have a much wider range of media, like digital TV and the Internet, to help form their opinions.
- The mass media are most likely to be influential on issues and parties which are new to people and about which people have little knowledge or experience.

The influence of the media on voting is most likely to take place over the longer term, by endlessly praising parties and leaders it wishes to win elections, and relentlessly attacking those it wishes to lose

- Floating voters are those most likely to be influenced by the media, particularly by party political broadcasts on television.
- Most of the media have, in the long run, supported the Conservative Party. This can create a long-term climate of opinion in which more people are favourable to the Conservatives, and in which opposition parties stand at a disadvantage. This support for the Conservatives from the media declined in the 1997, 2001 and 2005 general elections, when there was much more support for Labour, but it became very evident once again in the months before the 2010 general election.

THE TELEVISED PARTY LEADERS' DEBATES

For the May 2010 general election, there were for the first time ever in Britain three live televised debates between the leaders of the three main political parties (the Labour Party, the Conservative Party and the Liberal Democrats). This meant the electorate, for the first time, had an opportunity, on live television, to directly assess and compare the personalities and policies of the party leaders. The Liberal Democrats had the chance to present their leader and policies to the electorate in a way that they were unable to before, because as a party they lacked the money and media backing the Labour and Conservative parties had for promoting themselves. This live televised debate had a major effect prior to the May 2010 election, as the electorate clearly liked what they saw of the previously almost unknown Liberal Democrat leader (Nick Clegg), with the opinion polls showing a large surge in support for the Liberal Democrats. This Liberal Democrat surge in support only occurred after the first television debate, and it can only be explained by the effects of that debate, combined with a very volatile and unpredictable electorate which was disillusioned with the two main Labour and Conservative parties. However, this media effect proved short-lived, and the apparent surge in Liberal Democrat support proved to be an illusion that vanished when people actually voted, and the Liberal Democrats ended up with five fewer MPs than they had in the previous Parliament.

THE 'SPIN DOCTORS'

'Spin doctors' really came into prominence in the 1990s in Britain, particularly in the 1997 general election. Spin doctors are people who, in general, work for political parties. Their job is to manipulate the media by providing a favourable slant to a potentially unpopular or controversial news item. The term comes from the idea of spinning a ball in sport to make it go in the direction you want it to. The aim of spin doctors is to grab favourable headlines (or ones damaging to other parties) in newspapers, or sound bites on TV and radio. By getting across their version of policy, controversy and events, in stories fed to ever more demanding journalists, they hope to make the media put across a good party image to voters.

Social class

Social class has traditionally been the single most important factor influencing the way people vote, though this has been of declining importance since the 1970s. In Britain, the Labour Party was traditionally seen as the party with policies representing the interests of the working class, and many working-class people have tended to vote Labour. In contrast, the Conservatives were associated with the interests of the middle and upper classes. However, in

Former Iraqi Information Minister Mohammed Saeed al Sahhaf was nicknamed 'Comical Ali' for his 'spin-doctored' insistence in 2003 that the American and British invasion of Iraq was being crushed, at the same time as American troops were fighting their way to a military victory just 1 mile away from where he was speaking in Iraq's capital city Baghdad

the 2000s, both major parties moved more to the centre, and tried to have a broad appeal to people from all social classes.

While in general the most disadvantaged social groups are still more likely to vote Labour, and the most affluent groups to vote Conservative, there is a weaker link between social class and voting between these two extremes. The pattern of voting in Britain since the 1970s suggests three major related changes have occurred.

Pragmatism

Pragmatism means that people vote for practical reasons. Pragmatic voters are those who will support whichever party appears to offer them the greatest personal gains, such as more money, lower taxes and mortgage rates, and a higher standard of living. The electorate has become more motivated by pragmatism, and will support whatever party they feel has the most practical benefits to offer compared to other parties.

Volatility

The electorate has become more volatile or unpredictable – voters of all social classes are less committed to any one political party, and are more willing to change the party they vote for if another party appears to offer them better personal benefits. The British Social Attitudes Survey in 2009 found one in

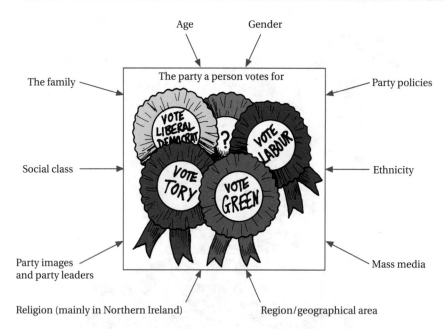

Figure 7.3 Factors influencing the way people vote

Activity

1 If there were a general election tomorrow, which political party would you vote for? Give reasons for your answer, explaining carefully what influenced you in making your decision.
2 Figure 7.3 summarizes the key influences on voting behaviour that sociologists have identified. In the light of the exercise above, how far do you think the findings of sociologists confirm or deny your view? Which influences do you think are the most important?

---

four people said they didn't identify with any political party. People are voting more for their own self-interest rather than out of party loyalty, and on the basis of a party's policies, its image and that of its leader, and how well it performs, or might perform, in government. Voters have less loyalty to any one party, and the support of voters swings to and fro between different political parties. This volatility was very clearly shown in the May 2010 election, with voters constantly changing their minds about which party to support during the election campaign, with the opinion polls showing frequent changes in the support for each of the three main parties, and with many voters remaining undecided how to vote right up to the day of the election.

Dealignment

There is no longer a clear alignment (a matching up) of particular social classes with one of the two main parties – in particular, the working class is no longer clearly aligned with the Labour Party, but neither is the middle class with the Conservatives. Most voters no longer show loyalty to a party according to their social class. **Dealignment** (a mismatch) between class and voting has occurred.

Dealignment in voting means there is no clear alignment (matching up) of particular social classes with one of the two main political parties, and most voters no longer show loyalty to a party according to their social class.

WHY DO PEOPLE ABSTAIN IN ELECTIONS?

About 40 per cent or more of the electorate in general elections, and as many as 70 per cent or more in local elections, abstain – they fail to vote. Disadvantaged groups, such as the least educated and the poor, and younger and older people are the most likely groups to abstain from voting. In marginal seats, where the difference between the votes of the parties is very small – sometimes as little as one or two votes – abstention can actually swing the election result.

Aside from factors such as apathy, forgetfulness, bad weather, being away on holiday or being kept in by illness (without a postal vote), people may make a positive decision to abstain for several reasons:

- In safe seats, where there has traditionally been a large majority for one party, voters may not feel it is worth voting since the outcome of the election is so predictable.
- It may be there is no candidate standing from the party people would normally vote for, or they may not support or understand the policies of any of the different parties. In 1997, an estimated 2 million former Conservative voters abstained, withdrawing their support from the Conservative Party, but unable to bring themselves to vote for any other party.
- Some voters might simply be very disillusioned with the political process. For example, they may think elections are a waste of time, since the policies of all the parties are too similar; they may not trust politicians and government; they may think councillors and MPs are out-of-touch with their concerns, or have a sense of powerlessness and think 'elections don't change anything anyway'. In such circumstances they may not bother to vote at all as a protest. For example, in the 2005 general election for Parliament, 44 per cent of people in the British Social Attitudes survey said they thought there was 'not much difference' between the Conservatives and Labour.

Such a lack of participation in voting is a serious matter in a democracy, as it may be that governments and councils are not really representing the feelings of the majority of voters.

OPINION POLLS AND ELECTIONS

Opinion polls are social surveys which try to find out people's attitudes on many issues, and they are widely used to discover how people intend to vote in elections. They most commonly use on-line surveys or interviews conducted over the phone.

The results of opinion polls provide the basis for reports about the 'state of the parties' which are regularly published in the newspapers and on Internet sites, such as the example shown below, and in election periods polls are conducted daily.

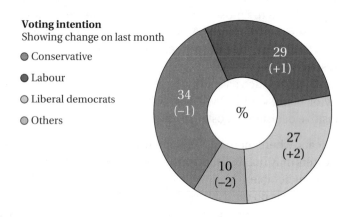

Voting intention
Showing change on last month

- Conservative
- Labour
- Liberal democrats
- Others

34 (−1)
29 (+1)
27 (+2)
10 (−2)
%

Opinion polls during elections are used to show how people feel about a range of features of the political parties, but most commonly reported is how people say they intend to vote. They are usually presented in a format like that shown here, showing the parties' share of the vote and how it has changed since the last poll

Activity

1 Do a Google search on 'opinion polls uk' or one at www.bbc.co.uk, or go to www.ukpollingreport.co.uk. Identify two recent opinion polls, preferably on voting, but otherwise on topics that interest you. Describe some things these surveys found, and also make a note of the number of people who were questioned, and how they were questioned, for example by phone, face-to-face interview, postal questionnaire and so on.
2 To what extent do you think public opinion polls give a true picture of what the public is thinking? Give reasons for your answer.

Why opinion polls are sometimes inaccurate

Opinion polls use sophisticated sampling techniques to obtain representative samples of the voting population. Often they can predict the outcome of elections accurately from asking no more than about 1,000 people. This is because the group they have questioned is a good representative cross-section of the entire population in terms of factors such as age, sex, ethnicity,

social class, and geographical spread around the country. However, sometimes the opinion polls fail to predict the results of elections accurately.

The reasons for this are quite varied, and many possible explanations are discussed in chapter 2 on the general problems of sampling and survey methods. Some possible problems with opinion polls are outlined below.

- They may not contain a representative sample of voters, which may lead to inaccurate results.
- Interviewer bias may mean people give inaccurate answers. People in face-to-face interviews may give the answer that they think is socially acceptable rather than what they really believe. For example, they may say they are prepared to pay higher taxes for better education and healthcare, but privately prefer (and vote for) tax cuts. There may be a sharp contrast between what people say to pollsters and what they actually do when it comes to voting. If a party is unpopular at the time, its supporters may be reluctant to admit to interviewers that they support it.
- The format and wording of questions may affect the results of the poll. For example, respondents prefer to agree rather than disagree with statements which are put to them.
- People may change their minds during the course of the election campaign, after the poll is conducted, when they have heard more arguments and have had more time to make up their minds. Because of this, opinion polls are likely to become more accurate the closer they are to the day of the election.

- Some of those interviewed may decide not to vote, or not be registered to vote because they are not on the electoral register, when it comes to the actual election, and this will distort the opinion poll's predictions.
- Opinion polls might themselves change the way people decide to vote and therefore the results of the election, as is discussed below.

How opinion polls might influence the results of elections

There is some evidence that published opinion polls might not simply reflect voters' opinions, but actually help to form and change them, and therefore affect the eventual election results. There are several reasons for this.

Complacency

If the polls predict a large win for one party, making its supporters complacent, they may not bother to vote, thinking that it is a safe seat and the result a foregone conclusion. This complacency, created by the opinion polls, might cost a party an election victory if too many of its supportes didn't bother to vote.

Tactical voting

If the polls predict that a certain party is going to win by a large margin, then supporters of another party which has no chance of winning might decide to vote for a third party in the hope of defeating the predicted winning party. This is known as **tactical voting**. An example might be committed Labour voters in a safe Tory seat, where Labour stands no chance of winning. If the opinion polls show that a Liberal Democrat is in second place, then Labour voters may decide to vote for the Liberal Democrat in the hope of defeating the Tory.

> **Tactical voting** is where, in an election, supporters of a political party which has no chance of winning vote for another party which is not their preferred choice, in the hope of defeating the predicted winning party.

The bandwagon effect

The bandwagon effect is where, if the polls show one party to be in the lead, undecided voters may want to 'jump on the bandwagon' and be on the side of what the polls suggest will be the winning party.

Defeatism

If the opinion polls show their preferred party has no chance of winning, then voters may adopt a view that defeat is unavoidable, and so not bother to vote. This would assist the predicted winning party.

The underdog effect

This is where people vote out of sympathy for the party that the polls suggest will lose, boosting its support.

Because opinion polls can affect the results of elections, some suggest they should be banned immediately before elections, and this has occurred in several countries, such as in France and Germany, where polls are not allowed in the last few days of election campaigns.

IS BRITAIN A DEMOCRACY?

Earlier in this chapter you may have discussed whether Britain is a democracy or not. Much of this chapter has emphasized the democratic features of modern Britain, and if you look back to figure 7.1, then you may agree that many of the features listed there are indeed to be found in modern Britain. However, despite its strengths, there are a number of weaknesses in British democracy.

Non-elected rulers

Democracy is meant to involve governments reflecting the interests of the people through elected representatives. However, the House of Lords and the monarchy are not elected, but both have considerable power in controlling which laws are passed.

Anglican archbishops and bishops have seats in the House of Lords, which plays an important role in making laws. But they are unelected, and unaccountable to voters

The voting system – first-past-the-post

Voting for the UK Parliament is by the first-past-the-post system, under which the party that gets most votes in any constituency (voting area) wins that constituency. In general elections, the representative of the winning party becomes the constituency's MP, and the party getting the most MPs usually forms the government. If the winning party does not have more than half of the MPs, giving it a majority over all other parties combined (an overall majority), then there is what is called a 'hung Parliament', and the party forming the government will not be able to win enough votes to pass laws without sharing power with, or at least getting the support of, one or more smaller parties. This happened in the May 2010 election, when there was a hung Parliament. Although the Conservatives had the largest number of MPs, they were only able to govern with the support of the Liberal Democrats, gained by sharing power with them in a Conservative – Liberal Democrat coalition government.

The first-past-the-post voting system means governments are often elected which represent only a minority of voters in the country as a whole. In fact, every government in Britain since 1945 has been elected with the support of less than half of the voting population. Figure 7.4 shows that, in the May 2010 general election, the number of MPs elected for each party in no way represented the parties' share of the votes in the country as a whole. Such circumstances mean that, while minority parties might collect a lot of votes in the country as a whole, they may get far fewer than their fair share of MPs, or none at all, in Parliament, and therefore no representation. **Proportional representation** – which means the number of MPs elected for each party reflects the share of the vote received – would ensure that minority parties and interests were more adequately represented. The hung Parliament in May 2010, and the unfairness shown in figure 7.4, led to growing demands for an overhaul of the voting system towards a fairer system, with backing from both the Labour Party and the Liberal Democrats. This led to the growing possibility in 2010 of a future referendum being held on changing the voting system to a more proportional basis.

Figure 7.4 shows the number of MPs that might have been elected for each party in May 2010 if perfect proportional representation had been adopted.

> **Proportional representation** is a voting system in which the number of representatives elected accurately reflects the proportion of the votes received.

Elite rule

As seen in the next chapter (see pages 411–15) wealth remains highly concentrated in the hands of a small upper class, which therefore has major influence in economic decision-making. For example, this class can decide where factories should be located and whether they should be opened or

Figure 7.4 General election results: United Kingdom, May 2010

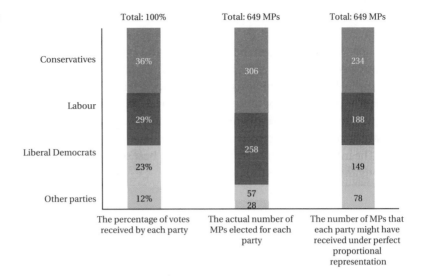

Total: 100% Total: 649 MPs Total: 649 MPs

Conservatives — 36% / 306 / 234

Labour — 29% / 188

Liberal Democrats — 23% / 258 / 149

Other parties — 12% / 57 / 28 / 78

The percentage of votes received by each party

The actual number of MPs elected for each party

The number of MPs that each party might have received under perfect proportional representation

closed down, and it can control the workforce through hiring and firing. Democratically elected governments cannot afford to ignore this power, as they might face rising unemployment and other social problems if the upper class decided not to invest its money.

Most of those in the top elite jobs who run the various institutions controlling society – like Parliament, central and local government, the civil service, the legal institutions (courts), the police, and the army – who wield enormous power and influence in this country, come from public-school and upper- and upper-middle-class backgrounds (see pages 225–8 on this). Even among Labour MPs, few come from working-class backgrounds. This raises questions about the extent to which working-class interests are adequately represented.

Unequal protest groups

As seen earlier in this chapter, not all interests are represented through protest groups, and some groups have a lot more wealth and power than others. It is the voices of the disadvantaged and the poor which are least likely to be heard, and even when many people are involved in new social movements, they rarely have much impact on those in power.

Deciding the issues

The political parties – not the population as a whole – often decide what the important issues are and which ones they are going to fight elections around. The mass media are mainly privately owned and controlled by a rich and powerful minority and have a conservative bias. They have an important role in forming public opinion and, like political leaders, can decide the issues around which elections are fought.

The points raised above suggest that perhaps Britain is not quite as democratic as many people might believe, and that not everyone gets an equal chance to express her or his opinions and influence decision-making. This is likely to be true particularly of those holding radical opinions who want to change the way society is presently organized. While democracy in Britain has many strengths and freedoms which must be defended, it also has its limitations. The interests of democracy are perhaps best served by removing the limitations and reinforcing the strengths.

SOCIAL PROBLEMS AND THE ROLE OF THE STATE

The government is the political organization which has responsibility for running and administering the state. The government is just one part of the state – Parliament, the civil service, local government (local councils), the police, the judiciary (legal system), the military, and all the major public services like health, education and highways are also parts of the state. A key role of the government and state is to maintain social stability, and this involves keeping social problems, like those discussed in chapter 1, under control.

Tackling social problems

The state carries an enormous amount of power, and often only the state has the power and resources to resolve social problems. Two examples of these, discrimination and unemployment, will be briefly reviewed, followed by a fuller discussion of the welfare role of the state in the UK.

Race, gender, age and disability discrimination

Race, gender and age discrimination are discussed more fully in the next chapter, but these, along with disability discrimination, are clear social problems as they disadvantage people in many ways, such as in employment, health and pay, and have negative effects on the quality of their lives. For example, disabled people often experience discrimination in so far as buildings, clubs, shops and workplaces aren't designed to cater for their needs, barring them from participation in important areas of social life.

While the state alone cannot resolve discrimination between individuals, it can make it difficult or illegal for such discrimination to take place in public services, by private employers and by individuals. There is a huge range of laws to tackle discrimination of various kinds. For example, the

What steps can the state take to reduce bigotry – like discrimination against people because of their race, gender, age, or disability – and promote tolerance in society?

Race Relations Acts outlawed racial discrimination in a range of areas, and public bodies now have a duty to promote equality of opportunity and good relations between different ethnic groups. The Equal Pay Acts and the Sex Discrimination Act attempted to tackle sex discrimination in education, pay and employment, and similar legislation exists to prevent age discrimination. The Disability Discrimination Acts of 1995 and 2005 gave disabled people protection against disability discrimination in a wide range of areas, including employment, education and access to goods, facilities and services, and public authorities are now legally obliged to promote equality of opportunity for disabled people. The Government's Office for Disability Issues (www.odi.gov.uk) is working to overcome discrimination and create more equality for disabled people.

The 2010 Equality Act aimed to promote further fairness and equality of opportunity; to actively tackle disadvantage and discrimination; and to strengthen existing protection against race, age, sex and disability discrimination. The Equalities and Human Rights Commission (www.equalityhumanrights.com) monitors and takes up cases of such discrimination.

These state activities to tackle discrimination are also found in a range of public bodies and services – for example, translation services and training in the NHS to reduce disadvantages arising from ethnic background, multicultural education in schools to promote racial harmony and understanding, and special efforts to improve the achievement in schools of some students from black and minority ethnic groups.

Unemployment

Unemployment is a social problem. For individuals, unemployment can mean a loss of identity, status and a sense of personal worth, as well as poverty, mounting debts and ill-health arising from poor diet and daily stress and anxiety. Social isolation may arise, with the loss of friendships formed through work, particularly as there is little money to spend on alternative activities, such as going to the pub with friends. Family life may suffer from these problems too, with more family breakdowns and domestic violence.

For society, unemployment may lead to more dissatisfied and angry people, with an increase in political unrest, such as riots, and more racism and scapegoating, as people try to find easy answers to their unemployment and try to lay the blame on vulnerable groups such as minority ethnic groups, young people, asylum seekers and migrant workers. Social problems such as poverty, homelessness, mental illness and rising rates of crime, suicide, alcoholism and drug abuse can all follow from high levels of unemployment. It is because these sorts of social problems may be created by unemployment that most governments take steps to keep it as low as possible.

Tackling unemployment   Government measures to tackle unemployment include the following:

- providing more retraining opportunities for older workers with redundant skills

- government job training schemes for the unemployed, to provide them with the skills to find work
- more vocational education, including key skills, so school leavers have more of the skills required by business and industry, making them more employable
- effective management of and investment in the economy, enabling British industry and British goods to remain competitive in the world economy, protecting British jobs
- a range of benefits from the welfare state to reduce the worst consequences of unemployment.

THE WELFARE STATE

The welfare state is the large grouping of services aimed at providing security for the entire population, and particularly for those who are most disadvantaged, like the poor, the sick, the unemployed and the disabled. It is through the welfare state in its widest sense that the government tries to tackle many social problems.

The welfare state originally began in the UK with the Beveridge Report of 1942. This recommended the development of welfare services aimed at the destruction of the 'five giants' of Want (poverty), Disease (ill-health and lack of healthcare), Squalor (poor housing), Ignorance (lack of educational opportunity) and Idleness (unemployment), and the creation of a society in which each individual would have the right to be cared for by the state from womb to tomb. The welfare state as we know it today came into effect on 5 July 1948 – the date of the foundation of the National Health Service.

The Beveridge Report of 1942 recommended tackling the 'five giants' of Want (poverty), Ignorance (lack of educational opportunity), Disease (ill-health and lack of healthcare), Squalor (poor housing), and Idleness (unemployment). These principles laid the basis for the state's role in tackling social problems we see in today's welfare state

The welfare state provides a wide range of benefits and services including:

- a range of welfare benefits through the social security system for many groups such as the unemployed, those injured at work, the sick and disabled, widows, the retired, expectant mothers, lone parents and children – for example state pensions, Job Seekers' Allowance, Incapacity Benefit and Income Support
- a comprehensive and largely free National Health Service, including ante- and post-natal care, hospitals, GPs, dentists and opticians (although increasingly more charges are payable – for example to dentists and opticians)
- a free and compulsory state education for all to the age of 16 (rising to age 17 from 2013), plus free pre-school education for 3- to 4-year-olds
- social services provided by local councils – such as social workers – and special facilities for the disabled, the elderly and children. Local councils are also responsible for housing the homeless, and for the adoption and fostering of children
- the National Minimum Wage, to help the poorest-paid and to prevent their exploitation.

Other providers of welfare

The welfare state, run by national and local government, is not the only provider of welfare. The informal, voluntary and private sectors also play important roles, often working alongside state provision.

Informal welfare provision

This is provided informally by family, friends and neighbours, and this often means care by women, as it is women who take on the main caring responsibilities in the family for the dependent elderly, the disabled and the sick.

Voluntary organizations

Voluntary organizations are non-official, non-profit-making organizations, often charities, which are 'voluntary' in the sense that they are neither created by, nor controlled by, the government. They employ both salaried staff and voluntary helpers, and are funded by donations from the public and grants from, or sale of services to, central and local government. They try to fill some of the gaps left by the safety net provided by the state, by providing help and information in areas where state assistance is too little or non-existent. Examples of such groups include the Salvation Army, which provides hostel accommodation and soup kitchens; Shelter, which campaigns for the homeless and helps with finding accommodation; Age UK; Mind, to help with mental health problems; and the Child Poverty Action

Group, which promotes action for the relief of poverty among children and families with children. The churches also provide a range of welfare support, particularly to the elderly.

Voluntary organizations have high levels of expert knowledge, and work in specialized areas – like domestic violence, homelessness, debt, mental illness, disability, rape and sexual abuse – where state provision may be under pressure, inadequate or non-existent. However, they often lack adequate funds to be as effective as they might otherwise be, and they do not exist in all areas where they are needed.

Voluntary organizations also play important roles as pressure groups, highlighting the weaknesses of the welfare state, and they frequently provide expert knowledge and make recommendations to governments for changes to improve social welfare.

The private sector

The private sector consists of profit-making private businesses, from which individuals or local and central government purchase services or benefits. This sector provides welfare services such as private hospitals, schools, care homes for the elderly, private pensions and medical insurance. Access to the private sector is generally only available to those who can afford it, and poor people may therefore not get services at all if the state doesn't provide or pay for them.

The politics of the welfare state

There are often bitter political disputes between political parties about what the role of the state should be in providing social welfare. There are two main political positions which are outlined below.

The social democratic approach

This suggests the state should be responsible for social welfare. It should provide 'womb to tomb' care, with universal provision of services available to all, like free education, pensions, full employment and free healthcare. The welfare state should tackle social problems such as unemployment, poverty and other disadvantages, and discrimination. This should be funded by progressive taxation, so those who earn the most pay the most tax. This approach, supporters argue, would help to promote a more cohesive, less divided and, therefore, more stable society.

The market liberal approach

Suppoters of this approach believe that individuals should take responsibility for their own welfare. They should be able to choose welfare provision from all those competing in the welfare market, including private companies and voluntary organizations, and they, not the state, should take responsibility themselves for obtaining it.

The social democratic approach above is seen as providing a 'nanny' welfare state, which is so generous that it undermines personal responsibility and self-help. It makes people unwilling to work to support themselves, and encourages some to avoid work by living off welfare benefits. The generosity of the welfare state has undermined the importance of support from families and the community. Money raised by taxation should not be wasted on providing welfare benefits or healthcare to those who are able to support themselves, and state benefits should be restricted only to the very poor, and those unable to work through sickness or disability. The rest of the population should pay for their own welfare.

These two competing political approaches to the welfare state have lessened as a divide between the political parties in recent years. This is because the views of all the mainstream political parties are changing. The soaring costs of the welfare state suggest the following will be the major concerns of all governments in the future:

- tackling dependency on welfare benefits by moving people into employment through 'welfare to work' schemes – getting people off welfare benefits and into paid employment
- cutting the soaring levels of state spending on welfare provision, particularly the rising spending owing to the health and pension needs of the growing numbers of older people
- making more people pay for the services they receive if they can afford it
- putting greater emphasis on provision by the voluntary and private sectors
- getting people to help themselves through the family and community, and encouraging people to save to pay for their own welfare services
- making welfare-state institutions like hospitals, surgeries, social services and schools more efficient, and introducing competition between them so they give clients better-quality services at lower costs, with more choice for clients. Welfare-state institutions are increasingly bg run more like private businesses.

Is the welfare state succeeding?

Huge sums of taxpayers' money are spent on the welfare state, and there are constant disputes about whether or not it is successful in tackling social problems like poverty and ill-health, and therefore whether more, or less, money should be spent on it. A few of these competing arguments are outlined below, some of which are discussed further in other chapters (particularly chapter 8).

IS THE WELFARE STATE SUCCEEDING?

Yes	No
• State support has eliminated absolute poverty in childhood and old age, and in periods of ill-health, unemployment and disability throughout our lives. The standard of social (council and housing association) housing has massively improved, and slums have disappeared.	• Many people still live a deprived lifestyle compared to most people, because welfare benefits are inadequate. There remain huge inequalities in wealth, income, education, housing, health and employment. Relative poverty and social exclusion remain serious social problems.
• All have access to free medical care, and the health of the nation has improved immeasurably.	• The welfare state is failing to cope with the demands placed on it. For example, there are often delays for hospital treatment, and there remain huge inequalities in health and access to healthcare (see chapter 9).
• All have free education from the ages of 3 to 18.	• The middle-class still benefit the most in education, and those from poorer families still suffer huge disadvantages (see chapter 4).
• Many vulnerable groups have a range of state agencies and other organizations to assist them, such as social services, GPs' clinics and Age UK.	• There are many vulnerable groups who slip through the safety net, or for whom there is inadequate or no state provision. They have to turn to a poorly funded voluntary sector, or just cope – or not cope – alone.
• Everyone is guaranteed 'cradle to grave' security.	• Generous welfare benefits create a nation of scrounging social misfits who are prepared to just live off benefits without ever working. The welfare state has undermined personal responsibility and self-help.

Activity

1 Do you think the state should be the main provider of welfare for all? What are the advantages and disadvantages of welfare provision by the state compared to the voluntary and private sectors?
2 Suggest reasons why informal welfare provision is mainly carried out by women. What consequences do you think this might have for women's lives and careers?
3 Suggest *two* ways in which private-sector welfare provision might create unequal access to welfare services.
4 Identify two social problems, explain why they are social problems and what steps the state is taking to tackle them.

CHAPTER SUMMARY

After studying this chapter, you should be able to:

- explain briefly what is meant by the terms *power*, *politics*, *authority* and *coercion*

- describe a range of ways that power is used in everyday life

- describe and explain the main features of a democracy, and how democracy differs from totalitarianism and dictatorship

- explain what is meant by citizenship, and identify some rights and responsibilities associated with it

- describe what is meant by active citizenship, the ways that people might participate or engage in the political process, and how this varies by social class, gender, age and ethnicity

- identify and explain some reasons why people don't participate in the political process

- identify ways in which people can influence power-holders in a democracy

- explain what pressure groups are and how they differ from political parties

- describe, with examples, the difference between insider and outsider pressure groups

- explain what is meant by a new social movement, with examples, and explain how they differ from political parties and pressure groups

- describe the methods protest groups use to influence those with power

- explain why some interests are better represented by protest groups than others, and why some protest groups are more effective than others

- identify the main political parties in Britain which put up candidates in elections, and briefly describe some of their main policies

- discuss the range of factors influencing voting behaviour

- discuss how the mass media might influence political attitudes

- explain why social class is becoming of less importance in influencing voting

- suggest reasons why people abstain in elections

- explain why opinion polls might sometimes fail to predict accurately the outcome of elections

- explain how opinion polls might themselves affect election results

- discuss the extent to which Britain might be regarded as a democracy

- describe, with examples, some ways that the state tackles social problems like discrimination and unemployment

- describe what is meant by the welfare state, what it does, and different political views of what it should do and how well it is working.

KEY TERMS

active citizenship
authority
charismatic authority
citizenship
coercion
dealignment

democracy
dictatorship
floating voter
globalization
insider groups
nationalism
new social movement

outsider groups
political party
politics
power
pressure group
proportional
  representation

rational-legal
  authority
tactical voting
totalitarianism
traditional authority
volatility

8

Social Inequality

Contents

CHAPTER 8

Social Inequality

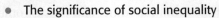

KEY ISSUES

- The significance of social inequality
- Social inequality as a social issue
- Social stratification
- Systems of stratification
- Four views of social class
- The class structure of Britain
- Social class inequalities
- Poverty
- Social mobility
- Changes in the class structure
- Gender and inequality
- Ethnicity and inequality
- Age and inequality

THE SIGNIFICANCE OF SOCIAL INEQUALITY

Most people would agree that few societies are really equal. The study of social inequality is of central concern to sociologists, because modern societies display such a wide range of inequalities. These include inequalities between rich and poor, between social classes, between men and women, between ethnic groups, and between age groups. Inequalities exist in a wide range of areas of social life, such as in job security, leisure opportunities, health, housing, income and the power to influence events in society. In Britain, income inequality – the gap between the rich and the poor – has grown rapidly since 1979, as shown in figure 8.1, and the gap between the two groups is now one of the largest in the European Union.

An understanding of social inequality provides a necessary starting point for the newcomer to sociology because it influences so deeply much of what happens in society.

SOCIAL INEQUALITY AS A SOCIAL ISSUE

Social inequality is an important social issue. In societies where there are the widest inequalities, particularly inequalities in income, compared to more equal societies, there are more social problems, like teenage pregnancy, crime and violence, there is less social cohesion, and people are, for example, more likely to be depressed and suffer mental illness, to be obese, to get harsher prison sentences if they commit crime, and to trust others less. While these disadvantages affect the poorest people the most, they also affect the rich. For example, the richest people in more equal societies have higher literacy levels than those who are similarly rich in more unequal societies, who also live shorter lives and are more likely to have their children die in their first twelve months of life. Inequality, then, seems to have harmful consequences for all, and not just for those who are poor.

Much of this book, and particularly this chapter, is concerned with describing and explaining a range of these inequalities.

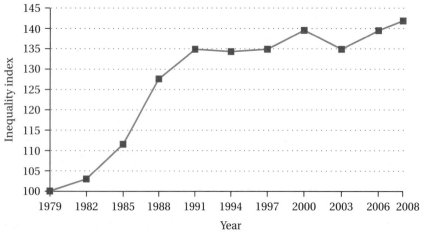

Figure 8.1 How inequality has grown in Britain, 1979–2008

This figure shows how inequality has risen in Britain between 1979 and 2008. It is measured using what is called the Gini coefficient (the equality index), which shows how income inequality has changed compared to a base of 100 in 1979. In 2008, inequality was 42 per cent higher than it was in 1979. *Source*: derived from R. Joyce, *Poverty and Inequality in the UK* (Institute for Fiscal Studies, 2009)

Activity

Refer to figure 8.1.

1 Between which years was there the sharpest increase in inequality in Britain?
2 In what year was inequality at its highest compared to 1979?
3 Much of the evidence in the paragraphs opposite comes from the Equality Trust, and more detail and explanation on the differences between less equal and more equal societies can be found at www.equalitytrust.org.uk.
   (a) Go to this website and explore how inequality influences *two* of the following issues: physical health; mental health; drug abuse; education; imprisonment; obesity; social mobility; trust and community life; violence; teenage births; and child well-being.
   (b) Refer to the 'remedies' section of the site, and suggest two remedies there might be to rectify or improve the two issues you've studied.
4 Make a list of what you consider to be the most important inequalities in society today. Explain in all cases why you think they are important in people's lives and how they affect the chances people get in life.

Social stratification refers to the division of society into a hierarchy of unequal social groups.

SOCIAL STRATIFICATION

Inequality affects not simply individuals, but whole groups of people, and such patterns of inequalities between social groups are called social stratification.

A stratification hierarchy

The word *stratification* comes from *strata* or layers, as in the way different types of rock are piled on top of one another to form rock strata.

Social stratification refers to the division of society into a pattern of layers or strata made up of a hierarchy of unequal social groups. These stand in relations of advantage and disadvantage to one another in terms of features

---

KEY TERMS USED IN THE STUDY OF SOCIAL STRATIFICATION

- **Economic inequality** refers to differences in all those material things which affect the lives of individuals, such as their wealth, their income, and the hours they work. These inequalities can be measured, and continue to exist regardless of whether people recognize them as important or not.

- **Life chances** are the chances of obtaining those things defined as desirable and of avoiding those things defined as undesirable in any society. Life chances include the chances of obtaining things like good-quality housing, good health, holidays, job security and educational success, and avoiding things like ill-health and unemployment.

- **Status** refers to the differing amounts of prestige or respect given to different positions in a group or society by other members of that group or society. Status involves people's social standing in the eyes of others. Status inequalities only exist as long as other people in a group or society continue to recognize them. For example, a vicar in a Christian society is generally given high status, but is unlikely to be given such status in a society practising witchcraft or voodoo.

- **Status groups** are groups of people sharing a similar status. For example, teachers form a status group based on a shared occupation, and teenagers generally share a similar status based on their age.

- **Ascribed status** is status which is given to an individual at birth and usually can't be changed. Examples of such status include a person's age, ethnic group, sex, or place or family of birth. Members of the royal family in Britain have ascribed status.

- **Achieved status** refers to status that individuals have achieved through their own efforts, such as in education, through skill, or via promotion at work and career success.

- **Status symbols** are things that show off people's status to others, such as the kind of job they have, the way they spend their money, the sort of house they live in, the car they drive, and their general lifestyle. All these things may be highly or lowly rated by other members of society.

- **Social mobility** is the term used to describe the movement up or down the social hierarchy between levels of a stratification system. For example, a person who came from a working-class family but became a middle-class doctor would have achieved upward social mobility. An **open society** is one in which social mobility is possible; a **closed society** is one in which no social mobility is possible.

such as income, wealth, occupational status, race, age or sex, depending on the stratification system. Those at the top of the stratification hierarchy will generally have more power in society than those at the bottom.

SYSTEMS OF STRATIFICATION

Sociologists have identified four major types of stratification system, which have important differences between them: slavery, the caste system, feudal estates, and social class.

Slavery

> **Slavery** is a stratification system in which some people are regarded as the property of others.

Slavery is a form of stratification in which a group of people are held against their will, regarded as the property of others, are controlled by their owners, forced to work, and bought or sold like any other possession.

Typical examples included Ancient Rome, Europe for over 400 years from the mid fifteenth century, and what is now the United States from the seventeenth to nineteenth centuries, with the enslavement of millions of Africans through the transatlantic slave trade.

Although slavery is now banned in all countries by a series of international laws and treaties, and was abolished in the British Empire and the USA in the nineteenth century, slave-like conditions are still found for millions of people today, including children, through human trafficking (illegal international trading in people) for forced labour or sex work in developed countries, and slave-like working conditions in less-developed countries. You can read more about contemporary slavery at www.iabolish.org, www.freetheslaves.net and www.antislavery.org.

The caste system

> The **caste system** is a stratification system based on Hindu religious beliefs, in which an individual's position is fixed at birth and cannot be changed.

The **caste system** is the most rigid system of stratification and is associated with India.

The levels of the social hierarchy are called castes, and this hierarchy is fixed and clearly defined. The social position of individuals is ascribed at birth in accordance with Hindu religious beliefs and customs. Hindus believe in reincarnation – that people are born again after death. Hinduism suggests that people's behaviour in their previous life will decide the caste they are born into after rebirth. Since people believe the social position they are born into (their caste) is god-given, they generally accept their ascribed caste position.

A caste society is a closed society, with no social mobility possible from one caste to another. Each caste is completely closed off from others by religious rules and restrictions, which ensure that very little social contact occurs

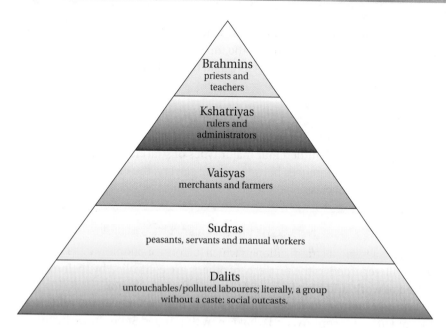

between members of different castes. The purity of each caste is maintained by **endogamy**.

This means that marriage is only permitted to a person of the same caste. Besides the choice of marriage partner, caste membership also determines social status and occupation.

In the Indian system, the Hindu religion divides the population into five major castes, shown in figure 8.2

Despite attempts by the Indian government to remove the inequalities of the caste system, the system still continues, as many people still accept the Hindu religious beliefs on which it is based.

It has been suggested that the apartheid regime in South Africa, which was only abolished in the 1990s, showed some similarities with the caste system. Here people were stratified according to ascribed racial characteristics (white, coloured, and black populations), with legal restrictions on mixing/marriage between different races, and with an almost 'religious' ideology of white supremacy.

Endogamy is where marriage must be to a partner of the same kinship or social group.

Feudal estates

Feudalism was typically found in medieval Europe.

The levels of the social hierarchy were called estates, and based on ownership of land. There was no legal equality between estates, and people in higher estates had more legal rights and privileges than those in lower ones. The lower estates had obligations and duties to those higher up the hierarchy, which were

Feudalism is a closed system of stratification based on land ownership and legal inequalities.

Figure 8.3 The feudal hierarchy

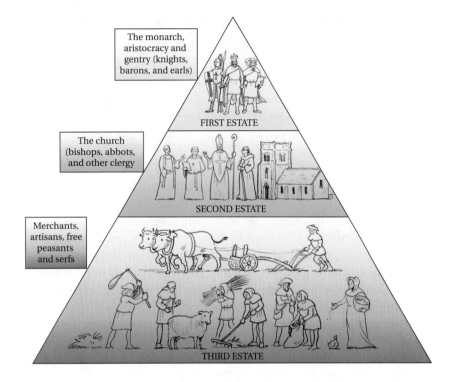

backed up by laws. For example, there was an obligation for serfs to work one day a week on the master's land. Membership of any estate was determined largely by birth, with social position, power, and status all ascribed at birth.

Feudalism was, like the caste system, a closed society, with social mobility from one estate to another extremely limited. However, some upward mobility to a higher estate was possible, for example through gifts of land as a reward for outstanding military service. In general, estates were preserved by endogamy, and inter-marriage was only rarely allowed between individuals of different estates. The feudal system of stratification looked something like the diagram in figure 8.3.

Social class

Social class is the form of stratification found in industrial societies, like contemporary Britain.

Social classes can be defined as broad groups of people who share a similar economic situation, such as occupation, income and ownership of wealth. Often, these criteria are closely related to each other and to other aspects of individuals' lives, such as their level of education, their status and lifestyle (for example, housing, car ownership and leisure activities), and how much power and influence they have in society.

> **Social class**
> is an open system of stratification consisting of broad groups of people (classes) who share a similar economic situation, such as occupation, income and ownership of wealth.

The main differences between the social class system and slavery, the caste and feudal systems are:

- Social class is based not on people as property, religion or law, but mainly on economic criteria such as occupation, wealth and income.
- The levels of the social hierarchy (social classes) are not clearly separated from one another: the divisions between social classes are frequently quite vague – it is hard to say, for example, where the working class ends and the middle class begins.
- Social class differences are not backed up by legal differences. All members of society in theory have equal legal rights, and those in higher social classes do not have legal authority over those in lower classes.
- There are no legal or religious restrictions on inter-marriage between people of different social classes. In theory people can marry whom they like; in practice people tend to marry someone in their own social class.
- Social class societies are open societies. There are no legal or religious restrictions on the movement of individuals from one social class to another, and social mobility is possible.
- The social class system is generally meritocratic. A **meritocracy** is a society in which social positions are generally achieved by merit – such as educational qualifications, talent, and skill – rather than ascribed from birth. However, the social class of the family into which a child is born can have an important effect on his or her life chances. Entry into the propertied upper class is still mainly through inherited wealth, and therefore social positions here remain mainly ascribed rather than achieved.

A **meritocracy** is a society in which social positions are achieved by merit, such as educational qualifications, talent, skill and experience.

'Look don't identify me by the size and shape of my body, my social class, my job, my gender, my ethnicity, my sexuality, my nationality, my age, my religion, my education, my friends, my lifrstyle, how much money I earn, the clothes I wear, the books I read, where I go shopping, the way I decorate my house, the television programmes and movies I watch, my leisure and sports activities, the car I drive, the music I listen to, the drinks I like, the food I eat, the clubs I go to, where I go on holiday, the way I speak or my accent, the things I say, the things I do, or what I believe in. I'm just me. Ok?'

Social class and status

An individual's social class and status are often closely linked, and a member of a high social class will usually have high status as well. This is because the amount of social respect individuals get is often influenced by the same factors as their social class – their wealth, their income and their occupation.

However, while an individual can only belong to one social class, he or she may have several statuses. For example, a person with a low-status, working-class job such as a refuse collector may achieve high status as a local councillor. Similarly, it is quite possible for two people to share the same social class but to have different statuses. For example, a white semi-skilled manual worker will find it easier to achieve status in a group of racist white workers than a black or Asian person, who may be given lower status simply because of his or her ethnic group, even if he or she has the same occupation and income as the white worker.

Activity

1 If you were trying to decide a person's social class or their status, what features would you take into account? Refer to the cartoon opposite, and list the issues that are mentioned there and any others you can think of.
2 Now put your list into order of importance, with the most important features first. Explain why you have put them in that order.

FOUR VIEWS OF SOCIAL CLASS

In the last activity, you listed the most important features that you would take into account in deciding a person's social class. The features you think important, though, may not be the same as those chosen by others. A similar dispute exists among sociologists. While most sociologists would agree that social classes consist of groups of people who share a similar economic situation, there are different views regarding exactly which aspect of that economic situation is the most important in defining a person's social class. The following discussion deals with four of the most common definitions and explanations of social class inequality that are used by sociologists: the consensus view of the functionalists, the conflict views of Marx and Weber, and the definition of class by a person's occupation.

The consensus view of social class

Consensus theorists believe that social class inequalities are both necessary and inevitable. Functionalist writers suggest this is because:

● Some jobs are more important than others in maintaining society, requiring specialized skills that not everyone has the talent and ability to acquire.

- Those who do have the ability and talent to do these jobs must be motivated and encouraged to train for these important positions with the promise of future high rewards in terms of income, wealth, status and power. There must therefore be a system of unequal rewards to make sure the most able people get into the most important social positions.

The difficulty with this approach is that there are many poorly rewarded occupations which can still be seen as vital in maintaining society. For example, a rich business executive can only become rich through the work of his or her employees, and a refuse collector is no less important than a doctor in maintaining society's health. In addition, not everyone in some of the vital jobs is motivated to do them by high rewards. No-one goes into teaching and nursing for the money, for example, but for reasons of job satisfaction and concern for the welfare of others.

Conflict views of social class

The Marxist theory of social class

Much sociological discussion about social class has been influenced by the writings of Karl Marx (1818–83). Marxists suggest that the main explanation for social class inequalities lies in the private ownership of the **means of production** – the key resources like land, property, factories and businesses which are necessary to produce society's goods.

For Marx, an individual's social class was defined by whether or not she or he owned the means of production. The concentration of ownership of the means of production in the hands of a small upper class brought to their

> The **means of production** are the key resources necessary for producing society's goods, such as factories and land.

According to Marx, society is split into two groups or classes: those who own the means of production (e.g. a developer with money to buy land to convert into expensive new commercial buildings) and those who work for wages (e.g. builders and construction workers). The builders are paid a fixed wage by the developer on whom they rely for their income, but the developer stands to make large profits out of the labour of employees

owners an unearned income in the form of profit, and laid the basis for social class inequalities in wealth and income.

Bourgeoisie and proletariat   Marx argued there were two basic social classes in capitalist industrial society: the class of owners of the means of production (whom he called the bourgeoisie or capitalists) and the class of non-owners (whom he called the proletariat or working class).

The proletariat, since they owned no means of production, had no alternative means of livelihood but working for the bourgeoisie. The bourgeoisie exploited the proletariat, making profits out of them by keeping wages low and paying them as little as possible instead of giving them the full payment for their work.

> The **bourgeoisie** is the class of owners of the means of production.
> The **proletariat** is the class of workers, who have to work for wages as they do not own the means of production.

The ruling class   The class of owners was also a ruling class, according to Marx. For example, because they owned the means of production, the bourgeoisie could decide where factories should be located and whether they should be opened or closed down, and they could control the workforce through hiring and firing. Democratically elected governments could not afford to ignore the power of the bourgeoisie, otherwise they might face rising unemployment and other social problems if the bourgeoisie decided not to invest its money.

The ruling ideas   The ruling ideas in society – what Marx called the dominant ideology – were those of the owning class, and the major institutions in society reflected these ideas.

> The **dominant ideology** refers to the ideas and beliefs of the most powerful groups in society, which influence the ideas and beliefs of the rest of society.

For example, the laws protected the owning class rather than the workers; religion acted as the 'opium of the people', persuading the proletariat to accept their position as just and natural (rather than rebelling against it), by promising future rewards in heaven for putting up with their present suffering; the bourgeoisie's ownership of the mass media meant only their ideas were put forward. In this way, the working-class were almost brainwashed into accepting their position. They failed to recognize they were being exploited and therefore did not rebel against the bourgeoisie, because they thought their position was natural and they could see no alternative to it. Marx called this lack of awareness among the proletariat of their own interests false consciousness.

> **False consciousness** is a failure by members of a social class to recognize their real interests.

Exploitation, class conflict and revolution   Marx predicted the working class would become poorer and poorer and society would become divided into two major social classes: a small, wealthy and powerful bourgeoisie and a large, poverty-stricken proletariat. The exploitation of the proletariat by the bourgeoisie, Marx believed, would eventually lead to major class conflict between the poverty-stricken proletariat and the bourgeoisie. The proletariat

A Marxist view of false consciousness and class consciousness

would struggle against the bourgeoisie through strikes, demonstrations and other forms of protest. The proletariat would then develop **class consciousness** – an awareness of their common working-class interests and their exploitation – until eventually they would make a socialist revolution and overthrow the bourgeoisie.

Communism   After the revolution, the proletariat would nationalize the means of production (which were formerly the private property of the bourgeoisie) by putting them in the hands of the state. The means of production would therefore be collectively owned and run in the interests of everyone, not just of the bourgeoisie. Capitalism would be destroyed and a new type of society would be created, which would be without exploitation, without classes, and without class conflict. This equal, classless society Marx called **Communism**.

> **Class consciousness** is an awareness in members of a social class of their real interests.

> **Communism** is an equal society, without social classes or conflict, in which the means of production are the shared property of all.

A SUMMARY OF MARX'S THEORY OF CLASS

Marx's theory of social class is based on a model of two social classes, defined by whether or not they own the means of production. The bourgeoisie (the owning class) is a ruling class which exploits the proletariat (the non-owning class). This exploitation gives rise to class conflict between these two major classes. The proletariat will eventually overthrow the bourgeoisie in the socialist revolution, and create an equal, classless society called Communism.

The strengths and weaknesses of Marx's theory of class   There has been much discussion of the Marxist view of social class, particularly whether it can still be applied in contemporary societies like Britain. One of the more obvious criticisms is that the revolution Marx predicted has not happened in Britain or any of the Western industrialized societies. While many of the class inequalities and conflicts which Marx identified remain in contemporary societies, the communist solutions he proposed do not seem to have worked in the way he foresaw. In those countries where revolutions did occur, Communism did not succeed in creating an equal society, and there emerged a new ruling class of people who were better-off than the majority. From 1989 onwards, a major wave of popular revolts shook Eastern Europe and the Soviet Union, and swept away the former communist regimes. There is now no communist country left in Europe, and only five in the entire world, in many of which large sections of the population are in poverty.

STRENGTHS

- There is still evidence of opposing class interests and class conflict, such as strikes and industrial sabotage in the workplace. The British Social Attitudes Survey has reported that over half of the population of modern Britain still believe there are strong conflicts between rich and poor and between managers and workers.
- The means of production remain mostly privately owned in the hands of a small minority of the population. There are still great inequalities of wealth and income in modern Britain, and widespread poverty: 10 per cent of the population own about 53 per cent of the wealth, and about 22 per cent of people are living in poverty.
- There remains much evidence of major social class inequalities in life chances, such as in health, housing, levels of educational achievement and job security.
- The owners of the means of production still have much more power and influence than the majority. For example, the major positions in the state, industry and banking are held by the privileged rich who have attended public schools, and they own the mass media.

WEAKNESSES

- While great inequalities in wealth and income continue to exist, the working class has not got poorer as Marx predicted. Living standards have improved vastly since Marx's day, and the welfare state and compulsory state education have given the working class a better lifestyle than Marx predicted.
- Compulsory education has given the working class more chances – though still limited – of upward social mobility, and the welfare state provides a safety net guaranteeing a minimum income for all. Housing, health and educational standards are much improved compared with the nineteenth century.
- Unemployment benefits help to reduce the more severe hardships which were associated with unemployment in Marx's day.

- Marx suggested only the two opposing classes of bourgeoisie and proletariat would emerge, but this approach does not easily explain the wide inequalities that exist between people who do not own the means of production. The past century has seen the emergence of a new middle class of professionals, managers and office workers between the bourgeoisie and proletariat. While these groups do not own the means of production, they benefit from exercising authority on behalf of the bourgeoisie and have higher status and better income and life chances than the working class. They generally have no interest in overthrowing the bourgeoisie.

Activity

1 Using your own ideas and the strengths and weaknesses of Marx's theory of class given above, decide whether, in your opinion, Marx's ideas are still relevant in any way in the modern world, or whether they are basically old-fashioned and out-of-date. Give evidence and examples of your own to back up your viewpoint.

2 To what extent do you think there are conflicts between groups of people in modern Britain, such as conflicts between rich and poor, managers and workers, and the unemployed and people with jobs? Suggest two reasons why you think these conflicts might exist, and two ways society could be made more equal in an attempt to reduce conflicts between people.

Weber's theory of social class

Max Weber (1864–1920) agreed with Marx that people's ownership or non-ownership of the means of production was important in creating social class differences and conflicts between classes. However, Weber suggested that differences in people's market situation were also important in creating social class inequalities.

'Market situation' simply means that some people are able to get higher incomes when they sell their abilities and skills in the job market because they have rare skills, talents or qualifications that are in demand – such as doctors and lawyers. It might also be because society values some skills and talents more highly than others and rewards them accordingly, as might be the case with football, film and music stars and other celebrities, or with some business executives or company owners. This means there are many different social classes differing in their market situations.

The difficulty with Weber's approach is that it does not easily explain the position of those who inherit their wealth and do not sell their skills in the labour market, as they live on unearned incomes rather than those earned through employment.

> **Market situation**
> refers to the rewards that people are able to obtain when they sell their skills in the labour market, depending on the scarcity of their skills, the demand for them and the power they have to obtain high rewards.

However, Weber thought that to fully understand social inequality and social conflict it was also necessary to look at status differences between people as well as their economic position. For example, status characteristics like gender, religion, age and ethnicity can all create conflicts between people regardless of their wealth and income. For example, there are conflicts between status groups like men and women, Protestant and Catholic (as in Northern Ireland), young people and older people, and between black and white people.

For Weber, therefore, society was divided by conflict between many competing social classes and status groups, rather than the two social classes Marx considered.

Defining class by occupation

Occupation or socio-economic group is the most common definition of social class used by governments, by advertising agencies when doing market research, and by sociologists when doing surveys. This is because a person's occupation is an easy piece of information to obtain, and people's occupation is generally a good guide to their skills, qualifications, experience, their income, their life chances and other important aspects of their lives. Occupation is also a major factor influencing people's power and status in society, and most people judge the social standing of themselves and others by the jobs they do.

There is a wide range of occupational scales in use, but three of the best known and most widely used definitions of class by occupation are the National Statistics Socio-economic Classification (NS-SEC), the Standard Occupational Classification 2010 (SOC2010) and the Institute of Practitioners in Advertising (IPA) Scale. The NS-SEC is used for all official statistics and surveys, and the IPA Scale is widely used in market research and many surveys, including opinion polls. These three scales are shown on pages 406–8, with a reference to what these classes roughly refer to in the everyday language used by sociologists, and in relation to the middle-class and working-class categories found in this book.

The middle-class occupations are generally non-manual, with people working primarily in offices, doing mainly mental rather than physical work. The term **white-collar workers** is sometimes used to refer to lower-middle-class clerical and sales occupations.

The working-class occupations are mainly manual, with people working primarily with their hands, in jobs requiring physical work.

The problems of defining class by occupation

While occupation is very commonly used to define social class, the use of occupation and occupational scales presents a number of problems for the sociologist:

White-collar workers are non-manual clerical workers, sales personnel and other office workers whose work is non-professional and non-managerial.

Table 8.1 The National Statistics Socio-economic Classification (NS-SEC)

This occupational scale is based upon occupational status and security of income, prospects of economic advancement, and the amount of authority and control at work.

Social Class	Commonly called	Examples of occupations
Class 1 Higher managerial and professional occupations	Class 1	
Class 1a Large employers and higher managerial occupations	Upper middle class	Large employer, higher manager, company director, senior police/fire/prison/military officer, newspaper editor, football manager
Class 1b Higher professional occupations		Doctor, solicitor, engineer, teacher, airline pilot
Class 2 Lower managerial and professional occupations	Class 2 Middle class	Journalist, nurse/midwife, actor, musician, junior police officer (constable), lower manager
Class 3 Intermediate occupations	Class 3 (Non-manual)	Secretary, air stewardess, driving instructor, footballer, telephone operator
Class 4 Small employers and own account workers	Lower middle class	Small employer/manager, self-employed publican, plumber,
Class 5 Lower supervisory and technical occupations	Class 3 (Manual) Skilled manual workers / upper working class	Lower supervisor, electrician, mechanic, train driver, bus inspector
Class 6 Semi-routine occupations	Class 4 Semi-skilled manual / working class	Traffic warden, caretaker, gardener, supermarket shelf-stacker, assembly-line worker, shop assistant
Class 7 Routine occupations	Class 5 Unskilled manual / lower working class	Cleaner, waiter/waitress, bar staff, road worker
Class 8 Never worked and long-term unemployed	The poor, and sometimes the underclass	Long-term unemployed, long-term sick, never worked

- The use of occupation excludes the wealthy upper class, who own property and have a great deal of power but often don't have an occupation. Occupational scales therefore do not reveal major differences in wealth and income within and between social classes.

Table 8.2 The Standard Occupational Classification (2010) (SOC2010)

This occupational scale ranks occupations according to their similarity of qualifications, training, skills and experience

Social Class	Commonly called	Examples of occupations
Class 1 Managers, directors and senior officials	Class 1	Senior sales manager, police officer (inspector and above), senior manager or administrator in national and local government and large companies
Class 2 Professional occupations	Upper middle class	University or college lecturer, teacher, doctor, solicitor, architect, vicar, social worker, pharmacist, civil engineer, librarian
Class 3 Associate professional and technical occupations	Class 2 Middle class	Surveyor, computer programmer, nurse, youth workers, journalist, airline pilot, laboratory technician, police officer (sergeant and below), fitness instructor
Class 4 Administrative and secretarial occupations	Class 3 (Non-manual) Lower middle class	Clerical worker, secretary, receptionist, market research interviewer, school secretary
Class 5 Skilled trades occupations	Class 3 (Manual) Skilled manual workers /	Bricklayer, electrician, plumber, motor mechanic, butcher, baker, chef/cook, computer maintenance and installation engineer
Class 6 Caring, leisure and other service occupations	upper working class	Hairdresser and beautician, nursery nurse, travel agent, child-minder and related
Class 7 Sales and customer service occupations		Sales rep, sales assistant, supermarket check-out operator, call centre operator
Class 8 Process, plant and machine operatives	Class 4 Semi-skilled manual / working class	Assembly-line worker, packer, bus/lorry/van/taxi-driver, tyre and exhaust fitter, driving instructor
Class 9 Elementary occupations	Class 5 Unskilled manual / lower working class	Farm worker, refuse collector, postal worker, road sweeper, cleaner, hospital porter, waiter/waitress, bar staff, traffic warden, shelf-filler, school crossing patrol attendant

- Groups outside paid employment are excluded, such as housewives and the never-employed unemployed. Housework is not recognized as an occupation.
- Social class is based primarily on the occupation of the highest-earning member of the household, but the use of a single head of household may ignore dual-worker families, where both partners are working. Such

Table 8.3 The Institute of Practitioners in Advertising (IPA) Scale

Advertisers are mainly interested in selling things to people, so their scale ranks occupations primarily on the basis of income. They obviously want to know how much money people have so they can target their advertising at the right people. This scale is very widely used in surveys of all kinds.

Social class	Commonly called	Examples of occupations
Class A Higher managerial, administrative or professional occupations	Upper middle class	Opticians, judges, solicitors, senior civil servants, surgeons, senior managers (in large companies), accountants, architects
Class B Intermediate managerial, administrative or professional occupations	Middle class	Airline pilots, MPs, teachers, social workers, middle managers, police inspectors
Class C1 Supervisory or clerical and junior managerial, administrative or professional occupations	Lower middle class	Clerical workers, computer operators, receptionists, sales assistants, secretaries, nurses, technicians
Class C2 Skilled manual workers	Upper working class	Carpenters, bricklayers, electricians, chefs/cooks, plumbers
Class D Semi-skilled and unskilled manual workers	Semi-skilled and lower working class	Postal workers, bar workers, office cleaners, road sweepers, machine minders, farm labourers
Class E Those on the lowest levels of income	The poor	Pensioners (on state pensions), casual workers, long-term unemployed, and others on income support and the lowest levels of income

families have much better life chances than single-income households in the same class. Their combined incomes might even give them the lifestyle of a higher social class.

- The classes on occupational scales tend to be very broad, and disguise major differences within each class. For example, a grouping like 'professionals' may include both poorly paid junior NHS doctors and rich Harley Street private specialists. There are major differences in income and life chances between such people, yet they are placed in the same class.

THE CLASS STRUCTURE OF BRITAIN

Often, when talking of social class, sociologists will refer to terms quite loosely. Figure 8.4 illustrates which groups of occupations are generally

Figure 8.4 The class structure

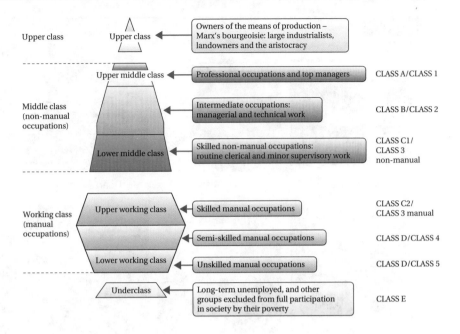

being referred to when particular social classes in contemporary Britain are mentioned. Note that the main division between working class and middle class is generally accepted as being that between manual and non-manual occupations. The controversial idea of the underclass is discussed later in this chapter.

> **Activity**
>
> 1 What social class do you think you belong to? Give reasons for your answer.
> 2 Think of all the differences you can between social classes in modern Britain. How would you explain the class differences you have identified?
> 3 Conduct a survey among people you know to see how they identify social class and what social class they would put themselves in, and why.

SOCIAL CLASS INEQUALITIES

Social classes do not exist merely in the mind of the sociologist: there are wide, measurable differences in life chances between social classes. The higher the social class of an individual, the more access she or he will have to society's resources – such as better housing, cars, food, holidays, income and job security – and the more influence he or she will have in society. The following section examines some examples of these class differences, and

Activity

Hot-dog seller

Dentist

Road sweeper

Housewife

Shop assistant

Sociology lecturer

Postal worker

Car mechanic

Bus driver

Firefighter

Member of
Parliament (MP)

Nurse

1 List all the ways you can think of that a person's occupation might affect other aspects of his or her life, such as family life, status in society, housing, health, leisure activities, beliefs and values, future planning, and so on. Make sure you explain precisely how the effects you mention are linked to a person's job.

2 Look at the twelve occupations shown in the pictures, and refer also to the occupational scales on pages 406–8. Rank the pictures 1–12 in four lists in order of: (a) pay, (b) status in society, (c) power, (d) class, numbering them 1–12, beginning with 1 as the highest. Give reasons for your rankings.

3 Do you think the gender or ethnicity of those doing any of these jobs might influence the pay, status or power that is given to the jobs? Explain your answer, with examples of particular jobs.

further examples are discussed in other parts of this book (see particularly chapters 4 and 9 on inequalities in education and health).

Inequalities in wealth and income

- **Wealth** refers to property which can be sold and turned into cash for the benefit of the owner. The main forms of wealth are property such as housing and land, bank deposits, shares in companies, and personal possessions.
- **Income** refers to the flow of money which people obtain from work, from their investments, or from the state in the form of welfare benefits. Earned income is income received from paid employment (wages and salaries). Unearned income is that received from investments, such as rent on property, interest on savings, and dividends on shares.

The distribution of wealth and income

Figure 8.5 shows that in 2005 the poorest 50 per cent of the population owned only 6 per cent of the wealth, while the richest 5 per cent owned 40 per cent. A quarter of the population possessed over three-quarters (77 per cent) of the nation's wealth. This pattern becomes even more unequal when you exclude the value of people's homes with over half of wealth owned by just 5 per cent of adults. These figures are official figures from HM Revenue and Customs (HMRC), the government's tax collectors, and they therefore under-estimate the inequalities of wealth, as the wealthy have an interest in concealing their wealth to avoid taxation.

As figure 8.5 shows, income is also unequally distributed, with the richest fifth (20 per cent) of the population getting 43 per cent of total income in 2008–9 – more than twice their fair share if income were equally distributed, and more than the bottom three-fifths got between them. The poorest fifth

---

Activity

Study figure 8.6 and answer the following questions:

1 Which group increased its share of income between 1979 and 2008–9?
2 Which group suffered the least cut in its income share between 1979 and 2008–9?
3 By how much did the percentage share of the poorest fifth of the population fall between 1979 and 2008–9?
4 How might the evidence in figure 8.5 be used to show that the rich were getting richer between 1979 and 2008–9 while the poor, in comparison, were getting poorer?
5 Draw a pie chart to illustrate the distribution of income in 2008–9.

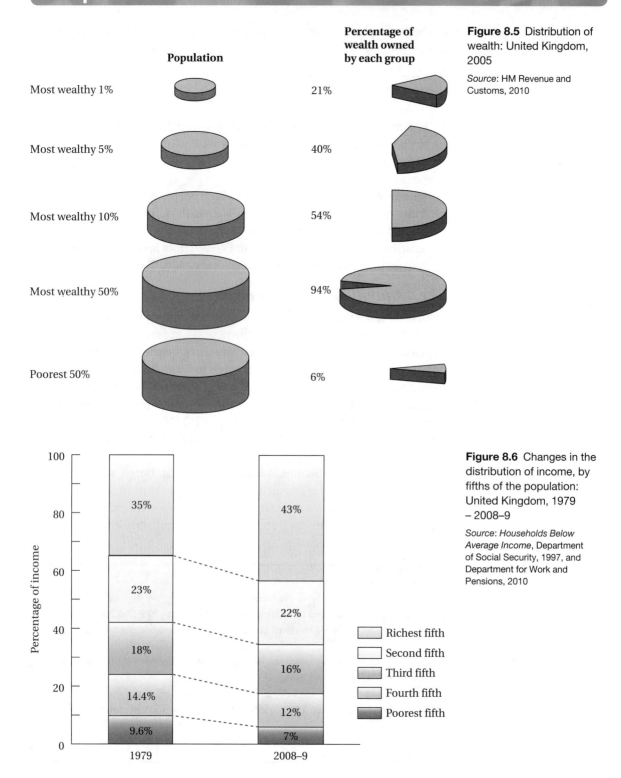

Population

Percentage of wealth owned by each group

Most wealthy 1%   21%

Most wealthy 5%   40%

Most wealthy 10%   54%

Most wealthy 50%   94%

Poorest 50%   6%

Figure 8.5 Distribution of wealth: United Kingdom, 2005

Source: HM Revenue and Customs, 2010

Figure 8.6 Changes in the distribution of income, by fifths of the population: United Kingdom, 1979 – 2008–9

Source: *Households Below Average Income*, Department of Social Security, 1997, and Department for Work and Pensions, 2010

Richest fifth
Second fifth
Third fifth
Fourth fifth
Poorest fifth

The UK Income procession

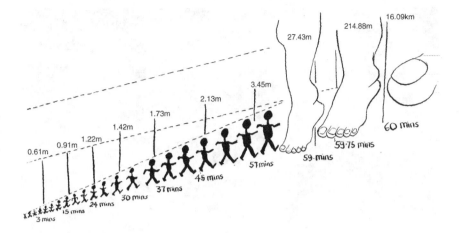

got only about 7 per cent, only about a third of their fair share if income was equally distributed.

Who are the rich?

The rich are:

- *The traditional aristocracy.* They are major land owners, such as the Duke of Westminster, who owns sizeable chunks of London, Cheshire, North Wales and Ireland, forests and shooting estates in Lancashire and Scotland, and properties in North America and the Far East. According to the 2010 Rich List published by the *Sunday Times,* the Duke of Westminster is Britain's third-richest person, with an estimated wealth of £6.75 billion (£6,750,000,000).
- *The owners of industry and commerce* – the corporate rich of the business world. This includes Sir Richard Branson of Virgin, Britain's eighteenth-richest person in 2010, with estimated assets of £2.6 billion.
- *Stars of entertainment and the media,* such as former Beatle Sir Paul McCartney (£475 million), Sir Mick Jagger (£190 million), Sir Elton John (£185 million), Simon Cowell – the force behind TV shows *Pop Idol, The X Factor, Britain's Got Talent,* and *American Idol,* on £165 million, David and Victoria Beckham (£145 million) and the relatively impoverished Robbie Williams (£90 million) and Sean Connery (£80 million).

Most wealth is inherited, with those inheriting doing nothing to earn their riches. Most of the rich live on unearned income from investments rather than from employment. The starkness of these inequalities is made clear by the Queen, one of Britain's richest women, with personal assets estimated at £290 million in 2010. If she were to pop this into her local building

The Queen is one of Britain's richest women, though there are other women and men who are *much* richer. Her wealth could produce an unearned income every year, after tax, that would take an employee on average wages about 205 years to earn. Do you think such inequalities can be justified? Explain why or why not

society, even during the recession in 2009–10, she would receive at least £8 in unearned income each minute of every day every year (after tax). This is an hourly rate of about eighty times as much as someone on the national minimum wage in 2010, and her unearned income each year after tax would take a full-time employee on average wages (and who was never ill) about 205 years to earn, and the Queen would still have her original £290 million.

High earners and the self-made rich do not necessarily put in more work than those who receive low pay; it is simply that society places different values on people in different positions, and rewards them more or less highly. Senior executives in large companies, bankers, and music and film stars and other celebrities will probably not have to work as hard for their high incomes as an unskilled manual labourer working long hours in a low-paid job.

Attempts to redistribute wealth and income

The massive inequalities in wealth and income which have existed this century, and the inequalities in life chances these have caused, have provoked various measures by governments to redistribute wealth and income more equally. Some of these measures are:

- *inheritance tax*, which is a tax payable when people give gifts of wealth either before or after death, and is intended to limit the inheritance of vast quantities of wealth from one generation to the next
- *capital gains tax*, which is intended to reduce profits from dealing in property or shares, and is payable whenever these are sold
- *income tax*, which is payable on unearned and earned income, and it rises as earnings increase
- *social welfare benefits* from the state, like Income Support, which are attempts to divert the resources obtained through taxation to the needy sections of society.

Why have attempts to redistribute wealth and income failed?

Despite these measures, attempts to redistribute wealth and income have been largely unsuccessful. Little real redistribution has occurred, and what redistribution has taken place has mainly been between the very rich and the lesser rich, and the gap between the richest and the poorest sections of society have actually grown wider in recent years. There are five main reasons for this:

1 Their investments often mean the wealthy can make their wealth grow at a faster rate than the rate at which it is taxed.
2 *Tax relief.* The state allows tax relief, money normally used to pay income tax, on a wide variety of things such as business expenses, school fees and private pensions. These are expenses which only the better-off are likely to have. This means that they pay a smaller proportion of their income in tax than a person who is poorer but who does not have these expenses.
3 *Tax avoidance schemes* are perfectly legal, and are often thought up by financial advisers and accountants to find loopholes in the tax laws and beat the tax system, thereby saving the rich from paying some tax. Such schemes involve things like living outside Britain for most of the year, investing in pension schemes to avoid income tax, investing in tax-free or low-tax areas like the Channel Islands, giving wealth away to kin well before death to avoid inheritance tax, or putting companies or savings in other people's names, such as those of husband/wife, children or other kin.
4 *Tax evasion* is illegal, and involves people not declaring wealth and income to HM Revenue and Customs. This is suspected to be a common practice among the rich.
5 *A failure to claim benefits.* Many people fail to claim the welfare benefits to which they are entitled. Some reasons for this are discussed later in this chapter.

Class inequalities in health and life expectancy

Despite the welfare state and the National Health Service, major differences in health continue to exist between social classes. Men and women from social class 1 on average live about seven years longer than those from social class 7. As shown in figure 8.7, over twice as many babies die at birth or in the first week of life (a **perinatal death**) or in the first year of life (**infant mortality**) in social class 7 as in social class 1.

Figure 8.8 shows how chronic sickness rises as one moves down the social class hierarchy (chronic sickness is long-standing illness or disability). The death rate from heart disease is about three times higher for men in social class 7 compared to those in social class 1. This is just part of a mass of evidence which shows that lower-working-class people suffer more from almost all diseases than those in the upper middle class.

These issues of inequality in health and illness are discussed further in chapter 9.

> A **perinatal death** refers to a still-birth or a death within the first week of life. **Infant mortality** refers to the death of a baby in the first year of life.

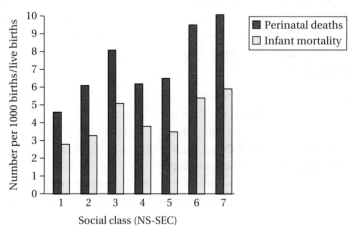

Figure 8.7 Perinatal deaths and infant mortality (for births within marriage only) by social class of father, England and Wales, 2008

Source: Health Statistics Quarterly 44, Winter 2009, Office for National Statistics

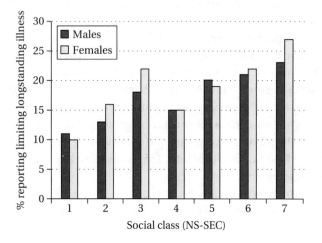

Figure 8.8 Chronic sickness (limiting longstanding illness) by social class and sex, Great Britain, 2008

Source: General Lifestyle Survey, Office for National Statistics, 2008

Activity

Study figures 8.7 and 8.8 and then answer the following questions:
1 Which social class has the highest level of infant mortality?
2 Which social class has about 10 perinatal deaths per 1,000 births?
3 Which social class has the lowest level of infant mortality?
4 What is the approximate difference between the number of perinatal deaths per 1,000 births in class 1 and in class 7?
5 What is the difference between the percentage of males reporting chronic sickness in class 1 and in class 7?
6 Which two social classes reported the highest levels of chronic sickness among females?
7 Figure 8.7 shows about two times as many babies dying within the first week or within the first year of life in social class 7 as in social class 1. Suggest explanations for this.
8 What does figure 8.8 suggest about the relative health of males and females? Do males or females appear the healthiest? Refer to data from figure 8.8 to back up your view.

Explaining class differences in health and life expectancy

These differences are often explained by the following features of working-class life, which are less likely to be experienced by those in middle-class occupations:

- longer working hours, with shiftwork and overtime
- poorer conditions at work, with more risks to health and safety through accidents and industrial diseases
- less time off work with pay to visit the doctor
- lower income, leading to poorer diets and housing
- more likelihood of working-class areas being at risk through industrial and traffic pollution
- poorer medical care in working-class areas, with longer hospital waiting lists and overworked GPs, and lack of sufficient income to make use of private medicine or purchase non-prescription drugs
- lower levels of education, which often mean less awareness of health and the services which are available, and less self-confidence in questioning the judgements of health professionals
- poverty in old age, due to the lack of an occupational pension and inadequate earnings while working to save for retirement
- smoking cigarettes, which tends to be more common in the working class
- higher levels of unemployment and poverty, and therefore more stress-related illnesses.

Class inequalities in employment

The different status of occupations is backed up by different terms and conditions of employment under which people work. These improve with movement upward through the social class hierarchy.

In general, those lower down in the social class hierarchy, compared to those higher up:

- get lower pay, despite working longer hours with shiftwork and overtime
- have shorter holidays
- work in more dangerous and less hygienic conditions, with greater risks of accident and disease
- are more supervised at work, having to clock in, getting pay 'docked' for lateness, and not being allowed time off with pay for personal reasons
- receive less training in their work
- are less likely to receive full pay during sickness, or to belong to an employer's pension scheme
- have much less job security: the risk of unemployment is seven times greater for an unskilled manual worker than for someone in social class 1.

Explaining class differences in employment

Class differences in employment are often explained or justified by the higher education, training and increased management responsibility of many non-manual workers, and the need to retain their commitment and loyalty to the firm and thus protect the firm's interests and investment. Even routine office workers often have some knowledge of the firm's secrets, such as profit levels, accounts, sales and orders, and the management might want to conceal knowledge of these from manual workers, particularly if they are submitting a pay claim. It is therefore in the firm's interest to try to retain the loyalty and commitment of non-manual staff. The tighter control and poorer conditions of work of manual workers suggest they are not trusted by management, are considered more dispensable, and can be more easily replaced.

Those in lower social classes often work in more dangerous jobs or unhealthy working conditions

POVERTY

Earlier it was shown that large differences in wealth and income remain in Britain, combined with a range of other social class inequalities. Nothing highlights more the extent of inequality in Britain than the continued existence of widespread poverty. A walk through the streets of any large city will reveal stark contrasts between the mansions, the luxury cars and the expensive lifestyles of the rich, and the poverty and hardship of many of those who are unemployed, sick or old, who are lone parents, who are homeless or living in decaying housing, and who are faced with a future of hopelessness and despair. Poverty is essentially an aspect of social class inequality, affecting above all those from the working class, because other classes have savings, occupational pensions and sick pay schemes to protect them when adversity strikes or old age arrives.

One of the key issues in discussing poverty, and certainly the most controversial, is the problem of defining what poverty is.

Absolute poverty

> **Absolute poverty** is poverty defined as lacking the minimum requirements necessary to maintain human health and life.

Absolute poverty or *subsistence poverty* refers to a person's biological needs for food, water, clothing and shelter – the minimum requirements necessary to subsist and maintain life, health and physical efficiency.

A person in absolute poverty lacks the minimum necessary for healthy survival. While the minimum needed to maintain a healthy life might vary, for example, between hot and cold climates and between people in occupations

Absolute poverty, shown here in Somalia, is generally associated with the less-developed countries like those in Africa, where famines and starvation occur, and people lack on a daily basis the minimum subsistence needs for biological survival
Credit: Gordon Browne

with different physical demands, absolute or subsistence poverty is roughly the same in every society. People in absolute poverty would be poor anywhere at any time – the standard does not change much over time. The solution to absolute poverty is to raise the living standards of the poor above subsistence level. Absolute poverty is most associated with the countries of the less-developed world, like those in Africa, where it remains a widespread problem. It is unlikely many people live in absolute poverty in Britain today, where poverty is basically relative poverty.

Relative poverty: poverty as social exclusion

Relative poverty involves defining poverty in relation to a generally accepted standard of living in a specific society at a particular time. This takes into account social and cultural needs as well as biological needs. Townsend has provided the classic definition of relative poverty:

> Individuals . . . can be said to be in poverty when they lack the resources to obtain the types of diets, participate in the activities and have the living conditions and amenities which are customary, or at least widely encouraged or approved, in the societies to which they belong. Their resources are so seriously below those commanded by the average individual or family that they are, in effect, excluded from ordinary living patterns, customs or activities.
>
> (P. Townsend, *Poverty in the United Kingdom* (Penguin, 1979))

Relative poverty is a condition in which individuals or families are deprived of the opportunities, comforts and self-respect which the majority of people in their society enjoy. Minimum needs are then related to the standard of living in any society at any one time, and will therefore vary over time and between

Relative poverty is poverty defined in relation to a generally accepted standard of living in a specific society at a particular time.

THE GLOBAL EXTENT OF ABSOLUTE POVERTY

- Around 1.4 billion people in the world are living in extreme poverty – on $1.25 (about 80p in 2010) a day or less.
- 878 million people are severely malnourished.
- One-fifth of the world's population are not expected to live beyond the age of 40.
- The world's richest 1 per cent of people receive as much income as the poorest 57 per cent.
- Nearly 1 billion people are illiterate.
- Easily preventable diseases, like pneumonia, diarrhoea, malaria and measles, kill nearly 11 million children under the age of 5 each year – 30,000 every day.
- About 1.1 billion people lack safe drinking water, and 2.6 billion people lack basic sanitation.
- 536,000 women die each year from causes related to pregnancy and childbirth – about one every minute.

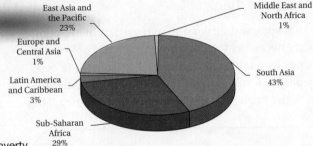

Figure 8.9 Income poverty

Distribution of people living on less than $1.25 (around 80p in 2010) a day
Global total: 1.4 billion people

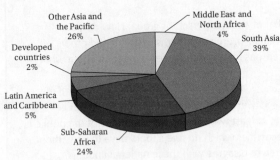

Figure 8.10 Hunger

Distribution of undernourished people 2004–6
Global total: 873 million people

Source: 2008 World Development Indicators, World Bank; *The State of the World's Children 2009*, UNICEF; www.globalissues.org; *The State of Food Insecurity in the World, 2009* United Nations Food and Agriculture Organization; *The Millennium Development Goals Report 2009*, United Nations

societies, as standards of living change. For example, those living in slum housing in Britain would be regarded as poor here, but their housing would appear as relative luxury to poor peasants in developing countries. Similarly, running hot water and an inside bathroom and toilet would have been seen as luxuries 100 years ago in Britain, but today are seen as basic necessities, and those without them would be regarded as poor by most people.

Social exclusion

The relative definition of poverty is closely linked with the idea of social exclusion. Social exclusion is where people are marginalized or excluded from participation in education, work, community life and access to services and other aspects of life seen as part of being a full and participating member of mainstream society. Those who live in relative poverty lack the resources and are denied the opportunities to live the normal life enjoyed by the majority of people, and are therefore excluded from full participation in society.

The consensual idea of poverty

A third idea of poverty is to ask the public what they regard as being poor, and what items they think are necessary for a minimum standard of living in Britain. In this way it is hoped to establish a widespread agreement (a consensus) on what ordinary people think makes up the minimum standards required for life in Britain at the beginning of the twenty-first century. The

Activity

1 Either alone or through majority agreement in a group, go through the *Poverty and Social Exclusion* list opposite, ticking those items which you think are necessities, which all adults should be able to afford, and no one should have to go without.

2 Compare your list with that of another person or group. How do your decisions compare with others? Were some items clear-cut and others borderline? Discuss the reasons for any differences of opinion about what count as necessities.

3 The *Poverty and Social Exclusion in Britain* national survey, conducted in 2000, found that items 1–35 were considered necessities by 50 per cent or more of the population. At least two out of three members of the public classed items 1–25 as necessities which no one should have to go without. How far does your list agree or disagree with these national findings?

4 The *Poverty and Social Exclusion* list was drawn quite a long time ago. Do you think there are things that might be regarded as necessities now that weren't in 2000? Say which items and give your reasons.

5 Do you think if you were in a very poor country you would have the same list of necessities? Give reasons for your answer.

Table 8.4 The Poverty and Social Exclusion Survey list

1. Beds and bedding for everyone
2. Heating to warm living areas of the home
3. Damp-free home
4. Visiting friends or family in hospital
5. Two meals a day
6. Medicines prescribed by doctor
7. Refrigerator
8. Fresh fruit and vegetables daily
9. Warm, waterproof coat
10. Able to replace or repair broken electrical goods
11. Visits to friends or family
12. Celebrations on special occasions such as Christmas
13. Money to keep home in a decent state of decoration
14. Visits to school, e.g. sports day
15. Attending weddings, funerals
16. Meat, fish or vegetarian equivalent every other day
17. Insurance of contents of dwelling
18. Hobby or leisure activity
19. Washing machine
20. Ability to collect children from school
21. Telephone
22. Appropriate clothes for job interviews
23. Deep freezer / fridge freezer
24. Carpets in living rooms and bedrooms
25. Regular savings (of £10 per month) for rainy days or retirement
26. Two pairs of all-weather shoes
27. Having friends or family round for a meal
28. A small amount of money to spend on self weekly, not on family
29. Television
30. Roast joint / vegetarian equivalent once a week
31. Presents for friends/family once a year
32. A holiday away from home once a year not with relatives
33. Funds to replace worn-out furniture
34. Dictionary
35. An outfit for social occasions
36. New, not second-hand, clothes
37. Attending place of worship
38. Car
39. Coach/train fares to visit friends/family quarterly
40. An evening out once a fortnight
41. Dressing gown
42. Having a daily newspaper
43. A meal in a restaurant/pub monthly
44. Microwave oven
45. Tumble dryer
46. Going to the pub once a fortnight
47. Video recorder
48. Holidays abroad once a year
49. CD player
50. Home computer
51. Dishwasher
52. Mobile phone
53. Access to the Internet
54. Satellite television

Source: adapted from David Gordon et al., *Poverty and Social Exclusion in Britain* (Joseph Rowntree Foundation, 2000). Reproduced by permission of the Joseph Rowntree Foundation

Poverty and Social Exclusion Survey above of some popular items, and the activity following, explore this idea of a consensual notion of poverty.

The controversy over poverty

The idea of relative poverty and its measurement have been particularly controversial. Many Conservative politicians attack the idea of relative poverty and the suggestion that many people in Britain are poor. Item A below presents this view. Item B presents an alternative view put forward by the Child Poverty Action Group, with which many sociologists would agree.

Activity

Read items A and B, and then answer the questions which follow.

Item A

Some conservatives attack the idea of relative poverty and the view that many people in Britain are poor. They argue that poverty in the old absolute sense of hunger and want has been wiped out, and it is simply that some people today are 'less equal' than others. They claim that the lifestyle of the poorest 20 per cent of families today represents affluence beyond the wildest dreams of the Victorians. Starving children and squalid slums have disappeared, and they point out that half of today's so-called 'poor' have a telephone, car and central heating, and virtually all have a refrigerator and television set. They argue that it is therefore absurd to suggest that more than a fifth of the population is today living in poverty. They claim the idea of relative poverty amounts to no more than simple inequality, and that the use of the concept of relative poverty means that, however rich a society becomes, the relatively poor will never disappear as long as there is social inequality. As one former Conservative minister commented, 'The poverty lobby would, on their definition, find poverty in Paradise.'

Item B

The Child Poverty Action Group (CPAG) supports the view that poverty should be seen in relation to minimum needs established by the standard of living in a particular society, and all members of the population should have the right to an income which allows them to participate fully in society rather than merely exist. Such participation involves having the means to fulfil responsibilities to others – as parents, sons and daughters, neighbours, friends, workers and citizens. Poverty filters into every aspect of life. It is about not having access to material goods and services such as decent housing, adequate heating, nutritious food, public transport, credit and consumer goods.

But living on the breadline is not simply about doing without things; it is also about experiencing poor health, isolation, stress, stigma and exclusion:

Poverty curtails freedom of choice. The freedom to eat as you wish, to go where and when you like, to seek the leisure pursuits or political activities which others accept; all are denied to those without the resources . . . poverty is most comprehensively understood as a state of partial citizenship.
(P. Golding, ed., *Excluding the Poor* (CPAG, 1986))

The gradual raising of the poverty line simply reflects the fact that society generally has become more prosperous and therefore has a more generous definition of a minimum income. The poor should not be excluded as the general level of prosperity rises.

Source: adapted from Carey Oppenheim, *Poverty: The Facts*, CPAG

1 With reference to item A, explain briefly in your own words conservative objections to the idea of relative poverty.
2 Explain in your own words what the former Conservative minister meant when he said 'The poverty lobby would, on their definition, find poverty in Paradise' (highlighted at end of item A).
3 On the basis of what you have studied so far in this chapter, what definition of poverty do you think the conservatives in item A support? Give reasons for your answer.
4 With reference to item B, identify three factors apart from material goods and services which the CPAG thinks should be taken into account when defining poverty.
5 Explain what is meant by 'exclusion' and 'poverty is most comprehensively understood as a state of partial citizenship' in item B (highlighted).
6 What definition of poverty do you think the CPAG supports? Give reasons for your answer.
7 Go to www.phespirit.info/montypython/four_yorkshiremen.htm and/or www.youtube.com/watch?v=Xe1a1wHxTyo. Explain how this comedy sketch illustrates, in a very amusing way, why poverty is best understood as a relative concept and can only be judged in relation to the lifestyles of others in the society to which a person belongs.
8 Discuss in your group whether or not you think poverty really exists in modern Britain, given the starving populations in Africa.

The **poverty line** is the dividing point between those who are poor and those who are not. The official poverty line used in Britain today is *60 per cent of average income* – the definition of poverty used by the European Union.

The measurement of poverty in Britain: the poverty line

The **poverty line** is the dividing point between those who are poor and those who are not. The official poverty line used in Britain today is *60 per cent of average income* – the definition of poverty used by the European Union.

Sociologists often also take into account those who are living on the margins of this poverty line, as those whose incomes are low often slip between being just above the poverty line and on or below it.

The extent of poverty in Britain

In 2008–9 in the UK:

- 13,400,000 people were living in poverty (below 60 per cent of average income) – 22 per cent of the population
- nearly a third (30 per cent) of all children were living in poverty.

The numbers of the poor, and the changes between 1996–7 and 2008–9 are shown in figure 8.11.

Activity

Study figure 8.11 and answer the following questions:

1. By how much did the percentage of the population living on below 60 per cent of average income decrease between 1996–7 and 2008–9?
2. What percentage of the population had below 60 per cent of average income in 1996–7?
3. How many fewer people had below 60 per cent of average income in 2008–9 than in 1996–7?
4. What percentage of the population were living on below 60 per cent of average income in 2008–9?
5. Suggest possible reasons for the decrease in the numbers of those living in poverty between 1996–7 and 2008–9.

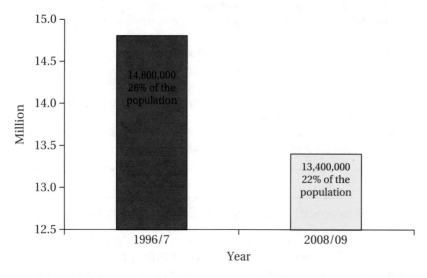

Figure 8.11 Numbers of people living in poverty (below 60 per cent of average income after housing costs): UK, 1996–7 and 2008–9

Source: Households Below Average Income (Department for Work and Pensions / Office for National Statistics, 2010)

THE FEMINIZATION OF POVERTY

Women are a bit more likely than men to experience poverty. In 2008–9, 21 per cent of all women lived in low-income households compared to 19 per cent of men, with 29 per cent of single women in low-income households compared with 24 per cent of single men. Women face a higher risk of poverty than men because:

- Women are more likely to be in low-paid and part-time work. In 2009, around two-thirds of low-paid workers were women.
- They are more likely than men to be lone parents with sole responsibility for children, leading to reduced possibilities for employment and dependence on inadequate state benefits.
- Women live longer than men and retire earlier (until 2020 when their retirement age will be the same as men's), and therefore spend a greater proportion of their lives beyond retirement age. However, because of low pay throughout their lives they are less likely than men to have savings, and are less likely than men to be entitled to employers' pensions.
- In many low-income households, it is often mothers rather than fathers who bear the burden of trying to make ends meet, and in the face of poverty sacrifice their own standard of living to provide food, clothing and extras for the children.

Who are the poor?

The identity of the major groups in poverty suggests that poverty is caused not by idleness, but by social circumstances beyond the control of the poor themselves. The unemployed, the low-paid, pensioners and the sick and disabled account for most of the poor. Those living in poverty (low-income households on or below 60 per cent of average income) in 2008–9 are shown below.

- *Those without work* – 53 per cent were workless.
- *The low paid* – 47 per cent were in full-time or part-time work. Many of the poor work long hours in low-paid jobs.
- *Pensioners* – 15 per cent were pensioners. Many elderly retired people depend on state pensions for support, and these are inadequate for maintaining other than a very basic standard of living.
- *Lone parents* – 18 per cent were lone parents. Lone parents are often prevented from getting a full-time job by the lack of affordable childcare facilities, or only take part-time jobs, which generally get lower rates of pay. The costs of childcare often mean lone parents cannot afford to work. The majority of lone parents are women, who in any case get lower pay than men.
- *The sick and disabled* – around a fifth of all disabled people were in poverty. Disability brings with it poorer employment opportunities, lower pay, and dependence on state benefits.

- *Children* – about 4 million children were living in poverty – nearly 1 in 3 (30 per cent) of all children.
- *Minority ethnic groups* – about two-fifths of people from ethnic minorities were living in poverty – twice the rate for white people. More than half of people from Bangladeshi and Pakistani ethnic backgrounds were living in low-income households, and about two in every three Bangladeshi and Pakistani children.

Figure 8.12 illustrates which groups made up most of those living in poverty in 2008–9, by family type and by economic status, and figure 8.13 shows the risk of being in poverty by various groupings.

> For the very latest data on poverty, visit www.poverty.org.uk.

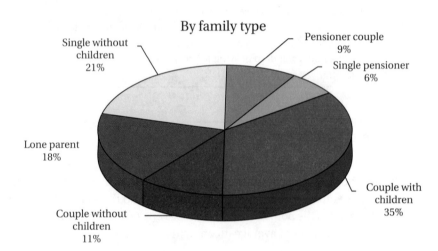

Figure 8.12 Who are the poor? There were 13,400,000 people living in low-income households (60 per cent or less of average income after housing costs) in the United Kingdom in 2008–9. This figure shows the family and economic features of those making up the total living on low incomes

Source: Households Below Average Income (Department for Work and Pensions, 2010)

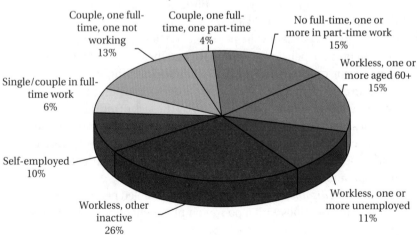

By family type

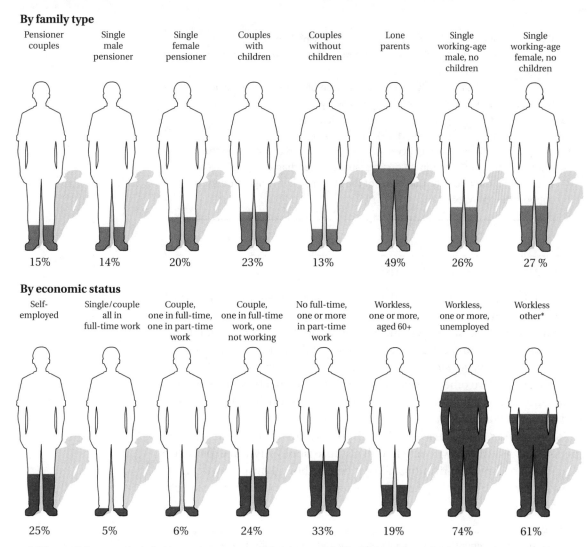

Pensioner couples	Single male pensioner	Single female pensioner	Couples with children	Couples without children	Lone parents	Single working-age male, no children	Single working-age female, no children
15%	14%	20%	23%	13%	49%	26%	27 %

By economic status

Self-employed	Single/couple all in full-time work	Couple, one in full-time, one in part-time work	Couple, one in full-time work, one not working	No full-time, one or more in part-time work	Workless, one or more, aged 60+	Workless, one or more, unemployed	Workless other*
25%	5%	6%	24%	33%	19%	74%	61%

* Other = all those not included in previous groups, eg. long-term sick, disabled people, and non-working lone parent

Figure 8.13 The risk of poverty: proportion of individuals in particular groups living in poverty (below 60 per cent of average income after housing costs): United Kingdom, 2008–9

Source: Households Below Average Income (Department for Work and Pensions, 2010)

Activity

Refer to figure 8.12.
1 What percentage of those living on a low income in 2008–9 were single pensioners?
2 Which family type made up the greatest proportion of those in poverty in 2008–9?
3 What percentage of the poor were made up of those who were workless? Refer to figure 8.13.
4 What percentage of self-employed people were living in poverty in 2008–9?

5 What percentage of couples with children were living in poverty?
6 What evidence is there in figure 8.13 that might be used to show that low pay is a cause of poverty?
7 What difference is there between the proportion of couples with children and that of couples without children living in poverty?
8 Which two groups overall have the highest risk of poverty?
9 Which group overall has the least risk of being in poverty?
10 Suggest how the evidence in figure 8.13 might be used to show that the poor are victims of unfortunate circumstances rather than being themselves to blame for their poverty. Could any of the evidence in the figure be used to support the opposite view?

Criticisms of the poverty line

Many people are critical of the definition of poverty simply in terms of income, because it takes no account of all the extras most of the population take for granted, such as coping with household emergencies, going on holiday, going out for a drink with friends, and taking part in other leisure activities. Poverty is not simply a matter of how much income someone has, but can also involve other aspects of life such as the quality of housing and the quality and availability of public services like transport, hospitals, schools and play areas for children.

Some aspects and consequences of poverty apart from shortage of income are shown below. While not all of those in poverty will experience all of these multiple deprivations, the list below shows how poverty can be like a spider's web, trapping the poor in a deprived lifestyle in many aspects of their lives.

> Poverty means going short materially, socially and emotionally. It means spending less on food, on heating and on clothing than someone on an average income. But it is not what is spent that matters, but what isn't. Poverty means staying at home, often being bored, not seeing friends, not going out for a drink and not being able to take the children out for a trip or treat or a holiday. It means coping with the stresses of managing on very little money, often for months or even years. It means having to withstand the onslaught of society's pressure to consume. It impinges on relationships with others and with yourself. Above all, poverty takes away the tools to build the blocks for the future – your 'life chances'. It steals away the opportunity to have a life unmarked by sickness, a decent education, a secure home and a long retirement. It stops people being able to take control of their lives.
>
> (Carey Oppenheim, *Poverty: The Facts* (CPAG))

● *Homelessness.* At the beginning of 2010, around 42,000 households were officially accepted as unintentionally homeless and in priority need by local authorities in England, though there were more homeless than this, such as those regarded as intentionally homeless, or not in priority need, or who simply don't come to the attention of local councils or other authorities.

Why do you think some people become homeless? How might being homeless affect other aspects of people's lives?

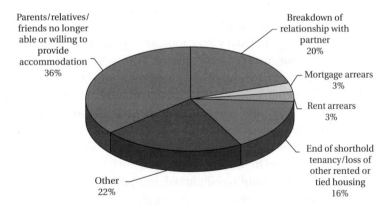

Figure 8.14 Reasons for homelessness: Households officially accepted as homeless and in priority need, by reason for loss of last settled home, England 2010

Source: Department of Communities and Local Government, 2010

- *Poverty in healthcare.*
  - There are fewer doctors practising in inner-city areas (where many of the poor live), and those who do are often overworked, because the poor have more health problems.
  - The poor are less likely to get time off work with pay to visit the doctor.
  - They face longer hospital waiting lists.
  - Many are not fully aware of what health services are available to them, and the poor tend to be less vocal in demanding proper standards of care from doctors.
- *Poverty at school.*
  - Inner-city schools often have a concentration of social problems, such as social deprivation, drugs, discipline problems and vandalism, and consequently a higher turnover of teachers.
  - Parents are less able to help their children with their education, and have less money than non-poor parents to enable the school to buy extra resources.
- *Poverty at work.*
  - *Poor working conditions.* These include a neglect of health and safety standards and a high accident rate; working at night and long periods of overtime because the pay is so low; lack of trade union organization to protect the workers' interests; lack of entitlement to paid holidays; and no employers' sick pay or pension schemes.
  - *Insecure employment,* often with high risks of job loss with very short notice of dismissal.
- *Poor health,* such as respiratory problems like asthma and infectious diseases, as a result of poor diet and damp, overcrowded housing.
- *Going short of food, clothing and heating,* and not being able to replace household goods or carry out household repairs and decoration. A survey in 2002 suggested that 1 in 20 mothers go without enough food in order to meet the needs of their children. Lone parents on income support are fourteen times more likely to go without enough food than mothers not receiving benefits. Many poor families have an unhealthy diet, not because they don't know or care about a nutritionally healthy diet, but because they can't afford it.
- *Isolation and boredom.* Making friends may be hard because there is no money to get involved in social activities.
- *Stress,* in the face of mounting bills and debts, perhaps leading to domestic violence, family breakdown and mental illness.
- *Low self-esteem,* brought on by dependence on others, the lack of access to the activities and facilities others have, and difficulties in coping with day-to-day life.

Tackling poverty

The main measures taken to help the poor have largely developed with the welfare state.

The welfare state provides a wide range of benefits and services including:

- a range of welfare benefits through the social security system for many groups such as the unemployed, those injured at work, the sick and disabled, widows, the retired, expectant mothers, lone parents, and children – for example state pensions, Job Seekers' Allowance, Incapacity Benefit and Income Support
- a comprehensive and largely free National Health Service, including ante- and post-natal care, hospitals, GPs, dentists and opticians (although some charges are payable – for example to dentists and opticians)
- a free and compulsory state education for all to the age of 16, rising to 17 from 2013
- social services provided by local councils, such as social workers, and special facilities for the disabled, the elderly and children. Local councils are also responsible for housing the homeless, and for the adoption and fostering of children.

The welfare state, run by national and local government, is not the only provider of welfare. The voluntary and private sectors also play important roles, often working alongside the state provision, and much welfare provision is provided informally by family, friends and neighbours. This often means care by women, as it is women who take on the main caring responsibilities in the family for the dependent elderly, the disabled and the sick.

There is more discussion of the role of the welfare state in chapter 7 – see pages 383–7.

The persistence of poverty: why the poor remain poor

The welfare state in Britain was originally seen as a way of providing 'womb-to-tomb' care, and of eradicating poverty. However, while it may have removed the worst excesses of absolute poverty, widespread deprivation remains in modern Britain, and the welfare state has yet to solve the real problems of relative poverty. Why is this?

Blaming the generosity of the welfare state: the dependency culture and the underclass (version 1)

Some Conservatives argue that poverty continues because the generosity of 'handouts' from the 'nanny' welfare state has, they say, created a **dependency culture**. This is where people develop a set of values and beliefs and

A **dependency culture** is a set of values and beliefs, and a way of life, centred on dependence on others.

A good way to remember the various explanations of poverty is to think of them as 'blaming theories' – where is the blame placed for poverty?

The explanations below variously:
- blame the *generosity* of the welfare state (the 'nanny state')
- blame the *inadequacy* of the welfare state
- blame the culture of the poor
- blame the cycle of deprivation
- blame the unequal structure of power and wealth in society.

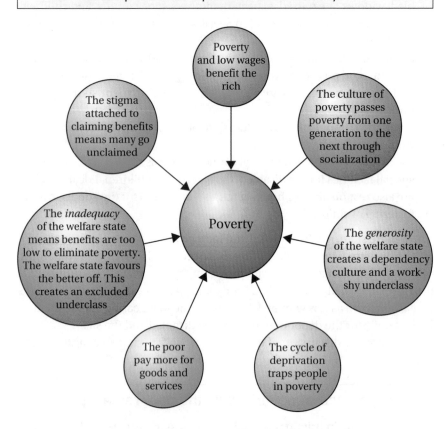

Figure 8.15 Why the poor remain poor

a way of life centred on dependence on others. They abandon reliance on work, the family and the local community, and are content to live on welfare state 'handouts', rather than taking responsibility themselves for improving their situation. The more the welfare state provides benefits for people, the less they will do for themselves, leading to a situation where people learn to become dependent on others. This discourages the poor from taking action to help themselves, and undermines self-help and self-reliance.

Universal versus selective, means-tested benefits   Such writers believe that universal welfare benefits (which are available to everyone regardless of income, such as the basic state pension, and free healthcare and education) should be withdrawn from all those who are capable of supporting themselves. These benefits should instead be targeted only at those who genuinely need them, such as the disabled and the long-term sick. Universal benefits should therefore be replaced by selective benefits, targeted by means-testing. Means-testing involves people having to pass a test of their income and savings (their 'means') before receiving any benefits, and only if these were low enough would they receive any benefits. The arguments over means-testing are presented in the box below.

ARE MEANS-TESTED BENEFITS A GOOD IDEA?

Yes	No
• Benefits are targeted only on those who really need them. People who are able to work should support themselves. Money is saved on universal benefits which most people don't need and shouldn't have. More money is available to invest in the economy, create jobs and cut taxes.	• Means-tested benefits, which are received only by the very poor, may lead to some people being worse-off if they take a low-paid job. They may lose means-tested benefits like housing or council tax benefits, and the extra they earn by working is not enough to compensate for the lost income. This 'poverty trap' discourages people from taking work. Universal benefits avoid this.
• Means-testing stops unemployment being an option for some people, and fights the welfare dependency culture.	• Because of the poverty trap, means-testing might drive people into a dependency culture and a reluctance to get a job.
• Families, communities and voluntary organizations are strengthened as alternative sources of support.	• Families and communities caught in the poverty trap are likely to be weakened by poverty and stress. Some will be encouraged to become 'benefit cheats' through concealing income and savings to get around means-testing. Universal benefits keep everyone's standards up to an acceptable minimum level.
• Selective means-tested benefits will enable more benefits for the most disadvantaged, by no longer wasting money on those who can afford to support themselves.	• Often the most deprived do not take up or make full use of even universal benefits, as they're unsure of how to do so. Means-tested benefits attach a stigma to those who claim them, and make it even more unlikely they will claim benefits to which they are entitled.

UNCLAIMED BENEFITS

Many poor people do not claim the welfare benefits to which they are entitled, particularly those which are means-tested. According to the Department for Work and Pensions' own estimates, released in 2010, between about 10 per cent and 53 per cent of those entitled to some income-related benefit were not claiming it, representing overall between £6.9 billion and £12.7 billion left unclaimed in 2008–9. This is between 18 per cent and 33 per cent of the money that was paid out. The failure to claim benefits is often because of:

- the complexity of the benefits and tax system
- inadequate publicity
- the obscure language of leaflets and complex means-testing forms, which means people often do not know what their rights are or the procedures for claiming benefits
- people's lack of confidence about whether or not they are entitled, or because they regard the effort involved in claiming as too great for the amounts involved.

The bureaucratic hurdles are often so great that many people are deterred from claiming what they are entitled to. This is particularly important as the poor are among the least-educated sections of the population. The mass media periodically run campaigns about welfare 'fraudsters' and 'scroungers' – with headlines like 'Stuff the spongers' – which help to attach a stigma to claiming benefits, which may deter some people from doing so. The establishment of the Department for Work and Pensions' 'Targeting Benefit Thieves' website (http://campaigns.dwp.gov.uk/campaigns/benefit-thieves/) may have further contributed to attaching such a stigma. A number of photos from previous and present campaigns are shown opposite.

Activity

Refer to the 'Unclaimed benefits' box above, and answer the following questions or discuss them in your group.

1. Do you agree or disagree with the view that the media give the impression that people receiving benefits are 'scroungers'? Give reasons for your answer.
2. Do you think most people receiving welfare benefits are deserving? How would you go about finding out?
3. Do you think benefits discourage people from taking more responsibility for their own lives? Give reasons for your answer.
4. Do you think it is reasonable that people should be expected to take a job even if they will be worse-off than if they received benefits?

The underclass – version 1: the poor as welfare scroungers and social misfits
Some have argued that the generosity of the welfare state, and the dependency culture, have created an **underclass** of people – right at the bottom of the social hierarchy – who have developed a lifestyle and set of values and attitudes which make them reluctant to take jobs.

The **underclass** refers to a social group who are right at the bottom of the social class hierarchy, who are in some ways cut off or excluded from the rest of society.

Do you think newspaper reports like the one from the *Daily Express*, from 14 October 2009, and campaigns like 'Targeting Benefit Thieves' might deter some people from claiming benefits to which they are entitled?

The Department for Work and Pensions' 'Targeting Benefit Thieves' campaign declares its aims to be 'to positively reinforce honest behaviour, create a climate of intolerance to fraud and to undermine its social acceptability'. By far the majority of benefit claimants are honest, but fraud (dishonest claims) is a serious problem which cost the government an estimated £1.5 billion in 2009–10.

(Reproduced by permission of the Department for Work and Pensions)

They are willing simply to live off the welfare state. Supporters of this view of the underclass also regard some of the poor as social misfits, pointing to their lack of morality, high crime levels, cohabitation, and large numbers of lone parents. However, many sociologists reject this view, arguing that the attitudes and values of the poor are no different from those of the non-poor: they want the same things as the rest of society, but just lack the means to achieve them. This alternative view of the underclass is explored below in version 2.

These ideas of the dependency culture and the underclass are also implied in the later 'culture of poverty' explanation (on pages 439–40).

Blaming the inadequacy of the welfare state: the underclass (version 2)

An alternative explanation for the persistence of poverty is offered by those who argue that benefit levels are too low to lift people out of poverty. From this viewpoint, the welfare state is not generous enough, and middle-class people gain more from the welfare state than the poor. For example, the middle class gain more from state spending on education, because they keep their children in education longer (in further and higher education). The middle class also gain more from the health service, partly because they are more demanding and assertive in their dealings with doctors, and partly because the middle-class are generally healthier. This means that doctors in middle-class areas are less overworked, and so are able to spend more time dealing with patients and their problems. Poor people, by contrast, get less time with their doctors and face longer hospital waiting lists. Tax relief on private pensions also benefits the middle class more, as they are more likely to have private pension schemes. In general, then, the middle-class gain more from the welfare state than the poor. This bias towards the middle class has been called the **inverse care law** – that those whose need is greatest get the least resources, and those whose need is least get the greatest resources. This is discussed more in chapter 9 on health.

The underclass – version 2: poverty and social exclusion This failure of the welfare state to provide sufficient help to the poor has led to an alternative view of the underclass to that discussed above. This alternative view suggests the underclass consists of disadvantaged groups whose poverty means they are excluded from taking part in society to the same extent as the non-poor. This excluded underclass consists of groups such as the disadvantaged elderly retired, lone-parent families and the long-term unemployed. These groups are forced to rely upon inadequate state benefits which are too low to give them an acceptable standard of living. This prevents them from participating fully in society, and gives them little opportunity to escape the poverty trap.

This view of the underclass suggests it is not the attitudes and values of poor people which are to blame for their poverty, but the difficulties and misfortune they face which are beyond their control, like unemployment, disability or sickness. The poor live depressingly deprived lifestyles, and want many of the things most of society already has, like secure and decently paid jobs and opportunities. In this view, it is government policies which have neglected to tackle unemployment, failed to improve the living standards of those on some benefits, and failed to give the poor the opportunities and incentives needed to get off benefits. It is this, not the attitudes of the poor, which leaves them excluded from full participation in society. This view suggests government policies should do more to tackle unemployment, improve the living standards of those on benefits (e.g. through higher pensions and benefit levels), and give incentives to the poor to get off benefits by ensuring there are enough decently paid jobs available. Only in this way will the excluded underclass disappear in our society.

> The **inverse care law** is the suggestion that, in the welfare state, those whose need is least get the most resources, while those in the greatest need get the least resources.

Activity

Two views of the underclass

Version 1

A group who have developed a lifestyle and set of attitudes which mean they are no longer willing to take jobs. They have evolved a dependency culture, which means they are not prepared to help themselves but are prepared to live off the welfare state. They lack morality, and have high levels of crime, cohabitation and lone parenthood. Their workshy 'sponging' attitudes and lack of social responsibility are the causes for their poverty. Most of the poor have only themselves to blame.

Version 2

A group whose poverty means they are excluded from taking part in society to the same extent as the non-poor, even though they want to. They consist of groups like the disadvantaged elderly retired, lone parents, the disabled and the long-term unemployed. Their attitudes are the same as those of the rest of society, but they are forced to rely upon inadequate state benefits which are not high enough to give them an acceptable standard of living. This prevents them from participating fully in society, and gives them little opportunity to fulfil their ambitions and escape the poverty trap.

Compare the two models of the underclass above:
1 Which view do you think provides the most accurate picture of poor people? Give reasons for your answer.
2 Suggest two solutions to the problem of the underclass for each version.

Blaming the culture of the poor: the culture of poverty

Another explanation for the persistence of poverty is the theory of the **culture of poverty**.

> The **culture of poverty** is a set of beliefs and values thought to exist among the poor which prevents them escaping from poverty.

This suggests it is the characteristics of the poor themselves, their values and culture, that cause poverty and social exclusion. It is suggested the poor form an underclass who are resigned to their situation. They seldom take opportunities when they arise, are reluctant to work, and don't plan for the future. They seem, in this view, to make little effort to change their situation, or to help themselves overcome their social exclusion. They won't use their initiative and involve themselves in mainstream society and try to break free of their poverty, even when opportunities to do so arise. Children grow up in this culture, and learn these values from their parents, and so poverty and social exclusion continue from one generation to the next.

The weakness of this type of explanation is that it tends to blame the poor for their own poverty, and implies that if only the poor would change their values, then poverty would disappear. However, if the poor do develop a culture of poverty – and this is hotly disputed – it may well be a *result* of poverty, and not a *cause* of it. For example, the poor cannot afford to save for a 'rainy day', planning for the future is difficult when the future is so uncertain, and it is hard not to give up and become resigned to being unemployed after endless searching for non-existent jobs.

TRAPPED IN POVERTY: THE POOR PAY MORE

One of the great ironies of poverty is that the cost of living is higher for the poor than the non-poor, and this hinders the poor in their attempts to escape poverty. The poor pay more because:

- They often live in poor-quality housing, which is expensive to heat and maintain.
- They have to buy cheap clothing, which wears out quickly and is therefore more expensive in the long run.
- They have to pay more for food as they can only afford to buy it in small quantities (which is more expensive), and from small, expensive corner shops as they haven't cars to travel to supermarkets. They also lack storage facilities like freezers for buying in bulk.
- The cost of house and car insurance is higher as a result of more theft and vandalism in poor areas.
- They pay more for credit; banks and building societies won't lend them money as they consider them a poor risk. Loans are therefore often obtained from loan sharks at exorbitant rates of interest.
- They suffer more ill-health, and so have to spend more on non-prescription medicines.

The culture-of-poverty explanation, and the earlier 'dependency culture' one, are convenient ones for those in positions of power, as they put the blame for poverty on the poor themselves. If these explanations are adopted, then the problem of poverty will be solved by policies such as cutting welfare benefits to the poor, to make them 'stand on their own two feet', and job training programmes to move them from welfare to work.

Blaming the cycle of deprivation

A further explanation for poverty is what has been called the cycle of deprivation. This suggests that poverty is cumulative, in the sense that one aspect of poverty can lead to further poverty. This builds up into a vicious circle which the poor find hard to escape from, and it then carries on with their children. Figure 8.16 illustrates examples of possible cycles of deprivation. The problem with this explanation is that, while it explains why poverty continues, it does not explain how poverty begins in the first place. The final type of explanation does try to do this.

Figure 8.16 Cycles of deprivation

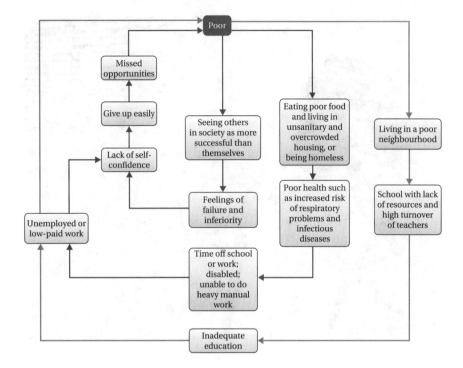

Blaming the unequal structure of power and wealth in society

These are structural explanations, which explain poverty in terms of the structure of society, with its unequal distribution of wealth and income and the inadequate assistance given to the poor. Poverty is seen as an aspect of social inequality and not merely an individual problem of poor people. These are mainly Marxist arguments, which suggest that the reason the poor remain poor is because they are exploited by the rich. Structural explanations suggests poverty remains for the following reasons:

● Low-paid workers provide the source of profits which enables the rich to achieve high incomes, and the position of the wealthy depends on poverty.

● Poverty ensures that the most undesirable, dirty, dangerous or menial low-paid jobs that most people don't want are done, as some people have no other choice than to do these jobs.

● The non-working poor help to keep the wages of the non-poor working-class down by providing a threat to their jobs, as they provide a reserve pool of cheap labour if wage demands become too high.

● The poor lack power to change their position, because they do not have the financial resources to form powerful groups to change public opinion, and they are often badly organized.

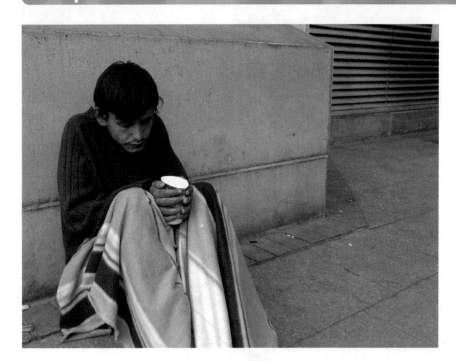

What factors push people into a cycle of deprivation and prevent them escaping from poverty?

In this view, it is not being unemployed, a lone parent, long-term sick, disabled, or old that causes poverty. Rather, it is government policy and the structure of society which mean some people face misfortune through no fault of their own, and are penalized for it by inadequate benefits, a deprived lifestyle and poor life chances.

Structural explanations suggest that any serious attempt to abolish poverty would involve a widespread redistribution of wealth and income. This would

---

Activity

1   Carry out a small survey asking people about poverty in Britain today. Do they think it still exists? What do they mean by 'poor'? Draw up a list of items and ask people whether they think they are essential for a basic standard of living. You could use the list of items in the *Poverty and Social Exclusion Survey* earlier in this chapter to help you. Try to draw some conclusions about the ideas of relative poverty, and the consensus view of poverty.

2   Imagine you have become the prime minister, with a huge majority in Parliament enabling you to carry through a successful campaign against poverty. Think carefully about all the explanations for poverty you have read of in this chapter, and the groups in poverty. Devise a series of policies which would help to reduce poverty. Explain in each case why you think your proposed policy would help to reduce poverty.

mean the creation of improved social services, higher welfare benefits, and more and better-paid jobs, with the introduction of higher taxes on the rich to pay for these reforms.

SOCIAL MOBILITY

Social mobility refers to the movement of people up or down the social class hierarchy, either during the course of the individual's lifetime or compared to the social class into which she or he was born. Modern societies are said to be open societies because social mobility is possible, and people can move up or down the social class hierarchy.

Why study social mobility?

The study of social mobility is important as it enables the measurement of how open society is. It can show how far there is equality of life opportunities in society, and therefore reveal dimensions of social inequality. Studying social mobility can show whether society is fair and meritocratic, and whether people's social position is achieved solely on the basis of their talents, abilities, skills and qualifications. Does everyone with talent and motivation, who works hard and plays by the rules, have an equal opportunity of succeeding and fulfilling their potential? Alternatively, studying social mobility can show whether the life chances of a child and their chances of success are largely a result of the social class into which they are born, and other factors like their gender or ethnic origin.

Measuring social mobility

Sociologists measure social mobility either by income, or by social class defined by occupation, using occupational scales like those mentioned earlier in this chapter. This means that there are problems with the measuring tools used in social mobility studies, as different studies may use different occupational scales, and those using occupational groups tend to produce slightly different results from those using income. This means it can be difficult to compare different studies.

There are two main types of social mobility that sociologists examine to see how open society is:

Inter-generational social mobility compares an adult's present occupation or income with that of the family she or he was born into.

- **Inter-generational social mobility** compares an adult's present occupational or income group with that of the family she or he was born into. This shows social mobility between two generations. For example, a refuse collector's daughter who becomes a doctor has experienced upward social mobility compared with the class into which she was born.

- **Intra-generational social mobility** compares an adult's present occupation or income with her or his first occupation or income, therefore showing how much mobility she or he has achieved in his or her lifetime. An example would be the person who began her or his working life as a small shopkeeper, but who eventually built up a massive supermarket empire.

> **Intra-generational social mobility** compares an adult's present occupation or income with her or his first occupation or income.

How much social mobility is there in Britain?

Social mobility in modern Britain is relatively limited, and most people stay in the broad social class they were born into. The main findings suggest:

Inter-generational social mobility

- A considerable number of children from working-class backgrounds now achieve upward mobility to the middle class. This is largely because there are declining numbers of working-class jobs, and growing numbers of middle-class jobs – there is 'more room at the top', enabling middle-class children to stay middle-class, while also enabling some working-class children to become middle-class.
- Nearly 80 per cent of working-class adults, and about three-quarters of those in the middle class, were born to parents of the same class.
- There is a close link between the social class of origin (the class people are born into) and the social class of destination (the one they end up in as adults) – at least 40–50 per cent of children today can expect to find themselves in the same class position as their parents, whether measured by income or by occupational group.
- Not everyone has the same chance of achieving upward social mobility. A child from a working-class background has only about half the chance of entering the upper middle class as an adult compared to one from the lower middle class. A child born into the upper middle class has about four times the chance of being in that class as an adult compared to one from a working-class background. For example, the typical doctor or lawyer today grew up in a family with an income two-thirds higher than the average family. This shows a clear lack of equal opportunity for all to have the same chance of getting the top jobs (see cartoon).
- Social class background is still the major factor influencing success in the education system, which is crucial for upward social mobility. Those from middle- and upper-middle-class backgrounds and those privately educated dominate the universities. Those 7 per cent of the population

The 1:2:4 pattern of unequal opportunity

Whatever the chance a boy from a working-class background has of reaching the upper middle class as an adult, a boy from a lower-middle-class family has about twice the chance, and a boy born into the upper middle class has about four times the chance of being in that class as an adult. This clearly shows an inequality of opportunity in the chances of upward mobility in Britain

who can afford to attend fee-paying private schools dominate the top institutions of power in the UK, with three out of four judges, one in two senior civil servants, over half the members of the professions, and a third of MPs privately educated.

- The propertied upper class still remains largely closed, as much wealth is inherited rather than achieved through work or talent. The best way to get rich in modern Britain is still to be born to rich parents.

Intra-generational social mobility

The chances of upward mobility during a person's career, such as moving from a manual job to a higher-status professional and managerial or technical job, have declined. Higher-status positions are increasingly filled directly by graduates from the education system, and most of these graduates themselves come from higher social class backgrounds.

> **Activity**
>
> Go through the following list, writing down for each one 'upward mobility', 'downward mobility' or 'no change', *and* 'inter-generational mobility' or 'intra-generational mobility'. Refer to the occupational scales earlier in the chapter (see pages 406–8) if you find any difficulty.
>
> 1 A nurse who decides to become a labourer on a building site.
> 2 The daughter of a miner who becomes a bank manager.
> 3 A teacher who decides to retrain as a social worker.
> 4 A doctor's son who becomes a taxi driver.
> 5 An immigrant from a poor farming background in Africa who gets a job in Britain as a farm labourer.
> 6 The daughter of a skilled manual worker who becomes a routine clerical worker.
> 7 A postal worker who becomes a traffic warden.
> 8 The son of a pilot who becomes a police constable.
> 9 The owner of a small shop whose daughter becomes the manager of a large supermarket.
> 10 A sales assistant in a shop who becomes a priest.

Obstacles to social mobility

While levels of social mobility have grown since the 1970s, there remain very large inequalities of opportunity, and a number of obstacles to social mobility and the development of a truly open society.

- Education is a key factor in enabling social mobility. Despite free and compulsory state education, there remains widespread inequality of educational opportunity, as seen in chapter 4. Many working-class children face a number of obstacles and disadvantages in the way of success in education, which mean they do not do as well as their ability should allow them to, and this restricts their chances of upward mobility. Middle-class families are generally in a better position to secure for their children a middle-class occupation, as they are more able to support their children in further and higher education in a wide number of ways.

- There remain biases in recruitment to the upper-middle-class elite jobs. For example, judges and top civil servants are recruited almost exclusively from people who have attended very expensive boys' public schools and then gone to Oxford or Cambridge University. This is a major obstacle for children from working-class backgrounds, who can't afford these schools and are therefore often denied the chance of getting into these top jobs.

- Women face a range of obstacles in achieving upward mobility, because of a number of factors which hinder their ability to compete in the labour market on equal terms with men (see later in this chapter).
- Disadvantages in education, and racism in education, training, and employment, often present obstacles to the upward social mobility of some minority ethnic groups. Consequently, a high percentage of people of African-Caribbean and Pakistani/Bangladeshi origin are represented in the working class.

Activity

1 Look at the table below, and explain how each of the factors might encourage or limit the possibilities of upward social mobility.
2 Suggest what steps you might take to ensure that the most well-paid and responsible positions in society are filled by the most able and committed people, regardless of their social class, gender or ethnic origins.

Factors encouraging social mobility	Factors limiting social mobility
• Family support for children, in the form of money, support in education, values and networks of contacts	• Inequality of educational opportunity and lack of success in education
• Raising educational standards and ensuring access to further and higher education for all	• Lack of family support
	• Poor attitudes, expectations and lack of ambition
• Equality of opportunity for all, based on meritocracy, with fairer recruitment policies by employers	• Barriers to some occupations, like the legal profession, for those from the 'wrong' social class or educational background
• Drive, ambition and a willingness to take up opportunities and take risks	• Racial and sexual discrimination
	• Childhood poverty

Conclusion on social mobility

Britain has one of the lowest social mobility rates in Europe. The chances of social mobility (compared to family occupation or income) have changed little since the early 1980s. Britain remains highly unequal, and the life chances of children remain closely tied to the social class of the families into which they were born. Children born to poorer families continue to have fewer chances of success in education, poorer employment opportunities and poorer health than those from more affluent backgrounds, creating barriers to upward mobility. Social class inequalities in social mobility (and also in gender and ethnicity, which are discussed later in this chapter) persist as major features of life in contemporary Britain, and most people do not achieve much upward social mobility from the family into which they are born.

CHANGES IN THE CLASS STRUCTURE

The changing occupational structure

At the beginning of the twentieth century, the majority of people in Britain were working in manual working-class occupations, with less than a quarter being considered upper- or middle-class. However, in the last 100 years, changes in the economy have occurred which have changed the occupational structure, and the non-manual middle class is now larger than the manual working class, although many so-called middle-class jobs are low-level and routine, and not much different from manual jobs in pay and terms and conditions of employment. These changes include:

- a growth in the tertiary sector of the economy, which is concerned with the provision of services, such as administration, sales, finance and insurance, transport, distribution, and the running of government services (like the welfare state and education). This has created more middle-class jobs, particularly routine, low-level, non-manual jobs
- a decline in semi-skilled and unskilled manual work, as technology takes over these tasks, and creates more skilled jobs
- a steady increase in the percentage of the workforce engaged in non-manual occupations, especially occupations such as routine clerical work and customer service work, as in call centres
- an increase in lower professional occupations, like teaching and social work.

These developments have led to a change in the shape of the social structure, with unskilled and semi-skilled manual occupational groups getting smaller, and skilled manual and lower-middle-class occupational groups getting larger. There has also emerged what some people regard as an underclass of long-term unemployed and other groups who are excluded by their poverty from full participation in society, as discussed earlier in this chapter. As shown in figure 8.16, the social structure has changed from the pyramid shape that existed about a century ago to the shape of a diamond.

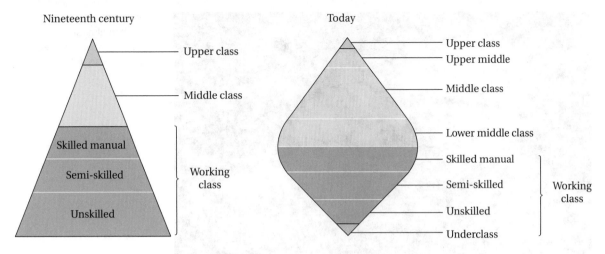

Figure 8.17 The changing shape of the class structure in Britain

The changing and declining working class: the traditional and new working classes

The traditional working class

The main section of the working class in Britain up to the mid twentieth century was what was commonly called the traditional working class. This was found mainly in the north of England, south Wales and Scotland, in traditional (long-established) basic industries, such as coal mining, docking, iron and steel, and shipbuilding. People worked in the same industry generation after generation and lived in social (council/rented) housing near one another and near the place of work. There was, as a result, a close-knit community living and working together, with high levels of involvement in community life and mutual support. These industries, the communities around them and the traditional working class have almost completely disappeared in contemporary Britain.

The new working class

Beginning in the 1960s, there was the emergence of a new working class, initially in the south of England, working in what were then newer, more technologically advanced manufacturing industries, like the production of cars and electrical goods. This new working class had greatly improved pay and living standards compared to the traditional working class, even exceeding those of some of the middle class. These highly paid, or affluent, manual workers could afford to buy their own homes and lived a privatized,

The traditional working class has almost completely disappeared in contemporary Britain

home-centred family lifestyle, with little involvement with neighbours or the wider community. They lived in what were formerly regarded as middle-class areas, and were able to buy the consumer goods which previously only the middle class could afford. This gave rise to the idea of **embourgeoise-ment** – that the upper working class was becoming more like, or merging with, the lower middle class.

Even though the lower middle class often has a bit more job security, the opportunity for more flexible working hours (flexitime), and generally work in more pleasant conditions, in contemporary Britain, in terms of factors like pay, home ownership, consumer goods and lifestyle, there is probably little separating the new working class from the lower middle class.

However, the new working class is today in decline, as manufacturing industries in Britain are closing down as production is moved to other countries where production costs are cheaper. As a result, working-class manual jobs of all kinds are today disappearing, and the working class is shrinking in size.

> **Embourgeoisement** is the idea that the differences between the middle class and working class are disappearing, with well-paid manual workers merging into the middle class.

The changing and growing middle class

At the same time as working-class jobs have been declining, there has been a growth in middle-class occupations, with a majority of people now engaged in non-manual work of all kinds, and particularly low-level routine non-manual work providing services to people, like administration, sales, insurance, financial advice, and customer services like call centres, rather than making products.

The new working class was found in more technologically advanced manufacturing industries, like the production of cars, and electrical and other consumer goods. The decline of manufacturing industries in contemporary Britain has meant this section of the working class, along with the manual working class in general, has been shrinking, with the middle class growing

The proletarianization of clerical work

Traditionally, those doing lower-middle-class occupations, like clerical and administrative work, had higher levels of education, higher pay, shorter working hours, and better working conditions and career opportunities than manual workers, and were seen as having a middle-class status and lifestyle. The proletarianization thesis suggests that these advantages, compared to the manual working class, have declined to such an extent that such groups are now virtually indistinguishable from the working class. For example, the pay of clerical workers has declined dramatically, and today is generally little better (and often worse) than that of manual workers; promotion opportunities have been reduced, as higher managerial jobs are often filled directly by university graduates rather than by people who have worked their way up; and the computerization of office work has reduced the skills of clerical work – this is called deskilling – and much clerical work has become more like routine and repetitive factory work.

The proletarianization of the lower middle class, combined with the embourgeoisement of the upper working class, have meant that, in terms of educational level, housing, lifestyle and living standards, there are few differences between lower-middle-class and skilled or upper-working-class occupations. There is now a 'bulge' in the middle of the social class hierarchy, as shown in figure 8.17 on page 449, with skilled manual workers and the lower middle class sharing similar status, rewards and lifestyles.

Proletarianization is the opposite of embourgeoisement. It is the suggestion that, rather than the working class becoming middle-class, some middle-class groups (particularly clerical and administrative workers) are descending into the working class.

Deskilling is the removal of skills from work by the application of new machinery which simplifies tasks.

Does social class still matter?

Many people today suggest that social class is no longer very important, often blaming sociologists for highlighting class inequalities which don't really have much impact on people's lives. Social class is thought to have little influence on people's lifestyles, and to be of declining importance today as a source of identity – how people see themselves and how others see them. They suggest that people today identify themselves not as being working-class or middle-class, but in terms of their gender identity or ethnic identity, or they create their own identities through the goods they choose to consume and the choices they make in how they live their lives. People are less influenced by their social class, close communities and work situations, and they can now choose, 'pick and mix', chop and change any identities they want from a range of different lifestyles presented to them through the mass media, and by the choices they make in their leisure activities and the lifestyles they express through their consumer spending.

However, even if people today don't identify themselves with their social class as much as they once did, this doesn't undermine the significance of social class. There are greater similarities between black and white children from working-class families than between working-class and middle-class children from the same ethnic group; there are greater similarities between women from the same social class than there are between women of different

Social class is like a goldfish bowl: you can't see the sides, but you'll soon realize they exist when you bump into them

social classes, and working-class women are likely to identify themselves more with other women of their own social class than they are with middle- and upper-class women.

Pretending that social classes don't exist will not make them go away, any more than not being able to see a plate glass door will stop you from hurting yourself when you walk into it.

Ask yourself why you don't buy expensive clothes, houses and cars, or travel first-class by train. Why don't you go to exotic foreign countries for long holidays several times a year? Why don't you eat out at restaurants all the time instead of cooking? Why don't you try to skip National Health Service waiting lists by paying for private medicine? What stops you from forging out your own identity by going on expensive shopping trips to buy goods to reinvent yourself?

Much of this chapter – and the chapters on education, crime and health – shows how, whatever anyone might think, social class and social class inequalities are significant features of contemporary Britain, and remain key influences on people's life chances.

Activity

What do you think are the most significant influences on your life chances, lifestyle and identity today? Is it your social class, your gender, your ethnicity or other things? Give reasons for your answer.

GENDER AND INEQUALITY

Stratification by sex is a feature found in most societies, with men generally being in a more dominant position in society than women. Our sex has major influences on how we think about ourselves, how others think about us, and the opportunities and life chances open to us. Men have traditionally been seen in a wide range of active and creative roles – as warriors, hunters and workers, as political leaders or successful business executives, as scientists, engineers, inventors or great artists.

And what roles have women been traditionally seen in? As housewives and mothers confined to the home and caring for their husbands and children. Even when working outside the home, women's jobs often seem to be an extension of their caring role in the home, looking after others as reception- ists, secretaries, nurses, teachers, social workers, shop and kitchen assistants, or cleaners. We might almost be forgiven for thinking that men and women exist in two different worlds, united only by belonging to the same species. Chapter 1 discussed the way these differences between males and females in modern Britain are constructed through socialization (see pages 19–35), and the sections below will examine some of the continuing inequalities between women and men which are, in part, a product of this socialization.

The sexual division of labour

The processes of gender role socialization outlined in chapter 1 often mean that women and men still have different experiences and expectations of life. Socialization still has the general effect of emphasizing girls' domestic responsibilities of housework and childcare, limiting their self-confidence, and pushing them, eventually, towards marriage or cohabitation. As seen in chapter 3, women continue to take on the major responsibilities for house-work and childcare, often alongside paid employment, as their primary roles in life. Boys, on the other hand, are still more likely to grow up conforming to the stereotype of the non-domestic, practical, unemotional, independent and assertive male, whose role in life is that of 'the provider, the protector and the impregnator'.

These patterns of socialization may be changing, for example through less gender stereotyping in schoolbooks and by teachers, and more role models of female success in education, the media and the labour market. Nevertheless, the narrow, stereotyped gender roles of thirty years ago are still adopted by many of today's children.

Whether there is a change or not, the different socialization of males and females continues to show itself in the **sexual division of labour** in the job market, with jobs being divided into 'men's jobs' and 'women's jobs', and with young men and women often continuing to choose different types of paid employment. Girls today have a strong awareness that they will one day have to balance work and a family, and many cope with this idea by aspiring only to undemanding careers. These divisions in the labour market, and the inequalities which women continue to face in a number of areas of social life, are considered below.

> The **sexual division of labour** refers to the division of work into men's jobs and women's jobs.

The changing status of women in Britain

During the twentieth century, there was a gradual improvement in the status of women in Britain, the outlines of which it is useful to list here. However, as will be seen later, women still face major inequalities compared to men, particularly the conflicting demands of family life and career success.

- Women have achieved more political equality with men, beginning with the powerful and often violent campaign waged by the Suffragette Movement at the beginning of the last century, and, by 1928, women had for the first time the same voting rights as men.

- Women today have equal rights with men in education. It is now illegal to discriminate against women or men by denying them access to certain subjects and courses at school or in further and higher education because of their sex.
- More types of job are seen as suitable for women today, and many more women are going out to work in paid employment. Women now make up about half of the workforce in Britain, which gives them more financial independence.
- Equal opportunity laws have helped women to get a better deal and overcome prejudice and discrimination. For example, laws like the Equal Pay Act (1970), the Equal Pay Act 1970 (Amendment) Regulations (2003), and the Sex Discrimination Act (1975) made it illegal for employers to offer different rates of pay to men and women doing the same or similar work, and to distinguish between men and women in work, leisure and educational opportunities. The Equality and Human Rights Commission helps to enforce these laws and to promote equality of opportunity between men and women.
- Women now have won equal rights with men in property ownership, and, in the event of a divorce, all property acquired during a marraige now has to be divided equally between husband and wife.
- Women have had equal rights with men in divorce since 1923.
- The welfare state has provided more support for lone-parent families, the majority of which are headed by women, and for women caring for dependent husbands and the elderly in the home.
- Girls have exceeded boys in educational success, and women are increasingly well qualified, and better qualified than men in the younger age groups.

> **Activity**
>
> Go to www.equalityhumanrights.com and investigate the kinds of things done by the Equality and Human Rights Commission in relation to gender inequalities. In the light of your findings, suggest three ways the Commission is fighting to improve the position of women, and to prevent discrimination against anyone because of their sex.

Why has the status of women changed?

The changing status of women in Britain over the last century can be explained by a number of factors.

The Suffragette Movement

The Suffragette Movement, which started at the turn of the twentieth century and lasted until 1918, aimed to achieve voting rights for women that were equal with men's in parliamentary elections. This involved a long and often violent struggle against men's ideas about a woman's role. It was the first major struggle by women for equality with men, and began to change the ideas held by both men and women about a woman's role. The success of this campaign gave women political power in elections for the first time, and MPs had to begin to take women's interests into account if they were to be elected.

Two world wars

During the First (1914–18) and Second (1939–45) World Wars, women took over many jobs in factories and farms which were formerly done by men, as the men went off to be soldiers. Women showed during these war years that they were quite capable of doing what had previously been seen as men's jobs, and this began to change people's ideas about a woman's role.

Compulsory education of children

Compulsory schooling since 1880, and particularly since 1944, has reduced the time necessary for the care and supervision of children in the family. Recent improved childcare provision, and access to school for all 3- and 4-year-olds has reduced this time further. This has given women with children greater opportunities to go out to paid work, with more authority derived from having their own income.

The suffragettes at the beginning of the twentieth century (around 1897–1918) were an important landmark in the long and continuing struggle for women's equality in the UK. The picture on the right shows Emmeline Pankhurst, a prominent suffragette who was arrested several times for her activism

The women's movement

The women's movement (one of the new social movements, discussed in chapter 7) first emerged in the 1960s (as the women's liberation movement), and was concerned with the fight to achieve equality with men in a wide range of areas. This movement was not a single group, but consisted of a large number of different women's groups with various aims, both in Britain and abroad. These groups were united by the need to improve the status and rights of women, and to end **patriarchy**, which is the dominance of men in society.

The women's movement challenged many ideas about the traditional role of women, particularly the stereotype that 'a woman's place is in the home'. It has campaigned for:

> **Patriarchy** is where power, status and authority are held by men.

- better nursery facilities
- free contraception and free abortion on demand, and 'a woman's right to choose' whether to have an abortion or not
- equal pay and job opportunities
- the removal of tax and financial discrimination against women
- freedom from violence against women
- the right of women to define their own sexuality.

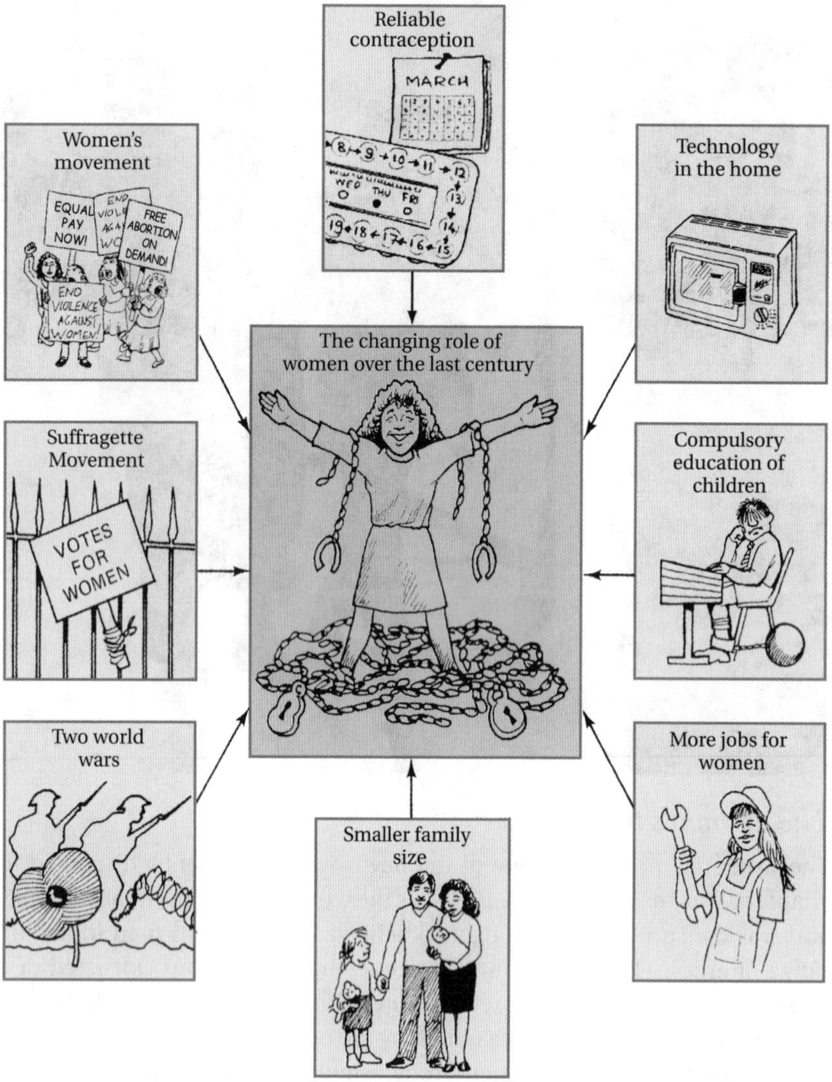

Figure 8.18 Why has the status of women changed over the last century?

The women's movement challenged many people's ideas about women, and has created a climate of expectation in which women now expect to be treated equally and not simply as lovers, housewives and mothers. It is mainly because of pressures from the women's movement that equal opportunity laws have been passed, and that **sexism**, or prejudice and discrimination against people because of their sex, is increasingly seen as unacceptable behaviour.

Reliable contraception

Modern contraception has become a much more reliable means of preventing unwanted children. Since the 1960s, the contraceptive pill has proven

> **Sexism**
> is prejudice or discrimination against people (especially women) because of their sex.

> **Activity**
>
> 1 *Either:* use the Internet and find out what you can about the kinds of actions carried out by women in their campaigns to achieve equality with men. You will find www.historylearningsite.co.uk/suffragettes.htm useful to investigate the suffragettes and the campaign for 'Votes for Women', and www. redstockings.org gives information on the women's liberation movement in the USA (where it started). The Fawcett Society (www.fawcettsociety.org.uk/) has a useful website to investigate current issues.
>
> *Or:* Interview some older female relatives about women's fight for equality in the women's liberation movement of the 1960s.
>
> 2 How do you think these activities might have changed both men's and women's views on women's traditional roles?

very effective, despite some health risks to women, and has enabled women to take control of their fertility, giving them more control over their lives.

Smaller family size

The declining size of families is both a cause and a consequence of the improving status of women. This has reduced the time spent in child rearing and given women greater opportunities to enter paid employment. A typical mother today spends about four years bearing and nursing children, and she can expect to live much longer than her nineteenth-century counterpart. This means, once a woman has had children today, she still has a long life stretching ahead to pursue a career. Increasingly, women are having fewer children, or none at all, and they are having them at an older age after they have established their careers.

More jobs for women

There are more types of job seen as suitable for women today, and legal obstacles to the employment of women have been removed in most cases. Although there still remains a lot of prejudice and discrimination by employers about the suitability of some jobs for women, the way women took over men's jobs during the world wars, and the pressures of the Suffragette Movement and, more recently, the women's movement have helped to erode hostility to female workers among many male bosses and workers.

This increase in employment opportunities for women has come about with the expansion of light industry, manufacturing and the tertiary sector of the economy. The tertiary sector is concerned with services, finance, administration, distribution, transport and government agencies, such as the NHS, the social services and education. The expansion of this sector has increased the number of routine clerical and administrative jobs which are overwhelmingly done by women. There has also been an increase in the number of jobs in the lower professions, such as teaching, social work, and nursing, which employ many women.

Maternity benefits and maternity leave now provide additional encouragement and opportunity for women to return to work after childbirth, as their jobs are kept open for them while they are absent having children. The fact that more women are working gives them greater financial independence and therefore more authority in both the family and society.

Technology in the home

Advances in technology have brought many improvements to the home environment, including better housing standards like central heating, labour-saving devices like freezers, washing machines, microwave cookers, food processors and vacuum cleaners, and manufactured foodstuffs such as canned and frozen foods, ready meals and fast food. It has been suggested that these improvements have reduced the time spent on housework. However, others argue that these developments have simply meant higher standards are expected. For example, automatic washing machines mean that washing is done several times a week instead of just once on 'washing day', and people change their clothes more often. This also creates, of course, more ironing. Similarly, vacuum cleaners mean that houses are expected to be kept cleaner than they used to be.

Activity

1 Despite the improvements in the position of women outlined above, suggest three obstacles or problems that women still face today that men don't.
2 Suggest how you might remove or overcome each of the obstacles or problems you have identified.

Women at work

Unpaid work: domestic labour

When talking about women at work, many people assume this refers to paid employment. However, it is important to remember there is one job which is performed full-time almost exclusively by women – unpaid housework or **domestic labour**.

This domestic labour of women is hardly recognized as 'real work' at all, and carries little status compared with paid employment. This is partly because housework involves women in cleaning up their own and their families' self-generated dirt, doing their own and their families' washing, etc. It is also because no qualifications are needed, and housework is carried out in the privacy of the home, with no recognition by others and no praise, only

Domestic labour refers to unpaid housework, including cooking, cleaning, doing the washing, childcare, and looking after the sick and elderly.

complaints if the work is not done. Many women who are full-time house-wives themselves often undervalue the status of their job, as is summed up in the phrase 'I'm only a housewife.'

Domestic labour has none of the advantages of paid employment, like regular working hours, 'clocking off' after work, chances of promotion, holiday pay or sick pay. As table 8.5 shows, housewives experience far more monotony, fragmentation and speed in their work than workers on even the most gruelling assembly line, but without the compensation of being paid for it.

Activity

Table 8.5 compares housewives' experience of their work with that of factory and assembly line workers.
1   Which group experiences the most monotony in their work?
2   Which group experiences the least speed in their work?
3   In which group did 31 per cent complain of too much speed in their work?
4   Suggest ways the evidence shown in table 8.5 might explain the finding that women who are exclusively housewives suffer more mental health problems than many of the population.
5   What differences are there between working exclusively as a housewife in the home and working in a factory which might make factory workers better able to cope with the monotony, fragmentation and speed of their work?
6   Table 8.5 was based on research in the 1970s. Do you think there have been any important changes since then which might make the experience of working exclusively doing housework less monotonous and fragmented, or make it require less speed today? Give reasons for your answers.
7   Suggest reasons why housework is often seen by many people as not 'real work'.

Table 8.5 The experience of monotony, fragmentation and speed in work: housewives and factory workers compared

Workers	Percentage experiencing:		
	Monotony[a]	Fragmentation[b]	Speed[c]
Housewives	75	90	50
Factory workers	41	70	31
Assembly line workers	67	86	36

[a] Monotony refers to the feeling that the work is boring and repetitive.
[b] Fragmentation refers to the feeling that the work is divided into a series of unconnected tasks not requiring the worker's full attention.
[c] Speed refers to the feeling that the worker has too much to do, with too little time to complete the task, and so has to work at too fast a pace.

Source: A. Oakley, *The Sociology of Housework* (Martin Robertson, 1975)

The Office for National Statistics has calculated that if the time spent on unpaid work in the home was valued at the same average pay rates as equivalent jobs in paid employment – for example, if cooking were paid as it is for cooks (around £21,000 a year, in 2010) or childcare as for nannies and childminders (around £17,000 a year), and caring as for care assistants (£18,000 a year) – it would be worth £739 billion a year.

Housework and childcare are still seen as primarily the responsibility of women. Even when both partners are working full-time outside the home in paid employment, it is still women who are in most cases expected to take the major responsibility for housework and childcare. This means that many full-time working women have two jobs to their male partners' one. The inequalities in domestic labour are discussed in more detail in chapter 3, pages 109–17 and you may wish to refer to these now.

The inequality of women in paid employment

Many of the factors discussed above explaining the changing status of women have brought about a large increase in the employment of women in the last forty years. In 2010, women made up nearly half of the workforce, compared with less than 30 per cent at the beginning of the twentieth century. About 70 per cent of women of working age were in employment in 2010, compared to 56 per cent in 1971. Much of this increase has been among married and cohabiting women with dependent children: less than 10 per cent of married women with dependent children were working in the early twentieth century, but this has now increased to about 72 per cent, including cohabiting women.

Although women have obtained job opportunities and rights previously denied to them, women's position at work is still unequal to men's. Much of this inequality arises because the central role of women is still often seen by a male-dominated society as primarily that of housewife and mother. The following section summarizes the key features of women's employment situation, and describes and explains the main inequalities women face in the labour market.

The sexual division of labour The sexual division of labour refers to the way jobs are divided into 'men's jobs' and 'women's jobs', with women generally working in different types of jobs from men, often in those having lower pay, poorer promotion prospects and lower status than men's. They are more likely than men to be in non-manual work, though this is usually in the more 'menial' non-manual occupations, such as routine clerical work and as sales assistants. Even those women in the professions are most commonly found in the lower ones such as teaching, nursing and social work.

As shown in figure 8.19, men are much more likely to be employed in the top higher managerial and professional group, and table 8.6 shows that few women in this group are in the highest-status and most well-paid and powerful professional jobs. Figure 8.19 also shows that women are mainly employed in jobs which are concentrated at the lower end of the occupational scale: in intermediate and semi-routine and routine occupations, like administrative and secretarial, personal service and sales and customer service jobs, many of which require little or no training. The fact that women are concentrated at the lower end of the salary and occupational status scale is known as *vertical segregation* in the labour market.

Women's jobs are also spread over a far narrower range than, and are of different types from, men's. This is known as *horizontal segregation*. Figure 8.20 shows that about three-quarters of women are employed in four main occupational groups: professional, associate professional and technical occupations (mainly in education, welfare and health); administrative and secretarial; sales and customer service; and personal services (like catering, cleaning, hairdressing and other personal services). As will be considered below, those occupations which are female-dominated are also often the lowest-paid.

Women are mainly employed in low-grade and low-paid jobs which are seen as 'female occupations'. These are often extensions of the traditional domestic roles of housewives and mothers into which many women continue to be socialized. These involve serving and waiting on people, caring for them, cleaning and clearing up after others – all jobs that women have traditionally done in the home. Such jobs include nursing, primary school teaching, secretarial and routine clerical work, low-grade catering work such as that of waitresses and canteen assistants, and working as shop assistants, supermarket 'shelf-fillers' and check-out operators. For example, secretaries serve their (still usually male) bosses, organizing the office to make things easier for them, making them coffee, and providing papers for and clearing up after their meetings; primary school teaching involves childcare; nursing is caring for the sick; catering involves cooking, serving and clearing up meals.

Part-time work　In 2010, around three out of four part-time workers were women, and about 43 per cent of women in paid employment worked only part-time, compared with 12 per cent of men. Surveys suggest this is closely related to women's responsibilities for children and other domestic tasks. Many working women are limited in the jobs they can do and the hours they can work because they are still expected to take responsibility for housework and childcare, and to be at home for the children leaving for and returning

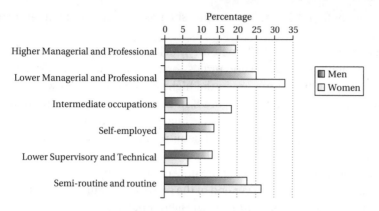

Figure 8.19 The occupations of men and women: UK, 2010

Source: *Labour Force Survey*, Office for National Statistics

Table 8.6 Women and men in top professional jobs: 2007–2010

Job	Women (%)	Men (%)
Senior civil servant (2009)	33	67
Senior police officer (2008)	14	86
MP (May 2010)	22	78
Cabinet minister (May 2010)	17	83
UK Member of the European Parliament (2009)	26	74
Local government chief executive (2008)	25	75
Armed forces senior officer (2007–8)	0.4	99.6
Lord Justice of Appeal (2010)	8	92
High court judge (2010)	15	85
Circuit judge (2010)	15	85
QC (England and Wales, 2009)	7	93
Barrister (England and Wales, 2009)	31	69
Partner in top 100 UK law firms (2008)	20	80
Trade union leader (2007–8)	21	79
Secondary school headteacher (2007)	36	64
General medical practitioner (GP) (England, 2009)	46	54
Directors in top FTSE 100 UK companies (2009)	12	88
All Senior Managers or Officials (2010)	33	67

Sources: NHS Information Centre; Bar Council; Department for Children, Schools and Families (DCSF); Equalities and Human Rights Commission; Ministry of Justice; Government Equalities Office; *Labour Force Survey*; Judicial Database; Judiciary of England and Wales; Office for National Statistics; Annual Civil Service Employment Survey (ACSES)

Figure 8.20 Occupational distribution of working women: UK, 2010

Source: Labour Force Survey, Office for National Statistics

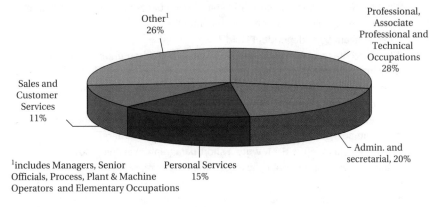

Other[1]
26%

Professional, Associate Professional and Technical Occupations
28%

Sales and Customer Services
11%

Admin. and secretarial, 20%

[1]includes Managers, Senior Officials, Process, Plant & Machine Operators and Elementary Occupations

Personal Services
15%

from school. There are still few workplaces today with childcare facilities which would allow working mothers to take full-time jobs. The presence of dependent children (under the age of 16, or 18 if in full-time education) and the age of the youngest child are the most important factors related to whether or not women are in paid employment, and whether they work full- or part-time. Figure 8.21 illustrates the importance of this link between dependent children and women's patterns of working in paid employment, and how these compare with those of men with dependent children.

Limited career opportunities   Women have more limited career opportunities than men for a number of reasons. Because of gender stereotyping at school and the wider gender-role socialization process, women, even when they have the necessary educational qualifications for the top jobs, often lack the self-confidence and assertiveness to apply for them.

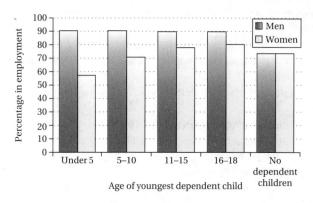

Figure 8.21 Employment Rates,[1] by age of youngest dependent child:[2] UK, 2008

Source: *Labour Force Survey*, Office for National Statistics

<hr>

Activity

Study Figure 8.21 and answer the following questions:

1 What evidence is there in figure 8.21 that, before becoming parents, men and women are equally likely to be in employment?
2 What is meant by a 'dependent child'?
3 What percentage of women of working age with children under the age of 5 were in employment in 2008?
4 What percentage of mothers, compared to fathers, with children under age 10 were in paid employment?
5 What evidence is there that having dependent children seems to have a far greater impact on the working lives of mothers than of fathers?
6 Using the data in figure 8.21, write a short paragraph explaining how the age of the youngest dependent child affects the employment rates of women.
7 Interview a sample of women in paid employment who have small children, and try to discover any problems or role conflict they experience at work and in the home arising from motherhood.

<hr>

There is widespread male prejudice about women in career jobs and senior positions. There is evidence that some men are reluctant to be supervised by female managers, and there is a common male belief that men make better bosses. It is often assumed by employers that any woman of childbearing age will eventually have children, and surveys suggest some employers try to avoid hiring pregnant women or those of childbearing age, and many continue to ask potential women employees about their family plans, even though such questions are illegal under discrimination laws.

<hr>

[1] The proportion of the population of working-age men (aged 16–64) and women (aged 16–59) who are in employment.
[2] Children under 16 or children aged 16–18 who have never married and are in full-time education.

Many employers still ask women discriminatory questions

Do you agree with the suggestion in the cartoon that the questions being asked at the interview discriminate against women, or do you think employers have a right to ask such questions? Do you think discrimination against women is still a problem in education, work and leisure activities?

Women with children, particularly, are often seen as unreliable because of the assumption they will be unable to cope with the demands of the job and balance work and family life, and will try to avoid work during school holidays, or be absent to look after sick children, although research has shown there is little difference in absence from work between men and women who share the same circumstances. Around three-quarters of all complaints of sex discrimination to the former Equal Opportunities Commission came from women, and it estimated that 30,000 women a year lost their jobs as a result of becoming pregnant.

Even successful women in career jobs often find they come up against what has been called the **glass ceiling** – an invisible barrier of discrimination which makes it difficult for women to reach the same top levels in their chosen careers as similarly qualified men. These factors mean women are often overlooked for training and promotion to senior positions by male employers.

In addition, women with promising careers may have to leave jobs temporarily to have children, and therefore miss out on relevant experience, training and promotion opportunities. Top jobs require a continuous career pattern in the 20–35 age period – yet these are the usual childbearing years for women, so while men continue to work and get promoted, women miss their opportunities.

The **glass ceiling** refers to an invisible barrier of discrimination which makes it difficult for women to reach the same top levels in their chosen careers as similarly qualified men.

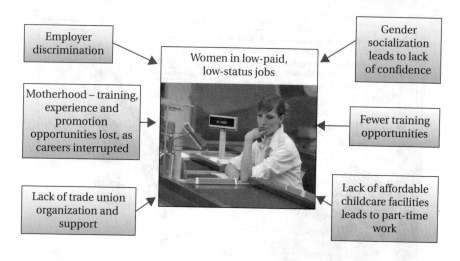

Figure 8.22 Why are women concentrated in lower-paid and lower-status jobs than men?

Finally, married or cohabiting women are still more likely to move house and area for their male partner's job promotion than for their own. This means women interrupt their careers and have to start again, often at a lower level, in a new job, which means the men are getting promotion at the expense of lost opportunities for their partners.

Limited access to training   Women are less likely than men to enter training for better-paid and more secure skilled work. Often women are denied training, and therefore promotion opportunities, because employers, parents, teachers, and sometimes the women themselves see training as 'wasted' on women. Employers, as a result of gender socialization, may assume women will leave work to produce and raise children. They may therefore be unwilling to invest in expensive training programmes for women. Rather, they prefer to employ women in low-skilled jobs where they can be easily and quickly trained and replaced. Of the small number of women who do obtain training, the vast majority are employed in 'feminine occupations' such as hairdressing, beauty and clerical work, which are generally low-paid with limited career prospects.

Lower pay   While the Equal Pay Act gives equal pay to women if they do the same (or similar) work as men, it has been shown above that women often do not do the same work as men, and consequently have no one to claim equal pay with. For example, many more women work in the low-paid 'caring' occupations than men, and there may often be no males to compare their wages with. In 2009 women made up around two-thirds of all low-paid workers, and 22 per cent of women in employment were on low pay, compared to 11 per cent of men. Women have fewer opportunities to increase their pay through overtime, shift payments or bonuses.

A 2009 report by the British Medical Association found that female doctors working in the NHS are paid thousands of pounds less than their similarly qualified male colleagues as a result of widespread discrimination and a hostile culture at work faced by women doctors with children

According to the Government's Equalities Office, in 2009 female part-time workers earned between 36 and 39 per cent less each hour than male part-time workers, and the average hourly pay of full-time working women was only around 83–87 per cent of that of men. The ten worst-paid jobs in Britain are all performed mainly by women. In a nutshell, this is because many women are concentrated in low-skilled and part-time work, which lacks promotion prospects and trade union protection, and often sick pay, holiday pay and redundancy payments – a situation which does not apply to the majority of men.

THE TEN LOWEST-PAID JOBS IN THE UNITED KINGDOM. . .

Leisure and theme park attendant
Waiter, waitress
Laundry and dry cleaning worker
Flower arranger, florist
Elementary sales work (e.g. counter assistant)
Elementary office work (e.g. routine office assistant)
Hairdresser
Retail cashier and check-out operator
Bar staff
School mid-day assistant

. . . and they're nearly all done by women!

Source: 2009 Annual Survey of Hours and Earnings (ASHE), Office for National Statistics

---

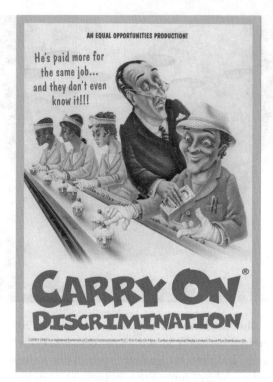

Reproduced with permission of the Equal Opportunities Commission (now incorporated into the Equality and Human Rights Commission)

Women and social mobility

Women have traditionally had poorer chances of mobility than men, with women being mainly concentrated in semi-skilled manual occupations, routine administrative, secretarial and sales work, and the lower professions such as teaching and nursing. However, the better performance of women in education, their growing participation in the labour force and equal opportunities policies at work are now giving women more favourable opportunities for upward mobility. Nevertheless, for the reasons considered above, women still face major difficulties in entering skilled manual and higher managerial, technical and top professional occupations. They have less chance of promotion than men, and many women experience downward mobility as they abandon careers with bright futures to take care of children, only to return to work at a lower status, and with less pay, than when they left. There are still very few women compared with men in the top elite positions in society – those small groups of occupations which hold a great deal of power, such as judges, leaders of industry, top civil servants, and MPs and government ministers.

Conclusion on gender inequalities

There have been great improvements in the position of women over the last century, particularly from the 1970s onwards under the impact of the women's movement. Attitudes have changed, and sexism has become less acceptable. Women have become more self-confident and assertive. They are now outstripping males at every level in education. Women are becoming more successful than men in many areas of the labour market, such as in the music industry and in business and the professions, like law and medicine, and are beginning to break through the glass ceiling to career success. Females often have better 'people' and communication skills than males, and these are the skills which are required for success in the new service economy – dealing with customers, orders, clients and complaints. The traditional stereotype of women as mothers and carers, with prime responsibility for running the home and family, is slowly being replaced by role models of strong, independent and successful women in all spheres of life, as women are beginning to achieve more success and influence in society generally.

However, women are still more likely to face poverty than men, and women alone head one in five families with dependent children. Women still earn less than men and have poorer career opportunities, and there are still few women in any of the top positions of power and influence in society. It is women rather than men who are more likely to face daily sexual harassment at work. Housework and childcare remain the primary responsibility of women, undermining their ability to compete with men on equal terms in paid employment, reducing their financial independence and restricting their power in society. As discussed in chapter 3, women remain overwhelmingly the victims of violence in the home. While women have gained much over the last century, there still remains some considerable distance to travel before women achieve equality with men in many areas of life in modern Britain.

Activity

This section has mainly focused on the inequalities facing women in paid and unpaid work.

1 What other inequalities do women face in their daily lives compared with men? Think about things like going into pubs alone, fear of attack and sexual assault, politics, and so on. List all those you can think of.

2 In the light of the issues raised in this chapter and your responses to the activity above, consider what steps might be taken to break down these inequalities. To help you do this, draw three columns. In the first column, list all the inequalities you can think of that women still face today compared with men; in the second column, list the causes of these inequalities; in the third column, list the changes that would need to be made in society to remove these inequalities.

ETHNICITY AND INEQUALITY

Race, ethnicity and minority ethnic groups

The idea of **race** refers to the attempt to divide humans according to physical characteristics (like skin colour) into different racial groups, such as Caucasian (white), Negroid (black African) or Mongoloid (Chinese). Such classifications have little scientific basis, and sociologists generally regard this as a rather pointless exercise, as it has no value in explaining human culture, such as social inequality. This is because human behaviour is largely a result of socialization, and cannot be explained by purely biological characteristics.

Ethnicity is a more valuable idea. This refers to the common culture shared by a social group, such as language, religion, styles of dress, food, shared history and experiences, and so on. An **ethnic group** is any group which shares a common culture, and a **minority ethnic group** is a group which shares a cultural identity which is in some respects different from that of the majority population of a society. This means that groups such as Travellers, the Polish and the Irish are all minority ethnic groups in Britain, as well as ethnic groups of a different skin colour, such as Asian, Chinese and black communities.

There is a wide range of ethnic groups who have emigrated to Britain over the years, such as the Irish, the Chinese, the Jews, the Poles, Indian, Pakistani and Bangladeshi Asians, and Black Africans, Black Caribbeans (together termed 'Black' or 'African-Caribbeans') and more recently people from Eastern Europe, such as the Czech Republic, Romania, Bulgaria, Estonia, Hungary, Latvia and Lithuania. However, when most people think of 'minority ethnic groups' they think of people of a different racial origin – of a different skin colour – and white people in Britain tend to think mainly of those of African-Caribbean or Asian origin, although recent immigrants and migrant workers from Eastern Europe are also becoming more commonly seen as a minority ethnic group. It is important to recognize that all minority ethnic groups do not share the same cultural features. For example, Asians and African-Caribbeans show especially strong cultural differences, and Indian Asians may be Sikhs (the largest group in Britain) or Hindus, while Pakistanis and Bangladeshis are more likely to be Muslims. Recent migrants from Eastern Europe come from a range of different cultural backgrounds.

Only about 8 per cent of the population of Britain are non-white, and these make up a small minority of all immigrants. Asians and African-Caribbeans together form about 5 per cent of the population of Britain. Well over half the minority ethnic population were actually born here, so it is mislead-

Race refers to the division of humans into different groups according to physical characteristics, like skin colour.
Ethnicity refers to a common culture, such as language, religion and beliefs.
An **ethnic group** is a group of people who share a common culture. A **minority ethnic group** is a group which shares a cultural identity which is in some respects different from that of the majority population of a society.

ing to regard them as immigrants, while over half of those who really are immigrants have lived here for more than thirty years.

The evidence on minority ethnic groups and social inequality

While some minority ethnic groups are doing very well in Britain, black and Asian people often face a series of disadvantages and poorer life chances than their white counterparts. Pakistanis, Bangladeshis and African-Caribbeans in particular face a series of disadvantages in Britain compared with the white majority, although there are differences within each group. Particular groups seem to suffer an 'ethnic penalty' in some situations – a range of inequalities which cannot be explained by any other factors apart from ethnicity, suggesting that the causes lie in direct and indirect discrimination. For example, in education, black pupils face higher risks of being excluded from school than white pupils committing similar offences, and have lower levels of achievement than those from similar social class backgrounds. As the government itself points out, 'if you are black, you are around eight times more likely to be stopped and searched by the police, six times more likely to be in prison and three times more likely to be arrested than someone who is white' (from *Tackling Race Inequality: A Statement on Race*, Department of Communities and Local Government, 2009).

Some of these inequalities and disadvantages are discussed in chapter 4 on education (see pages 213–16), chapter 5 on crime and deviance (see

She has good reasons to look worried – although some of those from minority ethnic groups are doing very well in Britain, many still face a series of disadvantages and poorer life chances than their white counterparts. Why might that be?

WHO SAYS ETHNIC MINORITIES CAN'T GET JOBS? THERE ARE OPENINGS EVERYWHERE.

COMMISSION FOR RACIAL EQUALITY

Reproduced with permission of the Commission for Racial Equality (now incorporated into the Equality and Human Rights Commission)

pages 257–62), chapter 6 on the media, (see pages 304–5) and chapter 9 on health (see pages 519–21). You should refer to these sections. This section will examine additional inequalities in employment, low pay, poverty, social mobility and housing.

Employment and unemployment

Nearly all minority ethnic groups are less likely to be in paid employment than similarly qualified white British men and women. During the economic recession of 2008–10, black and Asian unemployment grew at a faster rate than that for white people, and in 2009, nearly half (48 per cent) of 16- to 24-year-old black people reported themselves as unemployed, compared to 20 per cent of white people of the same age. Other findings show:

- African-Caribbeans, Pakistanis and Bangladeshis are less likely than white people to secure the best jobs. These groups are under-represented in non-manual occupations, particularly in managerial and professional work. They are hugely under-represented in Parliament and the top elite occupations. For example, only 4.3 per cent of senior civil servants were from minority ethnic groups in 2008. There have only ever been four non-white Cabinet ministers in Britain, and (in 2010) there were only 27 MPs (4 per cent of the total) from ethnic minority back-grounds. There are few black and Asian leaders in local government, and despite the relatively large number of minority ethnic group employees in the NHS, 99 per cent of chief executives are white.
- Black and minority ethnic groups are over-represented (that is, there are more of them than there should be given their proportion in the popula-tion) in semi-skilled and unskilled manual occupations, and they often work longer and more unsociable hours (shiftwork and night work) than white people. Black and Asian people are less likely to get employed

Figure 8.23 Unemployment rates,[1] by ethnic group: United Kingdom, April–June 2010

[1] The unemployment rate is the number unemployed as a percentage of all those active in the labour market.

Source: Labour Force Survey, Office for National Statistics, 2010

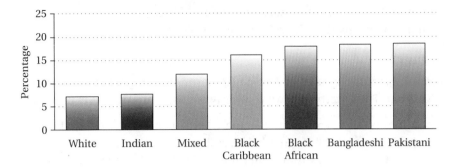

when competing with white British people with the same qualifications for the same job.

- People from minority ethnic groups are more likely to face unemployment, as shown in figure 8.23.
- Employment rates for Black and Pakistani/Bangladeshi men with university degrees are 6 per cent less than for White British men with degrees, and for women it is 11 per cent less than White British women with degrees. This gap widens to up to 44 per cent for those with no qualifications.
- Skilled and experienced women from minority ethnic groups are around twice as likely as white women to be unemployed. Black and Asian women frequently work longer hours in poor conditions than white women or men, and receive roughly three-quarters of white women's pay, even though they are on average better educated.

Lower pay

Black and Asian people have lower average earnings, even when they have the same job level as white people. On average, Pakistani and Bangladeshi men earn just over half the salary of white men, while African-Caribbean men earn about two-thirds. Asian women receive roughly three-quarters of white women's pay, even though they are on average better educated.

According to the Low Pay Commission (*National Minimum Wage,* Low Pay Commission Report, 2009), despite some specific ethnic minority groups, such as the Chinese, receiving higher earnings than white workers on average, ethnic minority groups:

- are more likely to work in low-paying industries, with security, hospitality and textiles employing the highest proportions
- are over 50 per cent more likely to be paid at the National Minimum Wage compared to all those employed
- have a significant proportion paid at the minimum wage.

The Low Pay Commission also found that many skilled migrant workers, like those from the Czech Republic, Slovakia, Hungary and Poland, were employed in unskilled low-paid work, and it identified migrant workers as a group that was particularly vulnerable to exploitation.

Poverty

Households Below Average Income (Department for Work and Pensions, 2010) and The Poverty Site (www.poverty.org.uk/) showed that in 2008–9:

- Minority ethnic groups were far more likely than white people to be in the poorest fifth of the population, as figure 8.24 shows.
- Two-fifths of people from ethnic minorities live in low-income households compared to one-fifth of white households.
- More than half of people from Bangladeshi and Pakistani ethnic backgrounds live in low-income households.
- 60 per cent of Bangladeshi families, 45 per cent of Pakistanis and 30 per cent of Black African families live in low-income households even when at least one adult is in paid employment, compared with 10 per cent of white families.
- Almost half of all children from ethnic minorities live in low-income households compared to a quarter of White British children.

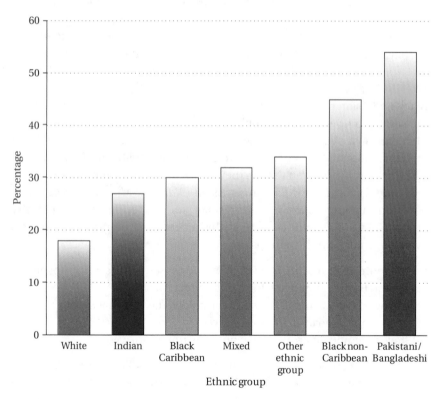

Figure 8.24 Percentage of each ethnic group in the poorest fifth of the population: United Kingdom, 2008–9

Source: Households Below Average Income (Department for Work and Pensions, 2010)

Social mobility

There have been relatively few studies of social mobility and ethnicity. However, the minority ethnic groups experience more upward and downward mobility than the white majority. While some minority ethnic groups are experiencing rapid upward mobility, and there is a rapidly growing black and Asian middle class, they still face a range of disadvantages. For example, while around 90 per cent of white British graduates are in middle-class jobs, only 56 per cent of Pakistani, 62 per cent of Indian and 68 per cent of African-Caribbean graduates are in such jobs.

Housing

Black and minority ethnic groups overall face the following housing inequalities.

- They tend to live in inferior housing to white people and in poorer and 'less desirable' areas of towns and cities.
- They tend to live in older properties than whites, and are more likely to live in a terraced house or flat.
- They face much higher levels of overcrowding than white households. Black and minority ethnic groups are six times as likely to live in overcrowded accommodation, and account for more than a third (36 per cent) of those living in overcrowded homes. Around 30 per cent of Bangladeshi households are overcrowded.
- They are more likely to live in rented accommodation, as table 8.7 shows, particularly in social housing (council or housing association properties), where they are often allocated the least desirable homes. Indian Asians, however, are more likely to be owner occupiers than whites are, although the quality of the Indian Asians' housing is often poor, and tends to be in the least desirable and cheaper areas.
- They are more likely than whites to be homeless. Around a quarter of those accepted as homeless by local authorities in England are from ethnic minorities, and ethnic minority households are around three times as likely to become homeless as the white population (from www.poverty.org.uk).

Explaining ethnic inequalities

The following explanations for ethnic disadvantage should be considered together, as they are cumulative, in that one aspect of discrimination or disadvantage can lead to further disadvantage in other areas. It is also important to remember that the social class and gender inequalities discussed earlier in this chapter also combine with ethnic disadvantages, and all three of these can combine to make ethnic inequality worse, such as in the case of

Table 8.7 Tenure by ethnic group of household reference person, England, 2008			
	Owner occupier %	Rented from social sector %	Rented privately %	All tenures (=100%) (thousands)
Minority ethnic group			
- Black Caribbean	49	41	11	269
- Black African	28	44	28	246
- Indian	74	7	20	387
- Pakistani	68	16	16	221
- Bangladeshi	38	47	15	92
All minority ethnic groups	50	26	24	1902
White	79	17	13	19 062
All ethnic groups	68	18	14	20 964

Source: Survey of English Housing (Department of Communities and Local Government, 2009)

Bangladeshi working-class women, who are probably the most deprived group in Britain. At the same time, it is also important not to develop crude stereotypes like 'ethnicity equals poverty', as that overlooks the great successes of some people from all ethnic backgrounds, particularly those of Indian and Chinese ethnicity, and it also disguises the fact that there are also widespread disadvantages facing the white British working class.

Social class

Many of the black and Asian population are working-class, and therefore face the same problems encountered by all working-class people, regardless of their ethnic origin. This would explain their disadvantage compared with the population as a whole. However, there is also evidence of additional racial prejudice and racial discrimination, discussed below.

Education

Underachievement in education, with some minority ethnic groups performing below their ability in the education system (see chapter 4), may partly explain why some minority ethnic groups are under-represented in managerial and professional work, and more likely to be found in unskilled and semi-skilled occupations. These occupations tend to be those most at risk in times of recession, which helps to explain the higher levels of unemployment among black and Asian people. However, discrimination might well mean that they are more likely to be singled out for redundancy when the axe falls.

The generally lower pay of Asian and African-Caribbean minorities which follows from these explanations might explain their inferior housing. However, there is evidence of discrimination among private landlords, letting agencies and council officials in allocating housing to black and Asian people.

Social capital

Social capital refers to the social networks of influence and support that people have, such as links of friends and family connections, and knowing the 'right people', who to talk to, who to get advice from, and who is in a position to help them (or their children) in times of difficulty or need, and to influence others in their favour. Possession of social capital is highest in the white middle and upper classes, and can provide a network of skills and support to help their children's education, finding the best schools, and connections to help them find jobs and take advantage of opportunities. Minority ethnic groups may either have weaker social capital, or less influential networks to help them take up opportunities.

> **Social capital** refers to the social networks of influence and support that people have.

Activity

1 Refer to table 8.7.
   (a) Which ethnic group is most likely to own the homes they occupy?
   (b) Which ethnic group is most likely to rent their home privately?
   (c) What is the difference in the percentage of white people who own their own home compared to all minority ethnic groups?
2 Look back over the section so far on ethnicity and inequality, and answer the following questions:
   (a) Which *white* minority ethnic group is most likely to be employed in low-paid work?
   (b) Which minority ethnic group is most likely to be unemployed?
   (c) Which minority ethnic group is most likely to be living in the poorest fifth of the population?
   (d) Which ethnic minority group appears to face the greatest overall disadvantages? Give reasons for your answer, and refer to some evidence.
   (e) Suggest two other forms of inequality facing minority ethnic groups *other than* those in employment, pay, poverty, housing and social mobility.
   (f) Minority ethnic working-class women are frequently the most disadvantaged social group of all. Drawing on your knowledge of gender, ethnic and class divisions, suggest possible explanations for this.

Racial prejudice and discrimination

- **Racial prejudice** is a set of assumptions about a racial group which people are reluctant to change even when they receive information which undermines those assumptions.
- **Racial discrimination** is when people's racial prejudices cause them to act unfairly against a racial group. For example, a racially prejudiced police officer might use his or her power to pick on black or Asian people more than white people, perhaps by stopping them in the street and asking what they're up to.
- **Racism** is believing or acting as though an individual or group is superior or inferior on the grounds of racial or ethnic origins – usually based on skin colour or other physical characteristics – and suggesting that groups defined as inferior have lower intelligence and abilities. Racism involves both racial prejudice and racial discrimination, and encourages hostile feelings and actions towards groups defined as inferior.
- **Institutional racism** is 'The collective failure of an organization to provide an appropriate and professional service to people because of their culture, colour or ethnic origin. It can be seen or detected in processes, attitudes and behaviour which amount to discrimination through unwitting prejudice, ignorance, and thoughtless and racist stereotyping which disadvantages minority ethnic people.' (Macpherson Report, 1999). (See the box on 'The Stephen Lawrence Inquiry and the Macpherson Report' on page 262.)

Activity

With reference to the definition of institutional racism given above, suggest ways that an organization might be unwittingly (that is, not consciously or deliberately) disadvantaging people from minority ethnic groups. An example might be not providing information in minority languages.

The 1976 Race Relations Act, amended in 2000, made it illegal to discriminate on the grounds of race in employment and housing, and to 'incite racial hatred', and this was strengthened by the establishment of the Commission for Racial Equality in 1976 (now incorporated into the Equality and Human Rights Commission). However, there is widespread evidence that racial discrimination in employment, housing and other areas continues, particularly against those with a skin colour other than white. Part of the problem is that it is difficult to prove racial discrimination. A black or Asian person who is turned down for promotion at work in favour of a white person may be told the white person was simply more suited to the job in some way.

The most straightforward explanation for disadvantages in employment is that they result from racism and prejudice by employers, who either refuse

to employ some minority ethnic groups, or employ them only in low-status and low-paid jobs, or refuse to promote them. This view has been confirmed by a number of surveys in which it was found that white workers received more positive responses in job applications than similarly qualified and experienced applicants from minority ethnic groups. For example, a 1990s survey by the Commission for Racial Equality found that white people were five times more likely to get interviews for jobs than black and Asian people with the same qualifications. Research in 2009 uncovered widespread racial discrimination in job applications against workers with African and Asian names (*A Test for Racial Discrimination in Recruitment Practice in British Cities*, Research Report No 607, Department for Work and Pensions, 2009).

The fear of racism affects where black and minority ethnic groups choose to live, as they seek to reduce the risks of racial abuse and attack by avoiding neighbourhoods they know to be racist and therefore unsafe for them. This restricts their choices in housing and the areas they can live in, even without the direct discrimination of racist landlords.

Are the inequalities facing minority ethnic groups reducing?

Grounds for optimism

Being black or Asian in Britain is often portrayed as a story of racial inequality, prejudice and discrimination. Yet the news is not all bad. The existence of institutional racism has now been officially recognized, and action taken to tackle racism in a wide range of public services and private organizations.

Activity

THERE ARE LOTS OF PLACES IN BRITAIN
WHERE RACISM DOESN'T EXIST.

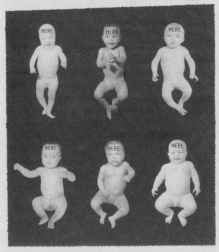

1 Refer to the 'Babies' poster from the Commission for Racial Equality (now incorporated into the Equality and Human Rights Commission). What point is the poster making?

2 Below are four possible explanations for racism. Study them carefully, discuss them in your group, and think of any other reasons why minority ethnic groups face racial prejudice and discrimination. Then, for each explanation, suggest a means of overcoming it.

   (a) *History*. Our society has a long history of white domination of African and Asian countries. Slavery and colonization were often justified on the basis of ideas about the supposed superiority of white people to those of other ethnic origins. These ideas still tend to linger on.

   (b) *Stereotyping*. A stereotype is a generalized, over-simplified view of the features of a social group, allowing for few individual differences between its members. Often the media portray degrading and insulting stereotypes of minority ethnic groups which fuel racism.

   (c) *Scapegoating*. Scapegoats are individuals or groups blamed for something which is not their fault. When unemployment, poverty and crime rates rise, it becomes easy to find simple explanations by scapegoating easily identifiable minorities, such as minority ethnic groups or asylum seekers.

   (d) *Cultural differences*. In any society where there are cultural differences between groups, such as in religious beliefs, values, customs, food, dress, and so on, there are bound to be conflicts from time to time between the minority cultures and the majority culture.

The Race Relations Act 1976 and the Race Relations (Amendment) Act 2000 have sought to tackle racism in all areas of social life, and every single public service in Britain, including schools, now has a legal obligation to positively promote race equality and better race relations.

In 2003 there were, for the first time, two non-white members of the Cabinet in Downing Street, and, in 2010, the number of MPs from ethnic minority backgrounds doubled, and Britain had its first-ever female Muslim Cabinet Minister in Baroness Warsi, who was also the first Muslim to become Chair of the Conservative Party. National and local government and some large private companies in Britain are trying to improve the under-representation of minority ethnic groups in important areas of social life, using measures like advertising jobs in minority ethnic newspapers, and race awareness courses for recruiting staff. Monitoring of job applications for ethnic bias is becoming increasingly common, and equal opportunities policies to combat discrimination are being adopted by schools, colleges, and private and public sector employers. Many schools now include multi-cultural education as an important part of the curriculum. In October 2003, Britain saw the appointment of a black chief constable for the first time in history.

In some areas, such as education, some minority ethnic groups are doing better and are much more likely to continue their education beyond the age of 16/17 than their white counterparts, and there is a growing black and Asian middle class.

Grounds for pessimism

Despite these reasons for optimism, this chapter has shown that major problems of inequality still confront the minority ethnic groups of Britain. Racist attitudes are still widespread. Three in ten people admitted to being 'very' or 'a little' prejudiced against people of other races in the 2007 British Social Attitudes Survey; and nearly one in five employees thought that there was some prejudice in their workplace against Asian employees, 13 per cent thought this in relation to black employees, and around a quarter of employees thought that their colleagues would mind if an Asian with suitable qualifications was appointed as their boss. One in three people thought that equal opportunity measures for black and Asian people had gone too far.

The 1999 Macpherson Report showed the continued widespread existence of real discrimination and prejudice and institutional racism in some key sectors of British society.

There are no black or Asian chiefs of the armed forces, few in the police force; and only 4 per cent of MPs in 2010 were non-white – under half their proportion in the population as a whole. Ethnic minorities remain under-represented in many high-status positions of power in contemporary Britain. There are more black and Asian university students, but black and

Black and Pakistani/Bangladeshi university graduates are far more likely to face unemployment than their white counterparts

Asian graduates face a higher unemployment rate than white graduates. Many black and Asian people are worse-off than white people with similar qualifications. More than half of people from Bangladeshi and Pakistani ethnic backgrounds live below the poverty line. Opportunities for Britain's minority ethnic groups, whether they be in education, jobs or housing, are still far fewer than for white people. Black and Asian people are still worse-off than white people as victims of crime and in their dealings with the law.

Activity

In three columns, as suggested below, make a list of all the inequalities facing minority ethnic groups, including those from the other chapters referred to at the beginning of this section, then in the second column put down some of the causes for the inequality you've identified, and in the third column suggest policies or steps that could be taken to overcome these inequalities.

INEQUALITY FACED   POSSIBLE CAUSES   POSSIBLE SOLUTIONS

AGE AND INEQUALITY

Age is not in itself a significant feature of inequality in contemporary Britain, and the age group to which you belong does not in itself have a major impact on your life chances, in the way that social class, gender, or ethnicity does.

Nonetheless, for the two extremes of the age range – children and young people (0–21) and older people (65+) – there are some significant differences from people of other ages.

The social construction of age

When something is a social construction, it means it is created through the individual, social and cultural interpretations, perceptions and actions of people. Age and age groups are social constructions, as how old you are is not simply, or even most importantly, a matter of biological development. The status allocated to people of different biological ages is created by society and social attitudes, and not simply moulded by biology, and there are often different norms, values and expectations of behaviour associated with different ages.

Attitudes to age vary between cultures. In some societies old people have high status as the 'elders' of a community, while in modern Britain older people generally tend to lack status and authority, though this can vary between ethnic groups. In the Asian and Chinese communities, for example, elderly people are still often held in high esteem. Social attitudes to people of different ages can change over time. In medieval times, childhood did not exist as a separate status. Children often moved straight from infancy, when they required constant care, to working roles in the community. Children were seen as 'little adults'. They did not lead separate lives, and dressed like, and mixed with, adults. Childhood was certainly not the specially protected and privileged time of life we associate with children today, with their legal protection, extended education and freedom from work.

The social construction of age means that we tend to think of people in terms of age groups in contemporary British culture, such as 'infancy', 'childhood', 'teenager', 'youth', 'young' and 'mature' adulthood, 'middle age' or 'old age'. The age group to which we belong can have important consequences for status in society, particularly for the young and the old, but often

These women are all of a very similar age. However, their levels of physical activity, independence and knowledge of the latest technology are very likely to determine which one you consider to be the 'oldest'

this is for quite short periods of time in the case of young people, as they grow up. The age group to which we belong does not generally have much impact on our life chances, and as the following section suggests, social class, gender and ethnicity are much more significant than age as sources of inequality.

Is age a significant source of social inequality?

Research by the Equality and Human Rights Commission (EHRC) (Michele Lee, *Just Ageing? Fairness, Equality and the Life Course*, EHRC, 2009) suggested that inequality between different groups within the same generation of people, such as middle-class and working-class groups, is greater than inequality between generations.

A **generation** refers to those born in the same 15- to 30-year periods.

The report said that the key basis of these social inequalities within generations, as well as any between different generations or age groups, was not mainly because of age, but because of social class, gender and ethnic inequalities, like those considered in this chapter. Inequalities among older people, such as those in income, poverty, health, housing, access to and use of public services, particularly health services, and life expectancy (how long people live) were primarily due to social class related factors. These included factors like the social class in which they grew up in childhood, their own educational achievements and occupations as adults, and periods of unemployment. For example, a person with no educational qualifications has a much higher risk of poverty, and a lower chance of being employed, in later life, than a person with educational qualifications. People from low-paid occupational backgrounds are more likely to be in poor health and living in poverty when they are older, even if they have been employed for all of their working lives.

The report also confirmed that gender differences created inequalities throughout life. Women in lower-classed occupations are less likely to be working in later life, and though women live longer than men, they spend more years in poor health, and are more likely than men to be in poverty when they are older. People of all ages from ethnic minority groups in the UK are more likely to have poor physical and mental health, and to have lower pensions in later life, compared with White groups.

The following sections therefore only identify some inequalities linked specifically to age, rather than social class, gender and ethnicity. However, it is likely that these inequalities are experienced in different ways by those from different social class, gender and ethnic backgrounds.

Young people and inequality

Inequalities among young people, say from ages 0 to 21, primarily arise from a desire to protect their overall health and safety, security and well-being, to protect them from exploitation and harm, and to prevent them from engaging in activities in which they are thought not yet to be mature or responsible enough to participate, such as marriage (age 16 with parent/guardian consent, otherwise age 18), driving a car (age 17) and voting and becoming a Member of Parliament or a local councillor (age 18). There are therefore a mass of laws which, in effect, give them fewer legal rights than those of other ages, and stop them from doing and buying things until they reach certain ages. There are also laws that try to protect them against exploitation – such as minimum wage regulations – and against child abuse and paedophilia. Some examples of these are shown below.

- Those under 14 (13 in some areas) aren't allowed to undertake paid work, except for odd jobs for a parent, relative or neighbour, babysitting, light work like a paper round, and some specially licensed sport, advertising, modelling or appearing in plays, films, television shows or other entertainment.
- Young workers (over school leaving age and under 18) are not allowed to work in a factory, construction work or transport.
- Those under school leaving age are not allowed to work during school hours or for more than two hours on any school day or 12 hours in any week, or before 7 a.m. or after 7 p.m.
- Those under the age of 16 (the age of consent) cannot legally engage in sexual acts.
- Shopkeepers cannot legally sell lottery tickets, aerosol paints and petrol to under-16s, or cigarettes, tobacco, solvents, lighter fuel, knives and alcohol to under-18s.
- Films, DVDs, video and computer games have '12', '15' and '18' age restrictions.

The Low Pay Commission pointed out that, in 2008, over 60 per cent of those aged 16–21 were employed in low-paying occupations, more than double the proportion of those of all ages. Young people are often at risk of exploitation when they are employed, and, like adults, are protected by a legally set National Minimum Wage. No employer can pay less than this legal rate without breaking the law. However, there are separate rates for 16- to 17- and 18- to 21-year-olds, which are both less than the adult rate. While this is a clear inequality, the reason given is so that young people aren't encouraged into work before they have finished the preferred options of education and training, which bring long-term benefits.

Young people are also particularly vulnerable to unemployment during periods of economic recession, as firms stop hiring and usually make their least-skilled workers redundant first.

Older people and inequality

One in four children born today can expect to live to be 100, and the average person can expect to live a quarter of their lives in retirement. In mid-2005 one in three people in Britain were aged 50 or over, and in twenty years' time, a quarter of all adults will be over 65 and the number of people over 85 will have doubled. Greater life expectancy means people may be in the 'older' age group for perhaps longer than in any other age group. This means that more people than ever before face an extended period of living with the social class, gender and ethnic inequalities discussed in this chapter, and that have blighted their lives, with these worsening as their health and income decline as they leave paid work and grow older.

People aged between 50 and 64 have the highest disposable income (uncommitted spending money) of any age group, and the 'grey pound' (older people's spending) is very important to businesses, and, increasingly, new businesses are opening up that market to older people and are dedicated to their needs, such as SAGA.

Age discrimination: ageism

Despite being a significant proportion of the population and a major market for business, older people often suffer prejudice and discrimination, with negative stereotyped assumptions that they are less intelligent, forgetful, 'grumpy' and 'moaning', in poor health, incapable and dependent on others, and so on – simply because they are old. Older people, particularly, are likely to encounter age discrimination or ageism.

Ageism can have detrimental effects on older people, and they may face being called derogatory (offensive and belittling) names and having negative media images ('dirty old man', 'boring old fart', 'grumpy old woman'), being infantilized (treated like infants/children), being denied a sexual identity, face barriers to proper medical treatment (such as not being referred to a consultant due to being too old) and losing jobs or facing obstacles to getting jobs on the grounds of age.

> **Ageism** is stereotyping, prejudice and discrimination against individuals or groups on the grounds of their age.

The Government Equalities Office in 2009 reported that one in four people aged between 49 and 63 said they were experiencing age discrimination, with nearly half of them saying they thought that discrimination in general would get worse as they got older. Of those aged 80 and over, 31 per cent felt discriminated against when trying to obtain quotations for motor insurance, travel insurance and car hire, compared with 2 per cent of those aged between 30 and 49.

Evidence from Age UK in January 2010 revealed half of motor insurers and a third of travel insurers automatically exclude people aged 80-plus seeking quotes, irrespective of their health status. From the age of 70, motorists have

Discrimination on age grounds is a major inequality facing older people. Ask a few of your older relatives if they have experienced any form of age discrimination

to declare any medical conditions and renew their driving licence every three years, even if there is nothing wrong with them or their driving skills. The employment rate of those over state pension age was 12 per cent (Autumn 2009), despite the fact that a majority of people say they would like to do some kind of work for longer than this. Many elderly people are discouraged by employers from continuing in work beyond retirement age, even if they are still perfectly capable of doing their jobs.

Age discrimination and harassment in employment were outlawed by the Employment Equality (Age) Regulations of 2006, and the Equality Act of 2010 banned age discrimination outside the workplace. However, like racial discrimination discussed earlier, age discrimination may turn out to be difficult to prove in some circumstances.

One more positive aspect of inequality in relation to older people that gives them advantages over all other age groups is the extra benefits that come from the state, such as free prescriptions, free eyesight tests and free off-peak bus travel for the over-60s, and free TV licences for those over 75. However, it might well be argued these benefits have been earned through a lifetime of working and paying taxes, and in all too many cases they do not do much to overcome the lifetime effects of the social class, gender and ethnic inequalities discussed in this chapter.

CHAPTER SUMMARY

After studying this chapter, you should be able to:

- explain why social inequality is an important social issue

- explain what is meant by social stratification

- describe the main features of slavery, the caste, estate, and class systems, and the differences between them

- define a range of key terms associated with social inequality, such as social class, status, life chances, social mobility, income and wealth

- describe the main features of consensus and conflict theories of social class, including those of Marx and Weber, and some problems of them

- explain why sociologists often use occupation as an indicator of social class, and explain the problems in the use of occupation and occupational scales

- outline the main social classes in Britain today, and describe and explain a range of social class inequalities, including inequalities in wealth and income, health and employment, and why attempts to redistribute wealth and income have failed

- explain the difference between absolute, relative and consensual definitions of poverty, and how the poverty line is measured in contemporary Britain

- describe aspects of poverty apart from lack of income

- identify the main groups in poverty in modern Britain, explain why each of them is poor, and give a number of explanations why the poor remain poor, despite the welfare state

- discuss the different versions of the view that the poor are an underclass

- describe some of the features of, and obstacles to, social mobility in contemporary Britain

- describe some of the main changes in the class structure in the past fifty years

- explain why social class continues to be of importance in contemporary Britain

- describe how, and explain why, the position of women has changed in Britain over the past century

- describe the main features of domestic labour

- describe and explain a range of inequalities facing women in paid and unpaid work

- explain why women get only about 80 per cent of the average male wage and are poorly represented in top jobs

- explain what is meant by the terms *ethnicity*, *ethnic group* and *minority ethnic group*

- describe and explain a range of inequalities faced by ethnic minorities in contemporary Britain

- explain what is meant by racial prejudice, racial discrimination, racism and institutional racism

- suggest some explanations for racism

- identify steps being taken to improve the position of the ethnic minorities, with examples

- describe how age is a social construction, some age-related inequalities, and assess how important age inequalities are in affecting life chances compared to inequalities arising from social class, gender and ethnicity.

KEY TERMS

absolute poverty
achieved status
ageism
ascribed status
bourgeoisie
caste system
class consciousness
closed society
Communism
culture of poverty
dependency culture
deskilling
domestic labour
dominant ideology
economic inequality

embourgeoisement
endogamy
ethnic group
ethnicity
false consciousness
feudalism
generation
glass ceiling
income
infant mortality
institutional racism
inter-generational social
  mobility
intra-generational social
  mobility
inverse care law

life chances
market situation
means of production
meritocracy
minority ethnic group
open society
patriarchy
perinatal death
poverty line
proletarianization
proletariat
race
racial discrimination
racial prejudice
racism
relative poverty

sexism
sexual division of
  labour
slavery
social capital
social class
social mobility
social stratification
status
status groups
status symbols
underclass
wealth
white-collar workers

CHAPTER

9

Health and Illness

Contents

Health and Illness

KEY ISSUES

- What is meant by health, illness and disease?
- The medical and social models of health
- Becoming a health statistic
- Medicine and social control: the sick role
- How society influences health
- The food industry
- Inequalities in health

In Britain, more people are suffering and dying prematurely of preventable diseases than perhaps ever before. We hear more and more stories of people with cancer, heart disease, asthma and eczema. If progress towards a civilized society can be measured by the health of a nation, we might sometimes be forgiven for thinking Britain is going in reverse. And if the health of the population is a measure of social justice, then Britain is as divided now as it has ever been. But it is not simply the hand of nature or fate that makes us sick. Poor health and premature death are not random lightning bolts that strike us out of the blue. Disease and premature death are not evenly or randomly distributed throughout society. Official statistics reveal a pattern of social class, gender and ethnic inequalities in health. These differences in disease and death provide strong evidence that sickness and health are not simply matters of fate or bad luck, but a product of the society in which we live.

While the message has been that medicine can cure us, all the major advances in health occurred before medical intervention. In Britain, the elimination of the killer infectious diseases of the past, such as TB, pneumonia, flu, cholera, typhoid and diphtheria, all took place before the development of modern medicine. It was social changes such as better diet, clean water supplies, sewage disposal, improved housing, and general knowledge about health and hygiene that improved health; medical improvements like antibiotics and vaccines were less effective because of malnutrition. This is shown most noticeably in the developing countries, where the major

Getting healthier is important to many people today – but what do you think makes us unhealthy in the first place?

advances in health have come about as a result of simple preventative measures such as clean water and sewage control.

Given the newspaper stories we read about medical breakthroughs, miracle cures, organ transplants, and so on, we would expect doctors and nurses soon to be out of business, as the health of the population improves. Surprisingly, perhaps, the opposite is the case. The financial demands of the NHS have rocketed, and more and more people are going into hospital, or are on waiting lists for treatment.

WHAT IS MEANT BY HEALTH, ILLNESS AND DISEASE?

> **Activity**
>
> 1 Write your own definitions, with examples, of 'health', 'illness' and 'disease'. Discuss, with examples, what your definitions might mean for promoting health and eliminating disease.
> 2 Try to think of ways in which views of being healthy might differ between: (a) a rich country like Britain and a poor African country, and (b) a person who lives in poverty in Britain and a wealthy member of the upper class.

The definitions of health, illness and disease are no simple matters. What counts as health and illness varies between different groups within a single society, such as between men and women, and between societies. Views of acceptable standards of health are likely to differ widely between the people of a poor African country and those in Britain. Even in the same society, views of health change over time. At one time in Britain, mental illness was seen as a sign of satanic possession or witchcraft – a matter best dealt with by the Church rather than by doctors. Similarly, what were once seen as personal problems have quite recently become medical problems, such as obesity, alcoholism, hyperactivity in children and smoking.

Suggest some reasons why what used to be seen as personal matters, like smoking, being overweight, and drinking too much alcohol, have come to be seen as social and medical problems

There is no simple definition of illness, because for pain or discomfort to count as a disease it is necessary for someone to diagnose it as such. There are also subjective influences on health: some of us can put up with or ignore pain more than others; some feel no pain; and many of us will have different notions of what counts as 'feeling unwell'.

- **Health** is probably most easy to define as being able to function normally within a usual everyday routine.
- **Disease** generally refers to a biological or mental condition that usually involves medically diagnosed symptoms.
- **Illness** refers to the subjective feeling of being unwell or ill-health. It is possible both to have a disease and not feel ill, and to feel ill and not have any disease.

Activity

The United Nations World Health Organization defines health as 'a state of complete physical, mental, and social well-being, and not merely the absence of disease or infirmity'. Some have argued that this definition goes far beyond a realistic definition of health, as it implies not simply the absence of disease, but also a personally fulfilling life.

1 Discuss how the World Health Organization might view the health of the long-term unemployed in Britain.

2 Using the World Health Organization's definition, how might 'good health' differ between: (a) people who live in a poor African country and those who live in modern Britain; and (b) people in Britain who live in an isolated village in the country and those who live in a town?

3 Discuss the view that 'good health is simply a state of mind'.

THE MEDICAL AND SOCIAL MODELS OF HEALTH

As seen above, there are different meanings attached to health. There are two main approaches, arising from different views of what the causes of ill-health are. These are often referred to as the medical and social models of health.

The medical model of health

The medical model has two main features.

- Disease is seen as mainly caused by biological factors, and recently by personal lifestyle factors such as smoking and diet. The sick person is

The social model of health focuses on the social causes of health and ill-health, such as whether or not there is safe waste disposal, clean running water and environmental pollution, and whether or not people have safe working conditions, and an adequate income to live a healthy life

treated in the same way as a car that has broken down. People become objects to be fixed by 'body mechanics' (doctors).

- The causes of ill-health are seen as arising either from the moral failings of the individual (such as smoking too much, eating junk food or not getting enough exercise) or from random attacks of disease. This is a bit like blaming car breakdowns on poor maintenance and lack of proper servicing, or on bad luck.

The social model of health

This model differs in two ways from the medical model.

- A strong emphasis is placed on the social causes of health and ill-health, and on how society influences health.
- Health and illness are not seen simply as medical or scientific facts. A choice exists as to whether people see themselves as ill or not, and those with power can choose whether or not to classify someone as ill. In most cases, 'those with power' means doctors and other medical experts.

BECOMING A HEALTH STATISTIC

The process of becoming ill is not as simple and straightforward as it might seem. People may respond to the same symptoms in different ways. While some may seek medical help, others may choose to ignore their symptoms. They may look for alternative non-medical or less serious explanations for them: bronchitis may become simply a 'smoker's cough', and symptoms of ADHD (Attention Deficit Hyperactivity Disorder) in children, such as excessive activity and disruptive behaviour, may be dismissed as them simply misbehaving.

For people to be labelled as 'sick' – and to be recorded as a health statistic – there are at least four stages involved:

1   Individuals must first recognize they have a problem.
2   They must then define their problem as serious enough to take to a doctor.
3   They must then actually go to the doctor.
4   The doctor must then be persuaded that they have a medical or mental condition capable of being labelled as an illness requiring treatment.

Activity

1   List all the factors you can which might influence each of the four stages involved in becoming a health statistic, which lead some people to visit the doctor and others not to. For example, in stage 1, you might consider a person's ability to continue her or his responsibilities to friends and family, pressure from relatives, friends and employers, and so on. Draw on your own experiences of what makes you decide whether you are ill, and whether or not to go to the doctor.
2   Discuss in a group what you think the most common influences on going (or not going) to the doctor might be.

The limitations of health statistics

This chapter refers to statistics on health in several places. However, like the crime statistics discussed in chapter 5, some of these statistics should be treated with care.

Health statistics may be inaccurate because:

- They depend on people persuading doctors they are ill, and are therefore simply a record of doctors' decision-making.
- Doctors may diagnose illnesses or the causes of death incorrectly, reflecting the state of the doctor's knowledge – and therefore recorded illnesses and cause-of-death statistics may not be accurate. For example, there may have been many AIDS deaths recorded as another disease, like pneumonia, before doctors discovered AIDS; many doctors still have difficulty in diagnosing ME (Myalgic Encephalopathy), also known as Chronic Fatigue or Post Viral Fatigue Syndrome, as its symptoms are similar to those found in a range of other medical conditions. Many doctors don't even recognize ME as a genuine medical illness, even though it was first identified in the 1950s and an estimated 250,000 people suffer from it in the UK.

Whether someone becomes a health statistic depends on the diagnostic skills of doctors, whether doctors recognize patients as having a recognized medical condition, and whether sick people themselves bother to go to a doctor at all

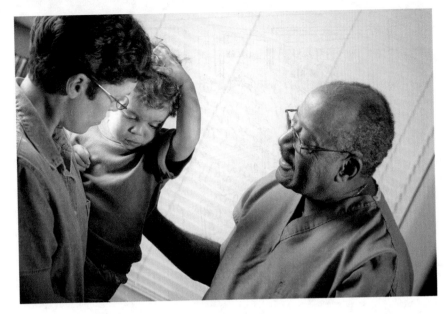

- Not all sick people go to the doctor, and not all people who persuade doctors they are ill are really sick.
- Private medicine operates to make a profit, and therefore is possibly more likely to diagnose symptoms as a disease.

MEDICINE AND SOCIAL CONTROL: THE SICK ROLE

Social control is concerned with maintaining order and stability in society. Sickness is really a form of deviance, and, when people are ill, they generally want to avoid normal social responsibilities because these are too demanding or stressful. The sick role – the pattern of behaviour associated with someone who is ill – is an escape route for the individual. This is because, when you are sick, you can quite reasonably and blamelessly abandon normal everyday activities, and often others will take over your responsibilities.

The **sick role** is the pattern of behaviour which is expected from someone who is classified as ill.

Allowing individuals to opt out into the sick role is potentially dangerous because the smooth workings of society may be upset if too many people adopt it. Imagine the disruption that would be caused in a school or factory where the teachers, students, managers or workers were always off ill.

Doctors play a key role in the social control of the sick by acting as gate-keepers of entry to the sick role, and preventing people becoming hypo-chondriacs and skiving on the grounds of illness. For example, they can stop people taking more than a few days off work on the grounds of illness by refusing to issue sick notes.

Features of the sick role

Rights

- Depending on the illness, individuals are excused normal social activities (for example, they are excused school or work). This requires approval by others such as teachers, employers and family members. The doctor often plays a key role in this process, by diagnosing the person as 'really ill', and issuing sick notes.
- Individuals are not seen as personally to blame for their illness: relatives, friends, and doctors are often very critical of those they do see as responsible for their own illness. Those who engage in excessive or binge drinking, for example, often don't get much sympathy for their hangover the morning after.

Responsibilities

Individuals have a responsibility – an obligation – to want to get well. When necessary, they are expected to seek and accept medical help and cooperate in their treatment. In other words, sick people are expected to do what the doctor orders, and they cannot expect sympathy and support if they don't try to get well. Even if people don't want to call in the doctor because they don't see their illness as serious enough to do so, they are still expected to stay in bed or take it easy in an effort to recover.

Figure 9.1 Some key social influences on health

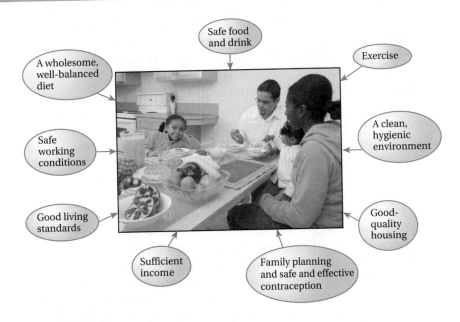

Safe food and drink

Exercise

A wholesome, well-balanced diet

A clean, hygienic environment

Safe working conditions

Good living standards

Good-quality housing

Sufficient income

Family planning and safe and effective contraception

> **Activity**
>
> With reference to figure 9.1, make a list of as many environmental, political, social and economic factors leading to poor health as you can think of, such as unemployment, pollution, or poor housing. Explain in each case how the factors you identify might influence health.

HOW SOCIETY INFLUENCES HEALTH

Figure 9.1 suggests a number of ways that social factors influence health. The fact that health is the product of society rather than simply of biology or medicine is shown by historical evidence that patterns of disease change over time. Changes which occurred during the nineteenth century and the first half of the twentieth century illustrate this well.

Improvements in health during the nineteenth and early twentieth centuries

In the nineteenth century, adult and child mortality (deaths) started to fall, and since then there has been a large and rapid population increase. For a long time this was thought to be due to the development of medicine. However, it is now agreed that it was due to a number of social and economic changes and the general improvement in living standards. These changes included:

- *Public hygiene.* The movement for sanitary reform and public hygiene in the nineteenth century helped to develop a clean and safe environment and higher standards of public hygiene. Safe and pure drinking water, efficient sanitation and sewage disposal, and paved streets and highways all helped to reduce deaths from infectious diseases.
- *Better diet.* Being well fed is the most effective form of disease prevention, as shown in the developing countries today, where vaccination programmes are not as successful as they should be because children are poorly nourished. The high death rates of the past were mainly due to hunger or malnutrition, which led to poorer resistance to infection. The nineteenth and early twentieth centuries saw improved communications, technology and hygiene making possible the production, transportation and import of more and cheaper food. Wages improved, and higher standards of living meant better food and better health.
- *Family planning and safe and effective contraception.* This led to smaller families, making possible a better diet and healthcare for children. This also improved the health of women, who spent less time in childbearing.
- *Housing legislation.* This increased public control over standards of rented housing, which helped to reduce overcrowding and the spread of infectious diseases between family members.
- *The war effort.* During the First World War (1914–18), unemployment was virtually eliminated. As part of the war effort, rents were controlled, food rationing was introduced, and minimum wages were established in agriculture. The resulting decline in poverty cut childhood deaths, especially among the families of unskilled workers in urban areas.
- *General improvements in living standards.* Higher wages, better food, clothing, and housing, laws improving health and safety at work, reduced working hours, and better hygiene regulations on the production and sale of food and drink all improved health.

All the above suggest that good health is more the result of government policy decisions and of economic development than simply of individual initiative or medical intervention.

The new disease burden

The infectious diseases of the nineteenth century were often called the 'diseases of poverty', since most victims were malnourished and poor. These have been replaced by 'diseases of affluence' – a result of eating too much poor-quality food, a lack of exercise, smoking and drinking too much, and so on.

A well-balanced diet is necessary for good health, and the lack of one makes people more vulnerable to disease. Despite the wealth of contemporary

Around one in four adults and one in six young people were officially classified as obese in England in 2009, with a similar pattern in Scotland, Wales and N.Ireland

developed countries, there is a problem of malnutrition in the form not of too little food, as you find in less-developed countries, but of too much of the wrong sort. As a result, advanced industrial societies experience health problems rarely found in simpler rural societies. The new disease burden includes obesity, and degenerative (worsening) diseases like cirrhosis of the liver, certain cancers, heart disease, respiratory diseases, diabetes, stomach ulcers and varicose veins. These kill or disable more people than they did in the past, and many more people are becoming chronically ill for longer periods in their lives than they did in the past.

In 2009 around a quarter of adult (over age 16) men and women, and one in six young people (aged 2–15) in England (with similar proportions in Scotland, Wales and N.Ireland) were officially classified as obese, and the World Health Organization predicts that, if current trends continue, almost 50 per cent of adults in Britain could be obese by 2025 through a combination of junk food and lack of exercise.

What are the causes of these new diseases?

It is generally accepted that the causes of these new diseases of affluence are mainly social and environmental, and therefore preventable. Public concerns over the food supply have been rising. There were major scares over BSE ('mad cow disease') in beef in the 1990s, and the linked human equivalent vCJD (variant Creutzfeldt-Jakob disease) had killed 169 people in the UK up to September 2010. Between 1982 and 2008, cases of food poisoning serious enough to be reported to a doctor rose by 500 per cent in England

and Wales, and there were around 70,000 such cases each year in 2002–9, and around 450 deaths in that period, with an average of around 55 people dying each year from food poisoning. *E.Coli* food poisoning outbreaks killed twenty people in 1996–7. A Food Standards Agency survey in 2002 found that around 12 per cent of the population – around 5½ million people – had experienced food poisoning in the previous twelve months as a result of food eaten in the UK. Many worry about GM (genetically modified) crops and foods, and the effects on health of the use of growth-promoting drugs in chickens was of continuing concern in the early 2000s. Some doctors have linked the rise in asthma to poor diet, with insufficient fruit and vegetables. The rise in heart disease has been blamed on factors such as smoking, stress, an inactive lifestyle (too many couch potatoes) and a diet high in sugar, salt and fats but low in fibre. In 2010, the Faculty of Public Health, which represents 3,000 leading public health specialists in the UK and around the world, called for the removal of artificial trans fats – found in many cakes, pastries, pies, chips and fast foods – from British food, to reduce the risk of heart attacks, strokes and diabetes. A 1997 British government report, *Nutritional Aspects of the Development of Cancer*, estimated that up to 70 per cent of cancer cases were linked to the type of food people ate. Diet was seen as ten times more important than the effects of job-related causes and of smoking on all cancers. The *Lancet* medical journal reported in 2003 that women eating too much food high in fat, such as butter, milk, meat, burgers, crisps, biscuits and cakes, were more likely to get breast cancer than others whose fat intake was low. A *Lancet* report in 2005 said that one-third of cancer deaths worldwide were caused by diet, lifestyle factors like smoking and alcohol, and physical inactivity and environmental pollution. This was confirmed by one of the most comprehensive studies of cancer ever. The World Cancer Research Fund's 2007 report, *Food, Nutrition, Physical Activity, and the Prevention of Cancer:*

Concerns over the nation's health have led to major public health campaigns to encourage people to eat better and give up unhealthy habits. These include (shown here) the Food Standards Agency's 'Eatwell plate', the Department of Health's 'five-a-day' campaigns to encourage people to eat better and exercise more, and the No Smoking Day campaign

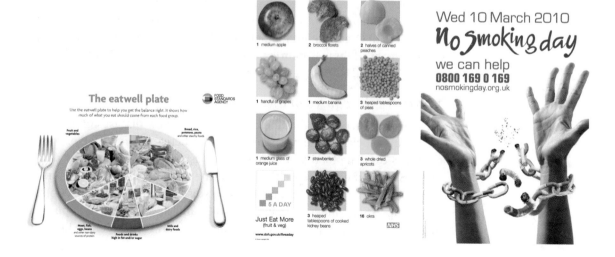

A Global Perspective, said that a third of cancers were caused by diet and lack of exercise, and could be prevented by people taking exercise, staying slim and abstaining from too much fast food, alcohol, red meat and preserved meats like ham, bacon and salami.

THE FOOD INDUSTRY

The British are now eating a more highly processed diet than at any time in history. We consume a whole range of factory-produced food, which is often low in nutritional value and may well be harmful to health, because of additives making up chemical cocktails of flavourings, colourings, preservatives and various drugs. For example, trans fats (mentioned above) have no nutritional value, but are added to foods to bulk them up and increase their supermarket shelf life. In 2007, the *Independent on Sunday* reported research suggesting that a common food preservative (E211 – sodium benzoate), found in a range of fizzy soft drinks like Fanta and Pepsi, had the ability to 'switch off' vital parts of DNA, risking cirrhosis of the liver and other degenerative diseases such as Parkinson's and Alzheimer's. A 2007 Food Standards Agency study on 300 randomly selected children found that hyperactivity rose after a drink containing additive combinations. This may explain why between 5 and 10 per cent of school-age children suffer some degree of ADHD (Attention Deficit Hyperactivity Disorder), with symptoms such as impulsiveness, inability to concentrate and excessive activity.

Revelations that large food processing companies were 'bulking up' chickens destined for schools, hospitals and restaurants with poultry skin, beef bits and pig waste, were of major concern in 2003. Highly processed junk

Activity

Why do we eat unhealthy foods? Food production is often in the hands of multinational firms whose primary concern is with making money. The points below suggest some reasons why many of the foods sold for mass consumption are of poor quality.

- The need for food products to travel
- The need for more imported food
- The need for foods to have a relatively long supermarket shelf life
- Marketing of a 'brand identity', with uniform colour, size and quality of foodstuffs
- The search for profit through marketing of factory-produced junk food
- Keeping costs down, for both the producer and the consumer

Study carefully the above, and figure 9.2, and try to think of as many ways as you can that nutritionally poor food, profits and poor health might be connected.

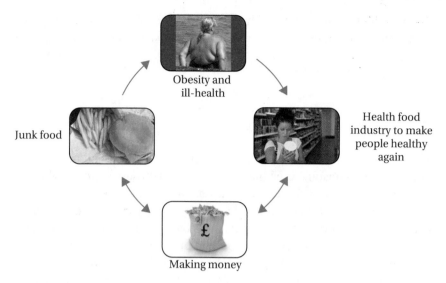

Figure 9.2 Making food and making money

food reinforces the trend towards a high-sugar, high-salt and high-fat diet which is low in vitamins, minerals, protein and fibre. Research in 2003 suggested that high doses of fat and sugar in fast and processed foods could be as addictive as nicotine and even hard drugs (like heroin and cocaine), causing hormonal changes creating a need for even more high-fat foods and generating obesity as a growing health problem. Why do people have unhealthy diets, and why do governments and food manufacturers allow unhealthy foods to be produced?

The activity opposite may have made you aware that many mass-produced foods are of poor quality.

The response to criticisms of the Western world's unhealthy diet is the health food industry. Its products are more expensive, such as wholemeal bread and organic vegetables, and the food and drugs industry makes a lot of money through its marketing of 'healthy' foods, vitamins and dietary supplements. It is estimated that around 10 million people in the UK use dietary supplements, despite warnings from the Food Standards Agency that excess vitamins can themselves be harmful to health.

The slimming or weight-loss industry – to offset the effects of obesity-producing junk food – is itself very big business. Vegetarianism and fitness centres have become money spinners, and we can now buy every manner of food which is 'low-calorie', 'slimline', 'low-fat', 'high-fibre', 'sugar-free', and so on. Health itself has become a product for companies to sell in a big way, while continuing to sell those products which often contribute to the original ill-health.

INEQUALITIES IN HEALTH

Social class differences in health

Official statistics reveal massive class inequalities in health. Nearly every kind of illness and disease is linked to class. Poverty is the major driver of ill-health, and poorer people tend to get sick more often, to be ill for longer and to die younger than richer people. Those who die youngest are people who live on benefits or low wages, who work in unhealthy workplaces, who live in poor-quality housing and who eat cheap, unhealthy food.

A 2010 report, *Fair Society, Healthy Lives* (the Marmot Review), calculated that if everyone were as healthy as university graduates (mainly from the middle class), with everyone without a degree having their death rate reduced to that of people with degrees, there would be 202,000 fewer early deaths each year among those aged over 30.

In contemporary Britain:

- The death rate in class 5 (unskilled manual workers) is about twice that of class 1. A person born into social class 1 (professional) lives, on average, about seven years longer than someone in social class 5.
- Those in the richest 5 per cent of the population, compared to those in the poorest 5 per cent, can expect to live seventeen years longer without serious or disabling illness of any kind: the poorest people don't just die younger, they also spend more of their shorter lives with a disability.
- In the first year of life, for every five children who die in class 1, eight die among unskilled workers. The risk of dying before the age of 5 is twice as great for a child born into the lowest social class as for one born into social class 1.
- Men and women in class 5 have twice the chance of dying before reaching retirement age than people in class 1. About 90 per cent of the major causes of death are more common in social classes 4 and 5 than in other social classes.
- Lung cancer and stomach cancer occur twice as often among men in manual jobs as among men in professional jobs, and death rates from heart disease and lung cancer – the two biggest causes of premature death – are about twice as high for those from manual backgrounds. Four times as many women die of cervical cancer in social class 5 as in social class 1. Women in the most disadvantaged classes are up to six times more likely than women in the most advantaged classes to die from respiratory diseases, five times more likely for heart and digestive diseases, and three times more likely to die from lung cancer and strokes.

- Working-class people, especially the unskilled, go to see doctors far more often and for a wider range of health problems than people in professional jobs.
- Semi-skilled and unskilled workers are more likely to be absent from work through sickness than those in professional and managerial jobs. Long-standing illness is around 50 per cent higher among unskilled manual workers than for class 1 professionals.
- Adults in the poorest fifth of the population, compared to those on average incomes, are much more likely to be at risk of developing a mental illness.
- All of the above are worse for the long-term unemployed and other groups in poverty.

These patterns of sickness and death provide strong evidence that it is society and the way it is organized that influences health, rather than simply our biological make-up.

The inverse care law

Social class differences in health are made worse through inequalities in the NHS. The inverse care law suggests that healthcare resources tend to be distributed in inverse proportion to need. This means that those whose need is least get the most resources, while those in greatest need get the least. Why is this?

- Poorer areas have fewer GP practices – so there are fewer doctors for those who are most likely to get ill, and poorer people therefore get less time with their GPs and poor working-class communities tend to have the most overcrowded facilities in the NHS.

> The **inverse care law** is the suggestion that, in the welfare state, including the National Health Service, those whose need is least get the most resources, while those in the greatest need get the least resources.

THE CHARACTERISTICS OF PEOPLE AGED 16–64 WHO ARE MORE LIKELY THAN MOST TO CONSULT THEIR DOCTOR

Those who:

- live in urban areas
- are council property tenants or live in other rented accommodation
- live alone
- are in social classes 4 and 5
- are unemployed
- are smokers
- are widowed and divorced
- are adults with young children
- work in construction, service and industrial occupations
- belong to a minority ethnic group

Source: adapted from Morbidity Statistics from General Practice, HMSO/Office for National Statistics

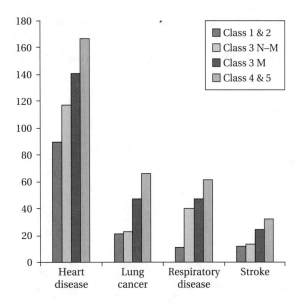

Figure 9.3 Mortality of men in England and Wales aged 35–64, by selected causes of death and by social class, 1997–9 (rates per 100,000 person years)

Source: Health Statistics Quarterly (Office for National Statistics, 2003)

Activity

Study figure 9.3.
1 Which disease shows the greatest difference in deaths between social classes 4 and 5 and social classes 1 and 2?
2 Which disease shows the smallest difference in deaths between social classes 1 and 2 and social classes 4 and 5?
3 Which social classes show the lowest deaths from lung cancer?
4 Identify *two* patterns shown in figure 9.3.
5 Suggest *two* possible social explanations for the social class differences in heart disease shown in figure 9.3.
6 Refer to the list of the characteristics of people aged 16–64 in the box opposite, and suggest reasons why each of the groups identified might be more likely to consult their GPs than other groups.

- Poorer people are more likely to be dependent on public transport, and so spend greater time travelling to hospitals and GPs, but they are also more likely to lose pay if they have to take time off work.

In contrast, those in the middle class:

- have more knowledge of illness and how to prevent it
- know more about the health services available and therefore get better service

- are more likely to fight against inadequate medical services
- are more self-confident, effective and assertive in dealing with doctors, and therefore get longer consultations, ask more questions, receive more explanations from their doctors and are more likely to be referred for further treatment
- have more money, so they are better able to jump NHS waiting lists by using private medicine.

Activity

The inverse care law

1 How does this cartoon illustrate the inverse care law?
2 Suggest reasons why people in deprived areas are more likely to suffer from poorer health and get worse healthcare than those in richer areas.

Explanations for social class inequalities in health

There are two main types of explanation for social class inequalities in health.

Cultural explanations Cultural explanations suggest that those suffering from poorer health have different attitudes, values and lifestyles which mean they don't look after themselves properly. Such explanations suggest that the victims of ill-health have only themselves to blame. Examples of this might include smoking too much, using too much salt or sugar, eating junk food, or not bothering to take any exercise. These types of factors are linked to a

Cultural explanations for social class inequalities in health tend to place the blame for ill-health on the victims themselves for having unhealthy lifestyles. To what extent do you think people are themselves responsible for their poor health? Or do unhealthy lifestyles arise from the family environment, or the material circumstances of people's lives, like social deprivation?

variety of conditions, including heart disease, cancer, strokes, bronchitis and asthma. Estimates suggest that alcohol abuse, for example, leads to around 9,000 deaths a year in the UK, and up to as much as 70 per cent of all cancers may be the result of a poor diet, along with other lifestyle factors.

Material explanations   Material explanations suggest that those suffering poorer health do so because of the inequalities in wealth and income in Britain. Those who suffer the poorest health are those who are the most materially disadvantaged, and lack enough money to eat a healthy diet, have poor housing, dangerous or unhealthy working conditions, live in an unhealthy local environment, and so on.

Figure 9.4 identifies a range of possible factors which might explain health differences, and you should now attempt the related activity beneath it.

Gender differences in health

As well as a pattern of social class differences in health, there is also a big difference between the health of men and women. At all ages, women's death rates are much lower than men's. Men's overall death rates are more than 40 per cent higher than those of women, and on average women live five years longer than men. Almost two-thirds of deaths before the age of 65 are male. After age 65, there are around 40 per cent more women than men in the population, and by age 85, women outnumber men by more than two to one.

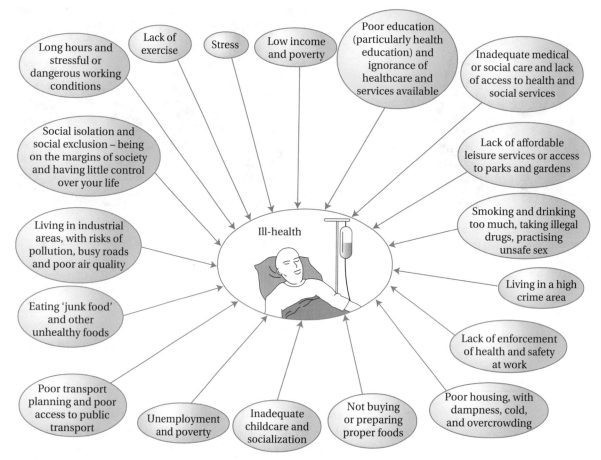

Figure 9.4 Cultural and material influences on health

Activity

Figure 9.4 suggests a series of points which contribute to social class inequalities in health. Study figure 9.4 and do the following activities:

1 Divide the explanations into cultural and material ones.
2 Suggest ways each point might explain class inequalities in health.
3 Suggest other reasons of your own for social class differences in health.
4 Do you think cultural or material explanations (or a bit of both) are better in explaining health inequalities? Give reasons for your answer.
5 Which of these factors do you think society can help to tackle, and which do you think are individual problems which only individuals themselves can solve? Give reasons for your answer.
6 In view of the explanations for social class inequalities in health, suggest policies and measures government and other authorities should take to reduce these inequalities.
7 Go to www.dh.gov.uk/en/Publichealth/Healthinequalities and identify and briefly describe four measures that the government is taking to tackle inequalities in health.

Women live on average about five years longer than men, partly because they take care of themselves better, but they also live more years with health problems of various kinds

Why do women live longer than men?

- Evidence suggests that boys are the weaker sex at birth, with a higher infant mortality rate, and women seem to have a better genetic resistance to heart disease than men.
- The process of gender-role socialization means men are more likely to be brought up to shrug off illnesses; they drink and smoke more, and use more illegal drugs, with all the consequences these have for health; they are more aggressive and take more risks; they are less careful in what they eat; and they are not socialized to show their emotions as much as women, and so have less outlet for stress.
- Women are more involved in family health, as they are more likely to be involved in nurturing and caring roles in the family, and sensitive to illness. Women are the biggest users of the health service, both for themselves and because it is generally women who organize the rest of the family going to the doctor's.
- Women are socialized to take care of themselves more than men, and they are more likely to visit doctors, which may mean they receive better healthcare.
- Men generally live more hazardous lives than women. The more dangerous occupations are more likely to be done by men – such as construction work – and therefore men are more at risk of industrial accidents

and diseases. In the home, men are more likely to do the dangerous and risky jobs, such as jobs using ladders and climbing on the roof. Men also make up the majority of lorry and car drivers and motorcyclists, and are therefore more at risk of death through road accidents.

- Men are more likely to work full-time and to work longer and more unsociable hours, such as overtime working and shiftwork, which can be harmful to health.
- Men retire later than women (age 65 compared to 60). Evidence suggests that the later retirement age of men could be an important factor in reducing their life expectancy (note: women's retirement age is planned to gradually increase to 65 by 2020).

Activity

1. Which of the reasons given for women living longer than men do you find most persuasive? Put them in order of importance, giving your reasons.
2. Do you think men's 'macho' behaviour is an important factor in shortening their lives? Suggest evidence for and against this from your own experiences.
3. 'The growing equality of women with men is a threat to women's health.' Explain this statement. Do you agree? How might this situation be avoided (apart from stopping women becoming more equal)?

Are women healthier than men?

The answer is 'yes' if we use only the indicators of death rates and life expectancy. However, statistics show that men, who in general die younger, don't

seem to experience as much ill-health as women, who live longer. Women are the major users of healthcare services and spend more years than men in poor health or with a disability.

Compared to men, women:

- go to the doctor about 50 per cent more often over the age of 16
- report more head and stomach aches, high blood pressure and weight problems
- consume more prescription and non-prescription drugs
- are admitted to hospital more often and have more operations
- go to see doctors about conditions like insomnia, tension headache and depression (which are often labelled as 'mental illness') about twice as often. In 2007–8, 56 per cent of those over age 16 in England using NHS specialist mental health services for adults were women
- receive far more prescriptions for tranquillizers, sleeping pills and anti-depressants

Women appear to suffer more depression and other mental illnesses than men. What social factors might help to explain this? Suggest reasons men might be less willing than women to admit they have a mental illness

- are off work with reported sickness more often and spend more days in bed
- in the 65–74 age group in 2006, women were two-thirds more likely to have rheumatism and arthritis than men in the same age group.

Why do women apparently suffer more sickness?

- *Stress.* Many women suffer a triple burden of being both low-paid workers, carrying responsibilities for housework and childcare, and managing family emotions. In many cases this involves having to manage limited household budgets with pressure to make ends meet, and a long day with little time to relax.
- *Poverty.* In low-income households, it is usually women who go without to ensure other family members get enough to eat. Women are therefore more likely to suffer the effects of poverty more directly than men.
- *Domestic labour* (housework). Domestic labour is rarely fulfilling (for further discussion on this, see pages 109–16 in chapter 3 on 'Families', and pages 460–2 in chapter 8 on 'Social Inequality'). Depression may be linked to the unpaid, repetitive, unrewarding, low-status nature of housework, in a society where only paid employment is really respected. The high accident rates at home might be influenced by the isolated nature of housework.
- *Socialization.* Women are socialized to express their feelings and talk about their problems more than men. Since women are generally the ones who 'manage' family health matters, they are often more aware of health and healthcare matters. Women may therefore be more willing than men to report physical and mental health problems. The higher rates of recorded illnesses among women could then be due not necessarily to greater health problems than men's, but to women's greater willingness to admit to problems and to take them to doctors. While women go to doctors for prescribed drugs like tranquillizers, men opt for non-prescribed drugs like alcohol. Men's higher death rates may simply be because they bottle everything up until it is too late.
- *Different diagnoses.* Due to gender roles, it may be that women are more willing to report symptoms of mental illness. Doctors are more likely to

Activity

1 Refer to the activity on p. 500 about the four stages involved in being labelled as 'sick' and becoming a health statistic, and suggest reasons why women might be more likely to end up as a health statistic than men.
2 Discuss the explanations suggested above for women apparently suffering more sickness than men. Do you think women really do suffer more ill-health, or do you think they are simply more open and honest about it than men?

see symptoms reported by women as mainly mental, while men's are seen as physical. Women are therefore more likely to be diagnosed as depressed or suffering from anxiety than men. Until recently, women had a much higher chance than men of being institutionalized in mental hospitals.

Ethnic differences in health

Social class and gender are not the only important factors in social inequalities in health; there are also some differences between ethnic groups. As with social class, social and economic factors, rather than culture and biology, are the main factors explaining the poorer health of minority ethnic groups in Britain. Compared to the white majority ethnic group:

- Black and minority ethnic groups are more likely to report themselves as being in ill-health, and generally have worse health than the overall population, but there are differences between diseases in different minority ethnic groups.
- African-Caribbeans seem more biologically vulnerable to developing sickle cell anaemia (a blood disease); they are more likely to suffer from hypertension (high blood pressure) and to die from strokes; and they are more likely to be diagnosed as schizophrenics and compulsorily committed to psychiatric hospitals for this and other mental illnesses.
- Those from ethnic minorities are much more likely to receive a diagnosis of mental illness than the White British, and one in five patients in

Overall, ethnic minority groups have poorer health. This is particularly true of older generations who may be reluctant to seek out healthcare or fail to find appropriate health information due to language or other cultural barriers

hospital for mental illness comes from a black and minority ethnic group background, compared to about one in ten of the white population.

- Asians (Indians, Pakistanis and Bangladeshis) suffer more heart disease, are 50 per cent more likely to have a heart attack, and are more likely to die from it, and have higher rates of diabetes.
- Most ethnic minority groups show higher rates of still-births, and child mortality generally within the first week, month or year of life.
- Most minority ethnic groups have higher rates of mortality.
- African-Caribbeans, Pakistanis and Bangladeshis are between 30 and 50 per cent more likely to suffer ill-health.

Why do some minority ethnic groups suffer poorer health?

Inequalities in health between ethnic groups result from many interlinking factors. These include:

- *Racism and poverty.* Many of the health problems of some minority ethnic groups arise for the same reasons as social class inequalities, as ethnic minorities are more likely than white British people to be among the poorest groups in society. Racism in society means some minority ethnic groups are more likely to find themselves living in the worst housing in environmentally unhealthy neighbourhoods, and to be unemployed or working for long hours in low-paid jobs in hazardous and unhealthy environments. Some research suggests that higher rates of recorded mental illness arise because psychiatrists vary their diagnosis of the symptoms of mental illness differently depending on the ethnicity of the patient, which may partly explain why one in five patients in hospital for mental illness comes from a black and minority ethnic group background, compared to about one in ten of the white population.
- *Diet.* Higher levels of heart disease may arise from aspects of the high-fat Asian diet, which also generates higher levels of obesity – itself a cause of heart disease and diabetes.
- *Language and culture.* Asian women are less likely to visit ante- and post-natal clinics, explaining higher levels of infant mortality. Asian women often prefer to see female doctors, and many find it difficult to discuss health issues with white male doctors, but the number of female GPs is lowest in those areas which have the highest concentrations of Asian households. Many older Asian women, and some older men, speak poor English, and this may create difficulties communicating with, and obtaining treatment from, doctors and other health professionals, and taking up screening services for things like breast cancer or cervical cancer. This is made worse by the lack of translation services in the NHS. Despite big improvements, there is still a lack of information available in minority ethnic group languages. Health professionals are often not sufficiently familiar with the religious, cultural, and dietary practices of different ethnic groups, hence their concerns may not be understood, nor their needs met.

Conclusion on health inequalities

This chapter has shown that health, illness, disease and inequalities in health are very much products of society rather than simply of biology or bad luck. As the 2010 report *Fair Society, Healthy Lives*, referred to earlier, pointed out, 'such systematic differences in health do not arise by chance, and they cannot be attributed simply to genetic makeup, "bad" behaviour, or difficulties in access to medical care, important as these factors may be. Social and economic differences in health status reflect, and are caused by, social and economic inequalities in society.' Social and economic life has major influences on the patterns of illness and death, and those who experience the greatest inequalities in health are the poorest groups in society, and these inequalities can be made worse by the effects of gender and ethnic group. So long as inequalities of wealth, income, education, occupation and social privilege continue, so will inequalities in health. The words of Dr John Collee, writing in the *Observer* newspaper in 1992, are still as true today as they were many years ago:

'Forget everything else I have written on the subject. There is one piece of health advice which is more effective than all the others. One guaranteed way to live longer, grow taller, avoid chronic illness, have healthier children, increase your quality of life and minimize your risk of premature death. The secret is: *be rich.*'

CHAPTER SUMMARY

After studying this chapter, you should be able to:

- explain what is meant by health, illness and disease

- describe the differences between the medical and social models of health

- suggest reasons why some people may seek medical help while others may not

- identify some problems with health statistics

- explain what is meant by the sick role, and identify the rights and obligations of it

- identify and explain a range of social factors which influence health and disease

- describe and explain social class, gender and ethnic inequalities in health.

KEY TERMS

disease

health
illness

inverse care law
sick role

Appendix: Reading Statistical Data

The evidence that sociologists use in their research comes in a variety of forms, but often consists of statistical data presented in the form of tables, graphs, bar charts, pie charts, and various combinations of these. These often prove difficult for newcomers to sociology to understand. This appendix is designed to introduce you to the use and interpretation of these forms of data, and give you practice in doing so. This should make it easier to read the tables and figures appearing in this book, and construct your own should you wish. Answers to all activities in this chapter (except the graphs you are asked to draw) are at the end of the chapter.

STATISTICAL TABLES

When confronted with a statistical table, you should first read carefully the heading of the table – this will tell you what subject the statistics refer to. Tables generally show the relationship between two or more factors, and the key thing to note is what the statistics refer to – whether they are in actual numbers or percentages and what units the numbers are in. For example, the numbers might be in thousands or millions or they might be in the form of numbers per thousand of the population.

Table A1 is derived from a series of official government statistics on divorce. The data in this table will be used to show the variety of ways in which statistical evidence can be presented.

Table A1 shows the relationship between a number of factors (shown in the left-hand column) and how these have changed over time (the dates shown along the top row). Notice that:

- The table refers to the different countries making up the United Kingdom. There are references to England and Wales, Scotland, Northern Ireland, Great Britain, and the United Kingdom.
- There are three ways in which the figures are expressed:
  - 'Petitions filed', 'decrees nisi granted', 'decrees absolute granted', and 'estimated numbers of divorced people who had not remarried' are expressed in *thousands*.

Table A1 Divorce: 1961–2001	1961	1971	1981	1991	2001
Petitions filed[a] (thousands) England and Wales	30	110	176	179	162
Decrees nisi[b] granted (thousands) England and Wales	27	89	147	161	147
Decrees absolute[c] granted (thousands) England and Wales	25	74	145	158	143
Granted to husband	11	30	42	44	44
Granted to wife	14	44	102	114	99
Scotland	2	5	10	12	11
Northern Ireland	–	–	1	2	2
United Kingdom	27	79	156	172	156
Persons divorcing per thousand married people England and Wales	2.1	6.0	11.9	13.5	13.0
Percentage of divorces where one or both partners had been previously divorced England and Wales	9.3	8.8	17.1	25.4	29.4
Estimated numbers of divorced people who had not remarried (thousands) Great Britain					
Men	101	200	653	n/a[d]	n/a
Women	184	317	890	n/a	n/a
Total	285	517	1543	n/a	n/a

[a] A petition is a request to a court to grant a divorce.
[b] A decree nisi is the stage before the divorce is finalized.
[c] A decree absolute is the final divorce, representing the legal termination of the marriage.
[d] Not available.

Source: Data adapted from *Social Trends; Population Trends; Marriage, Divorce and Adoption Statistics*; Office for National Statistics

- 'Divorces where one or both partners had been previously divorced' are expressed in *percentages*.
- 'Persons divorcing' are expressed as '*per thousand* married people' (this is known as the divorce rate).

> **Activity**
>
> Study table A1 carefully and answer the following questions to check whether you are reading the table correctly:
> 1 How many decrees absolute were granted to husbands in England and Wales in 1991?
> 2 How many divorced women in Great Britain in 1971 were estimated not to have remarried?
> 3 How many decrees absolute were granted in Scotland in 2001?
> 4 By how many had the number of decrees absolute granted in the United Kingdom increased between 1961 and 2001?
> 5 How many decrees absolute were granted to wives in England and Wales in 2001?
> 6 How many persons were divorcing per thousand married people in England and Wales in 1981?
> 7 What percentage of divorces in England and Wales in 2001 involved at least one partner who had been previously divorced?
> 8 What was the total number of divorce petitions in England and Wales in 1991?

DESCRIBING A TREND

When interpreting statistical data, you will often be expected to describe a trend, or how the pattern shown changes over time. In describing a trend, you should normally say whether there is an upward or downward trend, stating whether the figure has increased or decreased, and by how much, and give the starting figure and date and the finishing figure and date.

For example, with table A1 you might be asked: 'What trend is shown in the number of decrees absolute granted in the United Kingdom between 1961 and 2001?' Your answer might take the form: 'The number of decrees absolute has shown an upward trend, increasing by 129,000, from 27,000 in 1961 to 156,000 in 2001' (the figure of 129,000 being obtained by subtracting the figure of 27,000 in 1961 from 156,000 in 2001).

> **Activity**
>
> Using table A1, practise describing the following trends:
> 1 What trend is shown in the number of persons divorcing per thousand married people in England and Wales between 1961 and 2001?
> 2 What trend does the table show in the number of decrees nisi granted in England and Wales in the period covered by the table?
> 3 Comparing the number of decrees absolute granted to husbands and wives in England and Wales between 1961 and 2001, identify *three* trends that are shown.

GRAPHS

Statistics are commonly presented in the form of graphs. These show the relationship between two factors and how they change over time. These are shown on the vertical and horizontal axes, which are labelled to show what they represent. Trends can be spotted immediately by studying whether the line rises or falls between two dates. It is always important to note what the figures on the axes refer to – numbers, percentages, dates, and so on.

Figure A1, using the data given in table A1, illustrates how the number of decrees absolute granted in the United Kingdom has changed over time. Notice how the horizontal axis gives the date and the vertical axis gives the number of divorces (in thousands).

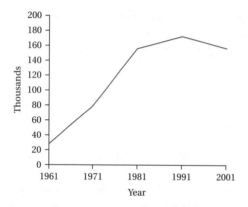

Figure A1 Decrees absolute granted: United Kingdom, 1961–2001

Activity

Using figure A1:
1 About how many decrees absolute were granted in 1971?
2 About how many decrees absolute were granted in 1991?
3 What trend is shown in the graph?
4 Using the data given in table A1, practise drawing your own graph to illustrate the changing number of persons divorcing per thousand married people in England and Wales between 1961 and 2001. Make sure you label the axes correctly and put a title on your graph.

Graphs may have more than one curve on them to show more information, and this is useful for making comparisons. For example, figure A2 shows that both the number of petitions filed for divorce and the decrees absolute granted (in thousands) have increased over time, and it is easy to see at a glance that there are large differences between them.

Activity

What does figure A2 show about the number of divorce petitions compared to the number of decrees absolute granted over the period covered by the graph? How might you explain this difference?

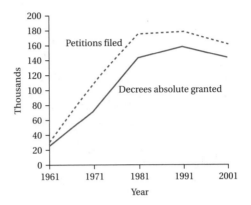

Figure A2 Divorces: England and Wales, 1961–2001

Cumulative graphs

Sometimes graphs may show how a total figure is made up by adding one set of figures to another. This is called a cumulative graph, as the figures 'build up' to the total. This is illustrated in figure A3 on page 528, using the data from table A1 on 'decrees absolute granted to husbands and wives in England and Wales'.

In figure A3:

 - The top line shows the total number of decrees absolute granted.
 - The bottom line shows the number of husbands granted a decree absolute.
 - The space between the two lines represents the number of wives granted a decree absolute.

By subtracting the number of husbands (the bottom line) from the total (the top line), it is possible to calculate the number of wives granted a decree absolute. For example, in 1991, there was a total of about 158,000 decrees absolute (point A), with 44,000 granted to husbands (point B). The number of wives granted a divorce is therefore about 114,000 (A minus B).

It is immediately obvious from looking at the graph that:

– Far more wives are granted divorces than husbands, as the gap between the top line and the bottom line is much wider than the gap between the bottom line and the horizontal axis.

– The gap between the curves widens over time (although it decreases slightly after about 1991), showing that the number of wives granted a divorce has grown at a faster rate than that of husbands granted a divorce.

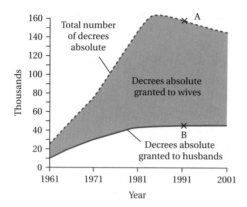

Figure A3 Decrees absolute granted to husbands and wives: England and Wales, 1961–2001

Activity

Referring to figure A3:

1 About how many wives were granted a decree absolute in 1961?
2 Identify three trends that are shown in the graph.
3 Using the data in table A1, draw a cumulative graph showing the estimated numbers of men and women in Great Britain who had been divorced but who had not remarried in the period 1961 to 1981. Don't forget to label your graph correctly and give it a title.

BAR CHARTS

Bar charts are another very commonly used way of presenting data and showing comparisons and trends in a visually striking way. Bar charts are constructed in much the same way as graphs, but columns are used instead of lines.

Figure A4 shows a bar chart comparing the estimated numbers of divorced people in Great Britain who had not remarried between 1961 and 1981.

Referring to figure A4, answer the following questions:
1 About how many divorced women were estimated not to have remarried in 1981?
2 About how many divorced men were estimated not to have remarried in 1971?
3 Identify two trends shown in the chart.

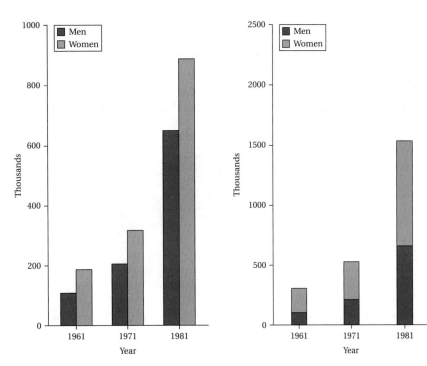

Figure A4 Estimated numbers of divorced people who had not remarried: Great Britain, 1961–81

Figure A5 Estimated numbers of divorced people who had not remarried: Great Britain, 1961–81

Cumulative bar charts

Bar charts may, like graphs, be cumulative and show how totals are made up. Compare figure A4 with figure A5, in which exactly the same information is presented in a different form (note, however, that the scales on the vertical axes differ between the two).

Activity

Using the data in table A1 (see page 524), construct a bar chart comparing the decrees absolute granted for divorce in England and Wales to husbands and wives for the years 1961, 1981, and 2001.

PIE CHARTS

Pie charts present data by dividing a circle into sectors, with the size of each sector being proportional to the size of the item it represents. Pie charts are very effective in showing statistics in an easily digestible and striking way. For example, using the data given in table A1, the number of decrees absolute granted to husbands and wives in England and Wales in 2001 might be presented as in figure A6.

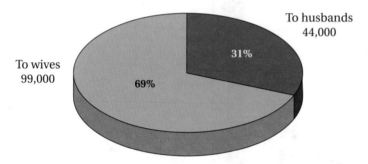

Figure A6 Divorces (decrees absolute) granted to husbands and wives: England and Wales, 2001

Activity

Draw a pie chart illustrating the way your 24-hour day is divided up between school/college work or paid employment, travelling to and from work, leisure activities, domestic jobs in the home, and sleeping and eating.

Throughout this book there are many examples of statistics presented in a variety of forms, often with activities to develop your understanding of them. You should not simply ignore them, but try to read and interpret them. They often contain important information which will help you to understand the text better.

Answers to questions in this chapter

p. 525   (1) 44,000. (2) 317,000. (3) 11,000. (4) 129,000. (5) 99,000. (6) 11.9. (7) 29.4 per cent. (8) 179,000.

p. 525   (1) Upward trend, increasing by 10.9, from 2.1 in 1961 to 13.0 in 2001. (2) Upward trend, increasing by 120,000 from 27,000 in 1961 to 147,000 in 2001. (3) All upward trends, although the wives' figure declined between 1991 and 2001, and the husbands' was the same in 1991 and 2001. Increasing by 33,000 for husbands, from 11,000 in 1961 to 44,000 in 2001; increasing by 85,000 for wives, from 14,000 in 1961 to 99,000 in 2001; and those granted to wives have increased more than those granted to husbands – by 85,000 compared to 33,000. The gap between them has therefore grown over time.

p. 526   (1) About 80,000. (2) About 170,000. (3) Upward trend, rising from about 28,000 in 1961 to a peak of about 170,000 in 1991, with a small decline after 1991.

p. 527   There are a lot more petitions than there are divorces granted. This suggests that some people who apply for divorce then change their minds for some reason before it is too late.

p. 528   (1) About 20,000. (2) There are four trends you could mention: total divorces increasing; divorces granted to husbands increasing; divorces granted to wives increasing; and the divorces granted to wives increasing far more than those granted to men.

p. 529   (1) About 900,000. (2) About 200,000. (3) There are three possible trends: the number of divorced men who had not remarried has increased; the same for women; and the number of divorced women not remarrying has increased much more than the number of men.

Glossary

Words in coloured type within entries refer to terms found elsewhere in the glossary.

Absolute poverty   Poverty defined as lacking the minimum requirements necessary to maintain human health and life. *See also* relative poverty.

Achieved status   Status which is achieved through an individual's own efforts. *See also* ascribed status.

Active citizenship   Citizens actively taking up both the rights and responsibilities of citizenship, particularly their responsibilities and not just their rights, and involving themselves as active members of the communities in which they live. *See also* citizenship.

Ageing population   A population in which the average age is getting higher, with a greater proportion of people over retirement age, and a smaller proportion of young people.

Ageism   Stereotyping of, or prejudice and discrimination against, individuals or groups on the grounds of their age.

Agenda-setting   The process whereby the mass media select the list of subjects to report and bring to public attention.

Anomie   Confusion and uncertainty over social norms.

Anti-school sub-culture   A set of values, attitudes and behaviour in opposition to the main aims of a school.

Arranged marriage   A marriage which is arranged by the parents of the marriage partners, with a view to background and status. More a union between two families than two people, and romantic love between the marriage partners is not necessarily present.

Ascribed status   Status which is given to an individual at birth and usually can't be changed. *See also* achieved status.

Authority   Power which is accepted as fair and just.

Beanpole family   A multi-generation extended family, in a pattern which is long and thin, with few aunts, uncles and cousins, reflecting fewer children being born in each generation, but people living longer.

Bias   A subject being presented in a one-sided way, favouring one point of view over others, or deliberately ignoring, distorting or misrepresenting issues.

Bigamy   Where monogamy is the only legal form of marriage, the offence of marrying another person while still legally married to someone else.

Birth rate   The number of live births per 1,000 of the population per year.

Bourgeoisie   Class of owners of the means of production.

Caste system   A stratification system (*see* social stratification) based on Hindu religious beliefs, in which an individual's position is fixed at birth and cannot be changed.

Cereal packet family   The stereotype of the ideal family found in the mass media and advertising. It is generally seen as involving first-time married parents and their own natural children, living together, with the father as the primary breadwinner and the mother as primarily concerned with the home and children.

Charismatic authority   Power seen as fair and just as it is based on a power-holder's personal charm and magnetism.

Chivalry thesis   The suggestion that paternalism or sexism on the part of the police and courts means they regard female offenders as a less serious 'threat' than men, particularly for minor offences, and treat women more leniently than men.

Citizen journalism   Where members of the public, rather than professional journalists and media companies, collect, report and spread news stories and information.

Citizenship   The legal, social, civil and political rights and responsibilities of individuals (citizens) living in a democratic society.

Class consciousness   An awareness in members of a social class of their real interests.

Classic extended family   A family where several related nuclear families or family members live in the same house, street or area. It may be horizon-tally extended, where it contains aunts, uncles, cousins, etc., or vertically extended, where it contains more than two generations.

Closed society   A stratification system (*see* social stratification) where social mobility is not possible.

Coercion   Rule by violence or the threat of violence.

Communes   Self-contained and self-supporting communities, where all members of the community share property, childcare, household tasks and living accommodation.

Communism   An equal society, without social classes or conflict, in which the means of production are the common property of all.

Compensatory education   Extra educational help for those coming from disadvantaged groups to help them overcome the obstacles they face in the education system and the wider society.

Conflict theory A sociological approach that emphasizes social differences and conflicts, with inequalities in wealth, power and status all creating conflicts between individuals and social groups. *See also* consensus theory.

Conjugal roles The roles played by a male and female partner in marriage or in a cohabiting couple.

Consensus theory A sociological approach that emphasizes the shared norms and shared values that exist between people, and sees society made up of individuals and social institutions working together in harmony, without much conflict between people and groups.

Consumer (or consumption) goods Products and services that people buy to satisfy their needs and desires, such as food, clothes, furniture, TVs and DVD players, computers for personal use, iPods and leisure activities, like paying to go to cinemas, clubs and concerts.

Corporate crime Crimes committed by large companies which directly profit the company rather than individuals.

Covert role A hidden role, where the researcher in participant observation conceals from the group being studied his or her true identify as a researcher, to gain access to the group and avoid disrupting its normal behaviour.

Crime Behaviour which is against the law – law-breaking.

Culture The language, beliefs, values and norms, customs, roles, knowledge and skills which combine to make up the way of life of any society.

Culture of poverty A set of beliefs and values thought to exist among the poor which prevents them escaping from poverty.

Customs Norms which have existed for a long time.

Dealignment In voting, no clear alignment (matching up) of particular social classes with one of the two main political parties. In particular, the working class (*see* social class) is no longer clearly aligned with the Labour Party, nor the middle class with the Conservative Party, and most voters no longer show loyalty to a party according to their social class.

Death rate The number of deaths per 1,000 of the population per year.

Democracy A form of government in which the people participate in political decision-making, usually by electing individuals to represent their views.

Demography The study of population.

Dependency culture A set of values and beliefs, and a way of life, centred on dependence on others. Normally used in the context of those who depend on welfare state benefits.

Deskilling The removal of skills from work by the application of new machinery which simplifies tasks.

Deviance Failure to conform to social norms.

Deviancy amplification   The process by which the mass media, through exaggeration and distortion, actually create more crime and deviance.

Deviant career   Where people who have been labelled as deviant (*see* deviance) find conventional opportunities blocked to them, and so they are pushed into committing further deviant acts.

Dictatorship   A form of totalitarianism in which power is concentrated in the hands of one person.

Digital divide   The gap between those people with effective access to the digital and information technology making up the new media and those who lack such access.

Disease   A biological or mental condition, which usually involves medically diagnosed symptoms.

Divorce rate   The number of divorces per 1,000 married people per year.

Domestic labour   Unpaid housework, including cooking, cleaning, childcare and looking after the sick and elderly.

Dominant ideology   The ideas and beliefs of the most powerful groups in society, which influence the ideas and beliefs of the rest of society.

Economic inequality   Refers to differences in all those material things which affect the lives of individuals, such as their wealth, their income and the hours they work.

Elaborated code   A form of language use involving careful explanation and detail. The language used by strangers and individuals in some formal context, like a job interview, writing a business letter, or a school lesson or textbook. *See also* restricted code.

Elite   A small group holding great power and influence in society.

Embourgeoisement   The idea that, with higher wages, the working-class (*see* social class) are becoming part of the middle class. The opposite of proletarianization.

Endogamy   Where marriage must be to a partner of the same kinship or social group.

Equality of educational opportunity   The principle that every child should have an equal chance of doing as well in education as his or her ability will allow.

Ethics   Ideas about what is morally right and wrong.

Ethnic group   A group of people who share a common culture.

Ethnicity   The shared culture of a social group which gives its members a common identity in some ways different from other groups.

Ethnocentrism   A view of the world in which other cultures are seen through the eyes of one's own culture, with a devaluing of the others. For example, school subjects may concentrate on white British society and culture rather than recognizing and taking into account the cultures of different ethnic communities (*see* ethnic group).

Extended family   A family grouping including all kin (*see* kinship). There are two main types of extended family: the classic extended family and the modified extended family.

False consciousness   A failure by members of a social class to recognize their real interests.

Feminist   Someone who believes that women are disadvantaged in society, and should have rights, power and status equal to those of men.

Fertility rate   The number of live births per 1,000 women of childbearing age (15–44) per year.

Feudalism   A closed (*see* closed society) system of stratification (*see* social stratification) based on land ownership and legal inequalities.

Floating voter   A voter who has no fixed political opinion, or is not a committed supporter of any political party.

Folk devils   Individuals or groups posing an imagined or exaggerated threat to society.

Gate-keeping   The media's refusal to cover some issues.

Gender   The culturally created differences between men and women which are learnt through socialization.

Gender role   The pattern of behaviour which society expects from a man or woman.

Generation   Those born in the same 15- to 30-year period.

Glass ceiling   An invisible barrier of discrimination which makes it difficult for women to reach the same top levels in their chosen careers as similarly qualified men.

Globalization   The growing interdependence of societies across the world, with the spread of the same culture and economic interests across the globe.

Hate crime   Any crime that is motivated by hostility and prejudice based upon a victim's identity, such as their race, disability, religion, beliefs or sexual orientation.

Health   Being able to function normally within a usual everyday routine.

Hidden curriculum   Attitudes and behaviour which are taught through the school's organization and teachers' attitudes but which are not part of the formal time-table.

Household   An individual living alone, or group living at the same address and sharing facilities.

Hypothesis   An idea which a researcher guesses might be true, but which has not yet been tested against the evidence.

Identity   How individuals or groups see and define themselves and how other people see and define them.

Illness   The subjective feeling of being unwell or unhealthy.

Income   The flow of money which people obtain from work, from their investments or from the state.

Infant mortality   The death of babies in the first year of life.

Infant mortality rate   The number of deaths of babies in the first year of life per 1,000 live births per year.

Insider groups   Pressure groups which have an active and close relationship with governments, with representatives providing evidence to, and being consulted by, them.

Institutional racism   'The collective failure of an organization to provide an appropriate and professional service to people because of their culture, colour or ethnic origin. It can be seen or detected in processes, attitudes and behaviour which amount to discrimination through unwitting prejudice, ignorance, and thoughtless and racist stereotyping which disadvantages minority ethnic people' (Macpherson Report, 1999).

Integrated conjugal roles   Roles in marriage or in a cohabiting couple in which male and female partners share domestic tasks, childcare, decision-making and income earning.

Inter-generational social mobility   A way of measuring social mobility by comparing an adult's present occupation or income with that of the family she or he was born into. It therefore shows how much social class mobility there has been between two generations.

Interviewer bias   The answers given in an interview being influenced or distorted in some way by the presence or behaviour of the interviewer.

Intra-generational social mobility   A way of measuring social mobility by comparing a person's present occupation or income with her or his first occupation. It therefore shows how much mobility an individual has achieved within her or his lifetime.

Inverse care law   In relation to the welfare state, including the National Health Service, the suggestion that those whose need is least get the most resources, while those in the greatest need get the fewest resources.

Juvenile delinquency   Crime committed by those between the ages of 10 and 17, though the term *delinquency* is often used to describe any anti-social or deviant behaviour by young people, even if it isn't criminal.

Kibbutz   A community established in Israel, with the emphasis on equality, collective ownership of property, and collective child rearing.

Kinship   Relations of blood, marriage, civil partnership or adoption.

Labelling   Defining a person or group in a certain way – as a particular 'type' of person or group.

Law   An official legal rule, formally enforced by the police, courts and prison, involving legal punishments if it is broken.

Life chances   The chances of obtaining those things defined as desirable and of avoiding those things defined as undesirable in a society.

Life expectancy   An estimate of how long people can be expected to live from a certain age.

Macro approach   An approach to studying society that focuses on the large-scale structure of society as a whole, rather than on individuals and small groups.

Marginalization   The process whereby some groups are pushed by poverty, ill-health, lack of education, racism and so on to the margins of society and are unable to take part in the life enjoyed by the majority of citizens. *See also* social exclusion.

Market situation   The rewards that people are able to obtain when they sell their skills in the labour market, depending on the scarcity of their skills, the demand for them, and the power they have to obtain high rewards.

Marketization   Where something is left to free market competition and the forces of supply and demand. In education, this refers to the process whereby schools and colleges become more independent, and compete with one another for students, and become subject to the free market forces of supply and demand, based on competition and parental choice.

Marriage rate   The number of marriages per 1,000 single people aged 16 and over per year.

Master status   The dominant status of an individual which overrides all other characteristics of that person, such as that of an 'ex-con'.

Matriarchy   Power and authority held by women.

Means of production   The key resources necessary for producing society's goods, such as factories and land.

Meritocracy   A society in which social and occupational positions are achieved by merit, such as educational qualifications, talent and skill. *See also* meritocratic society.

Meritocratic society   A society in which social and occupational positions (jobs) and pay are allocated on the basis purely of people's individual experience, talents, abilities, qualifications and skills – their individual merits. *See also* meritocracy.

Micro approach   An approach to studying society that focuses on small groups or individuals, rather than on the structure of society as a whole.

Minority ethnic group   A social group which shares a cultural identity (*see* culture) which is different from that of the majority population of a society.

Modified extended family   A family type in which related nuclear families, although living apart geographically, nevertheless maintain regular contact and mutual support through visiting, the phone, letters, email and social networking websites.

Monogamy A form of marriage in which a person can only be legally married to one partner at a time.

Moral panic A wave of public concern about some exaggerated or imaginary threat to society, stirred up by overblown and sensationalized reporting in the mass media.

Nationalism A sense of pride and commitment to a nation, and a very strong sense of national identity.

New social movement A broad movement of people who are united around the desire to promote, or block, a broad set of social changes in society. Unlike political parties or pressure groups, they are often only informally organized through a network of small, independent, locally based groups.

News values The values and assumptions held by journalists which guide them in choosing what to report and what to leave out, and how what they choose to report should be presented.

Norm-setting The process whereby the mass media emphasize and reinforce conformity to social norms, and seek to isolate those who don't conform by making them the victims of unfavourable public opinion.

Norms Social rules which define correct behaviour in a society or group.

Nuclear family A family with two generations, of parents and children, living together in one household.

Objectivity Approaching topics with an open mind, avoiding bias and being prepared to submit research evidence to scrutiny by other researchers.

Open society A stratification system (*see* social stratification) in which social mobility is possible.

Outsider groups Pressure groups that, for various reasons, do not have everyday active and close links with governments.

Overt role A non-hidden or revealed role, where the researcher in participant observation reveals to the group being studied his or her true identity and purpose.

Patriarchy Power, status and authority held by men.

Peer group A group of people of similar age and status with whom a person mixes socially.

Perinatal death Still-births and deaths within the first week of life.

Pilot survey A small-scale practice survey (see social survey) carried out before the final survey to check for any possible problems.

Pluralism A view that sees power in society spread among a wide variety of groups and individuals, with no single one having a monopoly on power and influence.

Political party   A group of people organized with the aim of forming the government in a society.

Politics   The struggle to gain power and control in a relationship, group or society, by getting in a position to make decisions and implement policies.

Polyandry   A form of marriage in which a woman may have two or more husbands at the same time.

Polygamy   A form of marriage in which a member of one sex can be married to two or more members of the opposite sex at the same time.

Polygyny   A form of marriage in which a man may have two or more wives at the same time.

Positive discrimination   Giving disadvantaged groups more favourable treatment than others to make up for the disadvantages they face.

Poverty line   The dividing point between those who are poor and those who are not. The official poverty line used in Britain today is *60 per cent of average income* – the definition of poverty used by the European Union.

Power   The ability of people or groups to exert their will over others and get their own way.

Pressure groups   Organizations which try to put pressure on those with power in society to implement policies which they favour.

Primary data   Information which sociologists have collected themselves. *See also* secondary data.

Primary socialization   Socialization during the early years of child-hood, carried out by the family or close community. *See also* secondary socialization.

Privatized nuclear family   A nuclear family unit which is separated and isolated from wider kin (*see* kinship) and the community, with members spending time together in home-centred activities.

Proletarianization   The process of decline in the pay and conditions of sections of the middle class (*see* social class), so they become more like the working class. The opposite of embourgeoisement.

Proletariat   The class (*see* social class) of workers, who have to work for wages as they do not own the means of production.

Proportional representation   A voting system in which the number of representatives elected accurately reflects the proportion of the votes received.

Qualitative data   Information concerned with the feelings people have, and the meanings and interpretations they give to some issue or event.

Quantitative data   Information that can be expressed in statistical or number form.

Race   Humans classified into different groups according to physical characteristics, like skin colour.

Racial discrimination   When racial prejudice causes people to act unfairly against an ethnic group.

Racial prejudice   A set of assumptions about an ethnic group which people are reluctant to change even when they receive information which undermines those assumptions.

Racism   Believing or acting as though an individual or group is superior or inferior on the grounds of their racial or ethnic (*see* ethnic group) origins.

Rational-legal authority   Power seen as fair and just as it is based on formal rules and laws. *See also* authority, charismatic authority, power, traditional authority.

Reconstituted or stepfamily   A family in which one or both partners have been previously married, and they bring with them children of a previous relationship.

Relative deprivation   The sense of lacking things compared to the group with which people identify and compare themselves.

Relative poverty   Poverty defined in relation to a generally accepted standard of living in a specific society at a particular time. *See also* absolute poverty.

Reliability   Whether another researcher, if repeating research using the same method for the same research on the same or a similar group, would achieve the same results.

Representative sample   A smaller group selected from the survey population for study, containing a good cross-section of the characteristics of the survey population as a whole.

Restricted code   A form of language use which takes for granted shared understandings between people. Colloquial, everyday language used between friends, with limited explanation and use of vocabulary. *See also* elaborated code.

Role conflict   The conflict between the successful performances of two or more roles at the same time, such as those of worker and mother.

Role model   Patterns of behaviour which others copy and model their own behaviour on.

Roles   The patterns of behaviour which are expected from individuals in society.

Sample   A small representative group drawn from the survey population for questioning or interviewing.

Sampling frame   A list of names of all those in the survey population from which a representative sample is selected.

Sanction   A reward or punishment to encourage social conformity.

Scapegoats   Individuals or groups blamed for something which is not their fault.

Secondary data Data which already exists and which the researcher hasn't collected her or himself. *See also* primary data.

Secondary socialization Socialization which takes place beyond the family and close community. It is carried out through agencies of secondary socialization such as the education system, the peer group, the workplace, the mass media and religious institutions. *See also* primary socialization.

Secularization The process whereby religious thinking, practice and institutions decline and lose influence in society.

Segregated conjugal roles A clear division and separation between the roles of male and female partners in marriage or in a cohabiting couple.

Selective exposure Individuals exposing themselves only to media output that fits in with their existing views and interests. *See also* selective perception, selective retention.

Selective perception Individuals filtering and interpreting media output so they only see or hear that which fits in with their own views and interests. *See also* selective exposure, selective retention.

Selective retention Individuals ignoring or forgetting media output that is not in line with their own views and interests. *See also* selective exposure, selective perception.

Self-fulfilling prophecy People acting in response to predictions which have been made regarding their behaviour, thereby making the prediction come true. Often applied to the effects of streaming in schools.

Serial monogamy A form of marriage in which a person keeps marrying and divorcing a series of different partners, but is only married to one person at a time.

Setting School students put into different groups or sets for a particular subject according to their ability in that subject.

Sex The biological differences between men and women.

Sexism Prejudice or discrimination against people (especially women) because of their sex.

Sexual division of labour The division of work into men's jobs and women's jobs.

Sexual orientation The type of people that individuals are either physically or romantically attracted to, such as those of the same or opposite sex.

Sick role The pattern of behaviour which is expected from someone who is classified as ill.

Slavery A stratification system (*see* social stratification) in which some people are regarded as the property of others.

Social capital The social networks of influence and support that people have.

Social class An open (*see* open society) system of stratification (*see* social stratification) consisting of broad groups of people (classes) who share a similar economic situation, such as occupation, income and ownership of wealth.

Social cohesion   The bonds or 'glue' that bring people together and integrate them into a united society.

Social construction   Something, like official statistics or the definitions of crime, deviance and health, that is created by people's interpretations and actions, and only exists because people have constructed it by giving it a particular meaning, interpretation and label.

Social control   The process of persuading or forcing individuals to conform to values and norms.

Social exclusion   The situation where people are marginalized (*see* marginalization) or excluded from full participation in mainstream society. Those who lack the necessary resources are denied the opportunities most people take for granted.

Social institutions   The organized social arrangements which are found in all societies.

Social mobility   Movement of groups or individuals up or down the social hierarchy.

Social policy   The packages of plans and actions adopted by national and local government or various voluntary agencies to solve social problems or achieve other goals that are seen as important.

Social problem   Something that is seen as harmful to society in some way, and needs something doing to sort it out. *See also* social policy.

Social stratification   The division of society into a hierarchy of unequal social groups.

Social structure   The social institutions and social relationships that form the 'building blocks' of society.

Social survey   A method of gathering information about some group of people by questioning them using questionnaires and interviews.

Socialization   The process of learning the culture of any society. *See also* primary socialization, secondary socialization.

Sociology   The systematic (or planned and organized) study of human groups and social life in modern societies.

Status   The amount of prestige or social importance a person has in the eyes of other members of a group or society. *See also* achieved status, ascribed status.

Status frustration   A sense of frustration arising in individuals or groups because they are denied status in society.

Status group   A group of people sharing a similar social standing and lifestyle.

Status symbols   Things that show off people's status to others, such as their house, their car and other products they spend their money on which give particular impressions to others.

Stereotype   A generalized, over-simplified view of the features of a social group, allowing for few individual differences between its members.

Streaming   Putting school students into the same group for all subjects according to their ability.

Sub-culture   A smaller culture shared by a group of people within the main culture of a society, in some ways different from the main culture, but with many aspects in common.

Survey population   The section of the population which is of interest in a survey.

Symmetrical family   A family in which the roles of husband and wife or cohabiting partners have become more alike (symmetrical) and equal.

Tactical voting   In an election, where supporters of a political party which has no chance of winning vote for another party which is not their preferred choice, in the hope of defeating the predicted winning party.

Totalitarianism   A system of government in which society is controlled by a small powerful group or an individual, and ordinary people lack any control over government decision-making.

Traditional authority   Power which is seen as fair and just as it is based on established traditions and customs. *See also* authority, charismatic authority, power, rational-legal authority.

Tripartite system   The system of secondary education established in 1944 in which pupils were selected for one of three types of secondary school according to their performance in the 11+ exam.

Underachievement   The failure of people to achieve as much as they are capable of.

Underclass   A social group who are right at the bottom of the social class hierarchy, who are in some ways cut off or excluded from the rest of society.

Validity   This is concerned with whether the findings of research actually provide a true, genuine and authentic picture of what is being studied.

Value consensus   A general agreement around the main norms and values of society.

Value freedom   The idea that the beliefs and prejudices of the sociologist should not be allowed to influence the way research is carried out and evidence interpreted.

Values   General beliefs about what is right or wrong, and the important standards which are worth maintaining and achieving in any society.

Volatility (in voting)   Where people's voting in elections has become less predictable, with voters less committed to any one party, with their support swinging to and fro between different political parties.

Wealth   Property which can be sold and turned into cash for the benefit of the owner.

White-collar crime   Crime that is committed by people in the course of their middle-class jobs.

White-collar workers   Non-manual clerical workers, sales personnel, and other office workers, whose work is non-professional and non-managerial.

Picture credits

Index

Using the Index

If you are looking for general topics, it is probably best to refer first to the contents pages at the beginning of this book, or at the beginning of each chapter. If you want to find a particular item of information, look it up in this index. If the item is not listed, then think of other headings it might be given under: the same information is often included several times under different headings. This index only includes the main references found in the book rather than every single occurrence of the theme and it is sensible to check the largest references first, such as, for example, pages 152–9 before 147, 148 and 177. The chances are that what you're looking for will be in the largest entry and this will save you time wading through a lot of smaller references.

Page numbers in **colour** refer to items in the glossary.